2016

ok
all through the
year.
Love
Ron & Carol

a special gift

presented to:

_____

from:

_____

date:

_____

This is my prayer—

that your love will flourish and you will not only love much but well.

—Philippians 1:9

The Women's Devotional Series

EDITORS

Carolyn
Rathbun
Sutton

with

Ardis
Dick
Stenbakken

Pacific Press®
Publishing Association
Nampa, Idaho | Oshawa, Ontario, Canada
www.pacificpress.com

Unless otherwise noted, Scripture quotations are from the King James Version of the Bible.

Scriptures quoted from AMP are from The Amplified Bible. Old Testament, copyright © 1965, 1987 by the Zondervan Corporation. The Amplified New Testament, copyright 1958, 1987 by the Lockman Foundation. Used by permission.

The Origianl Aramaic New Testament in Plain English- with Psalms & Proverbs, copyright © 2007; 8th edition Copyright © 2013. All rights reserved. Used by Permission.

Scripture quotations marked ASV are from the American Standard Version of the Bible.

Scriptures quoted from CEV are from the Contemporary English Version, copyright © American Bible Society 1991, 1995. Used by permission.

Scripture quotations marked DARBY are from the Darby Translation of the Bible.

Scripture quotations marked ESV are from The Holy Bible, English Standard Version® (ESV®), copyright © 2001 by Crossway, a publishing ministry of Good News Publishers. Used by permission. All rights reserved.

Scripture quotations marked GNT are from the Good News Translation. Copyright © 1992 by American Bible Society.

Scripture quotation from The Message. Copyright © by Eugene H. Peterson, 1993, 1994, 1995, 1996, 2000, 2001, 2002. Used by permission of NavPress Publishing Group.

Scriptures quoted from NASB are from The New American Standard Bible®, Copyright © 1960, 1962, 1963, 1968, 1971, 1972, 1973, 1975, 1977, 1995 by The Lockman Foundation. Used by permission.

Scripture quotations marked NCV are taken from the New Century Version®. Copyright © 2005 by Thomas Nelson, Inc. Used by permission. All rights reserved.

Scripture quotations marked NET are from the New English Translation, NET Bible® copyright ©1996-2006 by Biblical Studies Press, L.L.C. http://netbible.com All rights reserved.

Scripture quotations marked NIV are from the HOLY BIBLE, NEW INTERNATIONAL VERSION®. Copyright © 1973, 1978, 1984, 2011 by Biblica, Inc.® Used by permission. All rights reserved worldwide.

Scripture quotations marked NIrV are taken from the Holy Bible, NEW INTERNATIONAL READER'S VERSION®. Copyright © 1996, 1998 Biblica. All rights reserved throughout the world. Used by permission of Biblica.

Scripture quotations marked NJB are from The New Jerusalem Bible, copyright © 1985 by Darton, Longman & Todd, Ltd. and Doubleday, a division of Random House, Inc. Reprinted by permission.

Scripture quotations marked NKJV are taken from the New King James Version®. Copyright © 1982 by Thomas Nelson, Inc. Used by permission. All rights reserved.

Scripture quotations marked NLT are taken from the Holy Bible, New Living

You can obtain additional copies of this book by calling toll-free 1-800-765-6955 or by visiting http://www.adventistbookcenter.com.

Library of Congress Cataloging-in-Publication Data:

Living his love / compiled and edited by Carolyn Rathbun Sutton and Ardis Dick Stenbakken.
      pages cm
  ISBN 13: 978-0-8163-5739-0 (hard cover)
  ISBN 10: 0-8163-5739-0 (hard cover)
  1. Seventh-day Adventist women—Prayers and devotions. 2. Devotional calendars—Seventh-day Adventists. I. Sutton, Carolyn, 1944- compiler.
  BV4844.L58 2015
  242'.643--dc23
                              2015013954

May 2015

About the Editors

Carolyn Rathbun Sutton finds great joy in "being there" for other women, especially those struggling to find renewed purpose after a major life setback. She particularly enjoys helping women share with others their own personal stories of God's faithfulness.

Ardis Dick Stenbakken has had a zeal for women and women's ministries for many years. She loves to encourage women to use their God-given gifts and to learn how God led the women of the Bible. In 2004 Ardis retired as director of the General Conference Women's Ministry Department and now lives in Colorado.

Scholarshipping Our Sisters
Women Helping Women

There is an aspect of this book that is unique . . .

None of these contributors has been paid—each has shared freely so that all profits go to scholarships for women. As this book goes to press, approximately 2,200 scholarships have been given to women in 127 countries.

For more current information, or to contribute to these scholarships, please go to http://adventistwomensministries.org/index.php?id=52. In this way you too can help fulfill the dream of some woman—or even yourself—to attend college or university.

General Conference Women's Ministries Scholarship Fund

The General Conference Women's Ministries scholarship program supports higher education for Adventist women globally. Recipients are talented women of vision who are committed to serving the mission of the Seventh-day Adventist Church.

Among Friends, published in 1992, was the first annual women's devotional book. Since then, proceeds from 22 of these devotional books have funded scholarships for Adventist women seeking to obtain higher education. However, as tuition costs have risen and more women have applied for assistance, funding has not kept pace with the need. Many dedicated women who apply must be turned down.

Recognizing the importance of educating women—to build stronger families, stronger communities, and a stronger church—each of us can help. Together we can change lives!

There are many ways to support our sisters, such as . . .

- Praying for women worldwide who are struggling to get an education.
- Telling others about the Women's Ministries scholarship program. (Materials are available to share.)
- Writing for the women's devotional book. (Guidelines are available.)
- Your gift or pledge to support women's education.

To make a gift or receive materials, send us a postcard with the following information. (Our address is on page 8.)

Name _____

Street _____

City _____ State/Province _____

Postal Code _____ Country _____

E-mail _____

To contact us:

Women's Ministries Department
General Conference of Seventh-day Adventists
12501 Old Columbia Pike
Silver Spring, MD 20904

Phone: 301-680-6636
Fax: 301-680-6600
E-mail: womensministries@gc.adventist.org
Web site: http://adventistwomensministries.org
Scholarship application and devotional book writers' guidelines are available at our Web site.

Living His Praise

Praise: to express approval of (someone or something).*

Praise ye the LORD. . . . Praise him for his mighty acts: praise him according to his excellent greatness. Ps. 150:1, 2.

I will sing to the LORD all my life; I will sing praise to my God as long as I live. Ps. 104:33, NIV.

Jesus lived a life that quietly and continually praised His heavenly Father. Since heartfelt praise, exaltation, and worship of God drew Jesus closer to His heavenly Father, should we perhaps be more purposeful about living our lives as a continual praise?

Absolutely.

Of God, King David said, "You are holy, enthroned in the praises of Israel" (Ps. 22:3, NKJV). If, as David implies, God inhabits our praises, why do we so often forget to praise Him for His goodness?

And if we praised God not only for answered prayer, but also for hemorrhaged vocal cords, unpredictable grandchildren, potholes in the road, broken walls and even broken dreams, as do this month's authors, imagine how close, how unbelievably close, God could be.

* All definitions are taken from the *Merriam-Webster online dictionary.*

The God of New Beginnings

"Jerusalem lies in ruins, and its gates have been burned with fire. Come, let us rebuild the wall of Jerusalem, and we will no longer be in disgrace." Neh. 2:17, NIV.

When Nehemiah, exiled to Persia where he served as steward in the king's palace, learned of Jerusalem's lamentable situation, he cried. He also fasted and sought God's help and guidance. It seemed that lying among the rubble of Jerusalem's broken walls were also God's promises for His people along with their hopes that appeared to be destroyed.

Yet God heard Nehemiah's prayers and showed him how to proceed with the city's restoration and rebuilding. More important, God reminded Nehemiah that He is the God of new beginnings. One of Nehemiah's prayer requests during his months' long fast was that God would grant him favor in the eyes of the king, King Artaxerxes. Nehemiah was asked by the king one day why he looked so pale and sad. Offering a silent prayer for wisdom, Nehemiah carefully laid out Jerusalem's dilemma.

Not only did God grant Nehemiah favor in the king's eyes, but He also ordained that the king become the very channel through which Heaven would finance the restoration project. In addition, the king gave Nehemiah authority, despite the opposition of Israel's enemies in the surrounding nations, to head up the construction project. In so doing, Nehemiah was able to make secure both the city and its rebuilt temple, God's earthly center of worship.

The work was hard, the opposition fierce. But the wall was rebuilt. In gratitude, Nehemiah declared that all of Israel take part in a celebration of praise (Neh. 8:2) to the God of restoration and new beginnings. He said, "The joy of the LORD is your strength" (verse 10).

Do you have any broken places, relationships, or dreams? God can pick up the pieces and create a new beginning for you. He promises, " 'I will repay you for the years the locusts have eaten' " (Joel 2:25, NIV). At the start of this new year, Jesus offers restoration and will draw near to us—with hope and healing. For with God, nothing is impossible.

Believe this is a new day. A new and exciting year for you to experience with God as never before. "Enter into his gates with thanksgiving, and into his courts with praise: be thankful unto him, and bless his name" (Ps. 100:4).

Accept His restoration. His release. And have a happy—and most blessed—new year!

Maria Raimunda Lopes Costa

A Party for God

Give thanks to the LORD and proclaim his greatness. Let the whole world know what he has done. Sing to him; yes, sing his praises. Tell everyone about his wonderful deeds. Exult in his holy name.
Ps. 105:1–3, NLT.

Have you ever had a party for God? I know it may sound strange, but don't most people enjoy parties? They are times of fun, laughter, and a celebration of a life. So having a party to celebrate God would be wonderful. When I read the verses from Psalm 105, it seems like the psalmist is telling us to have a party for our heavenly Father.

Verse 3 begins with the word "Exult" (in the NLT) or "Glory" (in the NIV and KJV).

That word "exult" or "glory" is from the Hebrew word *halal,* which can mean "to make a show, to boast, to rave, to celebrate, to be [clamorously] foolish." So the psalmist is telling us that each day we should live a life of praise and glory to God. We should rave about God, be boastful in our praise of Him, and even be foolish in our praise of Him.

Many know my favorite word is *joy* and my favorite saying is, "Don't let anyone steal your joy." One way I have found to hold on to my joy each day is to begin my day by having a party for God and to continue that party all through the day. Each day I begin my morning devotional time with praise and thanksgiving to God. I give Him praise with psalms and hymns. And as the day—and my party for God progresses—I continue my praise and thanksgiving. I look for opportunities to tell someone about what God has done in my life.

At the end of my day as the party winds down, I end with a time of thanksgiving. Each evening before I go to bed, I write down five things that God has done for me that day. I want God to know that I love Him and thank Him for the things He has done in my life—little things and big things. And so I fall asleep each night with praise and thanks to God on my mind.

This all may sound really easy but it's not. There are times in my life, difficult times, when giving God praise and thanks is the last thing I want to do, yet I find that when I look at my life, no matter the trial, there is always, always some reason for me to praise and thank God. So try it. Have a party of praise and thanksgiving for God and let that party go all day long. Be foolish in your praise, rave about God's goodness in your life. Now that's a reason to celebrate!

Heather-Dawn Small

A Garment of Praise

"To console those who mourn in Zion, to give them beauty for ashes, the oil of joy for mourning, the garment of praise for the spirit of heaviness; that they may be called trees of righteousness, the planting of the LORD, that He may be glorified." Isa. 61:3, NKJV.

As soon as the plane landed in Beira, Mozambique, I felt that something was not right. I'd had a tight connection in Johannesburg due to a delay, and I was almost sure my bags had not made it through. Sure enough! When I passed through the immigration and ran to the baggage claim area, my fears were confirmed. No bags, no clothes, no nothing for five days. I was in a panic. What would I do? Then gradually I became aware of music, songs of joy outside the airport. I had been so upset about my situation that I had not even heard the amazing music. But as I listened, I realized I had two choices: to praise or to complain. I decided to praise.

Leaving the airport, I joined more than one hundred women who were singing—praising God for His blessings and thanking Him that I had arrived safely.

The days ahead were full of meetings, training, and fellowship. Did I miss my bags? Yes, at first, but I quickly learned to live without many things. I felt comfortable and happy. The ladies brought me a *capulana,* a piece of cloth that can be used in many ways. With the *capulana,* I survived the five days, rarely thinking about my lost bags. I was learning that if we will allow God to dress our spirit with praise, we will begin to sing again.

The day I left Beira, my bags were waiting for me at the airport. I praised God for bringing my things back, but I also thanked Him for teaching me to live with less. Today, when I face the same experience (and because I travel frequently, it happens often), I remember what God taught me in Mozambique, and my attitude changes immediately for the better. Why? Because when God dresses our hearts with praise, we are able to sing again.

Today is your day to sing. Maybe you are not waiting for luggage or material things; perhaps you are facing sickness, loss, or trials. Ask God to dress you with praise and help you to "give thanks in all things." You will discover changes in your thoughts and behavior, and you will never be the same. This morning, and every morning, you have the choice: to praise or to complain. Choose to praise. Choose blessings.

Raquel Queiroz da Costa Arrais

Rescuing Luke

O Lord, You preserve man and beast. How precious is Your lovingkindness, O God! Therefore the children of men put their trust under the shadow of Your wings. Ps. 36:6, 7, NKJV.

The white, blue-eyed kitten with gray on his head sat on the church porch. The bewildered expression on his three-month-old face suggested that someone had left him there despite the rainy downpour. I saw him as I arrived to play the piano for choir practice. Other choir members saw him too. We spoke kindly to him and petted him.

After practice, we discussed what to do. He purred when we gave him bowls of water, milk, and bread. What next? I couldn't take him because the three cats I already had wouldn't welcome him. No one else there could take him in, either. Sadly, we bade him goodbye.

Once home, I made phone calls, putting an ad on his behalf in two local papers. My friend Peggy suggested that I call Lorraine, a mutual friend who wasn't in choir.

Lorraine promised, "If nobody else shows any interest by Sunday and the kitten is still there, I'll take him to stay with me until I can find him a home." I prayed that the kitty would be there when she came to church. When Lorraine saw him, she named him Luke. And she did take him home with her.

On my end of things, the person taking my advertisement at the newspaper was reluctant to add Luke's name to the ad when I called to renew it.

"If he has a name, he's a pet," she insisted.

"But his humans deserted him," I explained. "His temporary rescuer named him. She names all the animals she takes care of. You can leave the name out if you feel you must."

"No, I'll go ahead and add it," she finally agreed. After Lorraine had kept Luke for at least a month, a kind couple read the ad and decided that they would like to have Luke. So they picked him up and gave him a permanent home.

When Luke was lost, he wasn't sure what to do. We, too, at times in life, may feel as if we're lost and looking at an uncertain future. But God, who cares about the smaller members of His creation, including sparrows (see Matt. 10:29–31), also cares about us. All we have to do is ask Him and then trust Him the way sweet, gentle Luke put his trust in us.

Bonnie Moyers

Anxious About Nothing

Be anxious for nothing. Phil. 4:6, NKJV.

eacher's aide had an anxiety attack today," said Melissa, placing her backpack on the dining table. "It wasn't pretty." (A recent favorite expression, she was using it whenever she could slip it in.) Chuckling to myself, I asked her what wasn't pretty. "Her exhibited behavior," said Melissa importantly. "She was really, really, really irritable and yelled at several of the kids." I raised an eyebrow. (Actually, it raised itself. Ever since childhood, my eyebrow tends to go up automatically when my brain thinks a question.) Melissa noticed my eyebrow and answered my unspoken question. "She put a bid on a condo three days ago and hasn't heard anything. So she can't sleep and naturally is very anxious."

"Too bad," I said. "Do you think her anxiety will alter the outcome of her bid?"

"Not a chance!" said Melissa, shaking her head. "That's the reason I reminded her of the scripture to be anxious about nothing." *Oops,* I thought to myself. That may not have gone over well. "It didn't go over well," said Melissa, echoing my thoughts. "She told me to mind my own business and said that scripture doesn't apply to this situation because there are some things that are perfectly acceptable to be anxious about." Melissa paused, chin in hand, and then asked, "What things are perfectly acceptable to be anxious about?" (I knew "perfectly acceptable" would be showing up again in conversation!)

"I believe the text means exactly what it says," I commented. "Be anxious for nothing." We discussed the difference between problem solving, evaluating options, making the best choice one can make at the moment with the knowledge and experience one possesses, and then letting it go—versus becoming embroiled in anxiety. "Anxiety triggers the brain to become irritable and to focus its attention and energy toward lower portions of the central nervous system," I explained. "Toward the brain stem, for example, that houses the stress response of fight-or-flight. Brain-function research has shown the negative impact anxiety can have on your brain, immune system, overall health, and exhibited behaviors. Be anxious for nothing!"

"Oh!" exclaimed Melissa. "So since the teacher's aide couldn't run away from school, she got irritable and yelled instead." Do you believe it is OK to be anxious? Think again.

Arlene R. Taylor

My Best Friend

A friend loveth at all times. Prov.17:17.

Through the years, I have been blessed with many friends. All are treasures and have a special place in my heart. However, my friends of fifty or more years with whom I have kept in touch, even when we live far apart, are extra special. Three couples whom my late husband and I have known since their and my childbearing years fit that category. The eight of us knew what it was like to live from payday to payday and still have fun together while raising and educating our children. My husband's passing in 2010 left only seven in our special group. These friends nurtured and supported me during that difficult time. Within a month of my husband's death, I had a birthday. Since these friends live about forty miles from my present home, the women wanted to get together to celebrate. My birthday gift from the three of them was a granite stone shaped like a brick and engraved with these words: "Friends forever."

One of my most recent friends has become my very best friend. In fact, he will soon become my husband. Aren't you glad God created us as social creatures needing relationships to enrich our lives? With friends we can laugh, cry, agree, disagree (though still be friends), worship, play, and work, while further bonding our relationships.

The Bible has a lot to say about relationships. The stories of David and Jonathan, Mary and Elizabeth, and Paul's friendship with Silas all illustrate the joys of friendship.

As dear as our friendships are, there is one that stands out high above the rest. That is our friendship with Jesus. His greatest desire is to be our very best and forever Friend. He promises to never leave us nor forsake us. He is a Friend that sticks closer than a brother. Jesus will never break our relationship. No matter where we live, what we do, or how good or bad we are, He will be there with us.

Jesus is always available to talk to any time we choose. We can get angry with Him, turn our backs on Him, and refuse to have anything to do with Him. Yet He will not turn away from us unless we tell Him to do so. Any time we want to get back in a relationship with Him, He welcomes us with open arms. He is truly the Friend who "loveth at all times." How I praise Him! With a Friend like that, what more could we ask?

Marian M. Hart-Gay

Snow That Lies

He was a murderer from the beginning, and abode not in the truth, because there is no truth in him. When he speaketh a lie, he speaketh of his own: for he is a liar, and the father of it. John 8:44.

I awoke today to a lovely sight—large, fluffy snowflakes floating past my bedroom window, covering roof, trees, and lawn in glistening white. Snowfall in the Pacific Northwest is not like the deep drifts of the Midwest and Northeast. Yet our snow here in the San Juan Islands can be quite deep for several days or weeks and then be gone within twenty-fours hours, leaving not a trace.

Beautiful snow can sometimes be deceptive. Beneath its lovely white blanket lie the lifeless remains of last summer's beautiful leaves, flowers, and grass. In reality, snow is cold, unforgiving, and possibly dangerous to health, life, and limb. Just a year ago, right here on Fidalgo Island, a poor inebriated local, Jim, stumbled into a snow drift, fell, and died there.

The deceptive aspect of snow reminds me of our enemy's promises that can also appear, sound, and feel beautiful, intriguing, and safe. But the enemy is a liar. Believing his deceptive promises leads to physical and mental agony and eternal death.

Some think our beloved heavenly Father's promises are dull and uninteresting. Next to the glowing promises of the evil one, they often seem so bland. God's promises are based on His love, His creatorship, and His knowing what will make us happy in the long run. Our eternal good and happiness is His goal for us. Trusting His promises involves our obedience to His law of love. Trust and obedience will result in better health, a more fulfilling lifestyle, an abiding contentment in Him, and eternal life.

God's Word states that He, the Creator of the universe, cannot lie. He is truth and purity personified. His many promises include the forgiveness of our sins. Even if they be "as scarlet, they shall be as white as snow" (Isa. 1:18). Snow that doesn't lie, that is. A cause for praise!

Beloved heavenly Father, may I always choose Your promises over the lies of the enemy. Thank You for loving me and wanting to share eternity with me. Thank You for giving us guidance in Your Word that promises eternity with You and life, health, and joy forever. In Jesus' name, I pray. Amen.

Darlenejoan McKibbin Rhine

Your Time to Make It Right

David pleaded with God for the child. He fasted and spent the nights lying in sackcloth on the ground. 2 Sam. 12:16, NIV.

"Go and tell Hezekiah, 'This is what the LORD, the God of your father David, says: I have heard your prayer and seen your tears; I will add fifteen years to your life.' " Isa. 38:5, NIV.

Daddy, I don't want to talk to Mom; she always loves and cares for people who take advantage of her," said the girl.

"Your mom is a beautiful lady; her heart cares and loves. Compelling her not to do this is like telling her to stop her heart from beating. She is going to be miserable if you take this freedom from her," replied her father.

After a week of not talking to her mother, the girl dreamt her mother died. *No, Jesus, I am not ready to see her go; please don't let her die! I promise You I will never avoid her phone calls again,* cried the girl. Falling at God's feet in the dream, she cried, *I promise I will never stop her from doing the right thing. Please let this be only a dream.* And it was. Never before had her prayers been answered so quickly. Very early that morning, her phone call awoke her mom.

Yet the dream about her mother's death kept haunting the girl. Three months after this dream, her mom fell and broke her arm. The doctors said she might not be able to use her arm again. *Lord, why did You let this happen to such a kind and loving person?* asked the girl. Soon the painful experience was over and her mother was able to use her arm again. Yet not much more time passed before her mother was diagnosed with cancer. The daughter fasted and prayed, like King David, for God to heal her family member. She asked God to give her sixty-five-year-old mother fifteen more years of life, as He had given King Hezekiah in the Bible. Yet just four months after the dream and after having asked her mother for forgiveness, her mother passed away.

Hearing this story, I wondered, How much time do *I* need to make it right with my friends, my family, and my heavenly Father? How much time do you and I have? We must each make choices right now. Praise God that He can give us the courage, strength, and time we need in order to make things right with others and with Him before it is too late.

Suhana Benny Prasad Chikatla

A Living Connection With Our Savior

The LORD shall make bright clouds, and give them showers of rain.
Zech. 10:1.

He will cause to come down . . . the rain, the former rain,
and the latter rain. Joel 2:23.

What are many of us praying for? For a living connection with our Savior, right? We do so as we worship, praise, pray, fellowship, and witness wherever we are. I've been thinking about what this living connection looks like in everyday life. My friend helps me better understand, for my friend tries to live every moment in connection with Christ. For example, every day when my friend takes her shower, she uses this time as an opportunity to sing hymns that praise and magnify God. Sometimes she composes songs to glorify Him.

Once, when my friend looked out of her kitchen window, she saw the shape of a lamb in the bright clouds of the sky. She felt it was God's reminder to her that the Lamb who was "slain from the foundation of the world" (Rev. 13:8) was coming some day soon to take her home. Sometimes my friend reminds God that she has laundry hanging out to dry—just in case it's within His will to hold back the rain until she can get her clean, dry laundry back into the house. My friend tells me that sometimes she prays not only for the rain that waters our soil but also for an outpouring of the latter rain. She is well acquainted with this text: "Be patient therefore, brethren, unto the coming of the Lord. Behold, the husbandman waiteth for the precious fruit of the earth, and hath long patience for it, until he receive the early and latter rain" (James 5:7).

Recently, I've been thinking about how my relationship with Christ relates to His promised latter rain. When I see a rainstorm washing over the earth, I remember that God wants to cleanse me as well through His indwelling Spirit. I recall His admonition: "Repent ye therefore, and be converted, that your sins may be blotted out, when the times of refreshing shall come from the presence of the Lord. And he shall send Jesus Christ" (Acts 3:19, 20).

Through our daily connection with Him, Jesus sends us the early rain—through His Holy Spirit—in order to prepare us to grow into His character. As He enables us, through His mercy and grace, to die daily to self, He makes us more and more like Him (see Gal. 2:20).

Now is the time to draw close to Jesus. Now is the time to open our hearts to the early rain so what we can praise Him and serve Him more fully during the time of the latter rain.

Yan Siew Ghiang

Will You Be My Best Friend?

So the LORD must wait for you to come to him so he can show you his love and compassion. Isa. 30:18, NLT.

From the backseat of the car, I heard a little voice say, "Grandma, will you be my best friend?" Oh, how those words touched my heart. Griffey already held a special place in my heart. Grandsons as well as granddaughters always do.

It had been several months since I had been to Denver to visit my daughter and her family. How big my grandson, Griffey, had grown! At three years of age, it's amazing how quickly they go and grow through various stages! What amazed me equally was how well he could communicate already. To say we enjoyed our time together would be an understatement. We laughed and hugged and read books and drove fire trucks and snuggled. Oh, how I love being a grandma! But when I heard him ask, "Will you be my best friend?" something in my heart absolutely melted. I replied, "Yes," while at the same time choking back tears of joy. I want to always be his best friend. I want to enjoy time with him and share life with him as he grows.

If we are so moved by tender moments like these, just think how God feels when we ask Him to be our "best Friend." There He is waiting for us. His Word tells us, "So the LORD must wait for you to come to him so he can show you his love and compassion" (Isa. 30:18, NLT). Just imagine the One who created the heavens and the earth waiting for us to come to Him, asking Him to be our best Friend, our Life, our Protector, and our Salvation. I want to share my life with Him; the One who created me and knows me better than I know myself . . . the One who says, "I am waiting for you. Will you be My best friend?"

When it was time to depart Denver for my trip back to Minnesota, I was sad to separate from my little Griffey, but I knew that I would leave a piece of my heart there with him. In fact, I would also carry him back home in my heart. As I got in the car to go to the airport, I hugged him and asked him, "Will you always be my best friend?" His coy little smile and sparkling eyes told me he and I would always have a special bond.

That is how I want my relationship to be with Yahweh. Always special! Always precious! Always joyful! Always trusting! Never lost!

Candace Zook

"Well Done"

His lord said unto him, Well done, good and faithful servant; thou hast been faithful over a few things, I will make thee ruler over many things: enter thou into the joy of thy lord. Matt. 25:23.

She seemed an unlikely candidate for favorite aunt. Aunt Florence was plagued with health problems from birth. She struggled with impaired vision, hearing, and intellectual capacity. Kidney troubles often caused her legs to swell. She also had an overbite of truly majestic proportions. Possessed of seemingly few "talents," Aunt Florence was still capable enough to be left in charge of my siblings and me when we were children.

My two sisters and I spent summer vacations at our grandparents' home in the small town of Antigo, Wisconsin. Living in their upstairs bedroom, Aunt Florence was available to take us children to magical places every afternoon. We'd walk—for what seemed like miles—to the abandoned train station, the water-filled foundation of a house long gone, the neighborhood park, or to the corner store for popsicles to cool us down in the summer heat. Our aunt knew names of bugs and birds and could whistle most local bird songs.

Indoors, Aunt Florence could always talk us into playing a game or listening to a story. We enjoyed curling up on her bed to hear tales of mission lands, even after our own reading skills had surpassed hers and we had, at times, to pronounce an unfamiliar word for her.

We slept in her upstairs bedroom, telling stories in the dark or sharing dreams we would never admit to our parents. Every morning, we'd see her roll out of bed and onto her knees. Her prayers were audible if you listened closely. She lifted each one of her family members up to the throne of grace, praying for our happiness, well-being, and salvation. Her prayers intensified as we grew older, our lives more complicated, our mistakes carrying bigger consequences. Her days ended as they began. On her knees. She praised God for the unshakeable certainty of the return of our Savior when she would hear Him say, "Well done."

Daily I treasure my legacy from Aunt Florence, a love and devotion I now carry on behalf of my own nieces and nephews that regularly send me to my knees. Whenever I am tempted to be less than a "good and faithful servant," I thank God for my memories of Aunt Florence—and am inspired.

Vicki Mellish

Grooved Road Ahead

Weeping may endure for a night, but joy cometh in the morning.
Ps. 30:5.

We usually read the sign "Grooved Road Ahead" with gritted teeth. This sign indicates that the traffic will be slow and the road will become bumpy and hazardous with our wheels pulling this way and that on the uneven surface. Yellow cones lining the roadway remind us that most of the road work will be accomplished during the dark of night, but how we wish for it to be over! How we wish for smooth roads right now!

A few days later as we merge onto the newly resurfaced highway, we notice the difference. There may be no sign proclaiming, "Hey, You Got Your Wish!" or "Thank a Construction Worker for Smoothing Out the Grooves!" but the misery is over. Memories of previous irritation about bumpy, grooved roads fade as we enjoy our comfortable new ride.

Spiritually speaking, do we not sometimes become impatient with the "grooved roads" in our own life journeys, those trials that irritate us? The annoyances that make us wonder, *Why me?* We want to scream out, "When will these trials pass? When will our smooth roads return?" We want to enjoy an easy, pleasant ride, forgetting that before the comfort must come the "road work" to refine our characters.

First, a section of road (that's us) is selected and marked off for repair and resurfacing. As with those who work on road surfaces, the Holy Spirit digs deep to remove the old layers. That can hurt! This removal process exposes damage caused by the frigid storms and torrid heat of life experiences. It even exposes damage resulting from our secret sins. The Holy Spirit is constantly at work on our characters, digging, grooving, examining, and preparing us for the new foundation and surface. Yet I am grateful to God for the heated and pressure-placed "asphalt"—those fiery trials of our faith—that repeatedly bring us to the foot of the cross. I am willing to tolerate the grooved roads in my town because I know that, in time, I will enjoy smooth new roads. May God heal my impatience during my character reconstruction as well.

Lord, give me the patience to wait, knowing that You are working in my life, and that the job is far from finished. Help me to have faith that You're leading, even when the road is bumpy. Help me to remember that after dark nights of reconstruction, joy comes in the morning.

Annette Walwyn Michael

Another Time in the Bus

"When the Son of Man comes, will he find faith on the earth?"
Luke 18:8, NIV.

Once more I was in a bus with the long eight hours ahead of me before getting to the city in which I worked. I was returning from a holiday during which my husband and I stayed in the home of some friends. It was very good to see them again and wonderful to spend some time in my home in Brazil. But now it was time to come back to Vitória da Conquista.

Soon after we got onto the bus, I noticed that the seat by my side was already occupied. Looking sideways, I saw a tall, strong boy. I thought, *How will I pass the night near this fellow?* The truth is that I judged the boy wrongly because to me he seemed very scary looking.

One hour into the trip, the bus had a problem, and we had to stop in the Federal Police area to wait for another bus. I was sleeping while we waited for the other bus. Two hours later, the other bus came. We climbed into the new bus and found our seats. I worried about the delay because I would have to begin work at seven the next morning. I started to talk to my seatmate. At first, we talked about our respective professions, the environment, religion, and lastly, about our spiritual experience. I was impressed with the boy's spiritual journey, conflicts, and sincerity. He took his relationship with God seriously, thought about his errors, and looked for divine guidance. He was a wandering sheep wanting to find the Shepherd's fold. I was surprised to find myself talking to a son of God who was still looking for Him.

I shared a little of my own return to the Lord with the young man and encouraged him not to give up. At the end of our conversation, he thanked me and said that I had helped him.

However, I felt as if I was the one blessed. Once more God reminded me that He can find faith in the most unexpected hearts. I silently praised God for the reminder that His sheep are all around us and we must be mindful of that. I also asked forgiveness for being judgmental, as I'd drawn conclusions about my seatmate based on his appearance.

The next morning, I disembarked before the final bus stop. My young seatmate was sleeping and I did not want to wake him up. While retrieving my bag, I asked God to continue guiding that boy—and others—to the safety of the sheepfold, toward rest and peace. And I thanked Him for being always so willing to do so.

Iani Dias Lauer-Leite

Trusting God in Times of Trouble

Even though I walk through the darkest valley, I will fear no evil, for you are with me; your rod and your staff, they comfort me. Ps. 23:4, NIV.

A number of years ago, we fell into dire financial straits when my husband lost his job. Emotional and financial turmoil resulted. To be honest, I felt as though life had spiraled down and there was no escaping this dark valley of despair. All around us seemed dark and dismal. I felt friendless, hopeless, and distressed because I felt no one understood our plight. Our daughter was a freshman in college; our son was a freshman in high school, and they both had needs. How could we maintain our children in church school under such financial constraints?

Often we read familiar Bible passages, such as Psalm 23, but we do not stop to interpret every verse. There are times in our lives when we face obstacles that we think are not surmountable, and we cry out to God for help. It is during these times that passages like today's scripture become our greatest help. I do believe that anyone who calls upon the name of the Lord will be rescued despite much weeping and supplication. Jesus is always the answer, but how often we fail to call upon Him when we are in the dark valley of despair. During our family's difficult time, God's still, small voice often impressed me to fast and pray. I would experience renewed strength and the reassurance that He would never leave or forsake us.

Then our electric bill came due and there was no money to pay it. I told no one, except the One who owns the cattle upon a thousand hills. I prayed, "Oh God, please have mercy! Send help so the utilities will not be disconnected." I went to the Bible where God reminded me that " 'Before they call I will answer; while they are still speaking I will hear' " (Isa. 65:24, NIV).

Sometime during this time of uncertainty, I went to the mailbox one day as usual. I opened an unexpected letter from my father who lived one thousand miles away. He had written, "I was impressed to go to the bank and withdraw some money to send you. It is enclosed."

Five hundred dollars! I had not asked for money or even complained about our needs. Yet God saw my need and, long before I called, He provided what we needed. The five hundred dollars paid the utility bill and bought groceries for our family. How we praised Him!

Trust the Lord when you're in the dark valley of despair. He has all the solutions.

Eveythe Kennedy Cargill

The Ultimate Protector

For God has not given us a spirit of fear, but of power and of love and of a sound mind. 2 Tim. 1:7, NKJV.

Have you ever experienced the feeling of personal violation? Three weeks ago, I did, my home was burglarized. A thief had broken in via the kitchen window. That evening, as soon as I walked through the front door, I realized that an uninvited, unwelcome intruder had invaded my family's personal space and ransacked our belongings. A plethora of strong emotions flooded over me.

I called the police and my insurance company. During the days that followed, I took immediate steps to make the house more secure. I had the front entrance door lock checked and adjusted. I replaced the back door with a metal door that had two locks. I replaced the kitchen window and put an additional bolt onto the door leading to the porch. I added two latches to the exit door on the porch and installed two alarms on the entrance and exit points. I was on a mission to prevent any future invasion. In spite of all I've done to secure my house, I'm still a bit nervous here, being again at home this first weekend after the invasion.

This morning, while having my personal devotions, I heard some noises downstairs and hurried to investigate. I discovered it was the "Hymns and Favorites" Internet radio station I'd turned on last night before I went to bed. Evidently, the computer had rebooted itself sometime during the night, stopping the music. I found the Web site and restarted the radio. The song being played was a prayer asking God for the protection that is found only in His loving arms, where there is no reason to fear.

Wow! What reassurance! my mind exulted. Aloud, I shouted, "I hear You, Father. Thank You, Jesus!" Isn't it amazing how, when we pray and praise, God speaks to our current situation and takes away our fears—sometimes as soon as the disturbing thoughts surface, if not even before? Satan seeks to keep God's children in a state of fear, but we needn't fear because we are covered by our Lord Jesus. God has "not given us a spirit of fear" but rather He's given us His power, love, and a sound mind. God has a plan for each of us, and He allows into our lives only those things that shape us into the people He wants us to become in order to fulfill His purpose.

Florence E. Callender

Led by a Child

A little child shall lead them. Isa. 11:6.

Ethiopian Adventist College is situated just about thirty kilometers away from Lake Langano in the beautiful Ethiopian Rift Valley. Every now and then, we missionary families were able to spend a weekend there to enjoy its beauty, relax, and spend quiet time with the Lord.

One weekend, we teachers, with our college students, were able to attend a retreat at this beautiful place. The students and teachers alike enjoyed the Friday evening vespers program and a good night's sleep. However, very early Sabbath morning, before six, we heard footsteps running toward our tent. Then we heard the sound of beating on the tent next to ours, which was occupied by Amarech, our family's helper. Emerging from our tent, we saw students trying to put out a fire that was destroying her adjacent tent. Quickly, my husband darted into what was left of Amarech's tent to turn off the gas tank she'd been using to cook breakfast.

"Why was your tent on fire?" we asked Amarech after the fire was finally extinguished. She told us she'd been cooking inside the tent and had decided to make a quick visit to the restroom. However, she'd left the flame on the stove burning.

"And I think I left a plastic plate too near the stove," she added. "It must have ignited and burned quickly. The tent was already halfway burned down when I got back." Her trembling voice betrayed fear of whatever consequences she might incur as a result of her carelessness. Everybody in our family ate breakfast in silence. Then our eldest son, Jojie, who was only about four years of age at that time, broke the silence.

"Mom? Dad? What are you going to do with Amarech? Are you going to fire her? You know she has been a very good worker. True, she made a big mistake this morning, but everybody makes mistakes." My husband and I exchanged glances, feeling moved by the forgiving spirit of our little boy. Of course, we had thought some consequence would be appropriate. Yet, after the informal mediation of a little child, we were sure that the only thing we could do was to forgive our helper—as God accepts the mediation of our Savior.

Amarech was forever grateful, remaining our loyal worker until we left Ethiopia years later. I praise God for using simple things, like a child, that remind us to love as He does.

Forsythia Catane Galgao

How Much Clearer Could It Be?

"With God all things are possible." Matt. 19:26, NIV.

For several years, I had been e-mailing back and forth with Jennifer, a young single mom in Africa. She was hoping to better her life with a career she would enjoy and also be able to support her children and herself. We often prayed together. She was finally able to get into a teacher's college where she could fulfill her dreams.

Jennifer arranged for her children to go live with her mother during the school year so she could both study and work hard to pay her tuition. Then last year Jennifer indicated she was short some funds in order to finish out the school year. Since her financial need was not a large sum, my husband and I were able to wire the needed funds to her school. She was so grateful for our help, and we all hoped she would be able to get through the second year on her own.

Then another e-mail arrived in which Jennifer told me she needed a bit more financial aid before she could take her exams. Normally, we would have been able to wire the funds to her, but we had had some unexpected expenses and were low on money ourselves. We let her know why we were unable to help her. She said she understood and would continue to hold us up in prayer that we would be able to meet our own financial obligations. She was not just thinking of herself but of us as well.

One morning, as my husband and I were talking about Jennifer's financial needs, I felt impressed to pray that if it were God's will that we help her, then would He please make that very clear to us that very day. Our mail usually arrives late in the afternoon, but that day it came right after lunch. As we went through the mail, there were two checks that we were not expecting at all. One was for a very small amount, but the other one was in the exact amount that Jennifer needed for her school account in order to take her exams. My husband and I looked at each other with tears in our eyes. We were speechless for a moment, and then we both agreed that it could not be any clearer that God had answered our prayers in a marked way. We went to the bank as soon as we could and wired the funds to Jennifer's school. Her need was greater than ours.

Though we were not able to help Jennifer, God was. With Him all things are possible. With gratitude, we glorify Him for answering our prayers for her—and in such a remarkable way!

Anna May Radke Waters

Touch Not My Anointed

My help cometh from the LORD, which made heaven and earth. He will
not suffer thy foot to be moved. . . . The LORD shall preserve thee from
all evil: he shall preserve thy soul. The LORD shall preserve thy going
out and thy coming in from this time forth, and even for evermore.
Ps. 121:2, 3, 6-8.

Years ago, I worked for a well-known armored car company in the Los Angeles area. In less than a year, the branch manager unexpectedly promoted me to cash vault/money room manager. My prayerful acceptance of the new position made me the only black and female manager at the company, though I was only in my twenties. I had recently come up with a successful solution to a major supervisor-caused problem. My superior noticed. I worked hard managing the money and doing billing not only for the cash vault but also for the coin room. This latter responsibility, however, irked the previous coin room manager, who began to plot my downfall, making my life miserable. By the grace of God, I always kept a cool head and refused to acknowledge negative attitudes directed at me. Often I felt like a sheep surrounded by wolves. I began each day with prayer. In a predominantly male business, I sometimes retreated to the women's restroom to have a cry, to pray, and to let the Lord put a calm smile back on my face.

One day Rex,* one of the managers, called me into a meeting. In front of a room packed with the other managers, he began firing off reasons why I was "not right for the position." The Holy Spirit gave me a strong response for each of Rex's accusations. At the end of the meeting, the branch manager blasted the other managers for wasting everyone's time and "acting like children," as he put it. "Our banking—and I—are very pleased with Sherilyn's work and have no complaints," he affirmed. Though hurt over the lies, I was grateful for the outcome, even though the men's disappointment increased their cruel treatment. Daily I asked God to move on my behalf. I praised Him, by faith, for doing so. I knew Satan could not remove me, unless God allowed it.

Arriving at work one morning, I spotted a large sign, posted at the entrance and saying that Rex was no longer an employee nor allowed on the premises. Soon after, I learned the other most offensive manager had been transferred to another location. I worked in peace for three more years until leaving for a better paying position with the Federal Reserve. The Bible says, "Touch not mine anointed" (Ps. 105:15). During any difficulty in life, God has your back too.

Sherilyn R. Flowers

---

* Not his real name.

I Will Get Home

For You formed my inward parts; You covered me in my mother's womb. I will praise You, for I am fearfully and wonderfully made.
Ps. 139:13, 14, NKJV.

There is an old song that has echoed in my head to an increasing degree lately. It is in one of the genres that over many years has been labeled as Negro Spirituals. It comes out of the slave experience. Its repeated verse says, "Sometimes I feel like a motherless child a long way from home."

It is a lament, for sure, and at times sounds like a dirge. Its minor key and solemn lyrics take me to a place of sadness, loss, and despair. At least, I have thought for many years that I traveled to that place called despair on the wings of that song.

Many women have taken that trip.

Then, more recently, I realized that the truth was just the opposite. For it was this song that sparked the recognition that I was about to sink to a low place. It was a warning and corrective. It said to me that I was about to allow life to beat me down and cause me to forget who and whose I am. It was my wake-up call. It was a lecture in reality.

For you see, the collection of Negro spirituals uses messages conceived and sung on multiple levels to communicate hope and give direction. That is, their overt messages were not their true meanings.

Often the words of these songs were the antitheses of their true messages. These seemingly simple songs were musical parables meant to give hope while sounding hopeless.

"Sometimes I feel like a motherless child a long way from home" really says to me, "Although it looks to you that I have no origin, no roots, and no place, I actually have a rich origin, the image of God, and a marvelous home a long way—physically and mentally—from this place of suffering."

It says my confident hope is to get back there some day.

We all have a home a long way from here; and the hope of every child of God is to get back there soon.

Another song reminds that if we are faithful, we will get there someday.

Ella Louise Smith Simmons

The Determined Dipper

Because the Sovereign LORD helps me, I will not be disgraced.
Therefore, I have set my face like a stone, determined to do his will.
Isa. 50:7, NLT.

Summer was waning. The occasional oaks were shedding rusty brown leaves under the canopy of towering evergreens. Our recreational vehicle was parked in a quiet nook at the end of the campground. With the pungent smell of pines and willows and the soothing, rippling music of the nearby Feather River, my husband and I felt enveloped in God's peace. Surrounding us were the mini-mountains of tailings left from California's gold rush of 1849. The river had produced vast quantities of gold for those long-ago miners, but the gold I was taking home cannot be measured in dollars and cents. It came from the rugged determination of a little bird.

One morning on my walk upriver through the campground, I ventured out on a ledge looking out over quite a stretch of the river. A small slate-gray bird caught my eye. It was a water ouzel, also known as the American dipper. Fascinated, I watched it. Constant deep-knee bends kept its body in perpetual motion even as the crashing waves it was facing threatened to topple it (from appearances, at least). In spite of the splashing foam rolling over it, the little bird held tenaciously to the slippery rock. In fact, it seemed that it appeared to enjoy the surrounding torrents of water. I watched the dipper periodically dive to the sandy bottom of the cold river in search of hidden aquatic insect larvae. Despite its repeated attempts, only once did I see it come up with a small sticklike worm in its mouth. These meager results, however, did not deter the bird from its constant search for food.

I discovered God had provided an amazing array of help for this unique creature: scaly nose plugs, strong claws, dense plumage, special eyelids to protect against spraying water, and an oil gland to waterproof its feathers. How can I not praise Him for providing what I need too?

As a great-grandmother of four, I realize the strength of my youth is waning. But the rugged determination of this little bird has inspired me. With God's help, I, too, am determined to use all the talents God has given me to draw others closer to Him. In the remaining years I have left, I have set my face as a stone, "determined to do his will" with all my strength, and to help hasten my Sovereign Lord's return. Will you do the same?

Donna Lee Sharp

The Biggest "Aha!" Moment of My Life

Commit your way to the Lord; trust in him. Ps. 37:5, NIV.

These past few years I have found myself face to face with many trials and tribulations—financial, emotional, and personal. I've been cheated in business transactions, lost a large amount of money to someone close to me who never paid me back and doesn't even speak to me anymore. I've experienced remarriage, the devastating death of my mother, and depression. The last two straws breaking the proverbial camel's back were when our cabinet maker suddenly died—just after I'd paid and contracted with him to do a huge job. This was followed by bad decisions from inexperienced and unprofessional workers.

During all of these crises, I've often thought, *Why is all this happening to me when life was so good before and things were so plentiful? I had a fantastic career and a great personal life with no major problems in it. Suddenly, my life has turned into one disaster after another! Why? Especially when I've always been a kind person and successful in business. In addition, I'm ethical, honest, and smart. Though I am trained to quickly understand challenges and make decisions to effectively deal with them, why am I now suddenly feeling so helpless? The challenges I currently face I can neither avoid nor solve!*

Such thoughts brought about worry, sleep loss, and episodes of weeping as I rehearsed my feelings of hurt, anger, and hopelessness. I felt at peace neither with the world nor with myself. How unlike the lyrics of a song I know that promises peace even if the world falls apart.

As I was talking to God one day about all my woes, He gave me an "Aha!" moment. He showed me that I had been trying to take control of everything in my life instead of allowing Him to be in charge. He impressed me that allowing Him to take control would roll the burdens off my shoulders. He would carry them for me! So I have asked Him to help me trust Him to be in control. I truly want to commit my way to the Lord and trust in Him. I want my life to praise Him, especially when I realize how very much He loves me and has a tremendous purpose for my life. Otherwise, He wouldn't have borne with me so long.

Thank You, God, for not giving up on me until I understood that it is actually my lack of faith that has not given me the internal peace that only a total surrender to You can achieve!

Joelcira F. Müller-Cavedon

Letting Go and Letting God

"So then, do not worry about tomorrow, for tomorrow will worry about itself. Today has enough trouble of its own." Matt. 6:34, NET.

I'm a very independent woman! I don't like asking for help. I'm more than willing to help others, but I don't ask for help! Recently, though, I've been quite handicapped.

I was on my way to the island of Samoa, via Auckland, to minister to the women there when I fell at the airport and fractured my right shoulder, although I didn't know that at the time.

Even as I lay on the floor in the terminal in Auckland, I refused help and wanted to stand up on my own! But I had to accept help from people who saw me fall and ran toward me—as I was unable to get up.

The pain was absolutely excruciating.

To make a long story short, I continued on my way to do my talks in Samoa, since the paramedics didn't think anything serious was wrong with me. I certainly wasn't screaming in pain! I don't know about you, but when I gave birth to my two children, not a sound came out of me, so why would this be any different?

When I got back to Sydney, however, I learned I had a fractured shoulder! I felt as if a big burden had been lifted off me. I wasn't just imagining the pain! Something was very wrong!

Since then I've learned to rely on my husband to help me shower, dry, and dress myself! My daughter drives me to the doctor; my fellow women's ministries leaders bring me food. Friends help clean the house and do other chores.

At first it was very hard, I have to admit, to accept all that help. Yet I've come to understand that we need each other, and I really appreciate the love I'm receiving.

At first, I worried about how I was going to do the simple things in life, such as take a shower. But I've learned a lot about humility as I'd never experienced it before. To be dependent on others for all things isn't easy, but it has taught me that I not only need them, but I need God even more than ever before.

And finally, I'm learning to let go of my independence and let God be the One in charge of my life.

Erna Johnson

The Divine Listener

"All those the Father gives me will come to me, and whoever comes to me I will never drive away." John 6:37, NIV.

One day, I heard three young boys talking. "I'm having problems with my parents," said one of them.

"What does that have to do with us?" asked another.

"Yeah," replied the third, "your parents are your problem, not ours." The first young man, crestfallen, ended the conversation.

Have you ever sought a sympathetic ear only to be shut out? After witnessing this exchange, I asked myself, "What would have happened if Christ had responded to people as did these two 'friends,' closing the door on someone in need of compassion?" How would we react if we were to tell God our problems and He ignored us and turned away from us, leaving us to suffer alone with our pain and uncertainty? Thanks to His great mercy, He does not do that. He says that if we know how to give the best to our children, He does much more for us (Matt. 7:11), and that includes listening to the problems we bring to Him. He also said that even if a mother forgets her children, He will never forget us (Isa. 49:15).

During His time on earth, Christ listened to problems shared by all manner of people: the tale of woe from the woman with the flow of blood, the confession of the tax collector Zacchaeus, the pleas of parents for demon-possessed children. He listened to little children themselves and to fishermen complaining about a bad night of fishing. He even listened to the thief on the cross.

Christ's mission here on earth was to reconnect the fallen human race with its Creator, reestablishing the bonds of love that had been broken. That is why He always listened attentively to each request and every cry. He supplied the needs of each person that approached Him and pointed them to His heavenly Father.

And still today the Divine Listener never shuts His ear to anyone. He is freely available to listen to us twenty-four hours a day. Let's give praise for the fact that unlike some phone numbers we dial, His number is never busy or "out of the area." After listening to our prayers, He will share guidance, comfort, and encouragement. May we also have for others the listening heart of Jesus.

Carmen Virgínia dos Santos Paulo

Heavenly Blessings

And it shall come to pass, that before they call, I will answer; and while they are yet speaking, I will hear. Isa. 65:24.

It seemed so small at the time that it happened. But at the end of the day as I reflected on how good my God is, I realized the miracle that God blessed me with that day.

I had awakened early. I ran out of my home without breakfast to a full day of seeing patients for six hours without a break. At about 11:30 A.M., I was seeing a patient but felt a little sweaty and light-headed. My sugar level was dropping. I needed a break and some food. My next patient, Dolores, brought me a gift in a little bowl—grape salad!

Before I could even ask my God, He had provided a healthy snack through Dolores. I was so thankful to her and to God. She wanted me to eat it while she told me what had been going on with her. I was grateful and complied. It was delicious and just what I needed to get me through the next few hours!

God promises to provide for our needs in every area of our lives (Phil. 4:19). Watch for the little heavenly blessings that come your way. If things are tough financially, you may find an unexpected envelope in the mail or your bills may appear less than they normally are. Someone at church may invite you to a potluck, which will save you money with groceries. If you are down emotionally, there likely is someone feeling worse than you. Look for that person. In blessing others you will be blessed yourself. Are you suffering from a physical ailment? God is still the Great Physician. He will either lead you to a physician who can help you with the correct diagnosis and treatment or He may choose to heal you. If healing is not what He chooses, don't forget that He won't leave you to walk your difficult journey alone. Claim the promises of Psalm 1 for yourself. In whatever He chooses for us, let's resolve to praise Him.

Ellen G. White wrote these comforting words: "Whatever your anxieties and trials, spread out your case before the Lord. Your spirit will be braced for endurance. The way will be opened for you to disentangle yourself from embarrassment and difficulty. The weaker and more helpless you know yourself to be, the stronger will you become in His strength. The heavier your burdens, the more blessed the rest in casting them upon the Burden Bearer" (*The Desire of Ages*, p. 329). Watch for those heavenly blessings!

Sharon Michael Palmer

God's Sound Effect

The voice of thy thunder was in the heaven: the lightnings lightened the world: the earth trembled and shook. Ps. 77:18.

At times God answers our prayers in the most unexpected and interesting ways.

My husband and I served as missionaries in Africa for some years. When he was working as an auditor, I accompanied him on some of his long trips. At times I would be asked to give a talk during the weekend religious meetings. On one of our auditing trips, the local church pastor invited me to give the sermon on the weekend.

At that time, I had just lost my mother, and my heart keenly felt the loss and loneliness. Early on the morning that I was scheduled to speak, I happened to open an envelope containing pictures of my mother. They brought me to tears. I cried for about an hour. A look in the mirror revealed my swollen eyes. I just could not stand up in front of a congregation looking like that! I prayed earnestly to be relieved of the speaking appointment. "Please, God," I asked, "send someone else to take my place. Spare me."

I went to church early, hoping to meet another pastor or other visiting missionaries—or *anyone* who could preach instead of me. Taking a seat in the back row, I watched as each person entered the sanctuary. Soon the time came for the preaching service and I had to prepare to go up front. God had not sent anyone, and I had to preach. I admit, however, that it was with a reluctant Jonah-like spirit.

Just minutes into the sermon, I told an African parable that involved the eruption of a volcano. With great expression, I dramatically stated, "Suddenly, a loud explosion split the air!" The word "air" was scarcely out of my mouth when a loud rumble of thunder jolted everyone in the church. I waited a few moments for the reaction to die down. I looked at the congregation and noted some amused looks. At the end of the service, a number of people commented on the "audio aid." One of the men asked, "Did you ask God for that thunder?" I admitted that I hadn't and that it had come as a perfect surprise, for the morning skies had been clear.

I like to think I heard God in that clap of thunder, rumbling His approval of my following through on the speaking commitment I had made—despite my emotional pain. What a God!

Bienvisa Ladion Nebres

When Do You Look Brightly Again?

"Moreover, when you fast, do not be like the hypocrites, with a sad countenance. For they disfigure their faces that they may appear to men to be fasting. Assuredly, I say to you, they have their reward."
Matt. 6:16, NKJV.

When my son, Luca, was three years old, we clashed over a subject of relative unimportance. Nevertheless, I stayed a little bit angry with him and carried my moodiness throughout the day, though trying not to let Luca see how I felt. When I later called my children for lunch, Luca came into the kitchen. He looked at me quite critically and asked, "Mummy, when do you look brightly again?" I had to laugh. Obviously, he could see through my face to my real feelings. Evidently, I'd looked at him "too darkly."

This small incident made it clear to me how important it is that we be aware that what we feel is what other people often see in us—especially if we're not very good actors! Spiritually speaking, the feelings and attitudes I harbor beneath a pretended façade can also affect the people I meet.

Am I a Christian churchgoer from my own conviction, feeling secure in Christ, or do I just "play church"? Do I read the Bible because of the need of it in my own life, or do I just want biblical knowledge to impress others? Does my outward concern for other people actually reflect a deeper prayer life with Jesus living through me? When perceptive people look past my "outward appearance," what do they see? Someone who is shining brightly for Jesus—and praising Him through my life? Or someone who is trying to mask the darkness inside? God has given us a promise to help us keep our focus on Him and our lights shining for Him: " 'Fear not, for I am with you; be not dismayed, for I am your God. I will strengthen you, yes, I will help you, I will uphold you with My righteous right hand' " (Isa. 41:10, NKJV).

My wish is to be able to focus on the fact that God is with me—no matter what mood I'm in. Little Luca's wise observation instilled in me a desire to not only "look brightly," but also to let His light truly shine from within. After all, Jesus said, " 'You are the light of the world. . . . Let your light so shine before men, that they may see your good works and glorify your Father in heaven' " (Matt. 5:14, 16, NKJV). Let's determine to "look brightly" for the glory of God.

Caroline Naumann

Lost Guide

When he hath put forth all his own, he goeth before them, and the sheep follow him: for they know his voice. John 10:4, ASV.

Kru Yai Noparat, our guide, was gone again. Though he was a forest ranger in the largest national park here in Thailand, he evidently hadn't been a guide very long. At least he was having difficulty staying with our group. As per our weekend plans, we students and teachers had enjoyed a hurried breakfast before 6:00 A.M. in order to complete one more scenic hike before our scheduled departure time of 10:00 A.M. We'd started off our hike, following our guide. Then he'd "disappeared." It was not the first time he'd left us, but this was definitely the longest stretch of time that he'd been gone. We'd followed the directions he'd given at the beginning of the hike and had hiked two hours before arriving at a beautiful stream.

"My heart is racing again," said Arlyn, one of the teachers. "I'd better go back to the trucks." As she started back up the trail, the rest of us paused to pray for her safety. And then we prayed that Kru Yai Noparat would come back. Not only was he our guide, he was also one of our truck drivers!

"We'd better try to retrace our steps," someone suggested. "If it took us two hours to get down here, we won't get back up to the pickup trucks in time to start the hike to our next camp." But four hours later, wondering if waterfalls had changed locations, we knew we were lost.

"There are lots of wild animals in this national park," observed one of my students in a nervous voice. "And look—leeches everywhere! These rocks are so slippery. But we can't phone anyone to tell them where we are because there's no signal out here. All we can do is pray, trust God, and just enjoy our hike."

When the guide finally reappeared, we were relieved, though he seemed to have difficulty getting his bearings in order to lead us back out. Later, when the students were role-playing the events of our eight-and-a-half-hour trek, I was amazed at how often prayer had been a part of our day's adventure! More than one student said, "Jesus was our real Guide. He never gets lost." How true! And His sheep know His voice. Let's praise Jesus for being our Guide today—and every day. He knows the way, and He will never leave us.

Rojean Vasquez Marcia

Do Actions Really Speak Louder Than Words?

"Yes, the way to identify a tree or a person is by the kind of fruit produced." Matt. 7:20, TLB.

I hemorrhaged a vocal cord in the spring of 2013 at the tail end of a rigorous schedule of radio shows and a concert tour of Australia. Extensive traveling, overuse, and—wouldn't you know it—acid reflux caused the problem. Although my voice had felt "fatigued" for several weeks, I'd not given it much thought, never having had problems in the past. I was faithful with the vocal warm-ups and cool-downs surrounding my events. Devastated, I looked at the photo of my bloody vocal chord at the laryngologist's office, not knowing if I'd be able to sing again.

I was put on strict vocal rest (no laughing, coughing, sneezing, or clearing my throat) for two weeks, which turned into four weeks. Fear of possible concert cancellations and postponements swept over me. Worst of all would be the event that couldn't be pushed back—my brother's wedding! It was smack dab in the middle of my physician-ordered silence.

I made a cute lanyard to hang around my neck with a sign that stated my predicament. *So how odd is it going to feel to attend such a joyous, family filled occasion without being able to express a thing?* I wondered. *I haven't seen some relatives for years, and now I won't be able to talk to them!* In the days leading up to the wedding, I hung out with my nieces and nephew who, surprisingly, didn't seem to mind my inability to speak. On the contrary, they seemed even more drawn to me. Unlike the adults who felt awkward around me (thankfully, I found a phone app that could speak when I typed), the children seemed to want to be with me at every waking moment. I learned that the two- and nearly four-year-old attentively "listened" to my guidance and leading though I could use only simple hand gestures and facial expressions. Remarkable! I didn't need words! Praise God! To this day, I remain their favorite "auntie." Not only did they win my heart, but I seemed to have made a huge impression on theirs.

I believe we sometimes put too much emphasis on words when communication is built on so much more (body language, energy, facial expressions, and actions). My damaged vocal cords experience has made me view the world differently and begs me to ask the question: If you couldn't verbally tell anyone you were a Christian, would they still know? If so, how? "By this shall all men know that ye are my disciples, if ye have love one to another" (John 13:35).

Naomi Striemer

January 29

Take Care of My Dad

Direct my footsteps. Ps. 119:133, NIV.

One day I was going through some of my children's old school papers and found a paper from my oldest daughter's folder. She'd titled it, "What Do You Want to Be When You Grow Up?"

I smiled and started reading because I wanted to see just how close she had come to her goal! You see, Kathy is an adult now with an LPN (licensed practical nurse) degree and is also in nursing school where she plans to earn an RN (registered nurse) degree. Kathy is also married with nine children and nine grandchildren. As I quickly read Kathy's childhood composition, I discovered that she had written several times, "When I grow up, I want to be a nurse so I can take care of my dad."

Well, after Kathy became an adult, her dad became legally blind. Recently, he'd been dealing with some medical problems during which time he'd been hospitalized for three days of testing. During that time our son, who lives two and a half hours away, came and stayed with the rest of us until Dad came home. Kathy couldn't come at the time because of her work and busy nursing school schedule.

One day she phoned and said, "Mother, school is out for the summer. I will be able to take a family leave. I want to come and help take care of my dad." So that is what she did, giving me a much needed break as well. Kathy's dad cooperated fully and was ecstatic to be able to have his own private nurse. He was also proud that the nurse was his daughter.

Kathy's dream of becoming a nurse so she could care for her father had come true. God had planted that desire in her heart thirty-seven years earlier in preparation for this medical crisis as well as for the fulfillment of His divine plan for her life. When Kathy wrote her long-ago school paper, she had no idea that she was writing out God's plan for her life. Truly He had directed her footsteps!

Our Father in heaven has also ordered our steps. He knew us before we were born. He knows what we're going to do before we do it. He even knows the number of hairs on our heads.

How can we not worship You, God, for guiding our footsteps? Amen.

Elaine J. Johnson

38

Converted by His Wife!

How do you know, wife, whether you will save your husband? Or, how
do you know, husband, whether you will save your wife?
1 Cor. 7:16, NIV.

The Lord is with those who labor in His vineyard. Surely I can testify to that!
My husband, Edward, did not join me in baptism when I became
a Christian and joined the church in 1997. However, he did begin to
occasionally visit church with me. About ten years after joining the church,
I suddenly developed a desire to preach in a series of evangelistic meetings,
also referred to as a "campaign." Therefore, I was delighted when the church
headquarters in South Botswana offered an evangelism training course for lay
people—those who have never been formally trained as preachers. Having this
resource, our local church decided to hold an evangelistic series. My fellow
church members chose me as the preacher!

Humbled, I went to my marvelous Lord in prayer. "Lord, work for me as I
work for You. You know the burden I carry for my husband. Let me be able to
praise You at the end of the two weeks for what You have done!" This bold prayer
came from the depths of my heart.

By this time, Edward was regularly attending church with me but had never
made a decision for baptism. I was hoping he would go with me to the meetings
every day, but he came only three times. On the last day of the evangelistic
campaign, I preached about the importance of baptism. I shared the story of the
converted jailer, found in Acts 16. Then I made an appeal to the audience. "If,
like that jailer," I implored, "you do not want to lose more time before making a
decision for baptism, please raise your hand."

One of the hands that went up was that of Edward, my own husband!
Encouraged, I made a further appeal: "If you raised your hand, please come
forward." Edward rose and walked forward as I silently praised God's name.

When I later asked Edward why he hadn't made the decision for baptism
earlier, he responded, "I almost did during the last two baptisms I attended.
But I just couldn't." At that moment I realized God had reserved my husband's
decision so I'd clearly see how He was honoring my faith, my efforts for Him,
and my faithful prayers on Edward's behalf.

God's ways and timing are the best. So, praying wives (and others), be
encouraged!

Bogadi Koosaletse

Lost and Found

He shall call upon me, and I will answer him: I will be with him in trouble; I will deliver him, and honour him. Ps. 91:15.

I have to run by the grocery store before work to pick up some ice cream for our office get-together today. Can I get you anything?" asked my girlfriend over the telephone. I told her she could get a hot drink for me on this chilly Monday morning. About an hour later, she phoned again: "Can you meet me at the office entrance to get your drink?" Through the open window of her car, she handed me my drink.

"What's wrong?" I asked, noticing she didn't seem her usual cheery self.

She responded, "Being a sunny day today, I wore my favorite sunglasses but think I dropped them in the store. I'm on my way back there to see if anyone found and turned them in." Seeing her sad face, I offered to ride along with her. Before getting into her car, I carefully searched around the seat and on the floor, just in case her sunglasses had slid into some crevice.

"I've already looked everywhere in the car," she said, though I insisted on searching through the back seats and the trunk. My efforts yielded no sunglasses.

"No one has turned in any sunglasses," a clerk at the customer service desk told my friend back at the store, while I retraced my friend's in-store steps down the freezer aisle and through the checkout area. Still no sunglasses.

Lord, I prayed, *please help us find the sunglasses.* I continued praying and praising for what He would do. "It took me a long time to find sunglasses like those," my friend sobbed as we got back to the car. In silence, she tried to compose herself, while I continued my prayer vigil. We sat in the car a little while before my friend started the motor.

Lord, I continued praying, *this isn't really about sunglasses; it's about my friend knowing You care about the details of our lives.* I reached down to pick up my previously forgotten hot drink for a sip. In so doing, my hand hit something hard. I automatically picked it up. The sunglasses! In response to my friend's questioning—but joyful—look, I responded, "I don't know what happened. But I've been praying and the Lord just sort of put them into my hand."

I called. He answered. Just like He promised He would do—for all of us!

Jemima Dollosa Orillosa

Living His Love

Love: a feeling of strong or constant affection for a person.

"A new command I give you: Love one another. As I have loved you, so you must love one another." John 13:34, NIV.

Personal and intimate. Unconditional, yet undeserved. Free, yet not cheap. Endless.

These terms only partially describe God's love for us.

This month's contributors have experienced this love on ordinary days but in extraordinary ways. Through God's exquisite "painting" of nature, or in an unseen band of angels, or through the words of an apparently purposeless, post-divorce greeting card, or tucked in the words of a child reminding us to forgive. God's love is evident everywhere. These devotionals also illustrate opportunities God provides for us to "love Him back"—by sharing a financial blessing with someone in need, returning tithe, being patient about unanswered prayer, or giving one's all as did the mother who made an exhausting run to reach her incarcerated son before it was too late.

The best way to luxuriate in—and share—God's love is by living it. Savoring it, one moment at a time.

februazy 1

Love Covers ...

Love covers over all wrongs. Prov. 10:12, NIV.

As I knelt to hug her, my young Doberman pup leaped into my arms welcoming me home. Then I looked aghast at the living room carpet. Five pairs of my shoes lay scattered across the living room—all chewed. I had obviously not secured the closet door when I left for work. Bored, Sheba had entertained herself all morning. And she liked variety—one shoe each of the five pairs—and quality leather too. I gathered the shoes and drove them to the repair shop. Slowly I held up my favorite taupe shoes with the pointy toes. I smiled encouragingly at the repair man behind the counter. He sadly shook his head.

"Can't you even try?" I pleaded. Again he shook his head. I held up the apple-green ones that coordinated with my sage and cranberry dress. He shook his head, more emphatically this time. I showed him the sandals I had recently purchased for summer. Sadly, I left with my favorite shoes in a bag—to throw away. Fortunately, the store where I bought my shoes had a yearly sale going on and I was able to replace a few of my shoes.

That was only the beginning. Sheba chewed a new garden hose in half. Tore off the face of my antique teddy bear, the one I had treasured since age two—a costly repair. One day I returned to the car to discover that Sheba had chewed in half both front seat belts of my Camero! And one in back as well. I totaled up the cost years later to discover that my beloved Sheba had chewed hundreds of dollars worth of items. But still I loved her.

She was my 110-pound companion, gentle and loving. She rode with me on writing assignments for work, not left alone in the car, of course. She provided me with exercise walking her and protection too. Kids broke into my neighbors' homes, but not mine. She would lay her head on my shoulder as I gave her a hug. She would place her nose in my hand and look at me with soulful eyes. Eventually, she traded her puppy chewing for chewy bones.

I wouldn't say that I forgave Sheba seventy times seven as Jesus recommends in the Bible—but it was close. The Bible also says that love covers a multitude of sins. It does, really. Love covered for Sheba. Those of us who live in a family or a marriage, or have close friends, know that love covers a multitude of mistakes, mishaps, accidents, and even sins.

Edna Maye Gallington

The Policeman's Mistake

And we know that in all things God works for the good of those who love him, who have been called according to his purpose.
Rom. 8:28, NIV.

I clearly remember what it was like to visit prison for the first time. Before officials would allow me behind locked doors, they searched my belongings and also my person. I endured all this in order to visit my beloved fifteen-year-old son. He was a drug user and was in prison for robbing a store with a toy gun. He needed an advocate who loved him.

I was led down a small, unventilated hallway with two cells. In one of them was my child. When he saw me, he dragged himself—weeping—across the floor towards me. Seeing him in this tragic state was almost too much for me to bear. I could not contain an outburst of tears. Some ten minutes later, a policeman opened the door and called the name of my boy. "We are taking him to the forum to undergo an assessment by a social assistant and a psychologist."

Startled, I asked, "Can I go with him? I have just gotten here to visit him."

"You can go," replied the officer, "but not with us. You do have the right to speak in the forum if you can get there on your own." I knew where the building was located, but it was quite a distance from the prison. The policeman left with my son. Once outside, I began to run as fast as I could toward the building where my son would be assessed. While I ran, my mind raced to Romans 8:28, a promise from God that I continually claimed while I strained to keep up my pace.

Exhausted, I arrived at the forum just in time. A few minutes later, an official called to my son but addressed him by a name that was not his. Looking up at my son, the psychologist said, "This is not the guy who should be here!" The officer apologized and said he'd return my son to the prison and make the correct inmate exchange. Suddenly, spotting me, the psychologist asked, "Are you this young man's mother?"

I nodded.

"Then leave this boy here," the psychologist ordered. "I'd like to talk with both this young man and his mother together."

God used a prison official's mistake and my exhausting run to turn this situation into an opportunity for me to advocate on behalf of my son. Years ago, God also used mankind's sinful mistakes—and Christ's earthly "exhausting run"—to turn mankind's fall into an opportunity for Him to advocate on our behalf. What love! What unconditional parental love!

Vera Lúcia F. S. Ferrari

God Heals Animals Too!

A righteous man regards the life of his animal. Prov. 12:10, NKJV.

O LORD, You preserve man and beast. Ps. 36:6, NKJV.

Karamjit Kaur's buffalo was very sick.

The vet was called in and the medication started.

The uncertainty continued for a couple of months. Uncertainty, because Karamjit's family livelihood came from the buffalo's milk. And also uncertainty about losing the animal altogether. After all, the family was considerably attached to their animal and they were concerned about its well-being. It would be no exaggeration, in fact, to say that a special bond existed between the family and their animal. The buffalo had brought them blessings. They even considered the buffalo to be part of the family. Knowing there was little hope of the buffalo recovering, therefore, caused them great sadness.

One day, about the time the family was tempted to give up all hope of this situation becoming any better, a woman dropped by their house. She was a woman of faith.

"We are sure that our sick buffalo is not going to live much longer," they told her with heavy hearts.

"Have you thought about offering a prayer about your animal's situation?" she asked them. "Here is the phone number of Mrs. Sunila Gill. Her husband is the pastor of this area." The Karamjit family called the number. The party at the other end of the phone line prayed right then and there—over the phone—for both the buffalo and its family. Miraculously, the buffalo started showing signs of improvement!

The Karamjit family was so delighted that they invited Mrs. Sunila Gill and her pastor husband to their home for a prayer meeting. This is how a Bible study started in the home of this Sikh family. Meanwhile, their buffalo fully recovered and the family's faith—in a God who took care of their animal—was born.

God, in His great love, has His own ways of reaching out to people. He who caused Baalam's donkey to speak also put a healing hand on this buffalo, using it to convert a family. Karamjit's family is now attending church regularly and will soon be baptized. Amen!

Premila Masih

My Band of Shining Angels

"I will have compassion on you," says the LORD your Redeemer.
Isa. 54:8, NIV.

he nightmare of a disintegrating marriage had brought me to the nadir of my life, my grief and despair rivaling the bleak, midwinter cold that clawed at the windows and seeped under the doors of the old farmhouse. I moved numbly through the days and dreaded nights when sleep was fitful and troubled. It was on one of these nights that the ringing telephone pulled me back to unwelcome consciousness. My sister's almost reverent voice, reaching across many miles, informed me she'd seen my house in her midnight dream in the midst of snow-covered fields stretching away on every side. And suddenly, there—*there*! Standing shoulder to shoulder, arms linked together in an unbreakable circle that completely surrounded my house, she'd seen a band of shining angels. "I thought you'd like to know," she whispered, and hung up.

I turned to face the window. *Are they there, God? Are they, really?* My room was so still. So cold. Frozen, like my heart. A full moon's pale light fell in a fragile oblique across the floor, a sliver of moonbeam that might shatter into a thousand crystal splinters the moment my toe touched it. I wanted—no, *needed*—them to be there, my angels. There with me and my three children, sleeping across the hall. We were so alone. So unprotected. So unloved. I crept toward the window, knowing I would die if it weren't so. Knowing I couldn't live if I didn't look. Holy words swirled into my mind: *"Your Maker is your Husband. . . . The Lord has called you like a woman forsaken . . . a wife [wooed and won] in youth, when she is [later] refused and scorned. . . . For though the mountains should depart . . . yet My love and kindness shall not depart from you"* (Isa. 54:5–10, AMP). I leaned my forehead against the glass. *Promise, God? Promise?*

I lifted my eyes and first looked farther than I could even see, to where the snowy fields ended abruptly against the black night sky. Then, inch by inch, my gaze fell down the pane to the snow that drifted against the evergreens lining our moon-drenched yard below. I saw nothing, but in a moment of overpowering awareness, I knew they were there. My angels—shoulder to shoulder, arms linked, faces upturned to my window. *"I will not in any way fail you . . . nor leave you without support. . . . [I will] not in any degree leave you helpless nor forsake, nor let [you] down. . . . [Assuredly not!]"* (Heb. 13:5, AMP). And in these thirty-six years since, He never has.

Jeannette Busby Johnson

God Will Take Care of You

And my God shall supply all your need according to His riches in glory
by Christ Jesus. Phil. 4:19, NKJV.

I have experienced in my life what it means to have to do without or to have very few of the necessities of life. Being the eldest of ten children in an impoverished family, I learned early in life how to be unselfish and to share whatever I had with my siblings. If I had one apple or one small cake, I made sure to divide it among all of us. This set an example for the younger ones to follow. We also shared what we had with neighbors and friends alike.

Even though my parents were poor, they were still individuals who gave to others. People who were in need often called on them for help. Even though a person gives with no strings attached and expecting nothing in return, invariably God blesses the giver. So at an early age, I learned to trust in and pray to a God who is faithful to those who help others in need.

Years later, there were many times when I did not know how my tuition for high school and junior college would be paid, but God always came through for me. I worked part time on campus during the regular semester. I sold Christian magazines and books during the summer time to offset my educational expenses. Somehow, some way, I always had just enough money, so I did not have to drop out of school and interrupt my course of studies.

During the last semester of my college years, my bills backed up. I could not see a way out. Then a wonderful pastor and his wife, who were generous as had been my own parents, offered to help by allowing me to live in their home near campus, thus eliminating my boarding expenses. The pastor's wife even paid for my class dress.

With the help of my heavenly Provider, I graduated from college and landed a job in a church-affiliated school. There I was able to finish paying my educational debt. Two years later, God opened the way for me to move to the United States. Once again, I experienced financial difficulties as I was both working and studying. Yet I was able to complete a nursing degree.

Truly I can say it pays to trust God and give to others in His name. My impoverished parents were unconditionally generous, and God always gave back in one way or another. When we share His love, it has a way of finding us again and making a way out of no way.

Kollis Salmon-Fairweather

Wait It Out!

He shall call upon me, and I will answer him: I will be with him in trouble; I will deliver him, and honour him. Ps. 91:15.

I am not the one to initiate a pity party; however, it seems as if my whole world is falling apart. Satan has literally attacked my relationship with some loved ones. He's also attacked my finances and health. Perhaps you, too, are being tried and tempted in ways that threaten to weaken your faith. Yet, let's revisit the lives of three Bible characters who chose to remain faithful to God—even when under the enemy's attack. From their examples of faithfulness under fire, we can draw strength and resolve to stay true to God in our own difficulties as well.

I think of Job's faithfulness while enduring one loss after another. At one point in his trials, Job declared, "Though he slay me, yet will I trust in him." God eventually honored Job by restoring twice as much as he had lost. God allowed him to live an additional 140 years and see four generations of his descendants (Job 13:15; 42:10, 16).

Then there was Daniel, the Jewish exile surrounded by idolatry. He remained faithful to the living God despite royal decrees—on pain of death—demanding the contrary. Though Daniel's long life was not an easy one, God, in His love, chose to honor the prophet's faithfulness by delivering him in old age from death in a den of lions (Dan. 6:16, 23).

And remember Joseph who was sold into slavery by his own brothers? He was falsely accused of adultery and thrown into prison (Gen. 39:14–20; 41:1). God eventually honored Joseph when Pharaoh entrusted him to be governor over all the land of Egypt (Gen. 41:41).

As with the low points in the experiences of these Bible characters, you, too, may feel as if the enemy has pulled the pin out of a hand grenade and thrown it into the midst of your life. Yet we, like these men, can rely on God's love and wait out our trials. God will strengthen us as He strengthened them. Whether God chooses to honor our faithfulness this side of heaven or not, we can still say, along with Joseph, "Ye [whatever enemy we're facing] thought evil against me; but God meant it unto good" (Gen. 50:20).

As the saying goes, "When you feel as if you're at the end of your rope, tie a knot in it and hang on." Wait it out—by waiting on God. No matter what, He is still love (1 John 4:8).

Cora A. Walker

Trip Into the Past, Present, and Future

Only be careful, and watch yourselves closely so that you do not forget the things your eyes have seen or let them fade from your heart as long as you live. Teach them to your children and to their children after them. Deut. 4:9, NIV.

From my late parents' home we gathered many boxes containing old letters. My father had saved all letters and documents, nicely sorted and labeled. I also found my own letters to my parents. A little while ago, I started reading through letters I'd written my parents from Africa. Reading them was like taking a journey into my past. These letters were reminders of long-forgotten memories, events, and emotions.

One day, during this time, I ran across Deuteronomy 4:9 in my daily Bible reading plan. The words of the text stood out as if I'd never read them before.

The Bible book of Deuteronomy reports what Moses wanted to say to the people of Israel at the end of his life. He repeated all the important things in the experience of the people, how God had brought them out of Egypt and led them through the desert. He called upon them not to forget their experiences and not to forget to tell their children and grandchildren about them.

I treasure the memories of my family's experiences, especially ones directly related to God's leading. I don't want to forget either, so these old letters are important documents for me.

At present, my children are too busy to be interested in the past. Every new day they wrestle with current challenges in their lives. Yet someday they'll better understand how much we can learn from the past. Learning from the past is particularly important for believers. When we see how God has worked in the lives of other people, our faith grows. That is why Moses said, in essence, "Don't forget how God has led you. He knows best. Follow His directions and you will thrive. Tell your children and grandchildren so that nothing is forgotten!"

In the Bible, God has given us a treasured "box" full of important documents, letters, experiences, and stories. Through these, we can learn valuable lessons from "virtual" trips we take into the past. Furthermore, this Sacred Book is a faithful guide for our present-day lives. And not only that, but the Bible's prophecies tell us what will happen in the future. God's Word is our treasure box containing His informative and consoling letters of love to us. Let's read them!

Hannele Ottschofski

The Infinite Game

[Love] always protects, always trusts, always hopes, always perseveres.
1 Cor. 13:7, NIV.

Do you know Seth Godin? I love him. A few weeks ago, he wrote this powerful little piece about the Infinite Game. I just read it and cried.

The infinite game is the one you keep on playing, not to win or lose, but because the journey is all there is, and it's worth it. It's the game where you never stop giving. It's where you throw a slower pitch so the batter can hit the ball.

It's not about what happens in the long run—you getting the job, or reaching some great goal or whatever. It's about that daily laughter with your family and friends. It's that daily sense of peace when you look in the mirror and you don't have any of that shame and you don't have any of that stuff. And you're looking at yourself with that joy of, "You know what? I am who I am, and that's enough, and God is crazy about me!"

The cry and desire of my heart is that we do that for each other! That's what the journey of recovery is about—playing the infinite game. That's what step twelve in the Twelve Steps of recovery is about: "Having had a spiritual experience as a result of these steps, we tried to carry this message to others and to practice these principles in all our affairs."

We are asked to walk alongside each other in our recovery. To fight for each others' healing.

It's not about completing that project or making that fund-raising goal or even starting that new ministry. Those things only matter for one reason: to keep us in the game. The goal is only ever about helping the next person, the next family, stand up. That's what we do for each other in recovery.

Paul says, "I press on to take hold of that for which Christ Jesus took hold of me. Brothers and sisters, I do not consider myself yet to have taken hold of it. But one thing I do: Forgetting what is behind and straining toward what is ahead, I press on toward the goal to win the prize for which God has called me heavenward in Christ Jesus" (Phil. 3:12–14, NIV).

That's the infinite game! That's what God calls us to do.

Thanks for staying in the game!

Cheri Peters

Messages From God

"But ask the animals, and they will teach you." Job 12:7, NIV.

To say my sister, Tibby, loves animals would be an understatement. She has an amazing understanding and respect for animals more than anyone I have ever known. She has rescued and found homes for many animals and recently spent two years domesticating seven feral cats. She gave up her bedroom for six months, patiently and lovingly working with them to develop special bonds. They now sleep in her and her husband's laps and love to be indoors with them! Tibby has always seen God through nature and feels that God sometimes gives us glimpses of Himself through the animals that He created (Rom. 1:20). This was never more apparent than in the early morning hours of February 22, 2008.

Our dear mother was nearing the end of her life. Three years prior, Mama had come to live with us after my wonderful husband, Steven, finished her downstairs apartment. It was such a joy having her live there. My sister and her husband live only minutes away, so we were all able to spend some very special times with Mama that we will cherish forever.

One sad day, we called in hospice care to help with Mama. Around 4:00 A.M. the next morning, Steven and I went downstairs to sit with Mama. At that very hour, a soft animal sound awakened Tibby in her home. It was not a bark or a whimper but an audible *"woof."* Tibby looked out her bedroom window and saw two large and beautiful white dogs that she had never seen before. Directly under her window, they were looking up at her. She slipped outside and they quietly walked over, continuing to watch her. Tibby had a quiet sense of God's love surrounding her; a feeling that God was comforting her since Mama's failing health was on her heart. So when we phoned her at 5:00 A.M. to tell her the end was near, Tibby was not surprised. Our mother passed away peacefully at 6:09 A.M. that morning with her loving family surrounding her. The two white dogs never returned to my sister's home.

It will only be when Jesus returns and we are in our heavenly home that we will fully understand all of the amazing events that have taken place on this earth and all the messages of hope and comfort that our heavenly Father has sent to us. And we will have eternity to listen to Jesus telling us the rest of those stories.

Jean Dozier Davey

Senhor Jair

"Blessed are the poor in spirit, for theirs is the kingdom of heaven."
Matt. 5:3, NIV.

I met *Senhor* (Mr.) Jair in the most dramatic moment of my life, and I will never forget the lesson of humbleness I learned. I was born in the countryside, the daughter of a man whose family had many possessions. But due to a prolonged drought, we had lost everything. My father became an employee, but he taught his children about the pride and vanity of the Portuguese nobles.

I am the youngest sister of five siblings. I suffered some abuse in childhood, which led to an introverted personality and a huge social phobia. In my adolescence, we went to live in a large metropolitan area, and I went through several administrative jobs. I got married, had two daughters, and stopped working. However, my life was not going well. I was afraid of people and isolated myself. Because of a complicated financial situation, I joyfully received a proposal to work from home, sewing for productions, and my self-esteem improved a lot. Then, the same person invited me to work in her clothing manufacturing plant. Always quiet, but working hard, I acquired her friendship. She gradually discovered that I liked to read. She loaned me several books from a Christian publisher that brought me much peace. I had an advanced knowledge of the Bible and knew some truths. So, she invited me to visit her church. I was afraid and said I did not have appropriate clothing—or even social status. My answer was based on my pride. But she insisted, and I ended up going with my husband one evening.

I was shaking, but I was very well received in the most humble church I've ever seen. Sitting in the last bench was *Senhor* Jair. He was an elderly gentleman, wearing wide and shabby clothes and slippers on his feet. Wrinkles creased his weathered face, which exuded love and humility. One glance at this gentleman reminded me of my lame excuse for almost not attending church. I asked God for forgiveness, and I began to ask for transformation of my selfishness, vanity, and pride. I found in other—even well-dressed—members the same love and humility of the old man. Mr. Jair stayed with us a while, then disappeared. Nobody knew anything about him. But today I still remember the lesson of humility that he taught me—without saying a word.

Isn't it just like the Lord to have put Mr. Jair in my path, to teach me to be humble in spirit and love quietly as Jesus does?

Rose G. S. Matos

The Greeting Card

She is clothed with strength and dignity, and she laughs without fear of the future. Prov. 31:25, NLT.

It was a brand-new card. I didn't remember buying it, but there it was in my card file. The bright words, "Happy Birthday to Our Son-in-Law," elicited a whole range of emotions. My daughter's divorce would be final in a few days. The sad circumstance hadn't quite sunk in, but clearly I wasn't going to need this card anymore. I can't quite bring myself to throw it away, so I am thinking I will give it to my friend whose daughter is happily married. She'll be able to use it.

As parents, why do we implicitly believe we are preparing our children for happy lives? Answering my own question, I suppose we just cannot imagine they'll need to be ready for sadness or even heartbreak. But the reality suggests a more pragmatic view. My daughter is now part of the 50 percent of married couples who divorce. But numbers aside, I am grieving for her and praying for her. She is more than a statistic to God.

Past weathering the initial shock, she has willed herself to move on. She was feigning excitement yesterday when telephoning to describe the new rental house, carefully glossing over the fact that it's half the size of her current home. I will drive there next week to help her pack boxes. I will have to "buck up." It's no time to cry.

In truth, I'm relieved she does not assume things should be perfect. She doesn't operate under some misconception that trouble will never knock on her door. She gives herself permission to mourn but then sits down with genuine determination to plan a new budget.

I'm grateful she believes God is near to her, even now. She has felt His love in gentle comfort during sleepless nights. Turning to Him when nothing made sense, she has been blessed with insight and reassurance. In the beginning she was emotional, but now objectivity and thoughtful realism need to hold sway. With God's help, I know she will move into the next phase of her life with resolve and tenacity. The losses of today will fuel her hopes for tomorrow.

So what's a mom to do? I wish I could have protected her from this. But I need to move on too. Surely I can rest in the assurance that she has grown up to be a spiritual woman—her faith is strong. How I thank God for the blessing of a daughter—married or not!

Linda Nottingham

You Can't Outgive God

"Give, and it will be given to you; good measure, pressed down, shaken together, running over, will be put into your lap. For the measure you give will be the measure you get back." Luke 6:38, RSV.

We are living in difficult financial times. Jobs are hard to get. Many are struggling. They cannot make ends meet and live from paycheck to paycheck. It is a hand-to-mouth situation. If you are working at a job, your hiring company may have cut your hours. Working overtime is no longer an option for many people. Home foreclosures are occurring everywhere. Young families cannot afford to pay back student loans.

I am working for a company as one of its managers. I have worked there for seven years. I hear many coworkers lamenting that they can no longer work overtime. Yet since I have been working at this company, my employer has scheduled an extra two and a half hours of work for me every week. That means I am paid for ten hours of overtime every month. I am very grateful. Yet, in a way, I am not surprised because I know who is blessing me with these extra hours. It is God who keeps His promises. He promises in Malachi 3:10–12 that if we pay Him an honest tithe (10 percent of our gain), He will bless us. I pay an honest tithe on my earnings, and God watches over me, keeping His promises. For me, honoring God through my tithe-paying has been my "remedy" for overcoming financial struggles. Though I face challenges, God somehow enables the person who schedules our work hours to see my extra hours as "normal."

I have received so many blessings from God that I cannot count them. For example, I once had an eye surgery. I calculated that the combined bill from my doctors, the hospital, and other care providers would bring the bill to $8,000. My insurance company paid just $1,500 of that amount, leaving me with a bill of $6,500. But when all my medical bills arrived, the remaining total amounted to only $4,830. God had somehow taken care of the rest.

I've never failed to pay my bills on time because my pockets are protected by God. I believe He is honoring me, according to His promise, because I am honoring Him.

Father, teach me each day to count it as a blessing to return faithfully what belongs to You. For You are always more than generous with me. Amen.

Orpha Gumbo Maseko

From Ashes to Diamonds

*"To console those who mourn in Zion, to give them beauty for ashes,
the oil of joy for mourning,
the garment of praise for the spirit of heaviness; that they may be
called trees of righteousness,
the planting of the LORD, that He may be glorified." Isa. 61:3, NKJV.*

On Tuesday, September 19, 2007, Saint Lucia was a country in mourning. We watched as the remains of our former beloved prime minister, Sir John George Melvin Compton, were carted away in his favorite pickup truck. Tears were shed as the heavily starched state pall bearers bore his casket on their sturdy shoulders from the vehicle to the funeral parlor for cremation. It must have been hard for the prime minister's family to realize their beloved had been reduced to ashes.

I have always been fascinated by ash and dust as it relates to human beings. To me, they have always represented the true nothingness of everything. In his play *Hamlet* (Act II, Scene II), William Shakespeare aptly describes the paradoxical nature of mortals. "What a piece of work is a man! How noble in reason, how infinite in faculty! . . . The paragon of animals! And yet to me, what is this quintessence of dust?" In talking to God once, Abraham described his own lowly estate as "dust and ashes" (Gen. 18:27).

"Is this the sum of the human experience?" I asked myself the day we said goodbye to our prime minister. These were indeed depressing thoughts. Then, some time later, I read an amazing article on the uses of ash. Ash does have value, I learned.

According to findings in this article, the carbon released during cremation can be captured as a dark powder and then heated to produce graphite. The writer of this article continued by stating that graphite, when sent to a lab, can be synthesized into fancy gems that resemble colored diamonds. I thought, *If a scientist can take cremation ash and turn it into "diamonds," just imagine what God can do with us while we're still living!*

You may feel that your life is one great sweeping of dust and ashes right now with no purpose. Yet remember that He who so wonderfully and fearfully formed us from dust of the earth has promised to give eventual "beauty" in the place of our ashes. What is love—what is it—if not this? Despite brokenness, we are all diamonds in the making. God transforms!

Judelia Medard-Santiesteban

Love Letters

Then they that feared the LORD spake often one to another: and the LORD hearkened, and heard it, and a book of remembrance was written before him for them that feared the LORD, and that thought upon his name. Mal. 3:16.

If ever there was a "romantic," it was Andrew. Soon to be married, Andrew came to me, asking me to create a special hand-made book to house the love letters exchanged between him and his soon-to-be bride. Andrew's plan was to surprise her with this romantic offering as a wedding gift, a place where their letters of love could be kept and cherished forever and ever! He gave me clear specifications. The cost: immaterial. The size: 9 x 12-inch pages with corner tabs in which to insert the edges of the letters. Nothing too fussy or "girlish." Nothing gaudy or overpowering, he said. Just stylish, sweet, artsy, tasteful, and durable as their love would be.

"I want her and me to be able to always look back on this anticipatory time in our relationship when our love was fresh, blooming, and frankly sweet," he said. "I want my bride to know for always how much I cherish her. I want to be able to read and reread about the love she cherishes for me as well."

I could not wait to get started. I chose off-white, handmade rag paper to symbolize purity and natural Asian skeleton leaves and raffia for embellishment. I prayed they would both love the book. It was as he wished—simple, natural, and yet possessing an artistic flair.

Working on Andrew's special memory book took my thoughts to another book mentioned in God's Word, a book of remembrance. In Malachi 3:16, God said He writes in this book the names of those that "feared the LORD, and that thought upon his name."

In fact, the whole Bible is a collection of God's love letters to us. It declares how His love led to the death of His dear Son on the cross in our place so that we may have eternal life through the blood which Jesus shed for us wretched sinners. God's love letters tell us He's preparing a place for us to live with Him. They share that, even now, He cares for each of us personally, individually, as if we were His only one true love. As Andrew's love letter book was for his beloved, the Bible is a timeless collection of love letters from our Bridegroom to His bride—you and me . . . *His* beloved. Let's read and reread them!

Cathy Shannon

February 15

The Healing Path of Forgiveness

Remember ye not the former things, neither consider the things of old. Behold, I will do a new thing; now it shall spring forth; shall ye not know it? I will even make a way in the wilderness, and rivers in the desert. Isa. 43:18, 19.

For if ye forgive men their trespasses, your heavenly Father will also forgive you. Matt. 6:14.

Have you ever been the recipient of forgiveness? It feels good, doesn't it! Have you ever offered forgiveness to someone who has done you wrong? If you are like me, you can identify with these questions. We all have experienced the reality of being hurt and having to make the decision of whether or not to walk down the path of forgiveness.

Yet walking down this path is possible only with Christ in our hearts. Alone, we would find it impossible to forgive. It is a journey that we are not capable of making on our own. God knows that apart from Him we cannot handle the emotional roller coaster that accompanies such a challenging process. But in His love, we can extend His love to others through forgiveness.

Forgiveness is a two-way street. Both the forgiver and the forgiven benefit equally from the process. We are admonished in the Bible that receiving God's forgiveness is conditional upon our first forgiving others. And again, we can do that only with His help.

Did you know, according to scientific journals, that we can experience greater levels of spiritual, physical, mental, social, and emotional well-being along the path of forgiveness? Let's briefly explore them.

Spiritually, forgiving others allows us to experience more oneness with God. We cannot achieve this oneness if our hearts are at odds with our fellow men.

Physically, forgiving others helps us experience fewer incidences of hypertension, heart attacks, diabetes, and insomnia.

Mentally, forgiving others enhances our own positive thought processes and helps alleviate depression and anxiety disorders.

Socially, forgiving others restores and strengthens relationships.

Emotionally, forgiving others removes the burden of guilt—for both parties.

Lord, help us choose the path of forgiveness today.

Althea Y. Boxx

God Is in Control

Before they call, I will answer; and while they are yet speaking, I will hear. Isa. 65:24.

God's providence is a great marvel. God does provide for our needs and often in advance. Have you ever experienced that? Sometimes it takes a while for us to realize what He's done for us until we look back later and see the marvelous things He has done in our lives.

In February 2009, I found myself in a wonderfully unusual situation. I'd been able to lead my physics students through the entire syllabus except for the very last section. They'd completed all the lab experiments and reports. This meant we were well ahead of schedule for completing the curriculum by March. I was elated. We would have a lot of time to review and practice answering past examination questions before the students would have to take their official external examinations that year.

Then, unexpectedly, I fell ill. I became so ill, in fact, that I had to miss teaching the rest of the school term. When I returned to school, I had only enough time to "crash teach" the last section of the physics syllabus, which we had not yet covered before my illness. Then it was time for my students to take their examinations.

According to the test results that year, my students did well, with only one of them failing the exam. I praised God for that outcome despite my illness-caused absence from the classroom. God knew that I would be missing out on seven weeks of teaching, so He had ensured—in advance—that my students' experiments and lab work would all be completed and recorded ahead of schedule. He enabled my students to understand key concepts so that we were able to complete most of the syllabus early. I need not have worried about my students during my illness. God had already made provision for them long before I became ill. Since that school year I have tried, in vain, to complete the same amount of class work as I did in 2009. God knew.

Ellen G. White, in *The Ministry of Healing,* wrote, "Our heavenly Father has a thousand ways to provide for us of which we know nothing. Those who accept the one principle of making the service of God supreme, will find perplexities vanish and a plain path before their feet" (p. 481). Each time you feel despondent, remind yourself that God is faithful and not only loves you but knows—and will provide—for all your needs.

Andrea Francis

Hiding Place

For if our heart condemns us, God is greater than our heart, and
knows all things. 1 John 3:20, NKJV.

It's two-thirty in the morning, a mere few precious hours from when my
babies will wake up and the daily grind will begin again. I'm exhausted, but
I can't sleep. I'm haunted by an uneasiness, a persistent sense of guilt and
inadequacy. For the last few days, I've felt a longing to crawl into my Father's
throne room, where I'm sure I can find a hiding place and peace.

I try to imagine what it would be like to slip into that quiet place for a bit of
rest. I don't need any special treatment. I'd be satisfied to curl up in a soft corner
somewhere—better yet, behind His throne where no one need see me but Him.
I expect my accusers might come bustling in behind me, nasty fingers drawn,
voices calling out my faults, which I can almost hear.

"She doesn't work hard enough!" "She wastes so much time!" "She's not
taking good enough care of her children, and they are snotty and coughing. (You
hear them now?)" "She stays up too late!" "She says lots of foolish things!" "She
doesn't appreciate her husband enough!"

"She is undisciplined!" "She doesn't keep up with the chores!" "She doesn't
contribute a penny to the family livelihood, though she's well-educated!" "She
has lots of ambition, but little motivation!" "She covets a bigger home and tighter
body!" "She thinks and says unkind things!"

And I'd stand trembling behind the throne ready to say, "It's true. It's all true,
and I'm so ashamed." But I wouldn't need to say anything because my Father
already knows everything. He doesn't need me to answer. The fingers pointing
towards me can't get through Him. In fact, they don't bother Him one bit.

I wouldn't need to hear what He says in response to the accusatory voices. I
wouldn't need to see what He writes in the dust. I just would want to hear Him
say to me, "Woman, where are your accusers?" And I would look up and find the
courtyard empty.

Then I'd give anything, just for a minute, to be a child again, to just crawl up
in His lap and, without a care in the world, fall asleep for a while and rest.

It's just three hours now until another D-day begins (Diaper Day, that is). Yet,
if I can't fall asleep, I'll still be resting in His heart and He in mine. That will be
three hours well spent.

Adel Arrabito Torres

Letters That Keep on Giving

See with what large letters I have written to you with my own hand!
Gal. 6:11, NKJV.

For the past several years, my mom, Lila, age seventy-seven, has lovingly told family members that if there's anything of hers they want after she passes, to please tell her now. She makes reference to the fact that from age seventy on, she is living in her bonus years, which could end at any moment. My daughter, Andrea, age thirty-seven, requested that Grandma Lila please sort through the huge box of letters and cards that she has been given from family and friends over her lifetime. Andrea wants to have back the ones she's personally written to her precious grandmother. So on the morning of Thanksgiving Day (U.S.A.), November 26, 2009, three days before Grandma Lila's seventy-seventh birthday, we began this task of sorting. Together we spent several sacred hours revisiting our bygone days, so that I could bring "priceless memorabilia" back to Canada for Andrea. She'll be blessed with encouragement and strength for her journey as she reads back through time and clearly sees how our family has been saved to serve our Lord.

One particular envelope caught my eye—not just because of its 32-cents "LOVE angel" stamp, but also because I recognized the handwriting of my Grandma Moore, Lila's mother. I felt impressed to read the letter addressed to my mom from her mom (postmarked Portland, Oregon, February 22, 1996). I'm glad that I've learned to completely trust and follow the prompting of the Holy Spirit. The letter was written on Thanksgiving Day stationery, and the apples adorning the paper made me smile (see Zech. 2:8). Toward the end of the letter, Grandma Moore had written, "Debbie [referring to me] sends me letters often to encourage me. She is a really good person, and tries to convince folks to do right. Even though her words fall on many deaf ears, she tries. It was a good feeling to see all the family that was here during my stay in the hospital. They took turns sleeping in a chair at night . . . that's all for now. Love and God bless you, Mom." Grandma Moore (age eighty-seven) passed away two months later, one week before Andrea's wedding.

Someday in Paradise, when Grandma Moore and I are reunited, she's going to shout, "Hallelujah! Praise God!" when she hears my life story. She'll also meet my many "forever friends" that I've made through the years as they've read my "letters" (devotionals) in the yearly devotional books through which I've been able to witness to others in the family of God.

Deborah Sanders

Is My Name Written There?

Nothing impure will ever enter it, nor will anyone who does what is shameful or deceitful, but only those whose names are written in the Lamb's book of life. Rev. 21:27, NIV.

On a recent trip from Fayetteville, North Carolina, to Oakland, California, my husband and I had a planned Christmas vacation with our children and grandchildren, along with a visit with my mother and kin in Ohio. We packed carefully. In place of a purse, I wore a container around my neck which carried our ID and medical cards along with our cash.

My knee implants activated the security buzzer at the airport's security check. An official asked me to remove the container hanging from my neck. Then he focused on my husband. Another agent X-rayed me to confirm that I did indeed have artificial knees. Finally, we were told we could go into the secured arrival/departure area.

Though both my husband and I have medical issues, we wanted to travel anyway. We did not mind going through the security check-in procedures. We knew that being with our loved ones would be well worth the discomfort and inconvenience of travel.

After weeks of enjoying time with our family, it was time to return home. While repacking, we couldn't find the security container with our ID and medical cards.

We desperately searched for it. Without our names on official documents, we did not have any way of getting on the plane—or home. Without our drivers' licenses, how could we prove our identity? *Father,* I prayed, *I know You have a master plan. Show us.* We learned we could confirm our identity some other way. Our mortgage company had copies of our drivers' licenses and faxed copies to us. After making several phone calls to the airline, we were able to confirm our return reservations!

Once again, a security agent singled us out at the airport. His supervisor approached us and asked, "Are you on any medications? If so, I need to see the containers with your names on them." When he read our names on the bottles, he allowed us through the gate.

As with that trip, I am willing to endure any "travel" inconvenience on my journey toward heaven. On that first resurrection morning, I want to be able to rise and enter the kingdom with my Lord because He'll have written my name in the Lamb's book of life.

Betty Glover Perry

"I Know the Plans I Have for You"

"For I know the plans I have for you," declares the LORD, "plans to prosper you and not to harm you, plans to give you hope and a future." Jer. 29:11, NIV.

Our vehicle wound its way down the narrow road, obscured by fog, rain, and mud so deep I was afraid we would become bogged down. Why had I come to this remote part of Papua New Guinea to share God's Word? I'd all but lost direction in my life over the previous two years. A post-divorce breakdown had caused my loss of faith and hope that God had any good plans for me. Yet when I was asked to come and share with these people in these remote—often dangerous—areas, God renewed my faith in His Bible promises.

Now I was traveling through areas where no new roads had been built in the last thirty years. Many people here had not ventured beyond their own villages for lack of transport. I smiled at the cries of "white merri" (white woman) as people caught glimpses of my face peering out the vehicle window. I knew God had brought me here for a reason. The first night I slept on a very thin mattress on the floor of a room barely large enough to fit my small bag in beside the bed. I ate supper in the cookhouse where food was prepared over an open fire.

As I rose soon after daybreak and made my way to the river to bathe in the fast-moving water, two women joined me. They seemed excited that I was there to bathe with them at dawn and I soon learned why. As we enjoyed the invigorating coolness of the river, they said they'd been praying for someone to come and tell them about God. They both spoke of dreams they had had—one many years earlier and the other during the previous year—in which they saw *me* coming to their village. From their dreams, they knew I'd be staying in the pastoral family's house and speaking in their church. The woman speaking of her dream, the most recent one, said, "I didn't believe the angel in my dream because no white woman would come to this remote area and live as we do. I only believed when I saw you step out from that vehicle yesterday."

I listened with amazement to these two dedicated prayer warriors for God. I thought back over my life and marveled at God who, through my divorce, dark days, and loss of faith, still had plans in place not to harm me, but plans to give me hope and a future. Later, as I traveled back to my home, I knew I would never doubt His love and leading in my life again.

Barbara Parkins

February 21

Paintings by Our God

"With all my resources I have provided for the temple of my God—
gold for the gold work, silver for the silver, bronze for the bronze, iron
for the iron and wood for the wood, as well as onyx for the settings,
turquoise, stones of various colors, and all kinds of
fine stone and marble." 1 Chron. 29:2, NIV.

I finally lifted my eyes from my devotional reading to look at the view beyond my bay window and almost gasped at the beauty. The sun had just struck the snow-covered foothills, and the clouds were just breaking around the peak of 14,259-foot (4,346-meter) Long's Peak.

What caught my attention were the colors. Have you ever noticed how God uses His paintbrush? He loves color and spreads it generously for us. And that morning the snow-covered hills were a glorious rosy pink. I sat quietly watching the color intensify and then fade. And I thought about other days and times when the colors of nature have caught my attention.

Think about how the world looks after a summer rain. The colors not only intensify but glisten. God's magic paint. Or how about the soft light of a late spring or summer evening as it paints fields and hills? This light is sometimes called a "sweet" light and is very hard for human painters to capture.

No human can paint like God paints the sky at sunrise or sunset. I'm sure you know the old saying, "Red sky at morning, sailors take warning; red sky at night, sailors' delight." I have seen some incredible, awe-inspiring sunrises here in Colorado—and they did precede a storm. And there have been innumerable gorgeous sunsets over the Rocky Mountains. What color choices! I have often thought that if I were to put such colors on canvas, it would probably look garish and unreal, but God paints it just right.

I have been privileged to visit some famous art in the Hermitage in Saint Petersburg, the Louvre in Paris, the Metropolitan Museum of Art in New York City, and the art museums in Washington, D.C. and Los Angeles. And even the museum right here in Loveland—Loveland is well known in the area for art of all forms, especially sculpture. I have enjoyed all of them, but none of them have filled my heart and spirit as have the paintings God has provided every day, no matter where I find myself. "And God [and I] saw that it was good" (Gen. 1:25, NIV).

Ardis Dick Stenbakken

New Song

And he hath put a new song in my mouth, even praise unto our God: many shall see it, and fear, and shall trust in the LORD. Ps. 40:3.

I pulled open the vegetable drawer in our refrigerator. An unusual scent wafted noseward. *I'll have to check that out soon,* I thought. In a hurry, I grabbed salad makings and proceeded with meal preparation. The next afternoon when I opened the vegetable drawer, a strong odor grabbed my attention. I pulled carrots and lettuce from the front of the drawer. Then cucumber and celery. From behind them, broccoli, cauliflower, and jicama. In the back corner of the drawer lay a bag with three squishy green onions. I'd used most of the rubber-banded bunch of green onions I'd purchased, and then forgotten the rest. They'd slid to the back and hid behind other vegetables. As I pulled out the bag, its folds slipped open. The putrid odor of onion rot spread. Bag at arm's length, I scurried outside to the compost bin and deposited the disgusting, stinking, half-liquid remains of three once-tasty green onions into the outdoor garbage can.

A few days later, I read Psalm 40 in my Bible. The phrase "new song" in verse 3 caught my attention. *Why a "new song"?* I wondered. *Why didn't he just say "song"?* I looked up the meaning of the Hebrew word for *new.* "New, new thing, fresh." New thoughts began to form. Our bodies change—cells die, new cells are born. Our emotions change—new sorrows pain us, new joys uplift us. Our spiritual lives change as well—we are either growing or dying.

As I spend time each day in God's Word, communicating with Him in prayer, serving Him in my daily life, my spiritual life changes. A text I've read before—maybe even treasured and memorized—explodes with new meaning. A hymn or gospel song touches my heart in a new way. As I grow in relationship with God, He puts new thoughts, fresh thoughts in my mind. He puts new songs, new praises in my heart.

New. Like fresh produce—crisp, valuable, delightful. But staleness exudes stench.

Similarly, a growing Christian exudes fresh and joyful perspectives. But yesterday's experience by itself is like green onions closed in plastic for way too long—gooshy, ooshy, and stinky.

God, I prayed, *keep me close and growing with fresh insights and new songs. Let my enjoyment of life with You inspire others to respect You, love You, and trust You.*

Helen Heavirland

Jesus in the Courtroom

"But when they arrest you, do not worry about what to say or how to say it. At that time you will be given what to say." Matt. 10:19, NIV.

ord, I do not know how else to prove my innocence, I prayed. *It is Your call, not mine.* I was waiting for the jury's verdict in a country that was not my own. Years earlier, I had immigrated and enrolled at a college to earn a certificate. I worked extra hard to pay my school fees and support my family. Then two months before my initial visa ran out, I approached the college authorities asking that the visa in my passport be submitted to the Home Office for renewal. I'd saved enough money to pay the fee to have this done.

In time, my passport was returned to me containing a new visa stamp, granting me two more years during which time I could remain in that country. I found a job and seemed to be settling in OK. The two years awarded me on my renewed visa passed quickly, and I would need to renew the visa once again. This time the company for which I was working agreed to secure a work permit for me. My manager wrote a letter on my behalf for me to take to the Home Office and submit along with my application for a work permit.

In person, I submitted my passport to the Home Office along with supporting documents. The officer waiting on me told me what day I should return to pick up my passport with the work permit. How excited I felt about getting my passport back! On the designated date, I walked into the Home Office. Nothing had prepared me for what was about to happen. I approached the clerk who had helped renew my visa the first time. "I remember you," he said. "Please follow me." On the other side of a doorway, two policemen were waiting for me.

One of them explained, "Your earlier visa stamp was forged. It's a counterfeit. You are under arrest for being in this country with false documentation." The case went to trial, and I cooperated fully with the authorities. My case was transferred to the jury of the Crown Court. Only God and praying friends sustained me during this trying time. After evidence was presented, the jury conferred and returned with their verdict: "Not guilty."

"Not guilty!" That's the *same* verdict God pronounces in heaven's courtroom when He sees the nail prints in the hands of Jesus and weighs the evidence of Christ's shed blood for me.

Regina Ncube

Scholarships Sent by God

Blessed be God, which hath not turned away my prayer. Ps. 66:20.

My grandmother was to me the most incredible person in the world. She used to take me with her to cottage meetings (Bible study given to people in their homes); and before I was ten, I frequently went with her to church every Sunday and Wednesday night. This godly woman instilled in me not only a fear of God but also a love for Him and a belief in the power of prayer.

We were not rich in this world's goods, but we were rich in faith and belief in God. As a young ambitious teenager, I desired to further my education but had not the means to do so.

One day our church pastor visited our home and asked, "Young lady, do you plan to go to college?"

"Yes!" was my prompt response. "But right now I don't have the money." Having taught for two years in one of our church's schools, I did qualify for a bursary, a two-year scholarship.

After following my pastor's advice to apply for a scholarship, my grandmother encouraged me. She fasted and prayed with me about the request. By God's grace, the scholarship committee favorably considered my request, and I received a full scholarship to Caribbean Union College (now University of the Southern Caribbean).

Many were the valuable lessons I learned and the friendships I formed. My relationship with God grew stronger as did my desire to serve in response to His love for me.

Upon graduation, I was dispatched to the area of His vineyard that God had planned for me. After two years of service on that island, our pastor, who then became a director of education, bid his congregants farewell.

Before he left, I said to him, "Pastor, someday I would like to get a bachelor's degree. When you get into the office, remember me." He suggested I apply for another scholarship. Again God blessed me—this time with a bursary to what is now the University of Northern Caribbean, from which I was able to graduate with a bachelor's degree in education.

God has provided me with Christian education at the tertiary level. As my grandmother modeled God's love for me, I am doing the same today for my grandchildren by encouraging them in their educational pursuits and helping finance their education.

Hyacinth V. Caleb

The Dream

But my God shall supply all your need according to his riches in glory by Christ Jesus. Phil. 4:19.

I don't typically remember what I have dreamt after waking up each morning. One morning, however, I woke up and had a vivid recollection of what I'd dreamt during the night. In the dream, I was on a volleyball court with my friends from church. At the end of the game, I went over to one of the ladies—a friend of mine—and handed her a one hundred dollar bill, telling her not to lose it. In my dream, I saw her tuck the bill into an undergarment for safekeeping.

Throughout the day, I couldn't stop thinking about the dream. I asked God what He wanted me to do. Surely, He did not mean for me to give my friend a one hundred dollar bill! With God I mentally tried to negotiate something smaller, like fifty dollars. It didn't work. In my mind's eye, I saw only the crisp one hundred dollar bill from my dream.

Finally, as I had no cash, I went to the bank's ATM and withdrew one hundred dollars. I put the money in an envelope and took it to church the following day. The woman (from my dream) was not there. Then I saw her teenage son and gave him the envelope, along with clear instructions to go straight home and give it to his mother. When he left, my immediate thought was that perhaps I shouldn't have relied so heavily on a teenager, so I decided to phone his mother. I said, "Your son is on his way home and has something from me to give you."

There, on the phone, I felt impressed to tell my friend about the dream. She began to laugh and scream, saying how much her heavenly Father loves her. When she finally calmed down, she told me that her youngest child was very sick. She'd taken her little daughter to the doctor. However, the medication he'd prescribed cost ninety-seven dollars. My friend did not have the money to buy the medicine for her child—nor did she know of any funding source. All she could do was make the choice not to worry and simply trust that God would provide. And He did. I was in awe of the amazing things that can happen when one is connected to God. What a humbling experience to be His answer to my friend's prayer!

Listen to that still small, Voice today. Reach out and bless someone. You will be blessed in return.

Sharon Long (Brown)

Yes, You Can. No, You Can't

By You I have been upheld from birth. Ps. 71:6, NKJV.

ge can play funny tricks on our minds. I know that it does on mine—especially in the areas of what I still can do and what I no longer can do. As I age, I like to think that I can do more than I physically can. This is a challenge for me because my life motto has been a saying attributed to D. L. Moody. It goes something like this: "Unless you try to do more than you think you can do, you will never do all that you could do."

On the other hand, we seniors sometimes think we're incapable of doing more than we do. So we take it easier than we should, and our bodies begin to weaken. Our muscles atrophy because we're not using them anymore. We've stopped doing activities that once made us strong in our younger years. Sometimes we're tempted to say, "I'm older now and less capable. I think I'll just coast." You've heard, haven't you, the saying "Use it or lose it"? People most often use this expression to describe succinctly how immobility leads to deterioration.

We need a balance between admitting to our age-related weakness and asking God for strength to keep us going in ways that are reasonable. After all, God is the One who has been holding us up all along. He isn't finished with us until His purpose through us is fulfilled.

What we say about exercise and the body is also true of the soul's strength. As we age, are we taking more time to "work out" spiritually? Are we spending more time than ever in prayer and the study of God's Word? Are we sharing what we know about His love with others?

Putting on a few more years doesn't mean we're entitled to sit around and do nothing—physically or spiritually. Consider how long God has been loving us and working on behalf of our salvation. So His soldiers don't automatically retire from His army at a certain birthday. There is still a spiritual war to fight. Are we daily putting on and wearing the spiritual armor that Paul described: the belt of truth firmly buckled, the breastplate of righteous living in place, the shield of faith held high, and the helmet of salvation assuring us of God's eternal protection (see Eph. 6:12–17)?

Even if you've been in the church for a hundred years, God will continue to fulfill His purpose in you. His love won't let go of you. So don't let go of Him!

Angie Joseph

The Ode to a Guarantor

He who is surety for a stranger will suffer, but one who hates being surety is secure. Prov. 11:15, NKJV.

A guarantor can be defined, in part, as a person who gives assurance as it relates to quality or performance. During childhood, though I liked singing psalms with my family or in other small venues, it was out of question for me to ever sing a solo or duet with someone else in public. I lacked the courage. I also loved reading, memorizing, writing, and reciting odes (a meditative poem). My first teacher promoted my love of poetry and encouraged my personal composition of poems, as did my botany teacher.

As a fifteen-year-old, I was once sitting next to a girl on a bus taking us to another church. As we in the bus joined our voices in song, my seatmate noticed and remarked on my voice. She proposed that we perform together in public a psalm of worship. Though wanting to decline because of my shyness, I still didn't want to offend her. She assured me a performance would go well, so I agreed. After gaining experience in public presentation, I soon became part of a musical group that praised God in worship services in different church programs.

Looking back, I now realize I needed someone who loved me enough to notice my abilities and encourage me to use them in ministry. I needed someone to support me and open up to me new possibilities and horizons. Sharing our gifts is really about bringing glory to God. Paul wrote, "For do I now persuade men, or God? Or do I seek to please men? For if I still pleased men, I would not be a bondservant of Christ" (Gal. 1:10, NKJV). My encouragers have included school teachers, church mentors, pastors' wives, friends, and many other people.

Today, the Women's Ministries Department of our church, through the sale of these devotional books, also encourages and supports young ladies around the world in order to help them get an education and live their lives to the fullest for God. At the same time, it is important that each of us notice the gifts of young women around us and kindly encourage them to be all they can be for God— using their gifts for Him. Our lives can be poetic odes investing in the future of those who need our encouragement to draw them out of their shyness by sharing God's encouragement (such as Isaiah 41:10 and Jeremiah 29:11). Will you be a guarantor for someone?

Raisa Ostrovskaya

God Will Watch Over You

He will watch over your life; the LORD will watch over your coming and going both now and forevermore. Ps. 121:7, 8, NIV.

Morris, my husband, was preparing to travel overseas for his uncle's funeral. Everything was in place, except for my nagging fear regarding his safety in his hometown. To worsen the situation, he had received a call from a stranger asking unusual questions and seeking information about my husband's flight.

We arrived in Atlanta from where his flight would depart, but during the night, sleep evaded me as I worried about his well-being. Sitting on the bed the next morning, exhausted from sleeplessness, I recalled the words of my grandson, Nikolas: "Gramma, if you pray, don't worry. If you worry, don't pray." Regretfully, I didn't heed his sound advice.

Up early, I opened my Bible and my eyes fell on these words: "He will watch over your life; the LORD will watch over your coming and going both now and forevermore." I interpreted this passage as God's affirmation that He would protect my husband.

At the airport, I walked with Morris as far as security officials would allow. Then I waved goodbye. On the ride back home, I thought again about the stranger's phone calls and prayed for God's protection of my husband. The following morning when I opened my women's devotional book, *Grace Notes,* my eyes fell on the following text. I stopped to read it: "For he shall give his angels charge over thee, to keep thee in all thy ways" (Ps. 91:11). Excitedly, I shouted, "Lord, thank You!" I prayed and started my day, confident of God's presence with my husband and me.

Approximately two hours later, while out and about, I was shaken when a police car appeared to follow me. I checked my traveling speed and played my favorite CD, singing along. Finally, the police car turned onto a side street. My husband arrived safely in his country and returned home safely.

I thanked God for His protection over both of us—and for His words of assurance that He will watch over us and keep us safe from harm.

Sister, are you facing turbulent times and do problems seem to overwhelm you? Give your concerns to Jesus, who watches over you and calms you with His love.

Shirley C. Iheanacho

Abuela Emma

Therefore we do not lose heart. Though outwardly we are wasting away, yet inwardly we are being renewed day by day. For our light and momentary troubles are achieving for us an eternal glory that far outweighs them all. So we fix our eyes not on what is seen, but on what is unseen, since what is seen is temporary, but what is unseen is eternal. 2 Cor. 4:16-18, NIV.

Mom called me late one evening. "Jenny-Penny," she started off using her nickname for me, "I just received a phone call from Cecilia. *Abuela* Emma is gone." I paused. *Abuela* means grandmother in Spanish and is a term of affection we used for Emma, a lady I have known all my life. She was not a blood relative but was the only *"abuela"* I had ever known. Years earlier, my parents, due to political unrest, left Chile as well as their respective families behind. So I grew up away from the majority of my extended family.

My parents met Emma while they were members of a Spanish-speaking church in Sydney, New South Wales. *Abuela* Emma lavished her love on my brother and me in the form of birthday money, hugs, weekly homemade cakes, and relationship advice during our teen years.

Unfortunately, *Abuela* began to suffer from dementia later in life. Her daughter needed to put her into a nursing home. Slowly, *Abuela's* illness took over her mind to the point that she no longer recognized her own family members. Then she was gone.

The news devastated me. My eldest sister and I were the only ones from our family who were able to attend the funeral. I spoke on behalf of my family and cried buckets. Then as the pastor conducting the funeral began to speak about the wonderful promise of eternal life for those that believe in the Lord, my tears stopped falling. A sense of peace washed over me as he reminded us of the second coming of our Lord Jesus. I experienced an overwhelming peace.

The pastor reminded us that one day God will wipe away all our tears. " 'There will be no more death' or mourning or crying or pain, for the old order of things has passed away" (Rev. 21:4, NIV). On that day, our faith in God's love will be replaced by sight!

Isn't that a wonderful and comforting promise? We don't need to be downtrodden about today because tomorrow brings a new future when we believe in Jesus, our Lord and soon-coming Savior.

Jenny Rivera

Living His Friendship

Friendship: the state of being friends; a friendly feeling or attitude:
kindness or help given to someone.
"I do not call you servants any longer. . . . Instead, I call you friends."
John 15:15, GNT.

"And you are my friends if you do what I command you."
John 15:14, GNT.

The following stories unveil two types of friendship: friendship with God and friendship with those around us.

Friendship with Jesus deepens when we crave His presence and listen for His voice through His Word. It deepens when we take hold of His power to overcome besetting sins. It deepens when we watch with Him in prayer during our own Gethsemane experiences, when—in the midst of life's thirsty, desert places—we seek renewal in the shadow of the Cross. Friendship with Jesus deepens when we realize He's not left us to journey toward our ultimate destination alone.

Friendship with others deepens when we honor a parent, comfort a spouse, do laundry for a sick neighbor, avoid gossip, advocate for the helpless, listen to the pain of a hurting heart, or return a shopping cart instead of leaving it out in the open to roll and dent someone else's car.

Friendship with Jesus motivates—even *impels*—us to treat others as He would treat them. Friendship with others leads us more deeply into intimacy with God.

A Day of Caring

Then shall they also answer him, saying, Lord, when saw we thee an hungred, or athirst, or a stranger, or naked, or sick, or in prison, and did not minister unto thee? Then shall he answer them, saying, Verily I say unto you, Inasmuch as ye did it not to one of the least of these, ye did it not to me. Matt. 25:44, 45.

I was visiting for a while in the hometown where I grew up and had attended church during my childhood and early adult years. During my visit, I learned at church that there was great concern for one of the members who was very ill. Some of us got busy with plans to travel to her home, which was many miles away.

The day came when we journeyed to this young woman's home. She and I had grown up together, even though she is older; so I was a bit apprehensive about seeing her again after so many years. We greeted her with warm hugs and words of comfort and cheer, but I could not ignore the immediate needs that I saw as we moved about her place. We did her laundry, cooked, cleaned her house, shopped for groceries, and ministered to her every need. The time came when we had to leave after our time spent together in labor, laughter, chatting, and remembrance of the days of long ago. We prayed with her as we ended these wonderful hours with her. Then with best wishes, hope for her prosperity, and good health for the future, we departed.

Sickness and suffering are so prevalent among us, that it seems we often regard them as commonplace. Sometimes we even forget to care. We become preoccupied with our own lives and happiness and our own comfortable surroundings. Often, when we are called upon to meet the needs of others, we refuse or neglect to do so for various reasons. Yet we need to remember that there may come a time when we will need the love and care of others. The Word of God encourages us to love and reach out to one another and to seek those things above and not the things of the earth. We are to pray with and for each other and trust in God. Furthermore, we are to live a caring life that gives to others and brings peace to ourselves as well.

I discovered great blessings on that day of caring when we visited our friend. Today, why not spend a little time caring for someone? You may experience a rich reward as well.

Help us, heavenly Father, to care for and bless others as we are blessed.

Elizabeth Ida Cain

Carried

My beautiful son didn't start talking until he was about three years old. He would simply point and grunt. He often lifted up his little arms to me and I understood that he wanted to be carried. When he started talking, he would lift his arms and simply say, "Carry me." I began addressing him affectionately as "Georgemichael-Carry-Me-Yergen."

I often told him, "One day you will grow into a great big man and Mommy will be a tiny old woman. Then you will have to carry me!" And I would laugh.

When he was about ten years old, I attempted to teach him some things about God. I wanted him to learn to use his Bible and see that God's Word could direct his life. I wanted him to develop his own personal relationship with Jesus. I asked him to get his children's Bible and find a verse that spoke to his heart. Once he chose today's text. I asked what this meant to him. He said, "Mommy, every day I have to carry this heavy book bag to school, and it really hurts my back and feet. I think that Jesus wants to help me with that." I was allowed to experience a special joy with him that day when he shared that he wanted Jesus to be his best Friend. His words reminded me that God, my best Friend as well, will carry every burden I must bear.

I don't know all that happened in my son's life through the years that caused him so much pain that he'd one day end his life. His father called me on the phone and said, "George is dead." Denial. Despair. Anger. Incomprehensible grief! Suicide? Unthinkable! There was no suicide note. My mind frequently whirls faster than a ceiling fan above my head. Dizzy doesn't begin to describe it. The world is so out of control, and I can no longer focus. Tears blur my view.

In one of my last conversations with my son, he told me that the poem "Footprints in the Sand" was a favorite. He was almost twenty-five years old, but he still needed to be carried.

I will see my son again on the resurrection morning. I can't wait to introduce you to him.

Whatever you are facing in your life today, no matter how bleak the outlook, no matter how great the obstacle, let God carry you through. This is my hope and my prayer for you.

Kathy Jo Duterrow Jones

Craving God

"Why do you spend money for what is not bread, and your wages for what does not satisfy?" Isa. 55:2, NKJV.

My heart was hungry. I was lonely, often discouraged. Looking for something to satisfy the empty ache in my heart, I too often turned to food. Chocolate. Ice cream. Cookies. Anything to soothe the emptiness I felt. To make me feel better. But it only lasted for a moment. It tasted good and felt good, but soon the familiar loneliness, discouragement, and hunger for more came back.

"Listen carefully to Me, and eat what is good, and let your soul delight itself in abundance" (Isa. 55:2b, NKJV).

Eat what is good. Delight in abundance. I knew God wasn't telling me to only eat healthy food. He was going deeper. This wasn't about food. This was about my heart. He knew my heart longing. He knew what would satisfy those empty places. The loneliness. The longing to be loved and accepted for who I am. To feel connected—like I belong. To know that I am wanted.

"Listen carefully to Me."

"Yes, I have loved you with an everlasting love" (Jer. 31:3, NKJV).

"I have called you by your name; you are Mine" (Isa. 43:1, NKJV).

God loves me. I know that. I've known that most of my life. It was His love that drew me to Him in the first place. As a child, learning that God loved me just the way I was caused me to commit my life to Him. But somehow as I grew up, I often lost that deep belief that God loves *me*. I know He gave Jesus to die for me, but the love part gets lost when I start thinking about myself and all the parts of me needing change, improvement. How could God really love *me* when I don't really love me?

What I really crave isn't chocolate or ice cream or cookies. What I really crave is what God offers: His accepting, powerful, always-there, life-changing, unconditional love. It alone can satisfy. I need to listen to Him and not the enemy who tells me I am unworthy, nothing, too bad to forgive again, and unwanted. I need to feed my heart on these truths that remind me of who He is and who I am in Him. Then I can be "rooted and grounded in love" and "filled with all the fullness of God" (Eph. 3:17–19, NKJV). Then my heart can be truly satisfied.

Tamyra Horst

Created in God's Image

So God created mankind in his own image, in the image of God he created them; male and female he created them. Gen. 1:27, NIV.

My mother told me that when she got married, my father wanted to have many children (as many African men used to do). The firstborn was a girl. My parents did not mind about the gender of the first baby they got. The second born was also a girl, and my father started complaining that he did not want girls—he needed boys. The third born was a girl. This disturbed my father, and he shouted at my mother that he was fed up with girls. He needed "real" children.

My mother tells me that she did all that she could to get a baby boy because, according to my father, he had no children yet. She prayed earnestly to God, and God gave her a baby boy. She named him Samuel. My father was happy this time. "You have just started giving birth to real children," he said.

Fortunately or unfortunately, the next three children were girls—these were the fifth, sixth, and seventh children. This further frustrated and disappointed my father.

My mother tried the eighth time to see whether she would get a baby boy. When she went to the hospital to give birth, my father did not even go with her. Instead, he sent a messenger to find out the gender of his newest child.

That baby was also a girl, the one who is writing this story. My father did not go to pay the medical bills. My mother and I were retained in the hospital pending payment of the maternity bills. Later, my maternal uncle went to the hospital and cleared the medical bills. As soon as my mother went home, Father married a second wife who would give birth to the kind of children that he longed for—boys. My father died a frustrated and disappointed man because the second wife he married gave birth to five girls, consecutively, and no boy.

This life experience has helped me conclude that all children are gifts from God. I am so grateful that He doesn't favor one gender or ethnicity or nationality above another. God created male and female in His image. May this knowledge enable us to accept, befriend, love, and care for all of God's children because all of us are heirs of God's gracious gift of eternal life.

Sarah Nyende

Fear Factor vs. Faith Factor

I sought the LORD, and He heard me, and delivered me from all my fears. Ps. 34:4, NKJV.

Our poor dog, Peaches! When he becomes fearful, he pants so hard. He barks. He doesn't know what to do with himself. He's afraid—afraid of thunder, afraid of gunshots, afraid of any loud noise. Why should he panic when none of those things have ever hurt him? He so often seems to live in his own personal "fear factor" world.

Last night when thunder started rolling, Peaches wouldn't stop barking. I let him into the house, and he hid under our kitchen table. He finds comfort being inside with us, as we're his best "friends." How similar, though, his behavior is to ours. When we're afraid, we want to be with someone. Someone else's presence helps our fear dissipate and vanish. Unfortunately, Peaches can't stay in the house overnight, as he's accident prone. Once I tried making him a corner to stay in, but he kept scratching to come out. Somehow that makeshift bedroom did not suit him. So, out he had to go onto the back porch to face his fears. He has a doghouse there, but he sometimes doesn't feel safe in it. He finds a spot way back in the shed where no one can see him.

One stormy night, I let Peaches into the house to stop his barking. He settled down right away. But soon my bedtime rolled around. I put Peaches back on the outside porch. *Bark! Bark! Bark! Let me back in!* Instead of satisfying his wishes, I went outside to be with him. He hid his head between my legs as I petted him and talked to him. He calmed down, and fortunately, so did the storm. No more thunder. No more loud noise. Peaches felt safe enough to sleep in his doghouse without a problem that night. *Thank You, Lord, for taking care of this storm.*

No one likes to be afraid. Sometimes, like Peaches, I live with a fear factor instead of with the faith factor. When I jog down the road in the morning, I often fear some loose dog will appear and try to bite me. I realize I can't really enjoy this time if I'm afraid. So now before I go out to jog, I pray, asking God to watch over me. Verses come to my mind, such as "My God hath sent his angel, and hath shut the lions' mouths" (Dan. 6:22). Surely, if God can handle lions, He can also keep dogs and other dangers from "biting" me.

Lord, Your words calm my fears. Remind us often that, like a good friend, You're always with us, offering us peace through Your Word, when fears threaten. Change our fear into faith.

Rosemarie Clardy

Bad News/Good News

And I will put enmity between thee and the woman, and between thy seed and her seed; it shall bruise thy head, and thou shalt bruise his heel. Gen. 3:15.

Has anyone ever said to you, "I have good news and I have bad news. Which do you want to hear first?" We usually answer, "The bad news," because we want the good news (whatever it is) to leave us with a sense of comfort and hope.

Our church was studying a book titled *The Great Controversy Between Christ and Satan* (Ellen G. White). As I read chapter 30, "Enmity Between Man and Satan," I first felt horrified then surprisingly relieved. I realized that the chapter first presented bad news, followed by good news that brought me both comfort and hope. That chapter helped me realize that before human beings were created on this earth, a war between Christ and Satan was already under way. And our gracious God created humankind, us, to be on His side of the war; His companions—on the winning side. What a Friend we have in Him!

But Eve, in the Garden of Eden, chose to doubt God's goodness. She chose to believe lies about His character told to her by Satan (disguised as a serpent). Eve acted on the lies, and Adam soon followed. Their choice to sin was the bad news, for it meant they now lived outside of friendship with God and in enemy territory. Then God came to them, promising to put enmity between Satan and humankind. Enmity was good news! But Satan knew that only death could satisfy the just demands of a holy God. He knew God had said Adam and Eve would die if they sinned. But imagine Satan's surprise when he realized God and His Son had a plan in place to pay the penalty of sin for all humanity—for all who would accept, in their place, Christ's sacrifice on the cross. God-placed enmity (His power within us) would not only allow us to choose His side of the great conflict, but it would also *empower* us to make that crucial choice.

Although Satan stole our first parents through deception, aren't you glad God plays by His own just rules? He doesn't deceive or force us back to His side. He gives us the gift of enmity to empower our choices. Jesus, while on this earth, gave us an example of how to depend on the Father's strength to make the right life choices. And the "good work" He began in us, He will finish. No wonder we can refer to both enmity and the gospel story as good news!

Lana Fletcher

Dr. Princess

Who forgives all your iniquities, who heals all your diseases.
Ps. 103:3, NKJV.

When I grow up, I want to be a princess-doctor," said Tori, my five-year-old great-grandniece. Pulling me toward her well-worn "doctor's office" desk, she added, "Come to my office and let me check your health." I sat on the floor in her toy area, and she went to work.

Tori (*pumping an air bulb, not attached to me*): Aunt Carolyn, your blood sugar is really bad.

Me: Do you mean my blood *pressure* is bad?

Tori: No, your blood *sugar*. I'm going to have to give you some medicine—with *no sugar* in it! Now let's check out your eyes (*pointing me to a little pretend eye chart*).

Me: I can read it all with both eyes—though my left eye doesn't see as well as the right one.

Tori: Then your left eye has to come out right now! I'll give you a new left eye and you'll be good to go. But first, Aunt Carolyn, I also took a picture of your bones that look like this (*handing me a clear plastic "X-ray" with something on it resembling the head of Donald Duck*).

Me: Well, I guess if that's what I look like . . . then that's what I look like. It's all good, right?

Tori: No, it's *not* good—and that means *more* medicine for you!

Me: Dr. Princess, can't *something* about me please be healthy?

Tori: That depends on your breathing test. Here, blow into this mask. (*I blow.*) Oh, dear!

Me: Now what's wrong? Isn't my breathing normal?

Tori: No, absolutely not! In fact, this test shows that you're not breathing at all! So here's more medicine and come back and see me in two days.

In a further exchange that evening, Tori said, "Aunt Carolyn, I can tell by looking that you're feeling better now. You don't have to come back to my office in two days."

This "medical" exchange with "Dr. Princess" made me chuckle. On a more serious note, it also reminded me of times I've wasted in "diagnosing" the perceived "diseases" I thought I saw in others. Times I could have better used by referring them to the Great Physician, who alone can give the correct diagnoses along with a healing touch.

Lord, fill me with Your Holy Spirit today. Forgive me for all the times I've played at being "doctor" instead of being still—in You—and then being a true friend to hurting hearts.

Carolyn Rathbun Sutton

Flight Delay

And we know that all things work together for good to those who love God, to those who are the called according to His purpose.
Rom. 8:28, NKJV.

My friend, Annie Korup, and I were delayed in customs over some routine checks of a brown rice packet that I had carried into Australia from Papua New Guinea. Our flight to Newcastle would board in fifty minutes. Missing the flight would incur additional charges to my special-fare ticket. To complicate matters, Annie was vision impaired and, in order to accommodate her special needs, we had to move at a slower pace.

After being cleared through customs, we lined up at the international check-in for our domestic connection. When we got to the counter, the Qantas Airlines officer informed us that we were booked on Jet Star instead. We must proceed to the domestic terminal to check in. I now knew that we would not make our connection with only thirty minutes to boarding time.

"Please, Lord," I whispered. "Take over here and get us to our flight in time. Protect Annie from danger as we will need to rush." I slipped my right arm under Annie's left and led her through the crowded terminal. I flagged down a taxi. Once inside the cab, I announced our destination and he reluctantly drove us to the domestic terminal for a twenty-dollar charge. I suspect he took an unnecessary detour because it seemed to take longer getting there than it should have.

At the domestic terminal, we found the long line at the security area to be disheartening. Something on Annie caused the security alarm to go off—twice. Another five minutes lost. By this time, I had lost all hope of arriving on time at gate 26, the last in the terminal.

Now we had a fifteen-minute walk in addition to a necessary stop at the newsstand to purchase a phone calling card. Without that we'd have no way to contact our Newcastle hosts, Robert and Julie Norris. All the while I prayed for God's intervention on our behalf.

Arriving late at gate 26, we found the waiting area empty. I slumped into a seat and pulled out my e-ticket to check our flight number on the overhead screen. What? Our connecting flight had been delayed by twenty minutes! *Thank You, God,* I breathed. Annie and I had a few unexpected moments to relax, eat, and arrive on time at our destination. Take heart! Though God may seem very "last minute," His promise assures us that He is always right on time.

Fulori Sususewa Bola

Not the End, but the Beginning

Behold, I will do a new thing; now it shall spring forth; shall ye not
know it? I will even make a way in the wilderness,
and rivers in the desert. Isa. 43:19.

It was over a year since my non-Christian husband had begun his twice-weekly, four-hour dialysis treatments in Port of Spain, a two-hour drive from Princes Town. One day, as the nurse took him off the machine, my husband's speech became jumbled and he started singing. The nurse recognized that his blood pressure was very high and phoned the doctor to come quickly. Concerned but prayerful, I watched the doctor question my husband. "How old are you?"

"Eighteen," responded my thirty-nine-year-old husband. Most of his other answers didn't make sense either.

"Take Mr. Marshall to the general hospital immediately," the doctor ordered. I had not been driving very long and did not know my way around the city. My husband, in his somnolent state, had to direct me to the hospital.

"Lord, please don't let my husband die tonight," I pleaded as a new doctor ordered a peritoneal (tube to the stomach) dialysis be done. Knowing the procedure would be painful, I asked, "Is my husband in any real danger?" The doctor replied with an explosive Yes!

I phoned my sister alerting her to have our church members pray for my husband. Alone with God, I alternately read from a book entitled *Pray for the Sick* and glanced up at a sign on the wall that read, "This Is Not the End of Anything, It Is Only the Beginning."

I prayed incessantly because, on top of all this, the nurses were on strike. The apparatus the doctors had set up was not working as it should, so I asked the one nurse on duty to stop it.

All night I prayed with my husband. We talked about the importance of his giving his life to the Lord. Sometime during that long, painful night, my husband surrendered his heart to a new Friend—Jesus. Today, nineteen years later, we are still thanking and praising the Lord together.

Do you need God to make a way in your wilderness right now? Remember that what you might see only as an end, God can see as the beginning of a "brand-new thing" He may be wanting to do for you. Ask for His power to hold on to His promises and trust that His love will carry you through.

Marilyn Thompson Marshall

Changes

For now we see through a glass, darkly; but then face to face: now I know in part; but then shall I know even as also I am known.
1 Cor. 13:12.

I remember visits to Grandmother's house in Moruga in Trinidad and Tobago when I was a child. These visits took place during the August holiday when school let out. We looked forward to these visits because it meant more room to run, trees to climb, and every treat we could think of, from homemade ice cream to pies to cassava pone. However, visits were not without their horrors, for Grandma would line us up to have senna pods tea (a laxative then used for an after-school worm-out). Ugh! That was the worst experience ever. The taste, the smell—even though she put milk in it and tried to disguise the flavor, you still knew what it was.

Another highlight was getting to use tweezers. Grandma would call me in particular, since I was the eldest, to pluck out the gray hairs on her hairline and nape (there were no hair dye sticks yet), a task that could take hours since there seemed to be a lot of gray hair.

The years went by and I watched my grandmother age, get sick and frail, and then go to sleep. I look at myself in the mirror now and see the gray appearing on my hairline. I look at my body and remember when I was slim and limber. Now to climb a flight of stairs might wreak havoc on my knees, and I don't have the same waistline. The years just flew by, bringing with them changes that were welcome and unwelcome, death and life, loss and gain.

One final change that I am looking forward to is one that will bring infinite peace and unending joy. Right now the changes that come to our bodies are changes of old age, sickness, and death. Even though we may exercise and eat right, because of sin, we still go through changes. The Bible says that right now "we see through a glass, darkly." Our understanding is limited and our eyesight is dim. But one day we will know as we are known; one day we will look in the mirror and see ourselves the way God saw us all along. One day Christ Himself will call our names. As we walk on those golden streets and look down at our reflections, we will see not the body that needs to be "wormed-out" or the gray hair that comes with age. Instead, as we look about, we will see robes of white covering hearts of praise, the healthy glow of a sin-free body, and, best of all, the eyes of our Father. Oh what a change that will be!

Greta Michelle Joachim-Fox-Dyett

Details

He that is faithful in that which is least is faithful also in much.
Luke 16:10.

Something had changed. When a coworker walked into our organization's medical office to pick up forms for her upcoming surgery, I could see that something was different about her. As we talked for a few minutes about her surgery, I noticed that her language was no longer peppered with curse words. She began to tell me about the recent decision she and her husband had made to commit their lives to the Lord. This was a radical change for them, and I could see the peace of God reflected in her face. Yet sadness tinged her joy because many of their old friends would no longer associate with them.

I was able to share with her how much the Lord meant to me and to encourage her to allow Him to govern in every area of her life—even in the little details. What Jesus would do should determine how we handle every situation of life. I gave her the example of how, after unloading groceries into my car at the store, it would be so easy to just abandon the shopping cart and drive off instead of returning it to a holding area. If I abandoned the cart, however, it could roll into another car and dent or scratch it. So even though I'm tempted to drive off and leave it, I try to do what I believe Jesus would in that situation—return the cart. After our conversation, my coworker and I hugged. She left for the hospital and I had a new friend.

Several weeks later, I was hurrying through the grocery store and ran into her. We caught up on our lives, discussing especially how she was healing from her surgery. Suppertime was approaching, so we both hurried off to finish our shopping. It was getting dark on this rainy winter day. My knee was hurting from my own surgery, and I really didn't want to push that shopping cart up to the holding area, but the thought crossed my mind, *What would Jesus do?* Slowly, I trudged with the cart up to the holding area. Suddenly, I heard my name. I looked up to see my friend pushing her shopping cart to the holding area too. She was laughing and said, "I'll never forget what you told me about doing what Jesus would do and taking the cart back."

How many little details of our lives testify to others of our commitment to reflecting Jesus in all we do and say? What would my coworker have thought of me if I'd not returned the shopping cart that day—and just driven off? What would she have thought of Jesus?

Sandi B. Cook

Prayer Gets Good Results

Therefore confess your sins to each other and pray for each other so that you may be healed. James 5:16, NIV.

My husband, Murray, has a grandniece named Heidi, who is a fully trained ambulance officer. Her police officer husband, Ian, often helped with the homeschooling of their four children. Yet their hearts' desire was to do volunteer work for the Lord. So they sold their home in Australia and moved near an orphanage in Nepal. In that country they secured housing in a high-rise apartment building and found themselves surrounded by many other families living there as well.

In her ministry with orphans, Heidi has been updating a medical file for each child since past medical documentation for the children has been sparse. She is bringing past records up to date so that it is easier to track any past medical problems that children have had as well as the treatment they've been given. More than 150 children reside in the orphanage. Some have the same names, which also complicates Heidi's record keeping. She is planning to run a basic first aid course for all the house-parents so they will know what to do when accidents happen or medical emergencies arise. And accidents do happen.

One day a little two-year-old boy, Yuv Raj, who lived in the apartment below Heidi's family, climbed over the balcony railing. From there he fell to the concrete below, landing on his head. He sustained a severe head fracture and brain injuries. Heidi immediately offered her medical expertise to help with the child. However, to secure a medical appointment in this part of the country, a person has to be in line at 7:00 A.M. in order to obtain a visitation ticket. Only forty tickets are issued at a time. Heidi stood in line on Yuv Raj's behalf and was able to secure ticket number 35 and obtain help for him. After Yuv Raj's accident, Heidi and Ian e-mailed friends and relatives in Australia to pray for the little boy's expenses and his healing. As a result of prayer, Yuv Raj began to recover. Yuv Raj is now giving high-fives to his friends back at school.

The prayers of friends and family have been the source of daily strength for progress in Heidi's challenging mission work. And prayer is your source of strength, as well, as you permit God to fulfill—through you—day by day, His ministry purpose for your life.

Joan D. L. Jaensch

Who Knows?

God sets the lonely in families. Ps. 68:6, NIV.

I had always been a homebody, living with my parents. However, in 2005, I decided I would have an educational adventure my second year of university by studying in another country. My intention, when I nervously left my family for a whole eight months, was to spend just this one year in England and then return home to finish my studies at the university, which my parents and sister had attended before me.

I comforted myself with the thought, *At least I'm coming home for Christmas.* So, not really having been away from home for any length of time, I obtained a passport and traveled by myself to Newbold College in England—with my plan in mind.

What can I say? Here I am, still living in the United Kingdom after seven years! And indeed they have been the best seven years of my life! God had a different plan for me. He knows how important my family is to me, but He also knows what's best for me. He knew that at nineteen, I needed to begin building a life of my own. I needed to grow and come to know myself as an individual independent of my parents. And God orchestrated His plan through a brand-new friendship with a very special person.

I had never even met anyone from Serbia, and now I am married to the most wonderful Serbian man whom I met in England. I couldn't be happier. God knew what He was doing, as He always does. Granted, both my husband I would like to see our families more often, but God has constantly shown us that He is taking care of us in everything. He has blessed us beyond our imagination and has faithfully guided us in His plan for our life together.

Everyday we make plans. Yet they are plans that don't always turn out as we expect.

God, however, the Almighty and All-Knowing, is in ultimate control of our lives, and He always has our best interests at heart. I am glad that He has that kind of control and not me.

May we, like our perfect Example and best Friend, Jesus, always seek God's plans for our lives. We will be happier as we seek to know His will and trust that He will see us through and guide us every step of the way. He has promised, "And my God will meet all your needs according to the riches of his glory in Christ Jesus" (Phil. 4:19, NIV).

Taylor Bajic

Witnessing as a Volunteer for Jesus

And this gospel of the kingdom shall be preached in all the world for a witness unto all nations; and then shall the end come. Matt. 24:14.

People witness for the Lord in many different ways. Some witness as homemakers, some as teachers, some as pastors, others are evangelists, and some write books to help us understand the Bible. I have been privileged to be a teacher, as well as a parent, a wife, a librarian, a nurse's aide, and a real estate salesperson. Now that I am retired, I have a new way to witness for the Lord—as a volunteer in the community.

I wanted to be able to make a difference for Jesus, so I now work as a court appointed special advocate (CASA) in my county's juvenile court system. I help children who have been removed from their parents for various reasons, such as physical abuse, domestic abuse, drug or alcoholic abuse, or just plain neglect. I deplore their dire circumstances, but I enjoy working through the details that help find safe, permanent homes for these children.

In preparation for this work, I took thirty hours of training and did thirty hours of independent study, which included observation in juvenile court. Each case is entirely different from any other. I learn something new almost every day. Part of my work involves collaborating with up to five lawyers as well as working with the Department of Children's Services and the judge of the juvenile court. In addition, there are the parents, of varying personalities, and children with whom I interact. Some of the children are mere infants born to a mother on methamphetamine. So babies are now tested for drugs that may be in their systems due to the mother's drug abuse.

Each child is appointed a case worker and is placed with a relative or in a foster home until the mother or parents have been arrested, placed on bond, and appear in court. If the case is a difficult one, the judge may request a CASA volunteer to work on the case as well.

If I am gratified to see my efforts as a witness and volunteer for Jesus result in hurting children finding a safe, permanent home, think of the joy that Christ—who volunteered to die in our place—will one day experience when He comes to take His children to their safe, permanent, beautiful, and eternal home!

Loraine F. Sweetland

Finding Joan

A man that hath friends must shew himself friendly. Prov. 18:24.

Joan Scher. Over forty years ago, this lady was sent to our country home. She was not well; she arrived with her six-year-old daughter, Belinda, and their dog. The only room to sleep in was in the nursery school room. The sofa opened up into a bed, and there they camped.

Belinda went off with my son John to Stanborough Park School, where my husband, Cyril, was teaching. I didn't know that Joan was an artist, but she transformed the nursery school walls with beautiful flowers and animals. She said that made her feel better, painting. It certainly made us all feel better. She had come for a short time but stayed for a long time.

When she was well again, she went back to her husband. They moved to Yorkshire, as she was a Yorkshire lass, and I thought that was the end of the story. It certainly was not. We actually went to stay with them in Yorkshire with our three children.

By this time, I was fully entrenched in my work with dyslexic children. We discovered that Joan was dyslexic. This would, at last, account for her struggles at school. Later on they moved to Kent. Our friendship was truly cemented then. We started to write books together. The bigger one was called *My Journey to Dyslexia*. Her artwork is just so gorgeous that it makes the book live. We have spent so many wonderful hours together. We have done lots of smaller books too. They are called the *How Books* and explain in colorful detail the steps to be taken to transform the life of a dyslexic child into a life of success: turning the *can't* into *can* (knocking off the "t" so that *can't* becomes *can*).

Joan is still painting, and although she is now eighty-three years of age, we still enjoy writing stories together. She can still illustrate them all in such a lovely way. Joan has a great sense of humor. She writes gorgeous poems in which her humor bubbles forth.

How fortunate that Joan came to our door so many years ago when she was so ill. Her faith was so weak then, but now we pray together for so many people. We never knew so long ago when the friendship began that it would result in a blessing that would go on and on.

Isn't it just wonderful how God gives us friends? We pray for each other and our friendship strengthens our faith and blesses others.

Monica Vesey

The Changing Seasons

And it shall come to pass, that from one new moon to another . . . shall all flesh come to worship. Isa. 66:23, KJV.

Recently, while reflecting on the changing beauty that the four seasons bring here in the Northern Hemisphere, I couldn't help but think of the impact that life's experience at different seasons of life can have on an individual. Let me share.

Just as a springtime environment gently nurtures a tender plant, so our early years, from birth through childhood, are best lived in a safe environment that meets our basic needs, whether physical or spiritual.

Adolescence and early adulthood usher us into the summer of our lives. In nature, summer heat and rain encourage a plant's rapid growth into maturity. I consider myself a "summer person," as that seems to be the season when my personal energy level peaks.

My favorite season, however, is autumn (roughly September to November where I live). Summer's green leaves become brilliant oranges, yellows, and reds that burst into our vision with magnificent splendor. Autumn is the time of year—and time of life—when we can enjoy the fruits of our labors. Well-tended gardens bring forth their bountiful yields, which, preserved by various methods, ensure sustenance during the less productive season of winter. Autumn brings to mind Christ's words, "Yes, the way to identify a tree or a person is by the kind of fruit produced" (Matt. 7:20, TLB).

All too soon winter follows autumn. I enjoy the first few snowfalls each winter season. Yet, after a blizzard or two, I start to feel like hibernating. However, regardless of the wintry weather, it holds no regrets for the farmers and gardeners who have worked well throughout the warmer seasons. They can rest from their labors, surviving winter's harsh winds and resting up for the work of the next seasonal cycle.

As with nature's seasons, so should it be with our seasons of life if we have been faithful to our heavenly traveling Companion. When the last cold wind blows across the landscape of our lives, we will be able to say, along with the apostle Paul, "I have fought well. I have finished the race, and I have been faithful" (2 Tim. 4:7, CEV).

Doreen Evans-Yorke

Right on Time

He has made everything beautiful in its time. Eccles. 3:11, NIV.

One Sabbath morning I sat in church, broken in spirit. Even during the sermon, feelings of depression overwhelmed me. I could not focus on the sermon without being reminded of my unanswered prayers, so I decided to just leave. At that moment, I heard the preaching elder say, "God will not take us out of the valley right now, but He promises to be with us."

That's it, I thought, *I am in a valley of depression.* As I got up to slip out, the elder was quoting Philippians 2:5, "Let this mind be in you, which was also in Christ Jesus."

To be honest, even though I was outside of the church, I still couldn't get home. I needed a ride. So I walked around to the back of the church, where I could be alone, wait, and just think.

I tried to memorize Philippians 2:5, realizing then that I needed a new "mind," a new character, to get out of this state of depression. Yet a wave of anger swept over me as I remembered the many times I had sought counsel in God's Word and prayed about my problems, many of which simply had not yet gone away. At that moment, I purposed to stop praying because I was not getting what I wanted anyway. Discouraged, I determined to work things through without any spiritual intervention.

A few minutes later, I caught a ride home with a church sister who was leaving the morning's service. Usually, I would have gotten out of the car at the main road, said goodbye, and then walked five minutes to my home. On this particular day, however, my friend drove me directly to my door. When I stepped out of her vehicle, the strap on one of my shoes broke. *Right on time,* I thought, *the shoe has served its time.* I disposed of that pair of shoes as soon as I got inside. Then something clicked in my mind. I'd been angry with God who hadn't answered all my prayers when I'd wanted Him to. Yet as I thought about my broken shoe, the Holy Spirit helped me understand that God will always be right on time for me too. *Yes,* I thought, *I am still in the valley. Yet, just as God prevented me from having to walk home with a broken shoe, He will not permit me to walk the rest of the road "home" with a broken life.*

In our weakest moments, we can know that God will demonstrate He has not forgotten us and will rescue us right on time. His delay is not denial, for His timing is always perfect.

Kimasha Pauline Williams

I Know You

I have called thee by thy name; thou art mine. Isa. 43:1.

I was a guest speaker at the Women's Ministries congress in Hartenbos, hosted by the Cape Conference in South Africa. Though the program was scheduled to end on Sunday at noon, I had to do my last presentation and leave early to connect to my next appointment on Monday.

After my presentation, I was left with only thirty minutes to get to the airport, which was thirty kilometers away. The women helped to carry my bags to the car as we said our goodbyes. We rushed to the airport with a terrific speed. Some ten minutes away, I started to gather my travel documents so that I did not waste any time when I get to the check-in counter.

I had my carry-on bag on my lap and I opened it up to get my handbag out. I discovered it was not there. I figured out that it could be in the car trunk, since my bags had just been thrown in due to time pressure. We sped to the parking lot and straight away opened the trunk to fetch my bag. It was not there either! I then realized it must have been left some thirty kilometers away. We telephoned the meeting place, and it was confirmed my bag was still under the last seat I sat in. I rushed to the check-in clerk, since there were only ten minutes before boarding closed. I wanted to see if they could check me in without my identity document. The clerk called his supervisor who said it was not possible but suggested that I see the police officer for an affidavit. The police officer said it was not possible to issue an affidavit without my proof of my ID.

I stood helpless and bewildered. I had no ID documents on me. Though willing, the person who took me to the airport was not allowed to take an oath that he knew me and my identity. No one was able to bear witness and testify that they knew me. I was finally checked in after producing a scanned copy of my passport on my computer. At my destination, I had to wait four hours at the airport for my handbag to arrive. I tasted what it means to have no one to bear me witness. In this world, people may not know or recognize you. You may have no credentials, but there is a God in heaven who knows you and me. He knows our sitting down and our standing up, the Lord who understands our thoughts. What an assurance! What a confirmation!

Dear Lord, I rejoice in the knowledge that You have known know me from the time I was in my mother's womb.

Caroline Chola

All the Days of Your Life

Honour thy father and thy mother: that thy days may be long upon the land which the LORD thy God giveth thee. Exod. 20:12.

Honour thy father and mother; which is the first commandment with promise; that it may be well with thee, and thou mayest live long on the earth. Eph. 6:2, 3.

I never fully understood what the fifth commandment meant about honoring one's parents until I reached my golden years and was on the receiving end of the commandment. More than ever, I appreciate that God asks children to honor parents even when we get old—rather than placing us, so to speak, on a shelf like some figurine to collect dust. Especially those of us who might develop dementia or Alzheimer's disease. God never intended that elderly parents be left to loneliness and depression but that, rather, they enjoy time with their children as long as possible.

What does it mean to honor our parents? It means cultivating a spirit of gratitude, because parents have done far more than we can ever know. They have made sacrifices for us that we only partially understand. The fifth commandment "is binding upon childhood and youth, upon the middle-aged and the aged. There is no period in life when children are excused from honoring their parents. This solemn obligation is binding upon every son and daughter and is one of the conditions to their prolonging their lives upon the land which the Lord will give the faithful. . . .

". . . The fifth commandment requires children not only to yield respect, submission, and obedience to their parents, but also to give them love and tenderness, to lighten their cares, to guard their reputation, and to . . . comfort them in old age" (*The Adventist Home,* pp. 292, 293).

No matter their age, children can smooth their parents' pathway to the grave with kindness, love, and help. This is God's plan. His own Son, Jesus, showed compassion and care for His elderly mother even as He hung on the cross. "When Jesus therefore saw his mother, and the disciple standing by, whom he loved, he saith unto his mother, Woman, behold thy son! Then saith he to the disciple, Behold thy mother! And from that hour that disciple took her unto his own home" (John 19:26, 27).

Honoring our parents is a sacred obligation and privilege all the days of our lives.

Camilla E. Cassell

Above All

Now unto him that is able to do exceeding abundantly above all that we ask or think, according to the power that worketh in us. Eph. 3:20.

For years we have been saving points towards airline tickets. Needing tickets in June, I phoned the airlines to book our flight and was encouraged to upgrade to a gold (credit) card, thereby saving 25 percent. The new card would take two weeks to arrive and would cost us $160 in annual fees. I didn't have the time to register, so I declined and bought tickets outright.

Needing tickets again in September, I was reminded—during that phone call—about the 25 percent savings if I had a gold card. Again, I declined. The next day while shopping, I realized I should have upgraded in June. We were building a house, charging large sums to our credit card, which translated into increasing points that could buy airline tickets. I went directly home, called the card company, and asked if I should I sign up today, would they give me the extra points retroactive from last June. The polite agent said they couldn't accommodate my request. When I asked to speak to his supervisor, the agent put me on hold.

I prayed earnestly. "Lord, please impress this supervisor to say Yes to my request. Lord, it's Your money we'd be saving, and I try to be a good steward."

Coming back on the line, the agent again said, "No, we can't fulfill your request." Disappointed, I silently asked God why He hadn't worked this out for us. The agent continued talking. "Though we can't help you starting from last June, we could award you five hundred points and not charge the annual fee for this year if you sign up today." Still thinking I was losing points by the agent not doing things "my way," I agreed to his latest offer. Just before the agent finished updating my information, he said, "We can also give you a 150-point bonus for three months if you spend two thousand dollars a month." (This is easy for a business like ours.) When I calculated and compared what I'd agreed to, I realized that I'd earned 235 points more by signing up that day than I would have, had the agent agreed to my first proposal. Plus, we had no annual fee to pay!

God is able to do exceeding abundantly more than we could ever ask or think. What a lesson I learned that day. When I stopped telling God what to do and how to do it—questioning His power, love, and concern for me—and just let Him "be God," how abundantly He blessed!

Beth Versteegh Odiyar

Listen to That Still, Small Voice—Part 1

Be still, and know that I am God: I will be exalted among the heathen,
I will be exalted in the earth. Ps. 46:10.

The day started in blessed communion with my best Friend in prayer and a time of Bible study. Then all too soon our family was scurrying about to prepare for church.

I praise His name that, after leaving my devotional time, I continued to listen to His Spirit. And God was able to use me that day in a simple but powerful way to touch a life.

After the Sabbath School program, I gathered my family together, and we found seats for the eleven o'clock church service. The service proceeded as usual. Yet, when we stood to sing, I glanced over my shoulder and saw a visitor slip into the seat behind us.

She was a beautiful, nicely dressed lady with an expensive-looking scarf draped stylishly about her regal neck. The woman's well-coifed hairstyle provided the finishing touch to her elegant demeanor.

The way she held herself suggested self-confidence. Her graceful, yet stately, mannerisms quietly created the aura of someone who is in perfect control of life. *Surely,* I mused, *this woman definitely has her act together!* Yet appearances can be deceiving, as I was soon to find out.

As we sung the opening song, I immediately heard a strong voice in my inner ear say, *"Turn around and greet that woman."* I thought, *I will, when it is more convenient.*

In my heart's stillness, I heard, *"Turn around and greet the lady."*

Fearful of appearing awkward and embarrassed, I continued to resist the strong impression. Again, I heard the voice say more strongly, *"Turn around now. Don't wait!"*

Now I realized this was the Holy Spirit was speaking to me.

Astonished, I wordlessly replied, *OK, Lord, I will listen.*

How easy it is for us to seek communion and friendship with God during our quiet time in the morning. Yet we go from that place of stillness into our busy days—and even to church—all too often forgetting that He wants us to keep listening for His voice and experiencing His close companionship throughout the day.

Vonda Beerman

Listen to That Still, Small Voice—Part 2

Speak, LORD; for thy servant heareth. 1 Sam. 3:9.

I turned around and faced the beautiful visitor. "Hi, I'm Vonda," I said. "I'm so glad you came to join us this morning. Where are you from?"

Taken aback, she said, "My name is Joan, and I live in a town nearby here." I smiled at her and turned to face the front of the church again.

A few moments later, Joan passed me a note. It read, "Thank you for acknowledging me. You don't know how God used you this morning." Then, before the sermon even started, she quietly slipped out of her seat and out the back door of the church.

By this time I was finally, and fully, in tune with the Holy Spirit's promptings and immediately obeyed the impression to follow Joan out. I caught her in the lobby before she had time to exit the church. "Are you all right?" I asked.

With tears coming into her eyes, she confided, "I've been watching a Doug Batchelor evangelistic series on TV, and God has convicted me that He wants me to worship on His seventh-day Sabbath. I was impressed to come to this church today, even though I visited here once before . . . and not one person acknowledged that I was here."

"I'm so sorry," I said.

Joan continued, "And until you introduced yourself, no one had said a word to me this morning either. So, in discouragement, I guess, I silently prayed, 'Lord, if You want me here in this church, please show me. Impress someone to speak to me.' " Just seconds before Joan was about to leave this church for good, I had spoken to her! Seconds before her leaving permanently, I spoke to her! We were both overwhelmed. "Someone is waiting for me in the car today," she explained, "but because God answered my prayer through you, I *will* be back!"

Thank You, I prayed. *Lord, I had no idea that Joan, like so many others, was discouraged, lonely, and searching for loving Christians who share her new convictions.*

Today, by God's grace, Joan is a baptized member of our church.

Friend, are you listening for His voice? Every moment is precious. Don't waste even one. Listen for that still, small Voice. Then obey it. He will use you in a mighty way!

Vonda Beerman

Earthquake!

Praise be to the Lord, to God our Savior, who daily bears our burdens. Our God is a God who saves; from the Sovereign LORD comes escape from death. Ps. 68:19, 20, NIV.

My friend and her elder sister moved into their first apartment in 1976. Later that year, the rest of their family joined them. They lived there comfortably for several years. Then one night my friend's father felt the bed shaking. Nervous, he suspected a large snake had made its way into the house and under the bed. But a quick search revealed no snake under the bed. The following day newspaper reports shared details of an earthquake in Indonesia. That explained the shaking.

After that experience my friend's family began to notice, from time to time, increasing tremors. One evening an earthquake struck, becoming so severe that many residents from the housing buildings on the next block scrambled out of their front doors, running into a large field for safety. But my friend's family stayed inside their apartment, as a younger child in the family was sound asleep. As the tremors continued, they noticed a hanging plaque above the door start to swing back and forth.

"Look!" shouted one family member. "The utensils on the kitchen counter are moving!" My friend remained on the shaking couch, praying for God's protective hand over her family and all the people in the city. Though it seemed the whole housing unit was shaking, she continued praying until the rolling movements stopped.

Praise the Lord God Almighty for His incredible wonders and His love! My friend's experience reminded me of the night on the Sea of Galilee when Christ's disciples cried out to Him as He slept in their boat in the midst a fearful storm. Upon being awakened, He calmed the storm (see Matt. 8:26). In the Bible, Christ predicted an increase of natural disasters toward the end of time just before He returns (see Matt. 24). Yet He also encouraged His followers to watch and pray " 'that you may be able to escape all that is about to happen, and that you may be able to stand before the Son of Man' " (Luke 21:36, NIV). Though we experience wonderful answers to our prayers now as we bring our burdens to Christ, the greatest wonder of all will be the day that He enables us to stand before Him, forever safe, in our heavenly home!

Yan Siew Ghiang

Could You Not Watch With Me?

"What! Could you not watch with Me one hour?" Matt. 26:40, NKJV.

Sometimes when I should be struggling to stay alert, I fall into lethargy. It just takes so much effort to stay vigilant. This story reminds me how dangerous it is to become apathetic when I should be observant.

We gaze intently at Jesus. " 'Love one another as I have loved you,' " He says. " 'Greater love has no one than this, than to lay down one's life for his friends' " (John 15:12, 13, NKJV). Did you catch that? Jesus is talking about death again! Here in the peaceful Garden of Gethsemane! But is He talking about Himself or one of us?

Jesus continues, " 'They will put you out of the synagogues; yes, the time is coming that whoever kills you will think that he offers God service' " (John 16:2, NKJV). Inconceivable! We shudder at the thought. Soon Jesus moves off to pray alone after counseling us to watch and pray. Suddenly, He is speaking again. We can't keep our eyes open even while He asks, " 'What! Could you not watch with Me one hour?' " (Matt. 26:40, NKJV). Again, Jesus finds us sleeping. James remains aware long enough to hear the Lord prayerfully groan about a cup of grave difficulty. The cup! James remembers Jesus predicting, " 'You will indeed drink the cup that I drink' " (Mark 10:39, NKJV). Even in sluggishness, James recognizes the cup is significant; but his eyes close. For now, James's cup is hidden in his stupor, hidden like Joseph's cup in Benjamin's sack of grain.

Jesus re-enacts Jacob's long night of wrestling as He grapples with His own epic battle. Tonight, all the disciples are engaged in a Jacobean struggle. They need prayer for power and protection; particularly Peter, John, and James, whose cup is revealed first as Herod's sword slashes open the grain sack of believers feeding on the Bread of Life.

Why have I come to the Garden of Prayer? Is my heart gripped in a life-and-death struggle against the enemy? Am I fervently praying to remain alert—not falling into temptation? Am I gripping the mighty right arm of God? Am I pleading for Him to uphold me when my cup is revealed; that I will have strength of purpose to faithfully drink the cup of the Father's will? Or am I too comfortable to recognize my heart is bowed in slumber, immune to the Master's plea to "watch and pray"?

Rebecca Timon

"Why Have You Forsaken Me?"

"My God, My God, why have You forsaken Me?" Mark 15:34, NKJV.

Sometimes in the loneliness of my heart, words do not even form and I simply weep. This story assures me that if I press close to His side, God fills the void.

During the Passover meal, Jesus predicts one of us will betray Him. We are stunned when John is first to exclaim, "Is it I, Lord?" Why would John think he could betray Jesus? Even now, John leans in, close to the heart of Jesus. We've seen the Son of Thunder walk with Jesus and respond to the Lover of his soul. It can't be so! John *loves* Jesus!

John follows Jesus closely during His arrest and arraignment. We follow along sadly with the crowd the next day when the beaten and condemned Man, our Master, is marched to the hill called Golgotha.

We are blinded by the unnatural darkness blanketing Jerusalem. In the emptiness of that black moment, Jesus cries out, "My God, My God, why have You forsaken Me?" But one disciple has not forsaken Him. In forlorn anguish, the Lord's head slumps. With eyes lowered and breath expiring, He focuses on the shadowy figure of John clinging to the foot of His cross. Jesus has no need to ask, "Friend, why have you come?" This disciple who loves Jesus more than anything—and knows Jesus loves him more than anything—is again leaning in as a lover, close by His side.

Look! Here is the grieving disciple who needs to be filled yet gives comfort to the crucified Lord. Here is a friend who sticks closer than a brother and will care for the weeping, heartbroken mother as his own. Here is a son for the mother to love. Here is the faithful follower being transformed into the beloved disciple who tells the whole wide world that Christ Jesus loves and saves, gives and lives.

And now Jesus looks at me whom He loves and asks, "My friend, why have you come to watch from afar? Will you forsake Me, or will you allow Me to love you completely, to fill your every need, and to provide for your future? Are you mindlessly following the crowd who reviles Me? Or will you draw near because you see the Son of Man dying to give you life? My beloved, will you truly believe that I love you more than anything?"

Rebecca Timon

How Much It Cost

God's mercy is great, and he loved us very much. . . . You have been saved by God's grace. Eph. 2:4, 5, NCV.

How many of us look forward to moving to a new location—especially if we have moved a lot during our lives? It's always stressful to leave our friends, family members, and the routine with which we are familiar and move to places unknown to us.

Often a move means new schools for our children, finding new doctors, learning where to shop for the best bargains, finding a house we can afford—and in a neighborhood that's safe. And then there's the sadness of missing old friends and the struggle to make new ones. Yet, in time, our new church congregation becomes our new church "family."

When we were young in the ministry, I never unpacked all of our belongings because I knew that at the beginning of the next summer, usually at camp meeting time, we would probably be moving again. Sure enough! Almost before we knew it, we'd be moving and off to a new adventure. However, as we grew older, moving became more like work than like adventure!

I wonder, can we even imagine the dramatic changes Jesus experienced when He moved away from His heavenly home to come live on this dismal planet for over thirty-three years? He left indescribable beauty, angelic adoration, harmonious friendships, and face-to-face communion with His Father. He left all of that to come to this earth as the sacrificial Lamb of God, who would live, suffer, and die among us. Knowing this, Jesus still "moved" to the new location.

By the age of twelve, Christ recognized His relationship to God, His heavenly Father. However, Jesus did not allow His humanity to play the victim. He embraced the crucial role He must play in order to save us. Hourly, He trusted His Father for strength and guidance. Knowing His earthly future, He was still joyful, forgiving, and full of encouragement to others. God's very Son, so ill-treated by those He'd come to save, was full of unconditional love, unselfishness, and forgiveness.

Think of it. His whole life was a sacrifice—for us. He considered you and me worth dying for! That should make us willing to give up everything for Him and prepare for the move that I'm really excited about—the move to the home He's preparing for us (see John 14:1–3).

Louise Driver

A Mystery No More

The angel said to the women, "Do not be afraid, for I know that you are looking for Jesus, who was crucified. He is not here. . . . Come and see the place where he lay." Matt. 28:5, 6, NIV.

Don't you just love a mystery? The Bible supplies one of the best, and women play an important role as it unfolds. The mystery began with a missing body. The women knew where it was supposed to be; Mary Magdalene and Mary the mother of Joses had watched Joseph of Arimathea and Nicodemus place Jesus in the new tomb on Friday (Luke 23:55). So Sunday morning, when they came again to the tomb, it was a shock to discover the body was missing!

It is a little hard to know just who came and went at what times, but Luke 24 says Mary Magdalene and other women ran to report the missing body to the disciples. It is no great surprise that the men didn't believe the women, but Peter and John did nevertheless go to check it out, and then left again. But Mary stayed behind, and as a result she discovered the solution to the mystery (Mark 16:9, 10)—Jesus was risen!

We know now, of course, that "there was a violent earthquake, for an angel of the Lord came down from heaven and, going to the tomb, rolled back the stone and sat on it" (Matt. 28:2, NIV). Like a modern conspiracy story, the soldiers were paid to lie about what had happened, but the women knew the truth, and you can be sure they told the other women they met around the mill stones, the wells, and in the marketplace. In fact, Mary preached the risen Savior! (Ellen G. White, *Evangelism*, pp. 471, 472).

That same day, Jesus walked with Cleopas and his wife on the road to Emmaus. You can be sure that both of them, in their own way and to their own audiences, witnessed that Jesus was risen. And they were not the only ones. Paul tells us that the risen Jesus appeared to more than five hundred individuals (1 Cor. 15:6). It was not a mystery anymore. It was a marvelous, redeeming, glorious fact that Jesus was risen! Alleluia!

This mystery is not like reading an ordinary mystery book and when finished we lay it down with satisfaction. It is something about which we need to make a decision. What are you, what am I, going to do about the risen Savior? It is we, each of us, who will finish the story. What is your decision today?

Ardis Dick Stenbakken

The Certainty of His Promise

" 'He will wipe every tear from their eyes. There will be no more death'
or mourning or crying or pain, for the old order of things
has passed away." Rev. 21:4, NIV.

From the balcony of the second-floor apartment where I live here in Brazil, I can see a beautiful palm tree. Whenever I can, I gaze on its beauty, and I also delight in watching the bird life that unfolds in the midst of its fronds. Turtledoves are very common in my country, so I wasn't surprised one day to see a couple of them perched on the branches. I suspected they were looking for a safe place to build their nest.

Sure enough! For the next several days, the two birds worked tirelessly. One would alight with a twig in its beak. Then it would flutter off, almost passing its incoming mate bringing in a long strand of dry grass to weave into the growing nest. How faithfully, carefully, lovingly, and uncomplainingly they worked. I was excited the morning I was able to catch my first glimpse of two little white eggs in the nest as the parent birds changed watch in the incubation process. I, too, looked forward to the day new life would peck its way through those tiny eggshells.

Then one afternoon, the sky grew dark. Suddenly, a strong storm descended on us. Through the window, I watched the palm tree swaying in the stiff breezes. I feared for the little nest. Then, with an aching heart, I watched as a windy blast tore the carefully crafted nest from the palm fronds, blowing from the tree. Sadly, I saw the two little eggs lying broken on the ground below. The good news, however, is that the parent birds survived and began rebuilding a new nest.

What an object lesson this was for me! This blustery loss suffered by two turtledove parents reminds me that human pain, on a much larger scale, wreaks havoc on millions every day, as Satan blasts his cruel, angry storms into our lives. Perhaps you've experienced one of these painful storms recently in your own life. Yet, because of who God is and what His Son did for us on the cross, we can take heart—as did those turtledoves—that better times lie ahead. So we keep up our courage. The risen Christ promised He would return and take us to a place where there will be no more tears, death, grief, or sadness. In the meantime, today, we can have the assurance that because of the indwelling Holy Spirit, we are never alone in our storms.

Maria Bellesi Guilhem

An Ordinary Tree

For thou hast been a shelter for me, and a strong tower
from the enemy. Ps. 61:3.

It was just an ordinary tree sharing its shade with weary travelers such as we were. After a long, hot day of travel inland, we pulled into a caravan (trailer) park to spend the night. And there it was—one solitary tree in the whole park! It offered the only shade on that property. Although another party of campers had set up camp in its shade on one side of its trunk, they welcomed us as we pulled under the thick branches on the other side.

My husband, Keith, and I sat relaxing outside. Looking up into the branches of the tree, we were amazed at the large number of birds that visited it in the late afternoon. At sunset many masked wood swallows settled in the foliage. After fluttering around a while, they began cozying up together on one branch, as is their normal behavior. We counted twenty-four swallows, all facing the same direction, on one branch as the sun set. Maybe this tree was their regular resting place. Whether it was or not, this was one of very few trees on the edge of the desert which, tonight, we were sharing with them.

In Dorothy McKellar's poem "I Love a Sunburnt Country," she relates her love of nature's beauty, diversity, and change that can be found in this land of Australia. I resonate with this love of hers. However, I know from experience that the farther one goes inland, the more barren the Australian topography becomes. Not only is it barren, but it's also isolated, hot, and dry. No drinking water. No trees. Those luxuries have been left far behind.

That one lone tree in the caravan park made me ponder the value of a tree. I wonder how often any given tree had provided shade to the weary. How many birds has it sheltered before being cut down?

And I remember another lone tree. The one to which the apostle Paul referred when he said, "The God of our fathers raised up Jesus, whom ye slew and hanged on a tree" (Acts 5:30). How could we ever calculate the value of that tree? Yet when we ponder its value and purpose, how grateful we can be. Indeed, it's the one tree for which I am most thankful. For in the shadow of the Cross—in the midst of the thirsty, desert places of life—this weary traveler finds shelter, refuge, strength, and rest.

Lyn Welk-Sandy

The Unknown Island—Part 1

"What sort of man is this, that even the winds and the sea obey him?"
Matt. 8:27, NRSV.

In his little book titled *The Story of the Unknown Island,* José Saramago* relates the story of a man who enters through the Petitions Door to his king's palace to request a boat. Determined that he should have his request heard, the man lies down in front of the Petitions Door and declares, "I will not leave here until my request is not only heard, but granted."

Seeing his determination, the king reluctantly abandons the comfort of his throne room and comes to the Petitions Door to deal with this impertinent man and his strange request: "Why do you want a boat?" asks the king.

"I want to set sail for the unknown island."

"There are no more unknown islands. All the islands have been discovered," sniffs the king with disdain.

Then the man responds, "I am a man of the earth, a land lubber, and even I know that all the islands, even those that have been discovered, are unknown and undiscovered until we disembark on them." Saramago here picks up on an ancient human theme: the quest. On the ship of life, all of us are on a quest that will fulfill our deepest needs and our highest aspirations. Finding that destination will take us through many trials and tribulations, but if we find that one thing for which our soul longs, we will find a profound and transcendent peace "which surpasses all understanding" (Phil. 4:7).

Jesus' disciples were, for the most part, fishermen and understood the potential dangers involved in arriving at the safe harbor. One night as they set out with Jesus to the other side of the Sea of Galilee, a "windstorm swept down on the lake" (Luke 8:23, NRSV) and threatened to capsize their frail vessel. Exhausted from the demands of the crowd that day, Jesus lay sleeping, even as the boat tossed to and fro and began to fill up with water. Desperate, as they realized that their efforts to bail water out of the boat were increasingly in vain, these seemingly helpless men cried out to their one last hope of survival: " 'Master, Master, we are perishing!' " Jesus woke up and "rebuked the wind and the raging waves" (verse 24, NRSV), and suddenly there was calm. Whether they realized it or not, these men had already disembarked on an undiscovered island called Jesus.

Lourdes Morales-Gudmundsson

---

* José Saramago, *El cuento de la isla desconocida,* trans. Pilar del Río (Madrid: Alfaguara, 1998); translations from the Spanish are mine.

The Unknown Island—Part 2

"I am the way, and the truth, and the life. No one comes to the Father except through me. If you know me, you will know my Father also. From now on you do know him and have seen him. . . . Whoever has seen me has seen the Father." John 14:6, 7, 9, NRSV.

The disciples could not imagine that the object of their spiritual quest was present right there in the ship of their lives. All they had to do was call on Jesus and the storms of life would be calmed. They couldn't know that about Him until they experienced Him for themselves, until they recognized Jesus as that Island of Safety and came to know Him even as they were known.

Their encounter with Jesus that stormy night on the Sea of Galilee deepened their knowledge of Him and of themselves.

On the one hand, their question mixed with awe and amazement, " 'Who then is this, that he commands even the winds and the water, and they obey him?' " (Luke 8:25, NRSV), was not so much a question seeking information, but an expression of awe in the presence of One whom they acknowledged as all-powerful. On the other hand, the recognition of their fragile faith led them to be overcome by the beating waves of fear.

When the protagonist in Saramago's tale (see part 1) asks the cleaning lady why she wants to come on this adventure to seek and find the unknown island, she responds that she wants to know who she is.

The man responds, "If you don't leave yourself, you will never know who you are" (p. 32).

Exercising faith is a form of leaving yourself, the self that was created by your parents' fears and frailties and by the social context in which you grew up. It takes faith to move beyond these formative messages that do not let us acknowledge God's invitation to take the faith journey toward Him through Jesus.

In pointing to their faith, Jesus lands His beloved disciples firmly on solid ground, assuring them that their fear arose not from God's absence, but from their own fragile inability to believe that Jesus was with them on their journey toward the Father, their ultimate destination.

Lourdes Morales-Gudmundsson

Living His Word

Word: the expressed or manifested mind and will of God.

In the beginning was the Word, and the Word was with God, and the Word was God. John 1:1, NIV.

"If you remain in me and my words remain in you, ask whatever you wish, and it will be done for you" (John 15:7, NIV).

Remaining in. Abiding in. These expressions are other ways to describe what it means to live in—and then live out—the principles and promises of God's Word, His will. The Holy Bible.

And when we live in this Word, what quiet, yet amazing, work God does in us!

This month's story collection introduces us to one writer who was impressed to imitate the godly example left by her late grandmother.

Another shares the lessons she learned while nursing an injured sunflower back to health.

Yet others found themselves living out God's Word while sharing a burrito with a stranger, cleaning out a toilet bowl, finding resolution to an MLD (major life disappointment), and watching a baby converse with an angel.

There is something about living God's Word—the mind of "the Word" in print—that turns the mundane into the holy.

Remembering Grandma

Then I heard a voice from heaven say, "Write this: Blessed are the dead who die in the Lord from now on." "Yes," says the Spirit, "they will rest from their labor, for their deeds will follow them." Rev. 14:13, NIV.

I remember that first day of April when we got the phone call. It was the kind of call you do not expect or want to get. My husband picked up the phone and talked to one of my cousins. At the end of the call, he became quiet. I sensed his discomfort as he said, "We have to go to Ndola right away! Grandma was involved in a car accident." I couldn't believe my ears—I'd just spoken to her the day before. Within ten minutes, we were on our way to the nearby town where Grandma was awaiting surgery in the hospital. How we prayed for God to be merciful and spare my sweet, kind, loving granny! I wanted my grandma to live for a long time so she could see her yet-to-be-born grandchildren. I wanted them to sit at her feet while she shared her affection for them, her wisdom, and, above all, her deep love for God with whom she daily walked.

Whether talking to family, church members, or strangers, the greatest passion of this beloved woman was to introduce them to God. A number of those she invited to church had accepted Christ. Though a newlywed of only four months, I still considered Grandma to be my spiritual rock. She was the first person through whom I glimpsed the love of God. She was the foundation of my faith, and I am glad to be standing strong today because of her example.

When we got to Ndola, we were met with great disappointment. Grandma had died. On that day I came face to face with the ugliness of death and the pain of losing someone close to me whom I loved deeply. Many people—whom we didn't even know—attended Grandma's funeral. What a wonderful tribute to this daughter of God who had lived her life well! An abruptly ended life cannot end that person's personal and spiritual legacy. And Grandma's legacy lives on. With gratitude and pride, I recognize the privilege I had of calling this great woman "Grandma."

Perhaps you, too, have lost a loved one. If so, take comfort from God's promise found in today's text. Though grieving, we can still praise God that the death of believers who lived out God's Word in their lives does not end their influence. Remembering the examples they left behind will encourage us to be strong and faithful—and strengthen our hope in the resurrection.

Judith M. Mwansa

The Little Pheasant

"And behold, I am coming quickly, and My reward is with Me, to give to every one according to his work." Rev. 22:12, NKJV.

Satisfy us in the morning with your unfailing love, that we may sing for joy and be glad all our days. Ps. 90:14, NIV.

I was walking through the wild lupins blooming in the front yard of my cottage when a sudden movement caught my eye. A small wild pheasant was creeping through the undergrowth. Approaching slowly, I spotted her nest containing a dozen brown, speckled eggs. I was thrilled at my find. I spoke reassuringly to her. Out of respect for the little pheasant's egg-setting and eventual motherhood-privacy needs, my family left the front yard unmowed for weeks.

Each day I carried fresh water and placed it just a few feet away from her. At first she threatened to run off when I came near but made no attempt to dart away. She simply hissed as I quietly approached. Over time she allowed me—and my grandchildren and other visitors—to approach her nest. Despite the summer's heat, the pheasant faithfully continued her vigil. Instead of hatching, though, the eggs began to rot and break.

The little bird's efforts had been wasted. Eventually, we had to remove the nest. My eyes filled with tears as I watched her hunt for her missing nest. I can only hope . . . next year.

The little pheasant's perseverance reminded me of Christ's faithful love toward us. Looking down over Jerusalem just before His crucifixion, He lamented, " 'How often I have longed to gather your children together, as a hen gathers her chicks under her wings, and you were not willing' " (Luke 13:34, NIV). Unlike the little pheasant, Jesus knew what the end result would be. He knew that many for whom He died would reject the free gift of eternal life that His sacrifice would offer. Will we accept His persevering efforts for us—through trust in His Word—to transform our lives? Will we allow His peace and contentment to fill our hearts so His faithful efforts for us won't be in vain? Now, whenever I see a pheasant, I think, *He is faithful.*

Dear Lord, help me to remember that You have given Your life to save me. Thank You for the heaven You will provide if I am willing to accept Your sacrifice. I pray for strength to walk the path that leads to eternal life with You in the earth made new.

Patricia Cove

Spring Cleaning—Outside and In

There is a way that appears to be right, but in the end it leads to death.
Prov.14:12, NIV.

Our church was having a spring cleaning day. Church members had the choice to work inside the church or outside. Since sunny days are rare in Rochester, New York, Gretchen (my gardening friend) and I elected to work outside. Our job was to pull weeds and wild grass from the brick-encased flowerbeds in front of the church. I took the left side of the brick encasement from the front stairs to the church sign. Gretchen went to work on the other side.

Around the flowers and bushes, I went to work pulling up weeds and wild grass that didn't belong there. I'd reach below the redwood chips and pull up the intruders by their roots. Most yielded easily as I yanked them out. After hours of flowerbed weeding, I thought I was finished.

However, two large plants seemed oddly placed in the context of the other flowering plants. When I double-checked with Gretchen, she assured me, "Those are weeds. Go ahead and pull them out." I was astonished, because their beauty had convinced me they were not weeds. Gretchen's expert eye knew the difference.

I yanked at the smaller of the two weeds, pulling with all my strength. It wouldn't yield. Its main root was at least an inch in circumference. A gardening tool helped me finally uproot it. I eyed the second beautiful weed. Its root was twice the size of the first. Even with a gardening implement, I couldn't budge it. I called for one of the deacons to bring his hoe. He chopped at the main root four times before managing to pull up the stubborn weed's foot-long root tentacles.

Sin can be like those deeply entrenched weeds. A sin can look beautiful to the untrained eye and so "right" to just leave in the soil of our hearts. Yet its roots are unconsciously and deeply embedded into our very souls, appearing as a good shrub. Only the expert eye of God can reveal to us what is truly sin. Like that deacon with a hoe, God's power, through the Holy Spirit, will uproot it, if we are willing to ask for His help.

Because Jesus is coming soon, He is "spring cleaning" in our hearts, the hearts of His saints. Let's cooperate with the loving Hand that alone can remove the "weeds" from our lives. Let's let the principles of His Word have their way in our lives. Then, more and more, our hearts will grow only those plants that bear the fruit of the Spirit and are beautiful to *His* eyes.

Evelyn Greenwade Boltwood

Right Place, Right Time

In all your ways acknowledge Him, and He shall direct your paths.
Prov. 3:6, NKJV.

Every day I pray, *God, put me in the right place at the right time to lift someone to You.* I also walk three miles most days up my country road. As I walk, I often pray for my neighbors and ask God to give me opportunities to meet them. One day, as I walked up the hill approaching Claira Emmerson's home, I saw her out in her yard pulling weeds. When she saw me coming, she got up and started walking toward the fence along the road. I did not want to stop because I was well into my aerobic exercise, but I slowed and greeted her.

"Good morning, Claira. How are you today?" I asked as I turned and stopped at the fence. I was surprised at the next words that came out of my mouth: "I was praying for you while I was walking by your home."

"Well, I have a prayer request," she quickly replied. "My daughter is in the hospital facing surgery in an hour, and she has convinced herself she will not make it through surgery. She is very fearful of dying."

"Surgery? In an hour? We need to pray for her right now," was my immediate response.

"Pray *here*? Right by the roadside?" she hesitated as she looked up and down the road. But she quickly consented and, oh, how I prayed, claiming Jesus' precious promises! I could sense peace coming into Claira's heart, judging by the big smile on her face as we finished.

As I walked on up the road, I took my cell phone out of my pocket and called my husband, who "just happened" to be—at that very moment—near the hospital Claira had referenced. He went directly Claira's daughter's room. After introducing himself, my husband was given the privilege of praying with the young lady just before the gurney came to take her to surgery. Her fear was gone! She disappeared down the hallway with a smile on her face.

At the hospital the next day, friends and family surrounded Claira's daughter, happily chatting. We didn't want to disturb the joyful scene, but she spotted us in the doorway. She pointed, saying, "Look, there's the man I told you about that prayed for me before surgery!"

Dear reader, accept my challenge today. Say this prayer and watch God answer!

Lord Jesus, put me in the right place at the right time to lift someone to You today. Amen.

Corleen Johnson

The Reoccurring Trial

But He said to me, My grace (My favor and loving-kindness and mercy) is enough for you [sufficient against any danger and enables you to bear the trouble manfully]; for My strength and power are made perfect (fulfilled and completed) and show themselves most effective in [your] weakness. Therefore, I will all the more gladly glory in my weaknesses and infirmities, that the strength and power of Christ (the Messiah) may rest (yes, may pitch a tent over and dwell) upon me!
2 Cor. 12:9, AMP.

I chose the Amplified Version for this text because I love the explanations in brackets throughout the verse. This version gave a familiar text new life.

How many times have you found yourself facing the same trial or a similar trial over and over again? I have. The one that comes to mind are the four knee replacement surgeries I have had between 2007 and 2013. More than once, I found myself asking God, "Why me?" "Why, Lord, did this one trial of fire have to come four different times in my life?" "What have I done to have such a difficult trial reoccur with such frequency and lasting, painful consequences?" Sound familiar? I think many of us go down that road of doubt and discouragement when we face a trial that seems larger than life, and far more when we face a reoccurring trial.

I can truly say that today's verse has been my compass through these years. Through my doubts and questions to God, these words have drawn my questioning mind back to these truths—God loves me. He cares about what happens in my life. He sees my pain and struggle. And He will give me all I need to face the trial.

I know it's hard to believe that when you are facing a difficult situation in life, especially those that we have no control over. It seems like God has forgotten about us. That life is beating us down and that there is no place to turn, no one to help, and no one who cares. But God cares. We just need to find our bearings. Like a ship lost at sea, we need to look to the compass of God's Word and find our direction back to the Giver of life and strength.

And so, through each surgery, each painful day of rehabilitation, and even now as I deal with the daily pain that has resulted from multiple surgeries on my knees, I can say with great assurance, "God is my strength, and His strength works best in my weakness." Hallelujah!

Heather-Dawn Small

I Was a Stranger to Him

You shall also love the stranger, for you were strangers
in the land of Egypt. Deut. 10:19, NRSV.

When I was in eighth grade, my brother, Willard (ten months younger than I and "Bubby" to me), hit his head really hard getting into a car one day. I even heard the loud thud. Soon he began having severe headaches, confusion, and slurred words. Hospital testing and brain scans didn't show anything abnormal, yet his maladies continued intermittently. One day at school, someone from the office told me Willard was in the sick room and didn't recognize anyone. The school nurse was there and said, "He'll know you. And your mother is on her way to pick you two up." Then she drew back the curtain where my brother lay on the cot. I was so glad to see him! "Willard, your sister is here to see you," she said. "Willard? Do you know who this is?"

My brother scratched his head for a second and said through slurred words, "I never saw her before in my life!" My smile quickly faded as my stomach churned. He didn't know me! The nurse, seeing that I was visibly shaken and fighting tears, gathered my brother's things together before we all walked outside where my mother was already waiting. After dropping me off at home, Mother drove my brother straight to the hospital. Home alone, I reminisced—Bubby and I biking through the neighborhood, ice skating on the school lake, roller skating with our church youth, even fighting over an Uncle Arthur's bedtime storybook. My connection with my brother was gone, perhaps forever. I cried and cried some more. Fortunately, about a year later, Bubby's mysterious confusion ended and he became his same old self again.

As I have contemplated Bubby's considering me a stranger that day at school, I realize that all of us have been a stranger to someone at one time or another—in the grocery store, the park, the gym, at work, and even at church. At times, we have longed for someone to welcome us into their circle, to appreciate us, to care about us. Those experiences can be frustrating, hurtful, and sad—just like what I experienced with Bubby that frightening day when he didn't know me.

Aren't you glad that Jesus entertained strangers when He was here on earth? He cared for people genuinely and proved God's love was for everyone, even strangers. Aren't we to do the same? Let's go the extra mile today in our actions and attitudes, lest by misrepresenting Christ we become strangers to Him.

Iris L. Kitching

Angels in the Nursery

"See that you do not despise one of these little ones, for . . . their angels in heaven continually see the face of My Father who is in heaven." Matt. 18:10, NASB.

Stories about angels and their interaction with us mortals grip us in a powerful way, filling us with wonder and courage and hope—and yes, longing—a celestial link with our true destiny. We hear often about their power to protect and rescue; their tireless efforts on our behalf. But something that happened many years ago opened my eyes to another facet of their heavenly personalities, one I had never thought of before.

My daughter, Suzy, was three months old, that adorable age when babies begin to coo and laugh when you talk to them. I had just given her a bath and dressed her up in her ruffly red dress. As a finishing touch, I attached a tiny red bow to her mostly hairless head with a dab of Scotch tape and laid her down for her nap. Her crib was positioned so that I could see her face whenever I looked down the hall from the kitchen.

But she didn't go to sleep. Instead, she began to laugh—soft, happy belly laughs, again and again. When I peeked around the door, she was looking up at the wall, little arms waving energetically. Then she'd hold very still for a few seconds, looking and listening intently, eyes never leaving that spot on the wall, before another bubbling laugh of delight overcame her. It looked for all the world as if someone was looking down at her, making her laugh. I was puzzled, but only for a moment, as a new idea flooded my brain: Suzy and her guardian angel were having a conversation! It made perfect sense: evidently, an innocent baby, fresh from the Creator's hand, guileless and as yet untouched by sin, is more than even an angel can resist.

One year I wrote each of my children a letter on their birthday, sharing stories I remembered about them from their childhood. I included this incident in Suzy's letter. Many years and life experiences later, she called me one night. "Mom, the strangest thing happened at work today. I got up from my desk where I'd been typing and suddenly felt as if there were angels in the room with me. I turned around to look, almost expecting to see them there. Of course, they weren't visible, but I felt their presence."

And indeed they were there with her. They had never left.

Rhoda Wills

God's Watchful Care

The angel of the LORD ncampet about them that fear him, and livereth them. Ps. 34:7.

Many years ago when my husband served as pastor in a rural west Jamaican church district, we were invited to an elder's home for a post–church service lunch. As we ate, I protectively cradled two children—my teething toddler daughter on my lap and my son still in my womb. We were enjoying the discussion around the table when someone suddenly asked, "Why is your baby's mouth watering so much?" I quickly turned my daughter's face toward me for a closer look. To my horror, I saw her mouth filled with little fish bones—so many, in fact, that she couldn't close her mouth (this explained the overflow from her salivary glands). I froze. My husband quickly took her from my lap and removed the bones from her mouth. They were bones I'd dropped on my plate while eating fish provided by our host. By God's grace, my daughter suffered no injury, as she hadn't swallowed any of the bones nor punctured her mouth.

For years, I was unable to forgive myself for that incident. How could I, an overprotective mother, have allowed this to happen? And on my very own lap? For a long time, I was angry with myself.

Pondering this incident today, I find valuable life lessons.

First, not even my protective care as a mother was sufficient to keep my child from encountering danger. I learned that all—adults as well as children—are ultimately protected by the Lord and must allow Him to do His work. Second, I realize I need to be more understanding and sympathetic of other people, such as the babysitter, who may also make mistakes.

I thank God for using this potentially tragic oversight on my part to teach me important lessons. Truly, as He promises in Romans 8:28, He uses "all things" to accomplish His purposes in our hearts and in our lives.

My children are adults now living on their own, and God continues His loving, watchful care over them. He is well able to protect and send His angels to deliver them as He may well have done the day our host family noticed our baby daughter's problem. Yet my daily duty is to consecrate my life to Him the first thing each morning—and to consecrate the lives of my children, for our mighty God is able to keep safely that which we have committed unto Him.

Jacqueline Hope HoShing-Clarke

Sunflowers

This short time of distress will result in God's richest blessing upon us forever and ever! So we do not look at what we can see right now, the troubles all around us, but we look forward to the joys in heaven which we have not yet seen. The troubles will soon be over, but the joys to come will last forever. 2 Cor. 4:17, 18, TLB.

Our garden has many types of produce: tomatoes, corn, beans, beets, and squash. But the plants that grow the best are ones we didn't even put in the ground. But we don't mind that they grow so well because they brighten our garden, as well as our lives. They are sunflowers. Some sunflower plants grow tall with only one large flower, nodding its bright face above the fence, while others are shorter and loaded with flowers. Not only do we enjoy their beauty, but we have also discovered they have another admirable characteristic: courage.

Since my husband can't walk very well, he often gets around the garden in a golf cart.

One day as he was approaching a sunflower plant, his foot hit the accelerator pedal instead of the brake. His golf cart leveled the poor sunflower plant.

"It's ruined," I sighed. "I'll pull it up." My husband objected, suggesting that we leave it where it was and give it some water so that "maybe it will grow." The downed plant responded to his tender, loving care. Soon the recovering plant produced showy flowers again.

When I saw how bravely that humble sunflower plant handled such a traumatic setback, I felt encouraged to face more courageously some health issues that had been bothering me. If God could help a plant in the garden, I was sure He could help me. I also observed another reason why the sunflower plant survived my husband's golf cart blow. It had a strong root system. I thought, *My faith needs to be rooted in God's promises like that sunflower plant is in the soil. Then—no matter how hard I'm hit by life's unexpected challenges, perplexities, or losses—I can still depend on the Water of Life. Christ will sustain me with His comfort, courage, and healing.* Eventually, natural remedies, physical therapy, and exercise helped relieve my physical pain.

Now, whenever I see a sunflower, I am encouraged, for I know that God will help me deal with my earthly setbacks until He comes to take me home. He will do the same for you.

Betty J. Adams

On My Own Power

For by grace you have been saved through faith. And this is not your own doing; it is the gift of God, not a result of works, so that no one may boast. Eph. 2:8, 9, ESV.

When you're a summer camp counselor, you don't get much free time. So when my friend, Amy, and I realized we both had a responsibility-free Sabbath afternoon in our schedules, we decided to relax away from the children with a paddleboat ride. After obtaining permission from the waterfront director, we put on life jackets, got into a boat, and gloried in our freedom.

Soon we became absorbed in our mutual heartfelt conversation, along the beautiful shores of Lake Rousseau, forgetting to continue foot-pedaling our bulky plastic craft.

"Look, Melodie," said Amy, interrupting me in midsentence, "we're on the other side of the lake!" I looked back at camp, which was now barely visible. "Should we head back?" she asked. I was about to assure her we were probably fine, when I saw a man swimming toward us.

"Hello, ladies!" called the middle-aged, Speedo-clad man (no doubt a resident of the cottage behind him). "Are you lost? I could pull you behind my Jet Ski anywhere you need to go. I'd love to rescue two lovely young ladies like yourselves!" Slightly skittish of this stranger, we assured him we were fine and determined to return to camp on our own power.

Yet the wind had picked up, we now realized, and lake ripples were quickly turning into waves. Paddleboats are not built for the high seas. Our newfound naval prowess, energized pedaling, singing, and mutual encouragement got us nowhere. Literally. We were stranded in midlake—and late for dinner. I prayed that God would somehow give our vessel unprecedented power, but no miracle came—until we heard the distant hum of a motor. Two fellow staff members were sputtering towards us in a dilapidated fishing boat, laughing at our expense. We would be saved! Swallowing our pride, we allowed our coworkers to tow us back to camp as the entire staff stood on the dock, cheering wildly.

At first I felt only embarrassment. But when safe and dry, I realized what a metaphor of salvation our predicament had been! Often we find ourselves drifting from God, away from His Word. Nothing we do in our own power can save us. Only when we surrender to the Power beyond ourselves can He rescue us and get us safely home. What will you surrender to Him?

Melodie Roschman

Are You Hungry?

"Is not this the kind of fasting I have chosen . . . Is it not to share your food with the hungry?" Isa. 58:6, 7, NIV.

I was starving. I was also on the run, hitting lunchtime on the road between appointments. *Taco Bell sounds good,* I thought. I pulled off the freeway, passing two men with signs on the off-ramp.

"Two bean burritos, please," I said into the intercom when it came my turn to order. I picked up my food bag at the window, pulled away, and crossed the street to park and eat in the lot of a large grocery store. It was immediately clear to me I couldn't eat both burritos in addition to the apple I'd brought from home. Ordinarily, I would have just tossed the burrito. But hadn't I just passed two hungry men at the corner? Perhaps it was meant for someone. But for whom?

Now, though, I would run into the restroom before heading out and eat my apple on the road. I was willing, but the Lord would have to provide me with someone to hand the food over to. I entered the restroom, seeing no one. When I approached the washbasin, I still noticed no one. But I was praying. "Lord, if there's someone You want this food to go to, please place that person in my—" I was thinking the word *pathway,* when I became suddenly aware that someone was, in fact, right next to me at the basin to my right. And as soon as I saw her, I knew—she was the person for whom the burrito was intended. A ragged backpack lay at her feet. She was tamping down her tousled hair with wetted fingers, cleaning up.

We didn't have much time; each of us must soon leave. I opened my mouth and what came out was, "Are you hungry?" She looked at me wide-eyed, speechless. I hastened to explain the situation, ending with an offer to go get the burrito.

"Oh, yes!" she breathed. Off I went, returning not only with the burrito but also the apple. She was outside the restroom, looking for me. I passed the meager offering over, said, "God bless you," received her thanks, and we parted. God clearly is working in my young friend's life; He performed a miracle just for her. I'm eager to hear the rest of Devin's story.

What is in your hand today that God would have you share with someone who is hungry? Hungry, especially, for Him? Just ask Him who and where they are. He'll be sure to show you.

Carolyn K. Karlstrom

God Said "No"

For God so loved the world that he gave his one and only Son, that
whoever believes in him shall not perish but have eternal life.
John 3:16, NIV.

I had longed for this day to come—the day I would give birth. My instructional birthing CD had prepared me for this experience. The baby's room was ready. My packed bag was ready to take to the hospital. I had supportive people who loved me and were rooting for me. It was the perfect day to welcome my soon-to-arrive little gift.

Then the first labor pain came. Ouch! Yet the midwife in my prenatal class had forewarned me that contractions would become stronger. So I braced myself, breathing and praying through them as we headed to the hospital. By now the contractions had become regular, but I'd dilated only one centimeter. Nine to go!

After several painful hours, and not much more dilation, the midwife suggested moving me from the labor room back to the prenatal ward. The examining physician, however, did not agree with her and insisted I stay in the labor unit where she could monitor the baby's progress. The midwife grumbled aloud to coworkers that I was not yet ready to give birth. So now I was in both physical and emotional agony, feeling as if I was a burden in the labor unit when I should be elsewhere. My family and friends continued praying for me as I secretly wondered if my painful contractions would ever end.

Meanwhile, my unborn son was distressed. He had swallowed meconium (fecal matter that accumulates in, and discharges from, the baby's intestines near time of delivery), and his heart rate was dropping with every contraction. The midwives soon realized that the physician had been correct in her assessment to keep me in the labor room. Now the doctor herself feared for the life of the baby. He could have died, but God said, "No." The physician decided to perform a last-minute caesarean operation to rescue him. And little Jude finally arrived!

As I reflect on that miracle birth seven years ago, I am reminded that, without emergency intervention—Christ's death on our behalf—we, too, were destined to die in our own filth and sin. But His Word assures us that God—in His love—said, "No." He sent His only Son to die our painful death so that we could experience new birth in Him. Breathe in His new life today.

Xoli Belgrave

Faithfulness, a Verb

Show me your faith without your works, and I will show you my faith by my works. James 2:18, NKJV.

I checked the bathroom. The shower looked clean. The floor, sink, and counter sparkled. But the toilet . . . ugh! No question about its condition. It needed cleaning! Our son was coming for the weekend. That meant family gatherings and friends popping in. That meant everyone would see the state of my bathroom. Fibromyalgia's stiff muscles often encouraged me to be blind to the bathroom's condition. Now I had to finish cleaning it.

I was out of energy, but the toilet had to be attended to. I stood with hands on hips, pondering the noxious object. Words from a recent Bible study class filtered through my despair.

"Faithfulness is a verb," the teacher had said. "It is a doing, an active response to faith."

My mind wandered. Due to deteriorating physical ability, I depend on God more. For instance, I struggle to attach the portable dishwasher hose to the faucet. Asking Him for help, I hold the hose in place and watch it pop on. When pain becomes more than I can bear, I turn to Him and pain retreats. Peace takes its place. Also, I count on His scheduling my life. Recently, I knew I needed more exercise but walking increases pain. A friend, whose pool is warmer than the YMCA's, invited me to swim with her. The warmer pool, the hot tub, the friendship, all combined to make exercise bearable. I knew God had intervened.

I believe. I have faith. I know God is interested in each detail of my life. But am I to lie in bed, expecting Him to propel me out of it, as He pulls my puppet strings? My head says "No!" and I take charge.

Traditionally, I try to make happen what I assume God wants. Until my own strength fails. Then I despair and wallow in misery. Now, I can no longer "make it happen." I know I am dependent on God. So, as I eyed the offending bathroom fixture, I began to connect my dilemma with the Bible-class teacher's Bible-based concept that *faithfulness* is an active response to faith in God's Word and power. The concept opened my understanding. Belief—faith that God cares and is willing to provide the energy, power, and opportunity to accomplish what is needed—calls for an act of faithfulness on my part. Doing and depending are not exclusive of each other.

With this principle in mind, I bent toward the needy porcelain.

Laurice Shafer

Really, How Is Your Faith?

Before they call, I will answer; and while they are yet speaking, I will hear. Isa. 65:24.

Talking and preaching about faith is easy, especially with blue skies overhead and no crisis in sight. But meet a crisis head-on, and the preacher of faith finds a need to search deeply regarding his or her degree of trust in the Lord and His Word.

When I got the news that my mother in Penang (Malaysia) was dying, I worked frantically on booking a ticket to fly from Seoul to Penang via Singapore. The first leg of my flight from Seoul to Singapore was confirmed, but I was put on the waiting list from Singapore to Penang. When I arrived at the Seoul airport that morning, I used every persuasive power I could muster to work on the airline agent, whom I hoped could assure me of a seat from Singapore to Penang. "My hands are tied," he told me. "Try your luck in Singapore." Though I could do nothing for the next seven hours but wait, I still wanted to worry about what would happen in Singapore. Could I get the connection to Penang?

Traveling on the Singapore-bound flight, I repeated Bible promises and surrendered my plight to God. An in-plane comedy movie and meal provided mild distractions from my dilemma. After my meal, the Lord suddenly gave me such peace that He would take care of every detail that I fell fast asleep. Exhausted from the past stressful months with Mom's illness heavily on my mind, I suddenly had peace and total confidence in God's leading and plan for this trip.

When I awoke, we were deplaning. In fact, we disembarked in the same terminal as my connecting flight! The airline counter was close and the waiting area just around the corner—perfect! I shared with the ticketing agent how I *had* to get on the flight to be with my failing mother. The compassionate agent assured me she'd do what she could. During the next hour, I encouraged my daughter, by phone, though we also made alternative plans in case it was not God's will for me to get on the desired flight. When the time came for me to check back with the ticketing agent, I became elated. Yes! A seat had opened up, even though the plane was full.

Despite my delay, I recalled how Mary and Martha thought Jesus was four days too late to heal Lazarus. Yet they learned, praise God, that He is always right on time!

Once again, my faith was renewed in a God who cares and who is surely good!

Sally Lam-Phoon

Give Me Water

Jesus answered, "Everyone who drinks this water will be thirsty again, but whoever drinks the water I give them will never thirst. Indeed, the water I give them will become in them a spring of water welling up to eternal life." John 4:13, 14, NIV.

"Give me your water, please." I will never forget hearing this request as many children surrounded me, asking for my bottle of water, when I was in Burundi for women's meetings.

Unlike some countries, Burundi has no lack of water resources. The problem is lack of proper management. In addition, the country's water system is still suffering the results of a thirteen-year civil war that destroyed much of its water infrastructure. When I looked at those poor children asking for water, my heart had compassion for them.

As Christians, we don't please God when four thousand five hundred children die every day because they lack something each of us takes for granted, a safe glass of water. Think of it—four thousand five hundred children, one every twenty seconds, a little life extinguished. The global water crisis is still the number one killer of children around the globe. Almost a billion people do not have access to safe water, and 2.5 billion lack the dignity of basic sanitation.

As I talked to the women and children in Burundi, they told me how a new water well in their village had changed their lives. Why was this so important? The average distance that women and children walk for water in Africa and Asia is six kilometers (3.7 miles). In some places, the women carry heavy loads of water (as much as twenty liters) on their heads. Over time, this severely damages the neck and spine. Now having a well in their village brings life, health, hope, and the promise of a better future for them and the generations to come.

In Africa, there is a saying: "Water is life." Water is not just important for life; it truly *is life.*

The Lord is our Source of life. He is the spring of Living Water, clear and pure, without cost, and sufficient for all our needs. He is able to bring life to your spirit and provision to your body. We just need to draw from Him daily. Go to the Living Water. And *be* the living water to someone. Be a well of clean water wherever you are. Jesus' invitation as you start your day is the same: " 'Come, all you who are thirsty, come to the waters' " (Isa. 55:1, NIV).

Raquel Queiroz da Costa Arrais

I Met John Paul

Love does no harm to a neighbor. Therefore love is the fulfillment of the law. Rom. 13:10, NIV.

An aunt introduced me to JP (John Paul) and his adoptive mother. JP is a young man who was born with no hands or feet. He has no tongue, and his chin is abnormally small. His articulation is hard to understand, and a swallowing problem has stunted his growth. Because of all these disabilities, school children ganged up on him chanting crude jingles they'd made up about his deformities. The outrageous and uncontrollable bullying caused school officials to discharge JP from school. His mother looked for another school to accommodate his needs in order for him to continue his education. Yet cruel treatment occurred in subsequent schools as well. Finally, JP's mother enrolled him in a Christian school. There the boy progressed academically, socially, and spiritually. He became such a role model that in March 2013, he was presented with a medal at graduation from elementary school for being the most well-behaved, highest-achieving student of the year. JP is now in high school.

JP's mom, besides being involved in church activities, had trained JP to reach out to other people on God's behalf. Mother and son work hard to bring honor and glory to God. Whenever an evangelist conducts a religious crusade in Palayan City, Nueva Ecija, they are part of the evangelistic team. What attracts people's attention to JP is first his physical appearance, of course. And then, amazingly, his organ playing! Crusade attendees are amazed that someone with his deficiencies can be so joyful and so useful. He is one of the friendliest members on every crusade team, encouraging people to return for the subsequent meetings to learn more about God and the revelation of His character through the Bible. Since JP has been involved with the crusade teams, over five hundred people have given their hearts to the Lord and been baptized.

Though most of us were born with hands and feet and a tongue, we still have "disabilities." Maybe not physical, but perhaps emotional or even spiritual. Perhaps, like JP, hurtful things have happened to us in the past. Yet, whatever our disabilities, God can redeem them, as He has John Paul's, for the advancement of His kingdom. Don't ever think you have nothing to offer God or others. Remember that God can even give life to dry bones (Ezek. 37:4)!

Esperanza Aquino Mopera

April 17

Traumatic Changes

"For I am the LORD, I do not change." Mal. 3:6, NKJV.

I had volunteered at the hospital on Thursday and was scheduled to play for church on Sabbath. So on Friday morning, with my mind rehearsing the day's to-do list, I headed to the grocery store—a trip that would change my life for months to come. Why? Because I left the store on a gurney in an ambulance! After an accidental fall in the store, I learned that my newly broken hip would require surgery, followed by recuperation time in a nursing center. Talk about unexpected change! But when this initial surgery went awry, more changes loomed on life's horizon during the four subsequent operations—all to correct complications arising from the first one. After weeks in the nursing center, I realized I needed to move to a more convenient location to accommodate my medical challenges.

With a heavy heart, I watched my new change-induced needs put a great strain on my already busy family as they chauffeured me on errands and helped care for my cat. Gradually, I accepted the reality that since driving was out of the question (another most inconvenient change!), I no longer needed a car. I sold it but not without feeling a pang of sorrow. I could no longer play organ or piano for church services. Too many changes, too fast these days.

During my recuperation time, I meditated on some of the great characters of the Bible and I gradually realized how traumatic changes had impacted their lives. Abraham moved from home without even knowing God's destination for him. Joseph's brothers sold him to slave traders far away from his father. Esther's beauty pulled her from a common life onto a queenly throne. Ruth left Moab to support Naomi. A Babylonian invasion changed the princely Daniel into a captive. Paul's theology and life changed when he met Christ on the Damascus Road. And, of course, Jesus changed His Godly image into a human form that suffered poverty and a painful crucifixion.

Yet God was the constant in each traumatic transition and life change. Not only did He sustain these people during their life-altering changes, but in every case, He also used the change itself to deepen His relationship with humanity and further His divine purposes.

How I thank God for bringing constant peace, promise, and relief to my oft-interrupted life! He'll do the same for you during any changes you're experiencing if you'll ask Him to.

Marilyn Petersen

Waiting It Out

To everything there is a season, and a time for every matter or purpose under heaven. Eccles. 3:1, AMP.

This morning the sun is gleaming through my window in glorious shades of gold and yellow, like the silky strands of hair on a child's blond head.

In the background stands a small brick church with a picture-perfect white steeple nestled among the evergreens that have endured the unpredictable storms of winter. Scattered throughout this lovely scene are a few flowering trees like the exquisite tulip tree with its blossoms of brilliant fuchsia etched in pearl. Although breathtaking in their beauty, they have come out too soon, prematurely, never realizing the few spring summerlike days were fleeting. And while nature's beauty slept, the icy winds of winter would plummet below freezing.

Cruelly, and seemingly without mercy, the remaining cold and windy temperatures of winter would wither the fragile faces that had so recently been drawn to the warmth of the sun's soothing rays.

As I contemplated the scene before me, I thought nature had a lesson to teach.

Sometimes we go through seasons of waiting. However, none of us likes to wait. We want what we want, and we want it *now*! This waiting may include waiting to earn a degree, waiting for the right job, waiting for a doctor's report, maybe waiting for the baby to be born. On and on the list goes.

I am learning that if I rush through the waiting time, I usually misjudge and my plans are then premature and fail to come to their fullest fruition. There are no shortcuts to being in God's time. It is a set time—time known only to Him. When everyone and everything are in their proper place, on that very day, at that very moment, God will move on every situation in our lives. In cold, lonely seasons of waiting, reassuring principles from God's Word help me endure.

For example, Ecclesiastes 3:11 says, "He has made everything beautiful in its time" (AMP). And Psalm 33:18 tells us how we should relate to this: "Behold, the Lord's eye is upon those who fear Him [who revere and worship Him with awe], who wait for Him and hope in His mercy and loving-kindness" (AMP). So let us worship Him now—no more waiting!

Cheryl Jane Shelton

April 19

Check in Counter

And I say unto you, Ask, and it shall be given you. Luke 11:9.

Each time I vacation in Nigeria (West Africa), my home country, I usually have some problem on the return journey. The most common problem is not enough cash to pay for excess luggage containing gift items I want to keep, since they're not available back home in Gambia.

Since yam tubers are not available in Gambia, I purchased some to give my children and friends. The night before my flight, I traveled from Ibadan, 130 kilometers from Lagos (the commercial capital of Nigeria), to the airport (a dangerous road trip after dark) so that I could spend the night at the airport, as my check-in time was at 6:00 A.M. I spent the night at the airport.

All night I sat up, keeping a watchful eye on my luggage. When check-in time arrived, I was the first in line. My heart sank when my suitcase tipped the scales at thirty-eight kilograms. My ticket allowed for a weight limit of only thirty kilograms. I did not have the money to pay the extra fee. Yet I was determined not to leave the yams behind.

As I pulled my luggage off the scales, I murmured a short prayer of utter dependence. "Please, Lord, help me to take these things home because of my children. You have told us in Your Word to at least ask, sharing the desires of our hearts."

A minute later, the counter attendant suggested, "Ma'am, why don't you remove the heavier items from your suitcase and place them in your hand luggage?" Quickly, I followed her suggestion, putting the yams in my transit bag. This lightened the weight of my suitcase—but not by much, it seemed. Concerned, I again lifted my big suitcase up onto the counter. The attendant nodded and tagged the suitcase, giving official permission for it to be loaded onto the plane. However, no one weighed my suitcase! I could not believe that the luggage would be accepted without my paying any money for excess weight. All the foodstuffs, of course, went with me in my hand luggage back to my family and friends. How grateful I was!

I thank God because it was He who impressed the counter attendant to help resolve my problem. I thank God because I asked and He answered, showing me the way. Someday soon, another "attendant" will process our "luggage" (our characters) at heaven's check-in counter. I praise God because Jesus Christ will be there to help us complete our journey home. Amen!

Taiwo Adenekan

The Race

Now there is in store for me the crown of righteousness, which the
Lord, the righteous Judge, will award to me on that day—and not only
to me, but also to all who have longed for his appearing.
2 Tim. 4:8, NIV.

The adrenaline was flowing at high speed early Sunday morning as fifteen-year-old Alex was primed for his first bicycle road race. Dad and Grandpa were not racing, so they got an early start just riding the race route on their bikes. The plan was that I would wait until the race started, then leapfrog ahead in the pickup to stop along the route and cheer as the bikers raced by. While I waited in the truck near the start line, Alex warmed up his nervous legs in the large parking lot. Dashing up to the pickup shortly before the start whistle blew, Alex yelled in a panic, "Nana, do you have any water?" In his excitement to have everything ready, he had failed to fill his water bottles—an essential requirement for a forty-mile (sixty-five kilometer) race. The bike was tuned up, he had his helmet and bike shoes, and the water bottles were nestled in the holders on the bike frame. But they were empty!

Jesus told a parable about some eager young people who failed to make adequate preparations. You know the story of the ten young women who were all excited about attending an evening's wedding festivities. Half of them planned ahead by bringing extra lamp oil, but they would not/could not share their oil with their less-prepared friends. What was the lesson Jesus was teaching? He wanted His audience to be thinking about the Second Coming and to understand that personal preparation is essential. We can't question God's desire that everyone be in heaven. "The Lord . . . is patient with you, not wanting anyone to perish, but everyone to come to repentance" (2 Pet. 3:9, NIV). Jesus made the ultimate sacrifice to make our salvation possible, so the variable is us! How can we be sure we're making adequate preparation?

"Who has the heart? With whom are our thoughts? Of whom do we love to converse? Who has our warmest affections and our best energies? If we are Christ's, our thoughts are with Him, and our sweetest thoughts are of Him" (*Steps to Christ*, p. 58). This means a daily connection, a daily filling of God's Spirit. I don't want to be an empty "water bottle." I want to be full to overflowing and ready for the race!

Roxy Hoehn

God and the Little Blue Book

"Behold, I am the LORD, the God of all flesh. Is there anything too hard for Me?" Jer. 32:27, NKJV.

In September 2012, my grandmother gave up her home in Georgia and moved in with my parents in Maryland. For a person one year shy of her one hundredth birthday, Grandmother gets around well and has a reasonably good memory. After Grandmother moved in with my parents, they informed her that rather than celebrating the Christmas holidays at home, we as a family would be vacationing aboard a cruise ship in the Caribbean. Of course, she was excited about the prospect of this trip.

However, there was one problem. While all of us had our passports, my grandmother did not. We began praying and researching what to do. In order to apply for a United States (U.S.) passport, one must have an official birth certificate.

Hurdle number one: Grandmother was born before 1921, the year birth certificates were issued, so she had no official record of her birth. However, we did have other documents, such as insurance forms. After several interviews with the passport clerk, our local office agreed to forward the information we did have to the United States passport clearinghouse. With this step now complete and a payment for expedited service included, we were certain that any day the little blue passport book would appear in my parents' mailbox.

Hurdle number two: Instead of receiving the passport in the mail, a letter arrived requesting an official letter stating that no birth date documentation existed for my grandmother's birth. Obtaining something like that would take weeks, so we petitioned—and paid—again. Soon a clerk from the State of Georgia Vital Records department phoned and said to my mother, "From your letter, I see how important it is for you to take your ninety-nine-year-old mother on this trip, so we'll help anyway we can to expedite the needed document." We know God touched this woman's heart to act at that very moment on our behalf.

Ultimately, the U.S. passport office accepted the state's document, and two weeks later the little blue passport arrived. Is there anything too hard for the Lord? Absolutely not. So what hurdle are you facing today? Is it too hard for Him? According to His Word, absolutely not!

Yvonne Curry Smallwood

Empty Nest Reminder

How often would I have gathered thy children together, as a hen doth gather her brood under her wings, and ye would not! Luke 13:34.

Since I became a mother, God has enriched my life with a unique understanding of His love for me. Today, once again, He let me experience one of my most significant spiritual lessons.

I had been trying to talk to my daughter all week. I was very anxious to know everything about her new life in college. For just a month I'd been experiencing the meaning of empty nest syndrome. I'd sent e-mails to her. No answer. I had called. She was not in her school residence room. I even spent a significant amount of money on a gift that I sent her by mail. Even this gesture of love had not elicited a response from her.

Today would be different, I hoped. Because it was Sunday, she would not be in class. I thought we could talk for a long time. She'd have lots of news to share with me. However, I was wrong. I dialed her up, and she answered! I was so excited. After just twenty minutes of chatting, we were just getting into a good conversation when she said, "Mom, I have to go. Really. I'm busy with a lot of things that I just have to do." We said goodbye and wished each other a good week, but I can't explain my disappointment. Of course, I couldn't force her to talk to me. I couldn't force her to tell me about her life. To talk, or not to talk, that was her decision.

Sadly, I recalled how deeply my heavenly Parent yearns for me to talk to Him. And why wouldn't we want to make time to chat, through prayer and His Word, with a Father who has provided for our needs—food, clothing, family, friends, a place to live, heavenly promises, everything! Yet how often we hastily say a few words, which we finish off with a quick "I love You" and "Amen." His heart must hurt over our careless handling of this relationship though He remains ever attentive, ever waiting until the next time we're in the mood, or sense the need, to talk with Him. In His love, He gives us the time and space to realize our need for Him.

After putting down the phone today, I had a good cry. But I also had a wonderful heart-to-heart chat with my perfect, patient heavenly Father, asking forgiveness for how I break His heart when I've not been "available." And I thanked Him for His unconditional love—anyway.

Eliane Ester Stegmiller Paroschi

Kept Alive by the Word—Part 1

But He answered and said, "It is written, 'Man shall not live by bread alone, but by every word that proceeds from the mouth of God.' "
Matt. 4:4, NKJV.

Empty. That's how Kelly Johnson described her life. By the time she was eighteen, she felt dead inside. My husband, Philip, and I had met Connie Jena, Kelly's mother, who was struggling with a daughter whose life brought her such pain. We became her encouragers.

In the fifth grade, Kelly was abused by a clergyman "for Jesus' sake." The product of a broken home, she lived interchangeably with a father who ignored her and a mother whom she clearly exasperated. When Kelly was raped as a teenager, her father blamed her because she "associated with riff-raff." Starved for attention and in need of money to help support herself at nineteen, Kelly began go-go dancing. At one of the clubs, she met the man she married, a man who would beat her so severely that he once detached the retina in her right eye with his boot tip.

Her calls to our home were often crisis calls as she tried to escape the abuse. After getting a divorce, Kelly moved in with her mother, drinking heavily. "I didn't want to feel," she said later. "I wanted to numb myself." Connie, Kelly's barely coping mother, called us frequently, torn between love for her daughter, yet rage at the disrespect Kelly showed her. Connie had her own cross to carry. While riding once in a bike-a-thon, this attractive, athletic woman with friends in high places and a rising career, became the victim of a teenage driver's mistake. Life became a nightmare of multiple surgeries and chronic pain. Finally, Connie gave Kelly an ultimatum: "Clean up your act or get out." This is when the now forty-something girl—struggling with a bipolar diagnosis, lost jobs, and lost relationships—came to the end of her rope.

"One night," she recalls, "I knelt by my bed and begged God to do what no one else could in my life. I cried all night, putting the baggage of my whole life—the pain and pointlessness—at Jesus' feet. Exhausted, I gave my burden to God. The drinking, the cigarettes, the emptiness, the pain . . . I gave it all to Him and then just cried till I was empty."

Then He began to fill her. "My need for cigarettes and alcohol was gone. Just as the Bible says, I began a new life that night. I buried myself in Scripture, even praying for those who'd hurt me. I let go of the pain. God was preparing me for my journey." How is God preparing *you*?

Cynthia J. Prime

Kept Alive by the Word—Part 2

For Your word has given me life. Ps. 119:50, NKJV.

T wo years ago, shortly after her conversion experience, Kelly woke up one morning unable to swallow. It was as if her esophagus was totally paralyzed. She choked on anything she tried to eat and vomited what did not choke her. Among other diagnoses, doctors told her that her stomach was not properly processing food and that she could no longer swallow. Kelly became a frequent visitor to the hospital emergency room as life-threatening complications developed. Physicians inserted feeding tubes into her abdomen, performing multiple surgeries and procedures to get nutrition into her body. Yet Kelly's "mess" became her "message."

Though her health problems continue, Kelly now inspires me—and many others—with her personal ministry. Every evening, she prayerfully selects scriptures to artistically embellish and text to individuals on her ministry list. A message board in a room, now her Prayer Board, displays a fresh scripture verse each day framed with Kelly's own beautiful artwork.

"I'm not comfortable with what's been happening to me," she says, "but God has used this illness to teach me something wonderful." It started one day when Kelly, worried and frustrated about her inability to eat—but praying—felt moved to open her Bible. The scripture under her hand was Luke 12:29, 30, " 'And do not set your heart on what you will eat or drink; do not worry about it. For the pagan world runs after all such things, and your Father knows that you need them' " (NIV). She says, "Isn't that amazing? God took the time to let me know that I would have to feed on His Word to live until He decides to heal my body." So Kelly's texted scripture messages (and attractive selfies) arrive with clockwork regularity. She also shares her faith with anyone who will listen. "I don't look like I am starving, though I don't keep down much. Even the doctors marvel. But I feed on God's Word. I live on prayer. And I have never been this happy in my entire life! If this is what God knows it takes to save me, it's OK."

Kelly continues to ask for our prayers as she struggles both to find answers to her medical dilemma as well as ways to support herself through her artwork. But her requests for prayer always end with an expression of thanksgiving, an encouraging thought from God's Word, and a chuckle at His creativity in finally getting His princess home.

Cynthia J. Prime

Hearing Before Doing

But be ye doers of the word, and not hearers only. James 1:22.

There is something within us women that makes us shift into high gear and lay out a whole new operational strategy when we know we're going to entertain a special guest. We clean, polish furniture, and cook. We take pride in being a good hostess.

Martha, being the gracious hostess that she was, warmly greeted her much-anticipated Guest into her Bethany home and then quickly made off to the kitchen to ensure that the meal would be ready. However, she got bogged down in the doing. She didn't get back to the living room to join her sister, Mary, who was hearing the words of Christ. Mary and Martha, being sisters, were close. Yet Bible readers remember them for contrasting reasons. My Bible study notes state that Martha "is remembered for her impatience and excessive concern for mundane matters." Mary is commended "for her special desire and discernment." Quite a dichotomy, then, between the two sisters. So Bible readers sometimes fault Martha for being spiritually bankrupt.

Yet Martha *was* serving. And what greater joy can a daughter of God have than to serve the Master? Martha truly did possess the gift of hospitality. Yet bustle alone does not constitute hospitality. Charles Spurgeon is credited with observing, "It's easier to serve than to commune." Perhaps that's why we, like Martha, become so encumbered with "much serving" (Luke 10:40). But guests visit to commune with us. So Christ's observation that " 'Mary has chosen what is better' " (Luke 10:42, NIV) shows that sitting first at His feet listening—before serving—is what consecrates our ministry for Him. We need the twin virtues that both Mary and Martha possessed: communion with Christ and service for Him. This balance—in that order—is vital.

Mary chose to listen to Jesus that memorable day in Bethany. And, yes, Jesus gently reprimanded Martha for not making the same initial choice. Yet she must have wasted no time in making that "better" choice because her subsequent intimate statement of faith to Jesus at her brother's tomb reveals she had gained a deep understanding of who Jesus was (John 11:27). And Christ must have approved of both her "hearing" *and* her "doing," for the last word-picture the Bible leaves us of Martha—following the resurrection of her brother—are these service-affirming words: "There they made him a supper; and Martha served" (John 12:2).

Judith P. Nembhard

More, More, More!

Delight thyself also in the LORD: and he shall give thee the desires of thine heart. Ps. 37:4.

My fifteen-month-old granddaughter and I went for our morning stroll in the garden. The day before, her granddad had introduced her to various fruits in the garden: oranges, tangerines, bananas, star fruit, coconuts, and cherries. I'd overheard him talking and had chuckled to myself thinking, *Poor child doesn't know what he is saying.* But they were enjoying a precious granddad-granddaughter bonding time. That was good enough for him. Now it was my turn to have this sweet little girl all to myself.

As I led her toward some trees in the yard, she stretched out her little hand and cried, "More!" As we approached the trees, her demands intensified: "More! More! More!"

More of what? I wondered. Then I realized that she was reaching out to the succulent red cherries hanging in clusters from one of the trees. This was the first time in years the tree had borne fruit. I reached up and plucked a cherry for her. She popped it into her mouth. Then she began picking cherries along with me for washing and eating later. And what a cherry feast she had later! As quickly as I placed one in her tiny hand, she'd eat it and smile, "More." How could such a small stomach hold so many cherries? Even when she'd eaten all the cherries we'd picked, she wanted more!

Though her visit with us is now over and she's gone back home to her parents, I still have the joy of reminiscing about that precious time with her. I also reflect on the many lessons I gleaned from her short visit. Her sweet, tender, expectant "More!" still rings in my ears.

This memory makes me think of how much *more* of Christ's love I need in my heart. How much *more* time I should be spending in His Word as I delve into His promises. How much *more* frequently I should be telling others about Him and His unfailing love. More! More! More! We all need *more.* Remember that old hymn—really, a prayer—entitled "More About Jesus"? That is the prayer of my heart as well.

I long to know much more about Him than I do, for more of His grace to flow through me to others, for more of the Holy Spirit's fullness to work in my life. Most of all, I long to experience more of the "love" that died for me. He is more than willing to give us *more.*

Gloria Gregory

MLDs

And my God shall supply all your need according to His riches.
Phil. 4:19, NKJV.

I've decided to coin an acronym: MLD stands for major life disappointments. I've decided it's long overdue we talk about them and officialize, while taming them a bit, as acronyms tend to do. A case in point: ADD became an official diagnosis, a household word, and an acronym; "admitting" the diagnosis no longer shamed parent or child. The same should be true of our MLDs. Many, but not all, of us have had them. They lurk behind even happy eyes and brave smiles. Here is my short list of some of the things that would qualify as MLDs.

1. Untimely bereavement: The loss of a child or young spouse hits harder than the loss of a ninety-five-year-old grandfather. These bereavements, notably suicide, bring unspeakable grief.

2. Chronic health problems: Especially strange, poorly understood illnesses such as fibromyalgia and irritable bowel syndrome. The sufferer often travels a lonely road.

3. Straying children: A true parent cannot sever emotional ties with a child any more than a river can stop its flow into a stream. A lost child makes that connection extremely painful.

4. History of abuse: Especially incest or domestic violence damage the bonding machinery, such that relationships come hard ever after. Not only are the victim's family connections forever compromised, but the sense of being a misfit around healthier people drives them into the very subpopulation that violated them in the first place.

5. Relationship failure: Relationships are delicate, intricate, and complicated. The best of surgeons must sometimes pronounce patients dead. It happens—sometimes in relationships.

The list goes on and on, enumerating as many sorrows as a fallen planet can choke out. But these fall close to home for me and for those I care about. I'm not writing to depress us. Rather, I'm setting us up for a solution. And here it is: Jesus saves from MLDs. Not the way we'd like Him to save. But in His way. For the person who lives for this world alone, an MLD drags them down like a lead boot in a foot race, unfortunate and unredeemable. But for a believer preparing for the coming of Jesus, an MLD provides a needed wedge between their spirit and things of the world. MLDs help spiritually even as they harm temporally. More than this, MLDs drive us to a higher Source of satisfaction—and to the power of His Word.

Jennifer Jill Schwirzer

Amelia

A nagging wife is like dripping that never stops. Prov. 19:13, NIrV.

We had never used a GPS (global positioning system) to know where we were, but when my husband, my sister, and I planned a trip to France, we thought a GPS would be a good idea. We tried it out and immediately decided that it needed a name. Despite her penetrating voice, "Amelia" got us safely to the airport, and we knew she'd be an asset on our adventure.

When we landed, I pulled out guidebooks and brochures, checked mileage, and announced where we were going. At first, Amelia was helpful, but once we headed into the countryside in search of a series of tiny rural churches, she posed challenges. For one thing, her French accent was dreadful. Neither Larry, Dana, nor I profess to speak French well, but we thought we'd be able to understand names of streets and towns. Often the driver would guffaw, "WHAT did she say?" We'd laugh when comparing words on the screen with her instructions.

But Amelia wasn't just unintelligible—she was also insistent. If we stopped to fill the tank with petrol, she would tell us to make a U-turn to return to the road. Or she would say, in a nasal tone that seemed to drip with annoyance, "Recalculating . . . recalculating." Drip . . . drip . . . drip. Her voice wore away at us like water on a stone.

We soon decided that she was programmed to take the shortest route possible. It didn't matter if the route was twisty and the streets narrow. She would not direct us to a time-saving highway; instead, she told us, "Turn left . . . turn right" every minute as we wound our way through villages. Drip . . . drip . . . drip. Occasionally, disgusted with our slow progress, we plugged our ears and navigated without her aid.

A few weeks after we returned from France, Larry and I packed the car, turned on Amelia, and headed to Alaska. When we reached the start of the Alaska Highway, Amelia announced, "Drive 2,026 kilometers and turn left." We grinned at each other as we contemplated more than a day of freedom from Amelia's micromanaging and nagging.

As Larry and I drove through the blessed quiet, I wondered if the lives of my students, my friends, and my family would be more positive if, on occasion, I, like Amelia, decreased my flow of advice and instructions and allowed them to find their own way in life.

Denise Dick Herr

The House

We were so blessed to live in a lovely ranch-style home. We lived on the end of a cul-de-sac where the kids could ride their bikes in the road. Their friends lived across the street—good people who went to church with us and shared the same values we did. Then things changed.

Due to political changes in the area, homes were being bought up left and right and made into group homes for troubled kids. Even the wonderful people across the road from us sold out. That house became a home for troubled, court-appointed girls. Though the girls were supposed to stay on their property, they'd sometimes drift over to our home and talk with our kids. I was concerned. So we prayed, "God, what should we do?" These encounters could undermine and devastate our own children's upbringing.

We decided to move, but to where? Should we build a home? Buy a home? Finally, we just moved out, rented a duplex, and began looking for land on which to build. We looked at newspaper ads, called realtors, and followed leads that friends—and friends of friends—gave us. But all to no avail. Months later, I said to my husband, "No more! I've packed away all the ads and realtor cards. I'm now leaving this situation in God's hands." My husband seemed dubious about my decision.

Weeks later, an acquaintance in church approached me and said, "I hear you are looking for land. Have you found any yet? If not, maybe we can help each other out."

"Why, yes, we're still looking," I answered. "However, the prices are always too high or the lot's too far from the kids' school." The woman invited us to come over to her house the next day. We met with the couple as we had arranged and sat down to talk. By the end of our conversation, we had purchased a five-acre parcel from her family only five minutes from our church and the children's school. We were ecstatic! Now we could build our new house.

I learned that when we stop trying to solve problems *our* way and simply put things into God's hands and trust His promises, He leads us to the right set of circumstances that will solve our problem—His way.

So today, in all thy ways, acknowledge Him and He will show you *His* way.

Marge Vande Hei

Little Bicycle Tour

Even though I walk through the valley of the shadow of death, I will
fear no evil, for you are with me; your rod and your staff,
they comfort me. Ps. 23:4, ESV.

We had planned to spend our family holiday riding bicycles instead of driving our car. To ensure the reliability of our bikes, we rode them to the repair shop. This twenty-kilometer jaunt was a nice little tour in itself as we rolled down bike paths and forest tracks. We had to leave our bikes to be serviced and were told we could pick them up Friday afternoon. Nice. That would provide us time for a less hurried and leisurely ride home. My husband drove us all home in the car.

Friday dawned warm and sunny—a perfect day for riding our bikes home from the shop. I packed a little snack for our return ride and some drinks. My husband drove us to the repair shop. Our bikes were serviced and waiting for us. It was already five-thirty when my children and I started home on our bikes and my husband drove home.

Soon, with only a few kilometers behind us, dark clouds unexpectedly eclipsed the sun. In fact, a cloud bank arose behind us. The sky ahead of us was still clear and bright, so we increased our speed in order to outrun the bad weather. A strong, cold wind began to blow. Stiff gusts blew tree branches, rustling their attached leaves, while leaves on the ground swirled about our bicycle tires. We heard a distant rumble, which meant that a thunderstorm was approaching quickly from behind. I was suddenly terrified. A raindrop brushed my cheek. Then I felt rain on my back. "Let's pick up our speed, children," I said, and we pushed ourselves to pedal faster. Passing a little village, I saw an archway. "Let's wait here a bit and see what the weather does," I suggested. As soon as we huddled under the archway, rain poured down. In buckets. We'd been saved from a downpour just in time. The storm was upon us. *I will fear no evil,* I mused.

Through sheets of driving rain, I spotted only a short distance away a pavilion. We relocated, bicycles and all, to this larger, drier shelter. For the next hour and a half—though cold but not wet—we ate snacks and played word games. Some local people secured the tent-pavilion to protect us from the elements. Later we headed home, much to my waiting husband's relief.

I thought, *We rode this afternoon through the valley of the shadow of death and thunderstorm, but God protected, sheltered, and comforted us.* He will do that for you today too.

Sandra Widulle

Living His Trust

Trust: belief that someone or something is reliable, good, honest, effective.

Those who know your name trust in you, for you, LORD, have never forsaken those who seek you. Ps. 9:10, NIV.

Trust in the LORD, and do good; dwell in the land, and feed on His faithfulness. Ps. 37:3, NKJV.

ow this can be a tough one! Living His trust.

Sure, we recall the trust it took for the children of Israel to stick their toes into the Red Sea. And that, of course, was before they even had a clue that God would part it for them and prepare a way of escape from their pursuing captors.

But that was then.

This is now.

Can living the trust Jesus modeled for us *really* enable us to deal with emergency surgery, push one's way back into life on the other side of sorrow, survive birthing a child, or live through an horrific incarceration as a teenager? The collective answer from the thirty-one women contributing to this month's devotionals swells into a resounding *Yes!*

We *can* live His trust; for He alone is trustworthy and always faithful.

Trust in the Lord

"I have seen their ways, but I will heal them". . . says the LORD.
Isa. 57:18, 19, NIV.

We were completing thirty years of work. My husband, Samuel Wohlers, had always had good health, but suddenly he started getting very sick. After numerous medical tests and appointments, medical specialists diagnosed him with cancer of the brain stem. This is not very common in adults; usually, this disease affects children, adolescents, and young adults.

We were faced with a difficult, long, and terrible battle for life. Our work was interrupted in order to accommodate an exhausting radiosurgical treatment and chemotherapy.

Daily we sought comfort and hope in the promises of God's Word. Months passed and the disease worsened. Samuel had to be hospitalized for nineteen days, twelve of them in the intensive care unit. As far as medical treatment was concerned, nothing more could be done. My husband had suffered significant losses and impairment of swallowing, mobility, vision, speech, and memory.

One night, lying in his hospital bed, he asked for us to pray before he went to sleep. I promptly grabbed my Bible to read a passage, a psalm. When I opened the Bible, my gaze was directed to Isaiah 57:18, 19. This wonderful promise from God seemed to be illuminated on that sacred page! I was dazzled, radiant with joy! I believed in healing! I trusted in my Lord! I was sure that God was doing the best for us.

Eight years have now passed since that day. The Lord allowed Samuel to walk again without using support. He can swallow with special care and do public speaking again to witness to the great love of God who heals and saves.

It is impossible to forget how God came with us into that "fiery furnace" during a trial that tested our faith and trust in Him. Truly we were "hard pressed on every side, but not crushed; perplexed, but not in despair; persecuted, but not abandoned; struck down, but not destroyed" (2 Cor. 4:8, 9, NIV). "Because of the LORD's great love we are not consumed, for his compassions never fail. They are new every morning; great is your faithfulness" (Lam. 3:22, 23, NIV).

Praise the Lord! Great is His faithfulness and compassion!

Elizeth de Carvalho Fonseca

Because He Said So

Let every soul be subject unto the higher powers. For there is no power but of God: the powers that be are ordained of God.
Rom. 13:1.

When I was pregnant with my first child, I truly looked forward to the pain of childbirth. Not that I enjoy pain. I knew it would be excruciating, but I knew the pain wouldn't kill me and that God would not give me more than I could handle. I was built for this, right? So I wanted to know what it was He thought (knew) I could handle. Wow! It was an empowering experience.

I think about other events in my life in those same terms. Life can be very difficult. But when I look at any life difficulties through the lens of childbirth, I know that I can make it through that too. When I was in labor, I never thought, *I can't handle this; this is too much.* Instead, I thought, *Wow. Well, this is much worse than I anticipated, yet it's pretty amazing that I can do this.*

At various points in our lives, we all find ourselves treading water somewhere between agony and depression. When we survive a difficulty in life, it means that you *can* do this. You *are* that strong. And the kicker? It's not really you. It's God. His strength is our strength. It may not seem impressive to let someone else do our work for us. To an offer of help, don't we often respond, "Oh that's OK. It'd be easier to do it myself"? At times it's hard to give over our burdens to God. However, that is exactly what He asks us to do. Accept His help and the peace that comes with it. There is more strength in an open hand than in a white-knuckle grip.

When we think, *I am not strong enough to do this,* we have to train ourselves to immediately respond with, "That's right. *I* can't do this. But I'm going to push through it because God *knows* that I can do this, since *He* is my strength." I would certainly never ask to have a lot of the pain and discouragement set before me, but it's a huge relief to know that I can endure it when I trust God to help me.

I have had three children and have never had to have an epidural (spinal injection for pain control) during childbirth. Yes, I'm bragging—on Him. Not on me. I'm pretty impressed with what God can bring us through and do through us when we allow Him to work on our behalf.

Jennifer Day

My Ever-Present Guardian Angel

The angel of the LORD encampeth round about them that fear him, and delivereth them. Ps. 34:7.

I talk with the Lord first thing in the morning, throughout the day, and the last thing at night. I try not to forget to invoke His presence whenever I leave the house and when I get into my car. On April 29, 2012, I was on my way to the Miami International Airport to pick up my daughter and her soon-to-be maid of honor. Since my daughter lives in a different state than I, we see each other only once or twice a year. Naturally, I was happily looking forward to seeing her and helping with the wedding preparations.

Though I am very familiar with the route to the airport, having driven it for twenty-seven years, I still somehow made a wrong turn, which put me in the lanes of opposing traffic—on a one-way street! Heavy, speeding traffic was headed straight for me! All I could do was call out to the Lord for His help.

Fearing for my life, I suddenly saw—out of nowhere—an opening onto a narrow dirt road. This road took me through a thick, wooded section before bringing me to an industrial area. However, some of the buildings looked abandoned. I saw no activity inside or out.

Thoroughly traumatized now by my close brush with death, I could no longer drive. My body shaking uncontrollably, I pulled off the road, alone and tearful. Yet how I thanked the Lord for His love, mercy, and protection—and from what He had just saved me from! I believe with certainty that His angels had been sitting right there beside me, controlling the steering wheel, and saving me from death or serious injury.

Cautiously, I got out of the car, went up to one of the buildings, and timidly knocked on a door. A very pleasant gentleman opened it. I explained my predicament. He kindly wrote down directions to the airport. I had no trouble finding my way there.

That experience has strengthened my faith in my mighty God. I believe that He kept me alive for a purpose. For His angels encamped around me that day and delivered me.

Have you remembered to ask God to go with you throughout your day's activities? If not, take a moment and ask Him now. He will hear. You can trust that He is "a very present help in trouble" (Ps. 46:1).

Eunice E. West-Haynes

My Little Sister

He restores my soul. Ps. 23:3, NKJV.

Having two older brothers was great but around the age of eight, I remember wishing my mother would have a baby. I loved babies! Babies were cute and fun. Our neighbors had a baby named Dougie. I had to content myself with mothering others' babies and playing with my dolls.

Several years later, my mother called me into her bedroom to tell me that she was pregnant. I was overjoyed! I was going to be the older sister of a real live baby doll to play with!

I was almost twelve when little Lynette Marie was born. Shortly after, she came home to spend her first evening with the family. I remember holding the baby bottle for her as she lay in her buggy. Mom was changing the diaper when she suddenly grabbed the baby and yelled, "Start praying!" I watched Mother attempt to resuscitate Lynette Marie, who had stopped breathing.

The next few days and weeks are just a blur in my memory. Before the saga was over, my little sister was declared to be grossly handicapped. Doctors urged my parents to place her in a state home. My heart was broken. I begged and begged my parents to keep her at home with us, promising that I would take care of her. Sadness filled my heart as my young mind grappled with apparently unanswered prayers and an anointing that did not produce a miracle.

What do we do in life when coming up against detours to our dreams—when those magical dreams become nightmares? Does God care? Somehow my family carried on, though sadness lived with us, and the hurt and pain continued on throughout the years.

Many years later now, my sister, almost fifty years old, lives in a family-type setting with twenty-four-hour caregivers in the very Massachusetts town where she was born. Along with my elderly father, I am now a coguardian for Lynette. I love my sister. I even have a small black-and-white picture on my desk that shows me sitting in a chair holding my sweet baby sister.

I reflect over this roller-coaster journey—the highs of joyful anticipation and the lows of disappointment—recalling my heartbreak when I realized that my little sister would be at home for only six months. Though I still don't understand why things happened as they did, I stand on firm ground today because I hold the hand of God. I live in His joy because I trust that someday I will have my questions explained by my kind, heavenly Father. And you will too.

Valerie Hamel Morikone

The Invitation

Save me, O God; for the waters are come in unto my soul. Ps. 69:1.

I sit quietly, listening to the sounds of the early morning. It is 2:30 A.M. My mind is filled with concern and fear: work, friends that are ill, family, deadlines, class plans, my students. The weight of my worry allows no sleep. My heart is heavy. I reach for the Bible on my nightstand and open the pages to Mark 14. The bold print on the chapter heading reads: "Jesus Walks on Water." I have read this story many times. In this early morning, the title appears more intriguing than ever. I read the story once, twice, and on the third time I see it: *the invitation.*

The scene comes alive in my mind: a turbulent ocean, a small boat carelessly being tossed in the ocean by heavy wind. Holding on to the side of the boat, Peter recognizes the voice of Jesus through the storm. Still, Peter seeks for more evidence. He asks: "Lord, if it is You, command me to come to You on the water."

The answer is delivered in the form of an invitation: "Come."

I can imagine Peter eagerly stepping over the side of the boat. I can imagine the wind blowing, water rushing past Peter as he looks ahead, focused on the image of Jesus. *"Come."* I wonder how the water felt under Peter's feet. I wonder what it felt like to take that first step forward. I *wonder.* What I *know* is that Peter begins to sink.

I know this feeling.

Called to move forward, the same invitation has been extended to me: "Come." Still, winds of doubt, stress, and worry all crash on me like heavy waves. Around me is a boisterous ocean: my life and its daily cares. Like Peter, the troubled waters of fear have entered my soul. I am sinking.

At 2:30 A.M., emotional waters are drowning my soul and like Peter, I call out: "Save me, O God." I hear my voice acknowledge my human frailty and feel the Holy Spirit's assurance that Jesus is extending His hand to me.

Heavenly Father, thank You for the invitation to "come" to You when doubt, daily concerns, and worries arrive at the shores of our lives. Thank You for the blessed assurance that in any storm You will not let me sink.

Dixil L. Rodriguez

The Jacket

Take delight in the LORD, and he will give you the desires of your heart.
Ps. 37:4, NIV.

On Mother's Day, I received an e-mail from my oldest daughter wishing me Happy Mother's Day and encouraging me to buy something nice for myself. I quickly responded, thanked her for remembering me on this special day, and told her that I could not go shopping for lack of funds. She asked me if I read her e-mail in its entirety, for she had attached a $100.00 gift certificate for J.C. Penney, my favorite store.

Sure enough. There was the gift certificate at the end of the e-mail. I was excited, thrilled, ecstatic. I assured her that I would go shopping and thanked her profusely for her thoughtfulness. I got some really good deals. J.C. Penney was also giving a $10.00 discount for purchases that were over $100.00. So I was able to purchase $110.00 worth of merchandise. With the purchases, I got a skirt that fit me perfectly. Of course, there was a jacket that matched, but I could not afford it. I was disappointed. But I still desired that jacket. Since there were several left in my size, I decided that in a few weeks I would go back to see if the price was reduced.

Two days later, I had a strong impression to go back to J.C. Penney. I did not feel that God was giving me that impression, so I shrugged it off—it had to have come from my great desire to have that jacket. However, the impression would not go away, so I decided that I would go back to the store. Only one jacket was left! I did not have much money. How could I afford it? Then I remembered a long-forgotten rebate Visa card in my wallet but was not sure if I had used up all of the $50.00 on it. As I handed the jacket and the card to the cashier, I asked her to check how much I had left on the card. She told me I had $7.65 left. I was blessed!

As I walked to my car, I looked at the receipt to see how much the jacket actually cost because the sale ticket indicated that it cost $23.99, down from $64.00. To my amazement, its price was $9.94! I could not believe my eyes. It was almost half the price I had paid for the skirt a few days before. I thanked and praised God for reassuring me that He is real and gives evidence of His presence in my life each day. He reminded me that all I need to do is delight in pleasing Him as He delights in pleasing me. I can trust Him not only to take care of my needs but also to give me the desires of my heart.

Mable C. Dunbar

Satisfied Desires in His Time and Way

The eyes of all look to you, and you give them their food at the proper time. You open your hand and satisfy the desires of every living thing.
Ps. 145:15, 16, NIV.

I had just completed my first year of graduate school. The next item on the calendar was a special visit home to Nebraska before starting summer work on the east coast. My sister, brother-in-law, and six-month-old niece were currently living in Bogotá, Colombia. They were coming into the country so we could meet the baby. My other siblings were also coming home for her baby dedication on Sabbath.

Thursday morning I was reading my Bible. Suddenly, Exodus 2:9 stood out: "Pharaoh's daughter said to her, 'Take this baby and nurse him for me, and I will pay you.' So the woman took the baby and nursed him" (NIV). Wow, that's a mother's dream! She had her baby back! Plus, she was paid to do something she wanted to do all along. That Sabbath morning the verse was still playing on my mind as I got ready for church. I was not sure why, but I asked God, *Is there something that I would like to do and could get paid for it?* A few hours later, I found myself sitting in the emergency room with the answer.

That morning, at the last minute, my ninety-six-year-old grandma's back began bothering her so much that she could not go to church. My mom had run next door to see if the neighbor could sit with Grandma for a bit. In her rush, Mom tripped and fell over our newly laid sidewalk by the garage. She returned to the house in shock, in tears, and cradling two obviously broken wrists.

Before leaving for the emergency room, I prayed. *God, You say You can work all things for good; please do. Also, order this day and the doctors that look after us. I'm trusting all of this to You.* Four hours later, we were home! The X-ray showed no osteoporosis, and the break was below the joint—no worry of future arthritis. Mom had wonderful doctors, realigned wrists, temporary splints, and a surgery scheduled for Monday. The baby dedication was postponed until Christmas. Unable to use her hands for at least the next four weeks, Mom would need twenty-four-hour assistance and personal care. Cheaper and more familiar than a caregiver, my parents asked if I would stay on and be my mother's caregiver. They would compensate my time. I welcomed the opportunity to be home, helping my mother and geting paid for it! God's way is best.

Dana Connell

Mother

He has also set eternity in the human heart. Eccles. 3:11, NIV.

We recently moved Mother into assisted living. Her growing physical frailty and declining cognitive ability necessitated a change.

Some of you have experienced the difficulty of trying to convince an unwilling parent of their need for more help. The sheer volume of work required to sort, pack, store, or dispose of a houseful of goods that are not your own is overwhelming.

I have moved often enough to know that packing will take time, and it was not difficult to anticipate that Mother would need lots of additional emotional support as well.

What surprised me, however, was the personal processing Mother's move triggered in me. My own mortality became more real, the sorrows and losses of aging more concrete. What will life be like without Mother to comfort and guide me? In what ways will my mind and body fail me in the coming years? Can I face my own inevitable decline with courage and grace? What is the meaning in a life that always ends in decay and death?

The old king who wrote Ecclesiastes grappled with similar issues.

"For the wise, like the fool, will not be long remembered. . . . What do people get for all the toil and anxious striving with which they labor under the sun?" (Eccles. 2:16, 22, NIV).

The answer the writer gives to this question I also see emerging in Mother's life. "A person can do nothing better than to eat and drink and find satisfaction in their own toil" (verse 24, NIV).

Mother lives in the present. She enjoys eating slowly and carefully. Her pleasures and sorrows are for the moment and quickly replaced. The possessions she needs are few and her wants are minimal. Amazingly, at the end of a very productive, overly busy life, time is the one thing she now has in abundance. Truly, "there is a time for everything" (Eccles. 3:1, NIV).

And so I find comfort and hope for my journey. No one knows what the future holds, but for today, I can eat and drink and find enjoyment in my toil.

I can leave Mother, and my questions, in the hands of God, who "has made everything beautiful in its time" (verse 11, NIV).

Cheryl Doss

Filled and Ready to Stand

Put on the full armor of God, so that you can take your stand against the devil's schemes. For our struggle is not against flesh and blood, but against the rulers, against the authorities, against the powers of this dark world and against the spiritual forces of evil in the heavenly realms. Therefore put on the full armor of God, so that when the day of evil comes, you may be able to stand your ground, and after you have done everything, to stand. Eph. 6:11-13, NIV.

Sometimes I make the critical, unfortunate mistake of going to the grocery store on an empty stomach. I've found that when I go shopping for food without first being filled, I tend to buy more than what I need. Suddenly, *everything* looks good, whether it be something healthy like fresh fruit or something toxic like cream-glazed doughnuts. Acting on impulse prompted by my appetite, I reach for the fresh fruit. However, I also fill my cart with doughnuts, cookies, and perhaps a slice of cake from the bakery. Of course, my body can do without junk food, but when I'm hungry, I reach for it regardless.

I recently thought of a parallel to these occasional empty-stomach grocery shopping experiences. Just as it's important for my stomach to be filled with healthful food before I go shopping, it is vital for my mind to be filled with the Word of God before I begin each day. Then I will trust Him and not myself. Whenever I begin my day with God through prayer and Bible study, I become equipped in Jesus Christ to face the wiles of the devil. I am prepared to experience victory over poor choices. But if I begin my day on "empty," I am more likely to make poor choices—in any area of my life.

God tells us in His Word to put on the *full* armor of God so that we can stand against the devil's schemes. One of those "schemes" in my life relates to food. There is a mind-body connection to spirituality—when our bodies are fed proper nutrition and are in prime fitness, our minds are clearer and more open to communication with God. But when our bodies are fed unhealthful foods, they affect the clarity of our minds, which will interfere in our communication with God.

Knowing this, I am resolved to make healthy choices every day, starting with the putting on of God's armor by spending time with Him. What about you?

Alexis A. Goring

Only Three Minutes

"Then he said, 'This is what I'll do. I will tear down my barns and build bigger ones, and there I will store my surplus grain. And I'll say to myself, "You have plenty of grain laid up for many years. Take life easy; eat, drink and be merry." ' But God said to him, 'You fool! This very night your life will be demanded from you. Then who will get what you have prepared for yourself?' " Luke 12:18-20, NIV.

Announced by lightning and thunder, the rain began pouring down on us. A maintenance crew of nine members were working on their job assignments. They'd almost completed the roof of the cafeteria's milk and eggs extension room when the storm hit. The maintenance director had just left the building site to run to his office to attend to another urgent departmental need. He'd been gone for just three minutes when someone called out a warning: "Men, take shelter in that nearby tree!" The men made a dash for the tree where they tried to shelter.

Then it happened.

Lightning struck the tree. Nine men fell to the ground. Three died instantly. Several onlookers quickly responded to the accident. Others, however, knowing the school had never experienced a tragedy of this magnitude, refused to help. "We can't help or the evil spirits will harm us." (They held the belief that helping someone struck down would be dangerous, especially if the injured one were to die.) A number of university employees, though, immediately assisted the injured, driving them to the nearest hospital in Antsirabe, thirty-five kilometers away.

I thought about the maintenance director who had not been under the tree because of business back at his office. His three-minute absence made the difference between his getting—or not getting—struck by lightning. Coincidence? Only God knows.

Many times we marvel at how quickly death occurs. This incident, which saddened us greatly, was a reminder for me to trust and live in God's love each moment of my life. In fact, several people at the university accepted Christ as their Savior after reflecting on this incident.

Lord, when it's my time to go to sleep in You and await Your second coming, let me be in a saving relationship with You. Keep me ready to meet You. Amen.

Evelyn G. Pelayo

Seek God First

"But seek his kingdom, and these things will be given to you as well."
Luke 12:31, NIV.

It is wonderful to read testimonies of God's love and hear how He has intervened in individuals' lives, answered prayers, and brought things to a positive conclusion for those who have been praying. We gain strength for our own walk with God.

However, as I write today, I am currently waiting for an answer to my own prayer. Yet I am learning a lesson from God, which I want to share. I believe He is using my situation to draw me closer to Him and show me that I need to seek Him first and "all these things will be given" unto me. I work as a not-yet-certified teacher of four- and five-year-olds. I love teaching and my goal is to achieve my teaching certification. In order to reach my goal, I studied part time for a degree that I achieved last year. I was then offered a place in a graduate teacher program (an employment-based route to earning my teaching credentials). I completed this program in June, achieving good grades on my classroom practice teaching.

The United Kingdom government stipulations require students to pass skills tests in both literacy and mathematics. I studied hard, took the tests, and committed my plans to God. Unfortunately, I did not pass the math skills test. I don't know why God has brought me this far but has not allowed me to achieve my goals.

Yes, I am disappointed, but I continue to make this situation a matter of prayer and trust in God to reveal His plans for me. I know that He is in control and believe that He will open a window. In the meantime, I need to seek Him first, for He has promised that if I do, He will provide whatever "things" are needed in my life.

In the meantime, I believe God is teaching me to wait and trust in Him. He is asking me to exercise faith in Him even before I receive an answer to my prayers—or know the outcome of this situation.

Perhaps, like me, you have been asking God for an answer to a prayer that you may not have received as yet. Whatever your situation—and no matter the outcome—continue to trust in God and believe that He loves you and wants only the best for you. Wait patiently on Him. Keep putting Him first in all things in your life. He will not let you down.

Karen Richards

Who Can You Trust?

"Now you must repent and turn to God so that your sins may be wiped out, that time after time your souls may know the refreshment that comes from the presence of God." Acts 3:19, Phillips.

Recently, I was talking with a friend in New Zealand. She's a leader of a recovery outreach project we're working on together. She told me, "God has raised you up, Cheri, for this time."

I just had to say, "We are asked to walk alongside each other in our recovery. At times, when I do that, I do it well and at other times I don't do it well, but God is faithful."

We are raised up to speak to each other. We're raised up to walk alongside each other. We're raised up so that—when I'm falling down—somebody who's more spiritual than I am at the time is going to grab me. Or when they're falling down, I can grab them. We're not raised up to stand in the position of God to each other. The only One who is faithful, consistently, is God. So, any praise goes to Him, for sure.

My friend reminded me of God's promise to pour out His Spirit on us so we can work alongside Him to bring each other to Him for healing.

The book *The Great Controversy* says that as we work with God and share what He says with each other, our faces will be "lighted up and shining" (p. 612).

When we walk alongside each other like that, we'll talk with each other honestly about our stuff, offering God's healing to each other, and our faces will shine with joy. It literally is because God is doing the work.

He's standing us up, giving us all that kind of cool stuff that comes with standing up for each other. He delights to heal us and give us His joy. "The more clearly we see that God is crazy about us, the more we'll trust that He takes deep joy in our recovery and that He can restore us to sanity" (*Steps to Christ,* Recovery edition, p. 17).

The joy of the Holy Spirit is so incredible that we can't help but say the next thing to encourage each other.

No wonder our faces are lighted up!

I say, "Amen! Bring it on! As He uses the least of us, there's no boasting, only joy."

Cheri Peters

Trust

"Restrain your voice from weeping and your eyes from tears, for your work will be rewarded," declares the LORD. "They will return from the land of the enemy. So there is hope for your descendants," declares the LORD. "Your children will return to their own land."
Jer. 31:16, 17, NIV.

I trust God. Most of the time. With most things in my life. But sometimes it's hard to trust that He is watching over my sons and doing what's best to lead them closer to Him. Their journeys haven't looked like I had hoped. They believed in God, but . . .

One morning I prayed and cried, begging God to move on their hearts and reveal Himself in a real way. I told God all the things I had done to teach them about Him. I recounted how we had taken them to church and Sabbath School. Sacrificed for them to attend Christian schools. I prayed with them each morning on the way to school and each evening before bed. On and on my list went. Now I wanted God to do His part. Show up and draw them deep.

Through my tears and ranting, I heard Him speak gently to my heart, *"I have loved you with an everlasting love; therefore with loving kindness I have drawn you."*

"I know You love me," I responded. "But please, help my sons know that You love them." I continued my begging and pleading.

And God continued whispering, *"I have loved you with an everlasting love; therefore with loving kindness I have drawn you."* I knew God was trying to speak to me. Reluctantly, I stopped and opened my Bible to the scripture my heart was hearing. As I read the passage, I turned the words of Jeremiah 31 into a prayer for my sons. Verses 16 and 17 stopped me in my tracks.

"Restrain your voice from weeping and your eyes from tears, for your work will be rewarded," declares the LORD. "They will return from the land of the enemy. So there is hope for your descendants," declares the LORD. "Your children will return to their own land."

God has such a sense of humor! There I was, recounting all my "work" on behalf of my kids, with tears and weeping, and God had a verse for that. And a promise that reminded me to trust Him. Even with my sons. He is working. He hasn't given up. He does persistently pursue them. And will relentlessly love them and draw their hearts to Him. My part is to trust.

Tamyra Horst

When God Does Not Answer Prayers

Rejoice always, pray continually, give thanks in all circumstances; for this is God's will for you in Christ Jesus. 1 Thess. 5:16-18, NIV.

When I arrived home one afternoon from school, my sister told me that my mother had tripped and fallen on the floor and could not walk. That accident brought a life-changing chapter to our family.

Mother was a busy lady. At the age of eighty-four, she still did all the household chores even if she was told not to do so. She insisted on grocery shopping, preparing the food, cleaning the garden, and every other little thing her hands could do to keep her busy throughout the day—until that morning when she fell. It was an accident that changed her lifestyle tremendously, an accident that limited her movement and made her so unhappy. As a very independent lady, it was difficult for her to accept her condition. She was not used to being served, fed, or bathed.

An X-ray revealed that she had a fractured joint and needed an operation. With an earnest desire to be on her feet again and go back to her usual routine, Mother decided to undergo hip joint replacement surgery. She had great hope that she could walk again. Unfortunately, when she was in the recovery room, she suffered a stroke and from then on she was unable to talk or walk again. Her health deteriorated, and after seven months of being bedridden, she passed away.

During that time, we prayed for her recovery. But God did not answer our prayers. As hard as it is for us to accept our mother's fate, my sister and I believed that there is a lesson God wanted us to learn from this experience. God showed us that He will see us through these sad moments in our life. He provided us with everything we needed to take care of our mother. Spiritual and financial blessings poured in. Relatives and friends gave us the spiritual and financial moral support we needed. We were not left alone by God.

A number of Bible characters going through trials did not always get the answers they wanted in response to their prayers. I am sure the apostles prayed for deliverance from prison. Yet incarcerated, they still believed. Though we never got the answer we wanted, God did not abandon us but made us feel loved and protected. This experience strengthened our faith in Him.

Minerva M. Alinaya

Lonely

"And surely I am with you always, to the very end of the age."
Matt. 28:20, NIV.

When I took those personality tests in college, I always seemed to teeter on the border between introvert and extrovert, somewhere between socialization *and* isolation. I come by this honestly as my mother is overly social—speaking, traveling, and happy in the middle of the loudest, busiest crowds. My dad, on the other hand, would probably be perfectly happy living in the woods somewhere with only bears and mosquitoes as neighbors. I am the offspring of these two opposites: craving isolation yet also craving socialization. Perfect for a singer/songwriter who enjoys the introversion of songwriting and the extroversion of performing.

Recently, after a small social gathering I organized had come to a close, it dawned on me that the reason I am constantly organizing and facilitating is because the little girl inside of me, the one who is struggling with her introverted side, is afraid of not being invited if she's not in charge of the invitations. Though it seems I have the teeter-totter between extroversion and introversion under control, I still find myself lonely sometimes and bury myself in my songs, telling myself, *I don't need people anyway.* But I do. One of my songs, "Circles," addresses this two-way pull: "Friends and foes / Aren't distinct always / I've had strong / And some fragile days / Sometimes I'm so lonely / I'm just speaking plainly / I feel a need for a bond of another kind."

When I wrote those words, I felt betrayed by my friends. I felt that if I disappeared, no one would notice. Yet I also found Jesus. I found He is enough to fill the widest, darkest gap of loneliness in my heart. Jesus went through long periods of loneliness (in the wilderness) and times when His close friends betrayed Him (Garden of Gethsemane). And finally, as He experienced the betrayal of the ones He created and the darkness of being shut off from the only One left, His Father in heaven, He was *utterly alone* (Matt. 27:46).

He experienced all this so the Holy Spirit could come and we'd *never* be utterly alone. "And lo, I am with you always, even to the end of the age" (Matt. 28:20, NKJV). One of the devil's favorite tricks is to make people feel isolated, but we have a Comforter, Counselor, and Helper through the Holy Spirit. Reach out to Him today. "And I will pray the Father, and he shall give you another Comforter, that he may abide with you for ever" (John 14:16).

Alison Brook

On Moving Mountains

"If you have faith as a mustard seed, you will say to this mountain, 'Move from here to there,' and it will move; and nothing will be impossible for you." Matt. 17:20, NKJV.

ut I don't have faith. I wish I did, but I just don't." I looked with longing at my friend, who for years had struggled with addiction. I had earnestly prayed for him, believing that someday he would have a moment of clarity and things would click into place.

Coming from a respected family and being an A student, his teachers pinned bright hopes on him. Blessed with an engaging personality and good looks, he seemed to have all anyone could wish for. Then he had fallen in with bad company. The effort that could have gone into bettering his life and the lives of others had gone into obtaining drugs. The sad result of this choice was his being in and out of prison all of his adult life.

Seizing upon a God-inspired thought, I picked up my Bible and said, "Look, God says He gives to everyone a measure of faith. And Jesus says that if you have faith only as big as a mustard seed, you can move mountains." Then I added, "Wait here. I'll be right back." In the kitchen, I rummaged through a drawer. Finding what I needed, I grabbed a can from the spice rack, sent up another prayer, and went back to my friend. From the set of measuring spoons in my hand, I chose the one-eighth teaspoon, filled it with mustard seeds, then repeated, "God says He gives to every man a measure of faith. This eighth teaspoon is the smallest measure I use in the kitchen, and you can see how many seeds it holds. If it takes faith only as big as *one* of these to move a mountain, just think what could happen in your life if you let God have your whole measure!"

It does seem that some people naturally have a greater faith. A childlike faith seems to find its way into some hearts more easily than into others. But God is an equal-opportunity God. He "is longsuffering toward us, not willing that any should perish but that all should come to repentance" (2 Pet. 3:9, NKJV). In exercising our mustard seed faith, pardon for sin is freely given when we come humbly to God, acknowledging a lack of faith to take hold of His goodness, and imploring His mercy and grace to set our feet in the path of righteousness.

So do you have a mountain of difficulty you need moved? In every peril of life, He has promised a way of escape—if we will lay our burden of doubt at His feet and leave it there.

Sylvia Stark

The Little Bird

Leave all your worries with him, because he cares for you.
1 Pet. 5:7, GNT.

When I was in my early twenties, I fell hard for a guy who had pursued me relentlessly for weeks until he finally had me, hook, line, and sinker. And then, he broke my heart.

It was confusing and entirely damaging for my ego and self-esteem.

I had truly come to the point of believing this guy was "the one" and had mentally worked so hard at subtly changing elements about him that I couldn't live without. I had him attending church, watching evangelistic DVDs, eating more vegetarian food, and giving up alcohol. I was so certain he'd change—right up to the big drop. He had come to the conclusion he loved me—just not everything that went along with me. A relationship would be "too difficult" with my rules and stipulations. It was abnormal! Who lived like me, other than me? he had insinuated.

I was so desperate to hang on to the doomed relationship that I was willing to do anything to get us back together. Even making specific plans to try alcohol for the first time in order to become more "educated" about my decisions. Thankfully, God had other plans as I woke up on that designated day with an out-of-the-blue fever of 102! I was on the verge of being delirious when Mr. Wrong called to cancel the evening date, saying, "I'm not messing with you and your God stuff. I think it's a sign."

I felt depressed, embarrassed, and disappointed with myself. By mid-afternoon, I was feeling better. I took a blanket and books to the nearby park and lay down to read. I hadn't been there ten minutes when I noticed a small bird nearby chirping very loudly. Suddenly, it hopped over and landed on my hand. I was in a state of shock while the little bird and I stared at each other. I thought, *I can't move or it will fly away.* Instead, it began singing while walking up and down my arm. It fluttered to my shoulder. It held my gaze the entire time as though it were looking into my soul.

Tears began to fill my eyes. I could sense in that moment that God was all around me. He had sent the little bird as reassurance of His love. I could trust Him.

Luckily, God didn't judge this young, foolish girl in her time of weakness. He just loved her back onto the right track.

Naomi Striemer

Daddy's Little Girl

See how very much our Father loves us, for he calls us his children, and
that is what we are! But the people who belong to this world don't
recognize that we are God's children because they don't know him.
1 John 3:1, NLT.

I once watched a father as he walked through his front door. He threw his arms wide open and called out, "Canddy!" Three-year-old Canddy raced towards him as fast as she could and threw herself into his embrace. He tossed her high in the air, then pulled her close, saying, "Canddy, do you know how much Daddy loves you?" Oh how I yearned for a daddy to fill my empty place! A thought occurred to me: *Why don't I try to establish contact with my own dad?*

I made plans, bought plane tickets from Puerto Rico to California, and packed suitcases. *What will I call him? How will we greet?* My stomach was in knots! Supportive family accompanied me to meet my father for the first time! My fantastic mother had taken the sting out of my growing up in a home with no dad. So I'd be strong, displaying her wonderful values.

Then, at last, there he was—standing—looking nothing like the picture to which I'd clung for years. We embraced. At that moment, deep down inside, I wanted to be Daddy's little girl. Loved. Cherished. Protected.

Reality quickly kicked in during that short visit. You see, my father is an alcoholic. The addiction cycle is horrific to experience in its entirety. The addict makes—and breaks—promises. Dad's actions continually betrayed his good intentions. Simply put, he loved the bottle more than he loved me. My deep disappointment was inevitable.

Maybe, as you read this, you think of your own father. Perhaps he, too, was absent, destructive, or failed to provide a safe shelter for his little girl. And you felt abandoned. Maybe you, too, have been longing to fill that empty place left by an earthly father. Yet as Daddy's little girl, you don't have to search for love anymore. Your heavenly Father has provided a safe and loving place for you. It's in His heart. And He's waiting for you with arms wide open.

No disappointments there. He will open to you His heart through His words in the Bible. He is the ideal, perfect Father. The Father you can trust. Today I know that regardless of an earthly father's love—or the absence of it—I'm still Daddy's little girl. And so are you.

Shelly-Ann Patricia Zabala

Have Faith in God

The LORD shall preserve thy going out and thy coming in from this time forth, and even for evermore. Ps. 121:8.

In addition to being the proprietor of a restaurant, I am also a licensed realtor. I sell, build, and manage properties. Some years ago, a particular property was sold while tenants were still living there. The tenants were aware, however, that ownership of that property was about to be transferred to another party. They agreed they would have to vacate the premises.

A real estate law states that a new owner cannot take possession of his or her purchase until the paperwork is completed and signed by an attorney-at-law.

Unfortunately, the buyers of this particular property—without authorization—prematurely approached and gained unlawful access to the property and to the house on it. Inside the house was a sick child who resisted the new owner and phoned his father.

"What is she trying to do?" responded the father, who now thought that *I* had authorized the unlawful take-over and an attempt to drive out his family.

Absent from my office for a time that day, I missed the ensuing excitement. Upon my return, staff members rushed to tell me what had happened. "It's so fortunate that you weren't here! Two gunmen, hired by the tenant family needing to vacate the purchased land, came here to the office looking for you!"

"Looking for *me*?" Now I was as shocked as my staff. *"Gunmen?"* I asked in disbelief.

"Yes!" answered another office worker. "And when they couldn't find you, they left in a rage! You must be very careful!"

I made a personal and risky decision. I would prayerfully visit the newly purchased property and trust God for a peaceful resolution to this misunderstanding.

"Oh, it's *you* . . . you—" screamed the angry tenant in a burst of curse words as I approached, praying. Then he calmed down enough to listen to my explanation. Soon he was apologizing for falsely accusing and threatening me. He offered me a beautiful puppy as a gift.

Have faith in God, my sisters. God has said that those who love His law will experience great peace (Ps. 119:165). And He has promised to watch over us daily as we come and go.

Ethlyn Thompson

May 20

The Dream Fulfilled

In all your ways acknowledge Him, and He shall direct your paths.
Prov. 3:6, NKJV.

As a young eye care professional in 1981, I dreamed of one day going to different places to help people see better. Yet two years later, in the wake of a personal loss, I came to the United States.

Away from home for the first time, I was sad and homesick. I didn't know what life had in store for me now. However, I claimed God's promise, "For I know the plans I have for you . . . plans to give you hope and a future" (Jer. 29:11, NIV). I would trust my heavenly Father with full control of my life. After all, He knows what would be best for me.

Years later, while working as an optician in Texas, I learned about the Gift of Sight International program, an organization that provides reading glasses to people in rural areas of developing countries. To my delight, I was chosen—one of twenty-six people—to participate in a two-week mission trip to Bolivia. We flew from Miami to Sucre. To my dismay, however, my suitcase never made it to our destination. Nevertheless, I was part of helping thousands of people see better with eyeglasses (even if I did have to survive for two weeks on just what I'd brought in my carry-on).

God had made my long-ago dream a reality! Subsequently, I went on other optical missions to the Dominican Republic, El Salvador, Ecuador, and the Philippines.

Since my husband shares my beliefs and supports my dreams and passion in life, I am enjoying an early retirement. This allows me—and sometimes, us—to participate in the mission trips. My husband has joined me on several trips to the Philippines, bringing more meaning into our relationship as we share God's blessings with others and help people see better.

What dreams do you have to honor God and help your fellow man? Talk to God about them. Then watch—even during times of personal disappointment—how He fulfills your dreams in His ways and in His timing.

Don't become discouraged if things don't happen as you think they should. He has promised that "all things work together for good to them that love God, to them who are the called according to his purpose" (Rom. 8:28). Your purpose and dream are important to God.

Rhona Grace Magpayo

Ministry of Sorrow

Sorrow is better than laughter: for by the sadness of the countenance the heart is made better. Eccles. 7:3.

I once heard a little story that went like this. A flood washed away a poor man's home and mill, taking with it everything he owned in the world. He stood at the scene of his great loss, brokenhearted and discouraged. The draining flood waters still swirled muddy pools across his property. To all appearances, the man had lost all he had ever worked for. Yet after the waters subsided, he saw something shining from the riverbanks that the flood had washed bare. That something was gold! Ironically the storm, which had apparently caused him so much personal loss, also revealed to him how rich he really was.

Life's floods sweep over us as well in various forms: bereavement, unemployment, divorce, loss of a loved one or even of one's reputation. The Bible is full of such "flood stories."

Take, for example, the family of siblings living in Bethany. The sudden illness of Lazarus left his two sisters, Mary and Martha, frightened and desperate. They sent word to their best Friend, Jesus, to come as quickly as He could. They well knew His power to heal. John 11:6 states that even after Christ received the message, He tarried where He was two more days before responding to the sisters' plea. Then Lazarus died! The sorrow was so great that even Jesus wept when He arrived on the scene—apparently four days late. Yet a demonstration of His resurrection power, as He called Lazarus from the grave, still encourages His followers today.

Earlier in the story, Jesus had said something that provides two clues as to why God allows so many floods into our lives. First, when Jesus received the message that His friend, Lazarus, was sick, He'd said, "This sickness is not unto death, but for the glory of God, that the Son of God might be glorified thereby" (John 11:4). And after He arrived in Bethany when Lazarus was still lying in the grave, Jesus added, "And I am glad for your sakes that I was not there" (John 11:15).

In addition to God being glorified through Christ's resurrection of Lazarus, this personal flood "ministered" to Martha and Mary by giving them an opportunity to declare whether or not they would continue to trust God, no matter what—even before they could see the gold.

May our floods always result in God's glory and our faithfulness until we see the gold.

Peggy S. Rusike Edden

The Lord Fought My Battles

"When I act, who can reverse it?" Isa. 43:13, NIV.

I studied journalism at the State University of Southwest Bahia. One semester, the radio journalism class schedules were transferred to Saturdays. Because I believe this is the day I should rest in God and worship Him, I prayed to God. At first, I was able to make arrangements with the professor so that I could attend classes with another group of students on another day. However, a few weeks later, the professor reneged. And then great battles began.

My mother prayed intensely and motivated other people to pray as well. I made a request to the secretariat of the institution to allow me to remain in the discipline. The request was accepted by the scholastic administrators of the course but not by the professor. The process was discussed in the plenary session of the department with decisions in my favor. A special class was created on Wednesdays with another professor. Dissatisfied with the decision, my original professor tried to stop that class with the intention of delaying my scholastic course by one year.

But God spoke to me! He told me, " 'You will not have to fight this battle. Take up your positions; stand firm and see the deliverance the LORD will give you' " (2 Chron. 20:17, NIV). With this assurance, I followed God's guidance. My request had now passed to the superior council of the university, composed of 350 teachers. At this time, God said, " 'Do not be afraid; do not be discouraged. Go out to face them tomorrow, and the LORD will be with you' " (verse 17, NIV). After an exhaustive meeting, the Lord gave me the final victory. The council not only authorized my new class arrangement but also made a declaration that, in the field of journalism studies, there should be no more mandatory classes scheduled for Saturdays.

But one concern persisted. My sister, Thais, who was also studying journalism, could theoretically find herself having to study under the same professor who persecuted me. Yet with faith, she exclaimed, "If it's not God's will, he will not be my teacher." And indeed, he never was. That particular professor got a leave of absence from the university precisely the same semester during which he would have been administering my sister's classes. Glory to God!

And God worked much more! He enabled me to finish the course ahead of schedule. The benefits of trusting God are many. With what problem do you need to trust Him today?

Thaiane Firmino

Learning to Trust

Yea, though I walk through the valley of the shadow of death,
I will fear no evil. Ps. 23:4.

One Friday I decided to visit my sick father. Two of my siblings and two friends were going to travel with me. My mom had earlier in the week visited me because I was feeling under the weather.

Now, feeling bad that Mommy left Daddy in his condition to come and see me, it was not difficult for me to come to the decision to return with Mom on Friday to visit him, as I was getting better. So we set out on a five-hour journey late Friday afternoon—six of us in the car.

After traveling for some time in a very heavy rain, we suddenly slid into a ditch that had been cut across the road, ruining one of the rear tires. It was obvious that the ditch was dug by hoodlums who take advantage of unfortunate victims like us by robbing them. My brother, who was driving, parked the car as we each stepped out. And it was just then that we realized we had no spare. What could have served as a spare had no rim.

We continued to drive at a very slow speed, praying that we could find a mechanic or a safe place to stay. After some time of driving on a badly ripped tire, we finally met two night watchmen guarding a gas station. We drove right into the station. These two men explained to us that the only mechanic in that area would not be able to leave town at that time of night. It was already after 10:00 P.M. and there was a curfew in the next town where he lived.

My worst fear was confirmed—we would all have to sleep in the bush near the nightwatchmen whom we didn't know. I exclaimed, "Mommy, these men are total strangers!"

Not moved by my outrage, Mom responded, "Let us pray." So we prayed. One by one, the others fell asleep. As for me, I kept intermittent watch. Just then, God spoke to me: *"Daughter, can you really protect yourself? Why not trust your life into My hands? I am here."* And that settled it. Finally, I managed to sleep.

By morning, my brother, in the company of one of the night guards, went to fix the tire, and shortly after we continued our journey.

Since then, I have learned to trust God more. He is the One who can keep me safe even when I walk through any fear, even through the valley of the shadow of death.

Mofoluke I. Akoja

Well Versed

For everything that was written in the past was written to teach us,
so that through the endurance taught in the Scriptures and the
encouragement they provide we might have hope. Rom. 15:4, NIV.

I am engaged in a battle to the death . . . with clutter. It's amazing how much stuff you can accumulate over thirty years of marriage, particularly if you never have to pare it down during a move. When I was sorting, tossing, and organizing the other day, I came across a box full of letters my husband and I had written to each other while we were dating.

As I read them, I couldn't help but wonder what our kids would think should they come across them in our "estate" (such as it is) years from now. Considered from that perspective, the letters were embarrassing. But even so, they reminded me of things I had forgotten, feelings that had dulled or changed throughout a long marriage. It wasn't that our love had died; just that it had grown up and matured. It wasn't the heady, unrealistic, ridiculous rush of those early days, which was just as well because, honestly, those letters made me blush!

In the same way, those letters are a sort of touchstone of the love I share with my husband though, God's Word is a touchstone of the love He has for us. He doesn't mean for it to stay on a bookshelf or on a table gathering dust. He wants us to read it so that He can interact with us through it. He can use it to remind us, admonish us, encourage us, and guide us. The Bible is God's living and active Word, and He speaks through it. But He can do that only if we expose ourselves to it. Better yet, if we hide His words in our hearts through memorization, He can call them to mind even when we don't have our Bibles on hand.

I find that God speaks to me so much through His Word that I've begun to write notes in the margin of my Bible next to highlighted scriptures to remind myself what situations or prayers particular verses are in response to. I come across them at random times, looking up texts during a sermon, for example, and am reminded all over again how much God cares for me and how involved He is in my life.

Now, if someone finds *these* "letters" after I am gone, they'll know just how much God loves me.

Céleste Perrino-Walker

At the Red Sea

I sought the LORD, and He heard me, and delivered me
from all my fears. Ps. 34:4, NKJV.

Have you ever "stood" on the shores of the Red Sea as did the fleeing Israelites the night they escaped Egypt? When some life challenge suddenly looms before me, I feel as if I am "at" the Red Sea with mirages of impossibilities before me. I look back and envision the enemy fast approaching. In any direction, I see no escape. I am overwhelmed. I can't rest. I can't sleep. I don't know what to do, where to go, how to get there. I am tired. I am defeated. No one understands. So I weep in silence.

Then in my distress, I look heavenward with a sincere heart and cry out, "Lord, help me! I cannot do this alone. Give me strength and wisdom to do what must be done."

And as Daniel cried out to the Lord and Gabriel was sent in response to his prayer, saying, "At the beginning of thy supplications the commandment came forth" (Dan. 9:23), an insurmountable release overwhelms me. A peace that passes all understanding overtakes me—instead of the enemy.

Yes, the Red Sea is still there, but somehow I see alternatives. A horizon appears on the other side of the challenge. I now notice new avenues of passage that I hadn't known existed. There is hope. A way has been prepared for me. My God has heard my prayer and sent relief! Why did I wait so long before praying?

I am often reminded of these famous lines: "What a friend we have in Jesus, / All our sins and griefs to bear; / What a privilege to carry / Everything to God in prayer!" We sing these words so fervently, yet continue to harbor pain, worry, and grief in our souls. Too often we arrive at the end of our rope before remembering to cry out to Jesus—when doing so would have diminished our distress at the first call of His name.

Perhaps you are standing at your Red Sea with seemingly no help on the horizon. Perhaps you have trials at home, at work, or at school. Perhaps you have tried everything, exhausting every ounce of energy. You have nothing more to give. With a trusting heart, call on Jesus. He is waiting to hear your invitation to involve Himself more deeply in your life. He already knows what you're going through. You have everything to gain and nothing to lose. Make the call.

Sylvia Giles Bennett

Flag a Pilot

But my God shall supply all your need according to his riches in glory
by Christ Jesus. Phil. 4:19.

Have you gotten to the end of your rope? Has time run out? We may not know why our plans are thwarted, but let's not doubt the providences of God. I think He enjoys surprising us in miraculous ways to solve our problems. My friend, Eric Rajah, experienced one of God's surprises in February of 2011.

Eric makes several trips to Kenya every year to assess the needs and plan new projects for his charitable organization, A Better World. After finishing his business at Masai Mara, he needed to fly to Nairobi and then on to Mombasa.

He arrived at the Mara airstrip at 9:30 to catch an 11:00 Air Kenya flight to Nairobi one morning. He watched as smaller planes came and went, but he was looking for Air Kenya, a larger plane. When the plane hadn't arrived by 11:30, he phoned the airline agent in Nairobi and inquired if there was a problem. He was told that another company plane had come and gone and he was not there. Much to Eric's disappointment, this was the last plane of the day.

As Eric thought of going back to the Fig Tree Hotel and rescheduling his flights, a small plane was ready to taxi off the runway. He ran and flagged the pilot and told him his dilemma. To Eric's surprise, the pilot said, "I will take you to Nairobi."

The stairs were lowered and Eric joined three other passengers and found a comfortable seat covered with a colorful Masai blanket. He paid the fare with a 25 percent discount and made it safely to Nairobi. As he stepped off the plane, he marveled at the gracious accommodation provided for him and how special he felt when the flight attendant said, "Glad you chose to fly 540. We look forward to seeing you again, and it was a pleasure to serve you."

When Eric went to the ticket agent to get a refund for the Air Kenya flight he had missed, he detected a bewildered look on the agent's face as to how he got to Nairobi before the plane had even landed. The original plane had landed at another airstrip to pick up some passengers and had gotten stuck in the mud. Unforeseen by Eric, God provided another plan so Eric didn't miss his important flight to Mombasa.

Let's flag our Pilot this morning. Perhaps He has a surprise for us today.

Edith Fitch

Eliana-Naghenjwa

A good name is rather to be chosen than great riches, and loving favour rather than silver and gold. Prov. 22:1.

Have you ever wished you would have been given a name other than the one you have? If yes, there is hope for you! Jesus promised "To him that overcometh . . . I . . . will give him a white stone, and in the stone a new name written, which no man knoweth saving he that receiveth it." (Rev. 2:17).

So what is in a name? Names are used to identify a person, thing, or place. Names also represent a person's character or who she or he is. I also think that a name can act as a prayer, every time one is called. As the old adage suggests: when you name it, you actually claim it.

When our first child was born, we wanted to name her after her paternal grandmother. She has a beautiful Pare (a tribe in northeastern Tanzania) name, "Naghenjwa," which means, "I am helped/saved." But we knew that a number of people would have a hard time pronouncing her name, so we thought to find another one that would complement it and still be easier for her to be called. We came up with three names, and while still contemplating which one to use, she decided to come a month earlier than was expected. We ended up choosing "Eliana," a Hebrew name which means, "The Lord has responded/answered." So she was called Eliana-Naghenjwa: the Lord has responded/answered; I am helped/saved.

This baby turned out to be a huge blessing from the time she was born until now when I write. You can't help but see that there is a special power that follows her. All the bad things that people warned us would happen with babies never happened with her. She is favored by everyone wherever she goes and in whatever she does. She is a delight to be with. I was impressed to think that every time she is called "Eliana-Naghenjwa," it is actually a short prayer reminding God that for this child, He has already responded/answered and helped/saved her.

What if your name were Mara, (Bitter, Ruth 1:20), Jabez (Sorrow, 1 Chron. 4:9), or any other meaning that gets reemphasized over and over? What name would you choose to reflect your trust in God? May your choice be a constant prayer and reminder to God that you are His.

Lynn Mfuru Lukwaro

His Plan Is Always Best

For your Maker is your husband—the LORD Almighty is his name—the
Holy One of Israel is your Redeemer; he is called the God
of all the earth. Isa. 54:5, NIV.

My husband and I had been separated for several months. Every day I prayed and prayed, pleading with God to restore my marriage. My children were suffering. One son thought that he was at fault. I was glad that our two oldest were away at boarding school and did not have to witness, on a daily basis, the disintegration of their family.

I was still keeping the books and doing the paperwork in my husband's business. One morning after I dropped the boys off at school, I went to work at the office. While I was paying the bills, my husband came into the room to show me a picture. "She's my girlfriend," he said. His words stabbed my heart like a knife, shattering all hopes for reconciliation.

Driving home, I cried out to God, "What am I going to do? What am I going to do?" God's answer to me was a little song that repeated over and over in my head.

"I will be a husband to you; I will be a husband to you." I had never heard either the words or the tune before or since. I like music, though it didn't play a big part in my life, but this was God's song to me.

Our home was not restored. *"I will be a husband to you; I will be a husband to you."* The song and its message built my courage during the next fourteen or fifteen months until the divorce was final. It supported me when the divorce papers arrived in the mail at the beginning of the older boys' graduation weekend. It carried me through months of looking for a teaching job after eighteen years outside the classroom, except for some substituting one year. It carried me through the sending out of many applications—with no response.

Those words sustained me through a move to a new town to teach in a private Christian school, a job that provided tuition assistance for both my college-age sons. I needed that song when it seemed that the paycheck wouldn't stretch to pay all the bills, whether for tithe or electricity. But I could trust my faithful Husband who always provided. Our needs have always been met. He healed my youngest son's stuttering. He healed my broken heart.

The heavenly Provider, Comforter, and Healer is your Husband too.

Kirsten Anderson Roggenkamp

Don't Be Late!

"Those who were ready went in with him to the marriage feast, and the door was locked." Matt. 25:10, NLT.

One Friday I was to fly from Sydney, my home city, to Hobart in Tasmania. I traveled to the airport by shuttle bus, usually a straightforward process. However, the shuttle bus was running late. Furthermore, the driver first had to deliver a family group to the cruise ship terminal near the city center before taking bus passengers to the international airport terminal. And all this before he could drop me off for my domestic flight. I had baggage to check in and knew that check-in would close at 1:30 P.M. The streets around the cruise terminal were jammed with traffic. We were running out of time to get to the airport. Everyone was stressed. I felt sorry for the passengers who were worried about missing their international flights. But missing my own check-in would ruin my travel plans. I could do nothing but pray.

The shuttle bus eventually reached the international terminal at 1:15 P.M. The other passengers quickly alighted. The bus driver looked a little relieved, but I continued to pray. We still had to get to the domestic terminal—on the other side of the airport! We finally arrived at 1:25 P.M. I headed straight for the Closing Flight counter. Several people were in line ahead of me. At last I handed over my bag for check-in. Turning from the counter, I looked at my watch again. It was 1:30 P.M. exactly! I sent up a silent prayer of thanks.

After a pleasant weekend in Hobart, followed by a day of work-related meetings, a colleague and I boarded our return flight, due to land back in Sydney just after 10:00 P.M. We were glad that the flight was on time because a delay could mean problems with Sydney airport's 11:00 P.M. curfew. (A few months earlier, on a delayed flight from Brisbane, my colleague had almost reached Sydney when the plane turned back to Brisbane to avoid breaking the curfew and incurring a substantial fine. This was a very frustrating experience for everyone aboard.)

The lesson here is obvious and pertinent: we are about to take the most important flight of our lives—to our heavenly home. "Check-in" closes soon. "Curfew" hour is approaching. We can't be late nor let any traffic jam dim our hope and trust in Him. Let's be faithful in prayer, for "He who testifies to these things says, 'Yes, I am coming soon' " (Rev. 22:20, NIV).

Jennifer M. Baldwin

When I Took My Eyes Off Jesus

And he said, Come. And when Peter was come down out of the ship, he walked on the water, to go to Jesus. But when he saw the wind boisterous, he was afraid; and beginning to sink, he cried, saying, Lord, save me. Matt. 14:29, 30.

I was the girl who showed up the earliest each week for Bible study, the one who never missed a church service. A bookworm and serious scholar, I graduated from high school with a 3.8 GPA (grade point average). Being the captain of my school's basketball team, I also graduated with two basketball scholarships for college. On my seventeenth birthday, I secretly exulted, "No more rules!" And like Peter in the passage above, I took my eyes off of Jesus. Two weeks after high school graduation, I drowned. Drowned in a life behind prison bars. Incarcerated for eleven counts of armed robbery and five counts of aggravated assault. I'd been the getaway driver of these crimes for "friends" who clearly didn't have my best interests in mind. So instead of entering college that fall, I faced up to 135 years in prison. How quickly I was sinking! Now I had no choice but to follow a whole new set of rules. My situation looked as though I would never get out—as if I would die in prison because of one wrong decision I'd made at the tender age of seventeen. Like Peter, I'd taken my eyes off of Jesus and was starting to sink.

Have you ever watched cartoon characters run off cliffs without falling? As long as the characters keep pumping their legs, they can run just as well in the air as if they were on the ground. But when they look down and recognize their dangerous circumstances, they panic and start falling through the air. Going off a cliff doesn't stop them. Rather, looking down does.

"For we walk by faith," wrote the apostle Paul, "not by sight" (2 Cor. 5:7). That means keeping our eyes on Jesus at *all* times—even in dire straits. During my eighteen months in the holding cell, awaiting my sentencing, I spent every day realigning my eyes towards Jesus. Praying for mercy. Praying for favor. Crying out as did Peter, "Lord, save me!" On "judgment day," I was sentenced to serve four years in prison instead of 135. I thank God that He didn't give up on me!

Walk by faith and not by sight. *Talk* by faith. Live, give, and love by faith. Hear by faith. By a faith that steps out of the boat, calls on Jesus, and takes His hand despite previous hurtful decisions. I learned that amazing things happen when you keep your eyes on Jesus.

Desireé Lee

It Wasn't Mine

Ask the LORD to bless your plans, and you will be successful in carrying them out. Prov. 16:3, GNT.

Although I had reservations about writing and sending a submission to an author compiling a devotional book, I decided to do so. As the clock wound down on the project's deadline, I found myself having to edit a fifteen-hundred-word document into a five-hundred-word document. On May 29, when I went through my manuscript, I clearly saw that I would have to completely refocus the piece.

Instead of panicking, I turned to God. After all, He was my inspiration in the first place. He knew exactly what needed to be done. My Bible study group prayed for me. And I prayed, believing that I was not working alone on this project. The refocus came easily. That heartened me. I was able to send in the submission two days earlier than the deadline. Again, I felt this was proof that the Lord was with me. I could not have done all that work on my own.

A quick e-mail back from the author of the project that same evening made me think it was an auto response. It wasn't. The author herself had written me. She shared that her sister and I have the same illness I'd referenced. I could tell that she had read my story with deeper understanding than I could have ever hoped. She asked me to share my story with her sister because she knew her sister often felt the same way I did about God's purpose for our lives.

Reading this author's response to me was literally one of the most amazing moments of my life. You see, the words were never mine in the first place. They were always God's, and He had a purpose for them! He had simply given me the story and the words when I trusted Him.

That night I felt as if God had reached down and given my heart a hug. That is the best way I can explain the experience—both then and now. I knew that even if my submission wasn't accepted for publication in the book, it would still be ministering to someone who needed my words—God's words. That was even more than I had hoped for.

God has a purpose for all of us. He is constantly working out His purposes for our lives, often in ways we often may least expect. He does this especially if we invite—and allow—Him to do so. What can you offer God today to be used for His purposes?

Maxine Young

Living His Obedience

Obedience: an act or instance of obeying.

And being found in fashion as a man, he humbled himself, and became obedient unto death, even the death of the cross. Phil. 2:8.

Jesus replied, "Anyone who loves me will obey my teaching. My Father will love them, and we will come to them and make our home with them." John 14:23, NIV.

When we trust someone, then we know it's safe to do what they ask of us. God is trustworthy, so what He asks of us is what is good for us. Obedience to the One who loves us supremely always takes us to a safe place where we find security and peace for our hearts.

True obedience comes from knowing that God loves us beyond understanding. Basking in this love creates a heart-desire to make choices that honor Him. That's why we pay attention to obedience even in life's little details. In the end, it's not about what *we* want to do. Rather, it's all about what *He* wants us to do—for our highest good and His greatest glory.

Heart-felt obedience *is* attainable. Especially when we remember that Jesus, with His blood, paid the debt for our rebellion in the Valley of Failure so that we can now use His strength to scale the Matterhorn of Victory.

Truth or Consequences?

"When Achan . . . was unfaithful in regard to the devoted things, did not wrath come on the whole community of Israel?" Josh. 22:20, NIV.

The Lord couldn't have been clearer: *All* the treasures of defeated Jericho must go into His treasury. Nevertheless, Achan "took some of them." "Them" included a handsome designer robe and some cash in the form of silver and gold—so *little* compared to the heaps of treasure everywhere. Who would know? Then the Israelites were badly beaten in the Ai battle. Someone had taken some of the devoted things, the Lord said. "I won't be with you anymore unless you destroy who did this."

Sure, Achan finally confessed his disobedience, but by then everyone already knew every sordid detail. We don't hear Achan apologizing for the hurt he's caused others, repenting of his theft from God—or even pleading that his family be spared from sharing his guilt. When we clutch sin close, we lose all perspective, blinded to its deadly reality, our reason overpowered by the serpent's hissed promises. When our covetous, sin-deadened faces are buried deep in the folds of the rich Babylonian robe, inhaling the fragrance of wealth, power, and position, we cannot hear the snake's evil chuckle of anticipation of the moment we will realize that it was all a lie and that we will never be able to wear our ill-gotten gain. It must remain forever buried, out of sight in the dank hole of despair, where its lovely colors will fade and its rich fabric will rot.

God first saw the slimy trail of Achan's sin in Lucifer, the "son of the morning," a sin that sent unfathomable horror reverberating throughout the universe. But His love-born plan, His Son's plan, was greater by far than all the covetous-born hatred and lies the evil one could fling at the descendents of Eden's perfect pair.

*Then for one last moment the Son stood before His Father's throne. And in the next moment, swifter than the speed of light, the Son became like a pinpoint of starlight in Mary's warm, dark womb.**

"He left His Father's throne above, so free, so infinite His grace; emptied Himself of all but love, and bled for Adam's helpless race; 'tis mercy all, immense and free; for, O my God, it found out me. Amazing love! How can it be that Thou, my God, shouldst die for me?" (Charles Wesley).

Jeannette Busby Johnson

---

* Concept from poem by Rhoda Wills.

Something of Tabytha in All of Us?

Trust in the LORD with all your heart. Never rely on what you think you know. Prov. 3:5, GNT.

I was happy to be moving into a dwelling that would be much better suited for "our" needs. I'd had enough of the Victorian terrace cottage with the postage stamp-sized "maintenance-free" garden plot. The one near the busy road that had claimed the lives of my mama and papa cats. Now, after six months, I'd move to a home with a proper-sized garden next to woods and away from speeding cars and heavy traffic, where my surviving cats would be safe.

On moving day, my cats trusted me to take them to their new home. Well, all my cats except for Tabytha. When I walked toward her to pick her up, she ran away and hid. Clearly, she had no intention of being relocated. She wanted to stay where she felt safe. She wanted to remain at the "old place." The rest of "us" moved. Since I still had access to the Victorian cottage for a little while, I'd return every day with the intention of retrieving Tabytha and taking her to our new home. Yet four days after our move, she seemed content without our being there anymore. Back and forth I went each day making vain attempts to gently coax Tabytha within petting (and grabbing) distance. But she continued to elude me, hiding in garden sheds or eyeing me from atop some distant roof. The efforts of friends and neighbors to catch Tabytha were also in vain.

One evening I decided to go up to the old cottage, though I knew Tabytha would be watching me from some inaccessible vantage point. Yet I resolved to outwait her this time. I sat down as if I was there for good. Slowly, eventually, Tabytha approached as I spoke softly to her. Soon her proximity and purring indicated I'd finally gained her confidence. They say that trust is a necessary prerequisite to obedience. At last, she came toward me at my call. Gently, I picked her up and drove her to our new home, which she now loves.

What should have been a simple transition to a far better dwelling turned out to be a lengthy, drawn-out, and complex affair simply because Tabytha couldn't understand enough to trust me with her safety. Sort of like what we put God through when we don't understand how safe He is to trust when attempting to move us to better places in our relationship with Him.

Dear Lord, I fear there is a bit of Tabytha in all of us. Help us to trust You and not make choices based only on our own understanding. Help us trust that You know what's best for us.

Laura A. Canning

A Gentle Nudge

Behold, I stand at the door, and knock: if any man hear my voice, and
open the door, I will come in to him, and will sup with him,
and he with me. Rev. 3:20.

One day when my husband arrived home from a mission trip, he announced he had brought a gift for me. The gift turned out to be a little girl in need of a home. Immediately, I hugged and kissed her. The girl was delighted to find a home where all of her needs were met, but she wasn't really ready to unlearn the past ten years of upbringing. We immediately started teaching her English. We homeschooled her until she caught up to her grade level.

The hardest place to teach her was at church, where she found it difficult to sit still. I often nudged her when she needed a reminder. She would ignore me. I would then gently pinch her. At that, she would dash to the far end of the bench, knowing I couldn't reach her there. She did not mind embarrassing me. But I must tell you that she eventually grew up and has brought me much joy. In our family, we give one another a gentle nudge when one of us needs help in public. A little nudge, a gentle word, to help better a behavior or situation.

In the Bible, God Himself tells us that He comes to our door and knocks gently. When we love Him, we joyfully listen to His voice and welcome Him into our hearts. And, oh, what a lovely time we experience together, talking and communing.

After Elijah's great victory on Mount Carmel over the prophets of Baal (1 Kings 18), God had more work for Elijah to do. But fearing the vengeful Queen Jezebel, Elijah fled into the desert. After days of flight, the exhausted prophet collapsed, asking God to let him die. Instead, God let His prophet sleep. Then He sent an angel to feed the hungry prophet. The angel approached Elijah with "a soft touch and a pleasant voice" that held "pitying tenderness" (*Prophets and Kings*, p. 166). At Mount Horeb, God could have shouted orders to him through the wind, earthquakes, and fire. Rather, God chose to reveal Himself in "a still small voice." Elijah's fear vanished. His confidence returned. He went back to work until God took him home to heaven—which is where He wants to take us some day as well.

In the meantime, let's be aware of—and obedient to—the gentle nudges of God's Holy Spirit. Let's open the door of our hearts to intimate and eternal fellowship with Him.

Birdie Poddar

Mountain Climbing

"Though the mountains be shaken and the hills be removed, yet my unfailing love for you will not be shaken nor my covenant of peace be removed," says the LORD, who has compassion on you. Isa. 54:10, NIV.

My husband has dreamed, since a teenager, of seeing the Matterhorn in the Alps on the border of Switzerland and Italy. We finally got there. This 14,693-foot (4,478-meter) mountain has four sides, which are so steep they are mostly snowless, although the surrounding mountains are beautiful and white year round. Conquering that summit stirs the hearts of about three thousand determined mountain climbers a year. What would motivate a climber to train physically and emotionally to face the hazards of the rocky cliff as well as extreme, volatile weather patterns? It's got to be an unquenchable desire in the heart to reach that highest point.

As Christians, when we have a driving desire to reach the heavenly summit, the devil seems to surround us with spiritual hazards. We can find daily climbing equipment in God's Word. Let's turn to His Word for the climbing equipment we need when we face challenges.

Depression—"Why, my soul, are you downcast? Why so disturbed within me? Put your hope in God, for I will yet praise him, my Savior and my God" (Ps. 42:5, 6, NIV).

Anxiety—"When I said, 'My foot is slipping,' your unfailing love, LORD, supported me. When anxiety was great within me, your consolation brought me joy" (Ps. 94:18, 19, NIV).

Sickness—"The LORD sustains them on their sickbed and restores them from their bed of illness" (Ps. 41:3, NIV).

Children—"All assemble and come to you; your sons come from afar, and your daughters are carried on the hip. Then you will look and be radiant, your heart will throb and swell with joy" (Isa. 60:4, 5, NIV).

Aging—"He gives strength to the weary and increases the power of the weak. . . . But those who hope in the LORD will renew their strength. They will soar on wings like eagles; they will run and not grow weary, they will walk and not be faint" (Isa. 40:29, 31, NIV).

Reading tombstone inscriptions in the village of Zermatt, I realized hundreds had lost their lives in unsuccessful attempts to reach the top of the Matterhorn. In our spiritual climb, we can be confident that the Divine Rope will hold us securely, enabling us to reach the summit!

Roxy Hoehn

Children

In all your ways submit to him, and he will make your paths straight.
Prov. 3:6, NIV.

hildren are something wonderful. A gift from God. When they are little babies, they are completely dependent upon us. But then comes the day when we as parents have to begin to let go, bit by bit.

Do you know, do you remember, the feeling of when your little girl or boy lets go of your hand to run after the other children in nursery school, and you have to leave him or her there and you go away?

You leave by the door you entered, and you close it between you and your little treasure. At home you again close another door. This has seemed like a long day's journey.

With every step you take, your heart pounds harder and your longing becomes stronger. The time until you can again wrap your arms around your dear child seems like an hourglass filled with all the sand on the beach of the closest sea. When it is finally time to pick up your child and he or she joyfully races toward you and gives you a big hug, you are sublimely happy!

How much greater are the feelings of our Lord! He created us! He sees where we are going! Not into a well-guarded nursery school, but away from Him, away from eternal life. And what about us? With every decision we have to make, however small it might seem, we should be aware of the fact that there are only two choices: We can choose the world, the miry pit that will defile us and even kill us! This is a decision against God and life. Or we can choose God, the clean path! We can choose life! And this is also a choice for yourself; a choice that no one else can make.

My wish for you, and for me, and for everyone at the beginning of each day is that we make the second choice every time and say No to disobedience against God; No to separation from God; No to the world; No to Satan; No to detours; No to whatever may be between you and Jesus.

I also wish that we say Yes to God; Yes to the room in our Father's house; Yes to life in eternity; Yes to peace in our hearts; Yes to light; Yes to love; Yes to . . . As children of the heavenly Parent, may we bring joy to His heart by saying *Yes* to the right choice!

Kerstin Dorn

Hold Your Tongue!

Do not let any unwholesome talk come out of your mouths, but only what is helpful for building others up according to their needs, that it may benefit those who listen. Eph. 4:29, NIV.

I love to dance, and I take it seriously. I am fifteen years old, in the eleventh grade, and I am taking advanced courses through Cambridge University, England. I don't have free time when school is over, so having a dance class means that I have built-in exercise a few times a week.

For our dance midterm, we had to choreograph a dance to be showcased in our winter concert. My teacher picked the groups, and I was placed in a group with four other girls. Two of the girls had a bad reputation, and I didn't know the other two girls. When we began rehearsing, I found the situation difficult at times as one of the girls was rude, bossy, and completely self-centered. Despite the hostile environment, we were making progress—until we all got sick.

Unfortunately, being sick caused us to fall behind. We had only four full weeks till the concert, and two and half of them were during a holiday break. As we struggled to finish choreographing the dance, ugly words were often spoken, but I always managed to hold my tongue. Recognizing our situation, the teacher helped us devise a plan to catch up—which included getting together during break.

I tried repeatedly to contact my group members, but I couldn't reach them. When the break was over and we met in class, I was told that they were too busy. I suggested that we get together over the weekend and finish the dance so that we could get full credit for our exam. The girl who had always been outspoken stated we should race off stage while she and her best friend danced a short duet to fill the missing time. She then stated that we could rush back on stage and pose at the end.

I couldn't believe she would say that. This dance was our midterm grade. I was angry, and it takes a lot to make me angry. In this situation, I am so glad that I had God with me. He knew I had had enough, and when I have had enough, I have problems "filtering" how I say what needs to be said. Just as I was about to lash out at her, our teacher started talking, and that kept me from speaking in a manner that wasn't Christlike. I want to be more Christlike. I pray that the words that come out of my mouth will build people up and not destroy. Don't you?

Lillian Marquez de Smith

Miracle at 11:59

Then gathered the chief priests and the Pharisees a council, and said,
What do we? for this man doeth many miracles. John 11:47.

I will not easily forget February to August of 2013. This period of time came with every type of challenge. One of the most critical examinations for an online degree program, consisting of four, fifteen-page research essay-type questions was due in early September 2013.

Because of sickness, jury duty, a burglarized home, the crash of my personal computer (subsequently down for long weeks), and ill health of family members, I could not meet the exam deadline. All I could do was still be faithful to God in my everyday life and inform my academic advisor that I could no longer pursue my intended degree. I must either quit the program or settle for an alternative and lesser degree. This predicament devastated me, and it certainly was not good news to my academic advisor either. She pleaded with me to reconsider, but I felt I was too sick to focus on this important, life-changing examination.

I was accepted into the alternate lower degree program but did not get around to clicking on the school's Web site "accept" and "submit" tabs for my response. With only two and a half weeks remaining before the final exam deadline of my preferred degree, I decided to give it my best—but didn't tell my academic advisor. On the last day of the course, I completed online, and submitted, the lengthy exam. It was exactly 11:59.

Twenty-four hours later, an e-mail message informed me that my coursework had already been evaluated. *How could this information be returned so quickly?* I wondered. *My work must be unacceptable!* I was shocked and nervous.

My heart raced at the speed of light as I read the next words, "Congratulations on Passing This Examination. Bravo!" I screamed with joy and excitement, while tears flowed down my red cheeks. I had to compose myself before my husband, who had come at my excited calls, could understand me and share in this miraculous turn of events.

My academic advisor was dumbfounded yet joyous. It was incomprehensible to her.

How could she have known that I was only the quiet, obedient instrument who had let God take the examination through me and work a miracle? Let Him work in you too.

Pauline A. Dwyer-Kerr

Chosen

"He didn't choose you and pour out his love upon you because you were a larger nation than any other, for you were the smallest of all!" Deut. 7:7, TLB.

I was at the end of one journey and at the start of another. It was quite exciting finishing the bachelor of education degree program and looking forward to teaching. That school year, I applied to a few school boards within my local vicinity to work as a replacement teacher. I had beamed with joy as I looked at the calendar of my daughters' school and noticed that none of their school holidays would be the same as mine. Being a single parent, this reduced the stress of finding a babysitter. I could go to work and, if necessary, they could care for their other sister who is intellectually challenged.

This seemed to be the perfect time to take on as many jobs as I could possibly get. However, by the middle of that week, I had not received any calls to teach. I then decided to spend the rest of the week doing some fun activities with the girls.

No sooner had I made plans with my family when I received two calls booking my services for Thursday and Friday, if I were available. Should I accept the two offers? I was undecided. I needed the money. I knew my children would understand. Yet, in the end, I chose to honor my family commitment.

While speaking to a friend that weekend about my dilemma, God impressed me that my choice had been one that honored Him. He chose me to be the mother of these children. I had promised them that we would spend time together that week doing things as a family. Psalm 15:4 tells us that keeping the solemn promises we make, even if they prove personally inconvenient down the line, is pleasing to God. He, too, is a promise keeper (Num. 23:19).

Yes, God had chosen me for a special purpose and ministry. He had chosen me to be a mother to these precious girls. I realized that although I had not earned any money from teaching that week, God had chosen to bless me with a wealth beyond compare. I am a chosen caretaker of these children who are precious in His eyes.

Dear God, thank You for choosing to love me so much. Help me always to seek You so that my choices will honor You. Thank You for choosing me to the ministry of parenting. Amen.

Georgina George

Little Choices

Whether you turn to the right or to the left, your ears will hear a voice behind you, saying, "This is the way; walk in it." Isa. 30:21, NIV.

When I was growing up, my parents logged timber with heavy equipment in the Colorado mountains. At the end of a thirty-mile, four-wheel-drive road, our family lived in a camper on the job so we could be together.

One day in December, my dad and four-year-old brother headed to town for fuel. After I finished my work, I curled up to relax and read *Little Women* until they returned. About four o'clock, I decided to bring in the wood. Here I was confronted with a decision: Should I put on all of my snow clothes for just five minutes to bring in the wood for our woodstove? Against all reason and habit, I took the time to put on hat, coat, gloves, snow pants, and boots. I brought in one load and was back at the wood stack when I heard my dad call for my mom. I turned and looked over the clearing where we were camping but did not see either of my parents.

"What?" I called back.

"The pickup truck and fuel trailer slid off the road and got stuck. I need Mom to bring the skidder to help pull the pickup out." The skidder is a machine somewhat like a large four-wheel-drive tractor. I rushed back inside to get my mom, but she wasn't there. Back outside, I talked with my dad; we decided I must go up the mountain to the job site, about a mile away, where my mom was working, because my dad was too tired to go.

Because I was suited up, I took a shortcut through two- to three-foot snow drifts, something I never liked doing. But time was essential because my dad had left my brother in the pickup to hike the six miles cross country in four feet of snow. Now it was getting dark, and overnight temperatures were going to fall below zero. Being dressed for the weather paid off. I reached my mom. She brought the skidder, and my parents rescued my brother before nightfall.

What really stuck out to me in this experience was the power my little choice had on bigger, more important outcomes than I had known at the time I made it. It's the little choices with which we need to be careful. Luke 16:10 could apply: "He that is faithful in that which is least is faithful also in much."

Melinda Ferguson

175

Weeds!

"The ground will sprout thorns and weeds, you'll get your food the hard way." Gen. 3:18, *The Message*.

Weeds are a part of my life. They show up in my lawn, taking away from the manicured look we work so hard to maintain. They grow prolifically in the garden. They release pollens into the air that cause many of us the agony of allergic reactions.

Yet yards, gardens, and fields are not the only places where weeds flourish. They can also spring up in our minds, choking out the fruit of the Spirit we would like to have growing there. As a child, I often heard the expression that equated an undesirable or unruly person to a "bad weed." This makes sense, doesn't it? For, indeed, thoughts influence behaviors.

Having encountered weeds so frequently in life, I've given a lot of thought to them and have arrived at several conclusions. I've seen that one reason most weeds get a bad rap is because of their obnoxious, piggish selfishness. They tend to take over a garden space, using up resources like water and soil nutrients. Yet they offer nothing to the gardener in return. Even little children can control weeds. I recall aiding our grandson, Kyle, when the three-year-old wanted to help his mommy weed her flowerbed. Little Kyle pulled and tugged at the weeds, working up a sweat. He knew the weeds needed to go, and he stayed with the task until he completed it. Today, years later, Kyle is a capable and persevering computer tech dealing with electronic "weeds" in computers. At an early age, he learned how to tackle weeds. When teaching, I used to tell my writing students that if they wanted good "produce" to result from tightly written essays, they needed to "pull those lazy words out" as a gardener uproots weeds. I'd tell them, "As writers, you're also gardeners." So are we. Especially in our minds.

The best definition I ever heard for "weed" is "something that's growing in the wrong place." So a weed can be a blade of grass in the soil, a tree, a word, or an un-Christlike action. God didn't tell Adam that *work* in the garden would be a curse. Instead, God said that *weeds* would be the cause of distress and labor. Yet for our asking, God, through the power of His Holy Spirit, endows us with the capability of uprooting weeds in our lives so that our hearts can produce the pure fruit of the Spirit. Let's be good gardeners every day. Happy gardening!

Betty Kossick

God, the Potter

Yet you, LORD, are our Father. We are the clay, you are the potter; we are all the work of your hand. Isa. 64:8, NIV.

A friend of mine was taking a ceramics class and invited some of us to go with her and learn how to glaze some pottery. To be honest, I had mixed feelings about it. I had never done any glazing before, and I wasn't sure exactly what to expect.

At my friend's class, we picked out which pottery pieces we wanted to glaze. After a quick crash course of what to do, we started. To begin with, I was quite hesitant. It took me some time to decide which glazes to use. Sample color tiles attached to each bucket of glaze helped inform my decision, though they couldn't truly convey what color the glaze would actually be. First of all, a lot has to do with how thickly the glaze is applied. The tiles show only what a thickly layered glaze will look like after firing (more on that in a minute). Also, layering one color of glaze over another will also alter the end result. Then there is the question of what technique to use for layering the glaze: spraying . . . brushing on . . .

After glazing my first piece of pottery, I started to enjoy the process. I don't know if I would ever get to the point that I'd find it to be a relaxing hobby as some crafters do, but I at least wasn't tense anymore.

In fact, I started thinking about how glazing pottery has some life parallels. For example, a person can do one's best to plan for a beautiful outcome in life—just as I tried to put together a pleasing color combination on my pottery pieces. But until the firing—life's unexpected trials, losses, and tests—one can't *really* know how it will turn out. All sorts of surprising things can happen. Firing changes everything!

The bottom line is that we are not really in control of very much—except for our power of choice. Which means, of course, that we *can* choose our responses to the firing process—even though we can't choose our trials. Our chosen responses under duress help determine our true colors. And if we're asking Jesus, our Creator, to walk us through life's trials and enable us to respond to them as He would, He will bring forth His beauty in our characters. Then, if we choose to believe that the Master Potter knows best, His beauty will be imprinted all over us.

Julie Bocock-Bliss

Escape From the Trap

Surely He shall deliver you from the snare of the fowler. Ps. 91:3, NKJV.

Figaro is the baby of our four cats—not only because he's the youngest but also because, even though he has grown to be second largest, he is still a playful kitten. He loves to play "fetch," and he believes that any piece of plastic food wrap in the house was put there as a toy for him. His favorite perch is on the broad shoulders of my son-in-law, Christopher, but the best game of all, according to Figaro, is "crawling inside." It can be in a basket, bag, box, or bookshelf; all that matters is hiding out some place that feels snug and secure to him.

One day Christopher was cleaning his office, which had become impassable with so many piles of paper. Figaro appointed himself chief helper. He'd leap to Christopher's shoulders from time to time as Christopher put more and more papers into the trash bag he'd started to fill. Then Figaro would conduct quick surveys to determine the focus of the master's attention before hopping squarely into the center of that focus, where he sat firmly and purred loudly. In time, though, his activity slowed enough that the office became tidy once more, and the trash bag was properly stuffed. Christopher hoisted the bag, which seemed overly heavy, out to the dumpster.

An hour or so later there was a frantic, ferocious uproar at the kitchen door. As Christopher opened it, a streak of fur burst past him and on into the security of the master bedroom. Following a hunch, Christopher set out to investigate the trash bag still in the dumpster. Sure enough, there was a huge, jagged hole in it through which Figaro had undoubtedly made his terrified escape.

As I listened later to the story of Figaro's deliverance from a free ride to the dump, I was reminded of God's promise that comes to us from the days of King David: "Surely He shall deliver you." When Figaro crept into that huge trash bag to sleep, it didn't seem like a dangerous trap at all. In my case, my busy activities and playful pursuits don't seem dangerous, either; they can even be quite a lot of fun. But then I notice sometimes that I've been cut off from my loving Master. That's when I'm thankful for the promise of One who gave Figaro strength and courage to break out of his snare. God will deliver me, too, even in those times when I have gotten myself into the cozy trap of lukewarmness.

Leonardine Steinfelt

Twisted Paper—Twisted Tongue

Even so the tongue is a little member, and boasteth great things.
Behold, how great a matter a little fire kindleth! James 3:5.

When I was around four years old, my sister and I were cleaning our room. I was given the task of emptying our little trash bin into a larger trash can in the bathroom. To get to the bathroom, I had to walk through the living room and the kitchen. On this soon-to-be unforgettable day, I passed the kitchen stove. The pilot light caught my attention.

I stopped and gazed, mesmerized by the wavy patterns and sporadic flashes of yellow sparking in the midst of the blue flames. No one else was around. So I reached into the little trash bin I was holding and drew out a piece of paper. I twisted the paper and held it toward the flame. My plan was to light the stove as I had seen my grandmother do so many times before. *Whoosh!* Fire engulfed the twisted paper in my hand. I quickly dropped it back into the trash bin, thinking the flame would die out. I emptied the little trash bin back into the bathroom's larger basket and returned our little bin back to the bedroom. I felt confident I'd gotten away with doing something I'd wanted to try for a long time.

"I smell smoke!" my uncle called out from another room in the house. He sniffed his way to the still-burning fire in the bathroom trash basket, putting it out before it caused too much damage. "What happened?" he asked pointing to the streaks of soot on the wall.

"Well," I said, "there must have been a twist of paper or something sticking out of the little trash bin I was emptying. Maybe it caught fire when I passed the stove." It never occurred to me that something that made me feel so grown-up could be so dangerous. Although I was spared physical harm, my embarrassment was as obvious as that soot-streaked bathroom wall.

Since then I've wondered if a "twisted" tongue isn't a lot like that twisted piece of paper. Many a tongue has kindled a great fire, damaging emotions and charring relationships beyond repair. Though we should know better, we sometimes drop a burning word about someone else into the listening ear of another, assuming the fire will just "die out." Yet too often the voracious flames leave spiritual "soot" on the walls of hearts and reputations. Only heaven-sent discretion, compassion, and a sanctified tongue can smother the fires kindled by twisted tongues.

Marea I. Ford

Human Discretion Is of No Use

Thou shalt guide me with thy counsel, and afterward receive me to glory. Ps. 73:24.

A few days ago when I opened the door to the garage, I realized that the left front tire of my car needed air. Immediately, I drove to the service station. As I drove up to the air pump, an attendant walked up to me and asked if I needed air. When I said "Yes," he proceeded to take the hose from its holder and walk toward the right front tire.

"I put twenty-eight pounds in the front and thirty in the rear," I explained.

"This pump does not have a gauge," he said. "I have to use my discretion." He pumped some air in each of the front tires. I thanked him and drove off. But somehow, I could not stop thinking about what he said: "I have to use my discretion."

While it may be quite acceptable to use discretion in many areas of life, there is one area where it may be dangerous to do so. In the matter of my salvation, I cannot use my human discretion to focus and direct my life. God has given me His Holy Word to guide me on my spiritual journey. I must follow the blueprint He has provided.

As I drove to work during that week and negotiated potholes on the country roads, I kept thinking the ride was unusually bumpy. I made several attempts to get the air pressure checked, but each time I tried to locate a functioning air pump, I was unsuccessful. Finally, in desperation, I called out to God as I drove through town on my way home Friday evening. "Dear Lord, I need to check the tires' air pressure. Please help me find a functioning air pump." Suddenly, I realized I was approaching a service station I'd forgotten about. Instinctively, I drove in and was relieved to find a working air pump and an attendant who was able to check the pressure in the tires and adjust each tire with the appropriate pressure. *What a God!* I thought. *He was on time in answering my prayer.* And what a difference the adjustment made to my ride as I drove home!

When we follow the guidelines that God has given in His Word, we will find that our lives will have meaning. We will be loving, kind, understanding, patient, and forgiving. We will avoid many pitfalls. We cannot use human discretion alone in seeking to know God's will. The Bible must be our guide. May God help every one of us to be firm in our determination to consult Him daily regarding the direction our lives must take.

Carol Joy Fider

Use What You Have

Then he said, Go, borrow thee vessels abroad of all thy neighbours, even empty vessels; borrow not a few. 2 Kings 4:3.

The prophet Elisha once told a young widow to take a jar of olive oil and fill the many jars she had borrowed from her neighbors (2 Kings 4:1–7). Stepping out in faith, she obeyed the prophet, and the Lord blessed her so much that she was able to pay off her creditors, rescue her sons from being sold into slavery, and still have enough money left over to live on. The Lord blessed the small amount of oil she had, along with her obedience.

Once, during a financial crisis, my husband and I could have lost everything. We had purchased a home, land, and some rental property. Years earlier, we made the decision to invest in real estate because it was the way to go back then. Our plan was to semi-retire at age forty.

Then a big recession hit the country. Chemical plants closed, and many people lost their jobs, including my husband. We had no money and had accumulated a lot of debt. Like the biblical widow, we didn't know what to do. My husband prayed, "Lord, help me!"

As an earlier Christmas gift, I had purchased for my husband a table saw he'd been looking at. When I asked him what he was going to do with it, he said, "Build a cabinet." He had no experience building cabinets. However, he etched out a drawing, measured what size it would be, purchased a sheet of birch plywood, and went to work. After cutting out the pieces, he started putting the cabinet together. Stepping back, he looked at his work. It was not coming out the way he wanted, so he decided to put it in the backyard where no one could see it. But a small voice kept saying, "Don't do that. Keep working on it." My husband obeyed. After putting all the pieces together, his first masterpiece was completed. Many more followed.

You see, the Lord had given us the table saw before the financial need was there. The answer to our financial blessing was in my husband's hands. And he would never have known that had he not obeyed God's voice. Later, Lionel learned another trade. In faith, with these two gifts, he started his own business and was able to pay our creditors—with money left over for us.

When you have a personal relationship with the Lord, trusting Him enough to obey Him, you can have the assurance He will turn problems into benefits both for you and for His glory.

Shirley P. Scott

Our Plan vs. God's Plan

I know what plans I have in mind for you, Yahweh declares, plans for peace, not disaster, to give you a future and a hope. Jer. 29:11, NJB.

Our family was on the move. In 1972, our church headquarters sent our family as missionaries to work in Brazil. We moved to Campo Grande in the state of Mato Grosso do Sul.

We were learning Portuguese; enjoying the people, sights, and foods; and had been in Campo Grande about two years when we were invited to do ministry in Belém, do Pará, rather than in Campo Grande.

We had questions: Where is Belém? How far is it from Campo Grande? How long will it take to get there? In the midst of our unanswered questions and packing our belongings for this long journey to the unknown, we were excited!

The movers had been contacted. Moving day arrived. Our plan was to have all our household items, clothes, everything put on the moving van. We would pack the car with all the necessary items, food, school books (for our children's long-distance home study), and several changes of clothing for the trip—a trip that would take, only the Lord knew how long. Finally the car was packed, and the movers had moved all but one piece of furniture out of the house—the refrigerator!

"Please, please put the refrigerator on the truck," I begged the movers in Portuguese "*Não, hoje, Senhora; amanhã.* (Not now, ma'am; tomorrow)." And they left.

Our plan was to have been in Presidente Prudente that day before nightfall. Arriving tomorrow would mess up our plans.

Yet it wasn't until the next day that the movers arrived, packed the refrigerator, and took off. Two adults, three children, school books, food, suitcases, and a dog piled into our two-door—and stuffed—Volkswagen. We set out for Presidente Prudente. A whole day late!

Approaching Presidente Prudente, that afternoon, we saw a sight that shocked us. Setting on the highway was an airplane that had made an emergency landing. And in the exact spot where we would have been had we traveled the night before.

I know the plans I have in mind for you . . . plans for peace, not disaster.

Carol Barron

Do You Hear What I Hear?

"The gatekeeper opens the gate for him, and the sheep listen to his voice. He calls his own sheep by name and leads them out. When he has brought out all his own, he goes on ahead of them, and his sheep follow him because they know his voice." John 10:3, 4, NIV.

On a summer vacation to England, my father decided to rent a car and drive to Wales. I will never forget how I felt after we spent a few days in Wales. Let me tell you about one experience.

Wales and London are about as different as night and day. As we made our way to Wales, we saw rolling hills. The countryside seemed to never end. The grass was green. Houses had thatched roofs. We saw lots of bed and breakfast inns, but most of all we saw sheep. Lots and lots of sheep. At the age of fifteen, I was amazed. I had never seen sheep in real life before. Sheep cannot live on the subtropical island where I am from.

Before night's end, we had stopped at a bed and breakfast to spend the night. After breakfast the following morning, our host led us on a tour of her farm. Among the many farm animals was a flock of sheep. When we asked her if it was true that a sheep can follow your voice, she told us to watch.

"Winston!" she called. To our amazement, a sheep, Winston, came walking out from among the flock. Our host greeted Winston, and the sheep returned to the flock. "Would any of you like to try to call him?" she asked. Of course, we would!

"Winston!" I called. Then I called again. Other members of my family called and called. Yet Winston would not come.

"Why won't he obey and come to us?" I asked our host.

She smiled and answered, "Because he doesn't know any of your voices—just mine."

Jesus told a parable of the Good Shepherd (John 10). A sheepfold has only one door. By entering in at the door, the shepherd would demonstrate to the sheep both his identity and his purpose. His sheep (just like Winston) would not follow strangers. Only the shepherd's voice.

Sisters, are you willing to step out from the crowd? Do you know the Good Shepherd's voice? Listen for it, and then follow Him today.

Dana M. Bean

My Two Fathers

And he arose, and came to his father. But when he was yet a great way
off, his father saw him, and had compassion, and ran, and fell on his
neck, and kissed him. Luke 15:20.

Today is Father's Day weekend, and memories of my father are flowing into my
mind like graceful and smooth waves back into the ocean. I loved him with
all my heart. He was caring, funny, respectful, charming, and thoughtful. He
played an important role in the lives of my six sisters and me. Around him we felt
secure, loved, and important. Even though our mother was the disciplinarian, we
respected our father and recognized his authority.

The highlight of our day was when he came home from work. As soon as we
heard the car coming into the driveway, we'd run to greet him with hugs and
kisses. He would enter the house with at least four little girls hanging all over
him. We fought over who would eat on his lap—it was a habit for him to have
dinner with at least two of us on his lap. He usually did fun things with us.

I remember him sitting in the kitchen with a can of delicious powdered milk
in his hand, and all of us in line with a glass of water and a spoon waiting our turn
to get our portions of powdered milk. He made simple things—such as changing
a flat tire—something amusing. There we were, with tools that we could barely
carry, trying to loosen the wheel lugs, to raise the jack and lift the spare to replace
a flat tire. Obviously, instead of helping, we made this process harder for our
father, but he made us feel that he could not have made it without us. When
we had nightmares or wet our beds, he always came to the rescue. What a warm
feeling to hear his comforting voice and feel his strong arms around us!

My father was, for all accounts, not perfect. He made some mistakes with
unpleasant consequences; but without any doubt, he shaped in our impressionable
minds a positive image of our heavenly Father.

I am more than sure that my Father God loves me and cares for me the same
way, and better, than my earthly father. I know that He carries me and lifts me up
in His strong hands. I am confident that He is my present Father in the absence
of my earthly one.

My hope is to live in heaven forever flanked by my two beloved fathers.

Hannelore Gomez

I Have a Father

See what great love the Father has lavished on us, that we should be called children of God! And that is what we are! 1 John 3:1, NIV.

I was nineteen years old and working in a country school. On the way to my parents' farm after work one day, my car got badly stuck in the mud. The more I tried to get out, the closer my car slid to the ditch. I carried rocks from the nearby woods and tried to push them under the wheels to provide traction. I even jacked up the car and created a bridge of sticks and stones under the wheels. Sometimes I could see a bit of progress, but after two hours of hard work, I realized that I would not be able to get the car out. The mud was up to the axles, the ditch was looming ever closer, and the mud hole in the road stretched far ahead.

Then, in the fading light of evening, I heard the sound of a vehicle approaching. Finally, someone was coming. Help was imminent. Over the hill appeared a red truck—my father's red truck! I stood on the roadside, eagerly waving to my hero—my dad. The truck got closer, sped up, and swerved around my car, just managing to pass by on the narrow road. Then it sped out of sight over the next hill. The sound of the engine gradually faded and died in the distance. And in my heart, my hope also faded and died. The darkness was falling, and now, so were my tears.

I needed a father, a father who would help me. I couldn't do it alone. As I dejectedly turned back to my car, I thought of other times when I felt that my father had been too hard on me. How could he leave his own daughter in this miserable situation? I questioned if he even loved me.

After a while, I heard another engine approaching. I looked down the road and over the hill came a tractor—a big, strong tractor with my big, strong dad driving it. "I couldn't stop with the truck earlier," he explained, "or it would have gotten stuck too." Then he chained up my car and pulled it out of the mud.

I have another Father who knows what I need. Sometimes I feel He keeps me waiting for help. Sometimes I wonder if He is too hard on me. Sometimes I don't understand His ways, and sometimes I even question His love for me. But in spite of my doubts, He eventually and always pulls me out of the mud. I am His daughter, and He loves me.

Shelley Agrey

Free Choice

I call heaven and earth to record this day against you, that I have set before you life and death, blessing and cursing: therefore choose life, that both thou and thy seed may live. Deut. 30:19.

When my oldest son became of age, I felt led to give him the choice of whether to continue attending church or not. I was confident that he would continue attending the church in which he'd grown up and where—in a gentle, loving spirit—he had accepted Christ as his Savior. When my son chose not to attend church that first Sabbath, I sent a prayer up to God and thought, *Maybe next weekend . . .* But my son continued choosing, in his newfound freedom, to stay home instead of attend church. My aching heart has witnessed this same choice of his for two years now. I've been so tempted to take back the freedom of choice that I gave him. Yet how can I do that? How can I, without breaking his trust in my word, *demand* his obedience?

Recently, through this ongoing situation, God has been reminding me that He also gives me the freedom of choice. He also continues to love and watch over His children even when they're making hurtful choices—to use drugs, drink alcohol, watch TV shows that negatively impact their lives, eat intemperately—or even shop wastefully or excessively. God, our heavenly Parent, stays close to us even when we're letting other "gods" of this world crowd out time that we might be spending in prayer, the reading of His Word, the enjoying of uplifting music, and attending church. I know how my heart aches for my son and how it breaks over the choices he makes. Yet how much more our heavenly Father's heart must ache and break over some of our daily choices, watching us lose out on so much of the abundant life and blessings He still makes available to us—just for the choosing. Matthew 7:11 states, "If ye then, being evil, know how to give good gifts unto your children, how much more shall your Father which is in heaven give good things to them that ask him?"

God's mercy and wisdom do not allow Him to take away our freedom of choice. He knows that it would prove Satan right, who wrongfully alleges that God is unfair. Patiently and lovingly, God waits for us to ask for His help in choosing Him in the very details of our lives. Join me in choosing Him today and every day.

Tammy Jamieson

Not Again!

"Ask, and it will be given to you; seek, and you will find; knock, and it will be opened to you." Matt. 7:7, NKJV.

It was well past midnight, and I had just completed work on a project to be presented the following day. Then I remembered some documents that would be required to substantiate a portion of the presentation. The desk was covered with several stacks of papers, but, recalling precisely in which stack the necessary documents had been placed weeks earlier, I proceeded, confidently, to search through the pile.

No sign of the documents in that pile, so I proceeded to examine the papers in all the stacks on the desk. No sign of the required papers. Where could they be? I was becoming anxious. Time was moving quickly. I needed to get some sleep because a full day lay ahead. Nevertheless, I continued to search. Those who know me are well aware of my impatience and unhappiness when I can't find things. I strongly dislike searching for anything; but if I must, then I will.

Finally, I lifted a silent prayer heavenward: *Lord, allow me to see the papers.* Then I returned to the original stack in which I was certain they had been placed. Carefully, one sheet at a time, I looked. Behold! Before too long, there were the "lost" documents! I breathed a sigh of relief and thanksgiving. Now I could retire.

I wonder, am I as determined and committed to diligently searching for, finding, and following the Way as I was in looking for and finding those documents? I fear that many times we exert great effort, strength, and time in attaining temporal, material, ephemeral things/goals to the detriment of everlasting ones. Unfortunately for us, transient objectives with immediate rewards appear more attractive than those that come with delayed gratification—those eternal rewards that demand sustained effort and a steady eye on the prize.

Perhaps our sights are not generally trained on the beyond, considering the apparent distance of the heavenly and eternal from our mundane minds. It behooves us to pray for guidance, courage, and understanding. To set our priorities wisely, investing as much—or even more—energy and time on eternal pursuits as we do on transient, oh-so-quickly passing ones.

Marion V. Clarke Martin

The Terraced Shrub Garden

Now unto him that is able to keep you from falling, and to present you faultless before the presence of his glory with exceeding joy, to the only wise God our Saviour, be glory and majesty, dominion and power, both now and ever. Amen. Jude 24, 25.

I once went to a thermal bath in the city of Aachen in Germany. While enjoying myself in the different temperature swimming pools, I noticed that there was also a small outside area for the visitors. So I went there and was quite impressed when I looked up a terraced, sunlit hillside with square-trimmed hedges running along the edge of each terrace. A circular building, like a shrine, nestled its six tall pillars in the shade of the trees on the hilltop—just behind waterfalls in the foreground. It was a beautiful terraced shrub garden with a step waterfall running through it.

Adventurous as I am, I wanted to explore this special place a bit more. I did notice a sign on the grass next to the waterfall that said "No Trespassing." Because I was not going to step on the grass, however, I thought my exploration would be OK. So I stepped on the cement walls, which framed the waterfalls, and I went all the way up to the shrine.

At that moment, a lady who was working at the terraced restaurant next to it, called out to me saying that I was not supposed to climb on these steps. I became embarrassed and headed back down immediately. However, I suddenly slipped and lost balance. Fortunately, I was able to intercept my fall by blocking it up with my hands; otherwise, I would have fallen on my back. What resulted was just a small bruise on my right foot.

Isn't it similar with sin in our lives? How often in my life have I entered Satan's territory without even being aware that I was on dangerous ground! How often did I need somebody to correct me, to tell me that I was wrong, before I actually realized my predicament?

This time, I got off the matter lightly. However, there are some sins I've committed in my life that have resulted in lasting scars. Had I only listened to the voice of the Holy Spirit those times! Had I only paid attention to the prohibition signs clearly outlined to me by God's Word and through the advice of godly counselors. Doing so could have spared me much trouble.

I don't want to be that foolish, adventurous girl anymore. I want to heed the warning signs and listen to the Voice that knows what's best for me. I'm sure you do too.

Daniela Weichhold

Not Only Knowing, But Living

Jesus replied, "Are you not in error because you do not know the Scriptures or the power of God?" Mark 12:24, NIV.

At some family meeting or in public, has anyone asked you to recite a Bible passage? Have you participated in contests in which the person who mentioned the greatest number of verses won a prize? Is it possible that it was very easy because you recited these verses by memory and at that point memory was on your side? From childhood, we are encouraged to learn Bible texts by heart. They are undoubtedly important to our lives.

The Bible mentions that there were at least two things that the Sadducees did not know: one, the Scriptures; another, the power of God. There is no doubt that the Sadducees were religious and that they could recite long passages of the torah. However, there is a difference between reciting words from Scripture and truly knowing their meaning—and believing what it says. How easy it is to be in the presence of Christ yet not to have Him in the heart.

I read an interesting story about a pastor and an actor at a social gathering. Someone asked the actor to recite Psalm 23. When he finished, the audience applauded him. Then the pastor was asked to recite the same psalm about the Good Shepherd. When he finished, listeners were shedding tears. When someone asked the actor why the difference in the response of the people, the actor answered, "I know the psalm, but the pastor knows the Shepherd."

There is a great truth in the answer of the actor! When we have the true Shepherd in our hearts, we know and live His words. This is the difference between knowing the faith and living the faith that we embrace.

The Word of God, through the Holy Spirit, gives us the power to know it, to understand it, and to live its teachings. Ellen G. White, in her book *The Great Controversy*, writes, "We should not engage in the study of the Bible with that self-reliance with which so many enter the domains of science, but with a prayerful dependence upon God and a sincere desire to learn His will" (p. 599).

God, who has guided your life and mine, has also given us wisdom to learn His Word—and the opportunity not only to recite it but also to live it.

Meibel Mello Guedes

Arguments Produce Quarrels

Don't have anything to do with foolish and stupid arguments, because you know they produce quarrels. 2 Tim. 2:23, NIV.

L ook what I did at Barbara's birthday party!" Melissa waved several sheets of paper, each covered with pictures connected by colored lines. "I haven't seen these for years," I said, setting aside my work. "Did you enjoy the game?"

Melissa nodded. "But Barbara got into an argument with Mayling. She's from Hong Kong. Barbara drew lines between a monkey and a calf 'cause they're mammals. Mayling connected a monkey with bananas and a calf with milk, 'cause that's what they eat. They both said the other one was wrong. It got pretty loud. I said I'd ask you who was right."

Taking a deep breath I smiled down into her eager little face and said, "Cultural neuroscience would say they represent equally valid, if different, perceptions. Different just means unlike; not necessarily right or wrong."

"Cul-tur-al neu-ro-sci-ence," Melissa articulated slowly. (I knew those words would pop up soon in her conversation.)

"Studies are discovering neurobiological bases for well-known as well as unexpected cultural differences. When research subjects were shown a variety of pictures, brain imaging studies revealed that different brain regions were activated based on whether the individuals were born and raised in Eastern or Western parts of this planet," I explained. "Westerners tended to activate brain regions that recognized objects and categorized them by similarity, while Easterners showed more activity in brain areas that processed relationships among the objects (as in food). Researchers believe that the brain has been shaped by culture and not vice versa."

"Wow!" cried Melissa. "Tomorrow I'll tell both girls they were right, based on cultural neuroscience research. (There it was!) Barbara's got a Western brain; Mayling's got an Eastern brain." She paused. "So how come people argue about stuff like that?" It was an excellent question. I had no answer. Indeed the world seems embroiled with arguments and quarreling: in families, schools, churches, politics, culture, and countries. It's past time to get serious about the apostle Paul's counsel (Titus 3:9) to avoid foolish controversy and meaningless argument.

Arlene R. Taylor

The Guard of Israel Does Not Sleep

Indeed, he who watches over Israel will neither slumber nor sleep. The
LORD watches over you—the LORD is your shade at your right hand.
Ps. 121:4, 5, NIV.

In my childhood, I remember seeing the fulfillment of this text many times.
My family lived in a wooden house, and my mother sewed clothes for others
in order to make some extra money. She was always up late at night on the
sewing machine so she could make timely deliveries to her customers.

One night, after my brothers and I went to sleep, my mother put a pan of
food on the fire and went to finish sewing a costume for one of her clients. It
happened that she fell asleep and went to bed, forgetting that she had put the
pan on the fire.

When we woke up, the neighbors were pounding on the door and trying to
break it down because the house and its vicinity were filled with smoke. We were
suffocating in the smoke, but the house had not caught fire. Amazing! The pot
had burned to coal, and smoke was pouring from it nonstop. Yet the only flame
we saw was the flame of the stove that had been cooking the food in the pan.
There was not even a spark of fire elsewhere in the house.

Again and again our neighbors exclaimed, "Only God saved you from being
burned alive in your sleep!"

Besides this incident of God's protection strengthening our trust in Him, He
had also shown His love and care for our dear neighbors whose home could also
have caught fire if ours had started to burn.

As human beings, we are flawed, and we forget things very fast. Among so
many tasks that we have in our lives, we, like my mother forgetting the pan on
the fire, can forget to put ourselves under God's care.

Today I pray to God so I can be awake to His Word, His love, and His soon
return.

*Lord, if by any chance I sleep and cannot wake up for Your will, if I am choking
on my duties and I'm not listening to You, send again Your children to wake me up.
Loving Father, thank You because You are the Guardian of Israel who does not sleep
and is attentive to the needs of each one of Your children. Amen.*

Nilva de F. Oliveira Boa Morte

I Will Bring You Home

"At that time I will gather you; at that time I will bring you home."
Zeph. 3:20, NIV.

One October I was driving home. It was late, it was dark, and it was raining. I noticed a big dog darting in and out of traffic on the road. *He's going to get hit,* I thought. He was dragging a chain. *Do I stop or not? It's a big dog, he may bite me. It's wet. How would I even get him in the car?* I was debating this as I drove right by him. Then I felt guilty all the way home. Finally in order to stop feeling guilty, I said out loud. "OK, Lord, the next dog you put in my path I'll put in the car!"

It's not surprising what God did next. Two weeks later, while driving home again I saw another big dog. This one was running up to every car that passed by. Stopping the car in the middle of the road, I peered out at him. What pleading eyes he had, as if to say, "Won't someone please take me to my home?" I jumped out, opened up my back door and pronounced, "Get in. You are going home!" Amazingly, he jumped in.

Picture wet, muddy dog on nice leather seats. I put the homeless dog out in our fenced back yard. Instantly he started running circles as if looking for someone. Knowing he was safe for the moment, I went to retrieve food, water, and a chair. He ate and drank like he was starving. After that I sat in the chair and placed both my arms around him and soothed, "God knows where your home is. Your people are probably praying for you right now. God is going to get you where you belong." I called several friends to pray for this dog, found directions to the shelter, and put him back in the car. As he was riding on the back seat (this time on a towel), I kept reminding him over and over, "God knows where your family is, and they will come back for you." Three days later I phoned the shelter to hear them excitedly say, "The dog's name is Junior, and his family came the very next day to get him. In fact, they were here every day looking for him until you brought him in."

Like Junior, most of us have run away from "home"—our walk with God— by going where we wanted to go and doing what we wanted to do. Yet, when we confess our lost condition to Him, He is right there beside us (where He always is). He's been interceding for us and watching for our change of heart, always eager to take us home to Himself again.

Diane Pestes

The Little Guest Room

"But about that day or hour no one knows, not even the angels in heaven, nor the Son, but only the Father." Matt. 24:36, NIV.

By the time I was nine years old, my uncle Volmar and my aunt Iolanda came to live on our farm. Because they had two children around the same age as my siblings and me, we were excited to have their company in our games and rides.

Months went by, and our friendship grew so close that we began to consider our cousins as our siblings. After a while, however, they had to move to a neighboring state. I cried a lot when they left, seeing the house so empty. But then I controlled myself as I remembered that they had promised they would always visit us during vacations and holidays.

When they came to visit, we received them with a lot of joy. An interesting fact about their visits is that they liked to surprise us, usually dropping in on us without any warning that they were coming. Although we were excited to see them, we were often unprepared for them.

Over time, however, we became accustomed to these unforeseen visits. In fact, we got into the habit of cleaning the guest room just prior to every holiday so that they wouldn't catch us unprepared for their visit. I was usually asleep when they arrived. Then I'd wake up and hug them all with excited cries of joy, happy the guest room was ready for them (and I was also happy that they usually brought along some very nice gifts for us).

Being ready for these surprise visits makes me think about the second coming of Jesus. When on this earth, He created bonds of friendship with His disciples. But after a while, He had died for us, been resurrected, and ascended to heaven. The disciples must have wept at His departure. However, Jesus promised that He would return one day—not just to visit His friends, as my uncle, aunt, and cousins did—but also to take all who believe in Him to His heavenly mansion. He promised there would never be a separation again.

We don't know exactly when He's coming back, but our hearts (our little "guest rooms") should always be prepared to receive Him. When Christ returns, those who are ready will receive the best present in the universe: a crown of precious stones and eternal life. But the best part is that we can enjoy His eternal presence always.

Mayla Magaieski Graepp

Just One

Therefore let him who thinks he stands take heed lest he fall.
1 Cor. 10:12, NKJV.

Have you sensed the tug-of-war battle for souls intensifying? Obedience to God strengthens us; but by disobeying, we lose our footing. Which direction are you leaning?

Just one bite of fruit didn't seem like much. But it was forbidden—the *one* they shouldn't touch. The test of Adam and Eve is repeated in our day. The serpent is subtle. This I well know. Having listened to his whisper to "innocently" search online for an old boyfriend, I momentarily let go of Christ's hand. This act of curiosity placed me on enemy soil and in proverbial quicksand. Finding nothing online, I stopped looking. But the whisperer was watching. He knew my Achilles' heel. Soon the former beau contacted me.

His request that I listen to one of our old love songs was one big mistake that took my mind and heart (and values) back thirty-three years. I was like a giddy teenager again. The more I listened to that one song, the more the rebellious spirit behind it had access to my mind. One short visit began with one long hug. Another big mistake as I ignored the counsel to be "reserved," reserving touch until committed to one another. Just one gift and one birthday card bonded us still more. Other temptations abounded. So did compromises—one here, one there, one more—till I was snug in the snare, convinced that my tolerance of his lifestyle would lead him to the Lord. Instead, it was leading me astray. His profession of undying love was flattering, another of the enemy's favorite tactics.

Praise the Lord, He freed me from the trap, though scars and pain remain. We often think "just one" won't hurt anyone. In this, we're sadly mistaken. One act of folly, one unguarded moment may have eternal consequences. And Satan knows that *one* may lead to two and three and four. He has the "skinniest toe," so we must never crack the door. We're being prepared for the final test of allegiance, passable if *God* comes first with our obedience to *His* voice. When tempted to take that one small bite, we must flee, turning from E-V-I-L to L-I-V-E.

What (or who) is *your* Achilles' heel? Nothing (and no one) is worth losing Heaven.

Let's dig our heels into righteous soil and stand firm in the truth, victorious with Christ in the tug-of-war. Let's never stray from our One True Love—"the *Just* One"—sent from above.

Clarissa J. Marshall

God's Protection

The LORD will keep you from all harm—he will watch over your life;
the LORD will watch over your coming and going both now and
forevermore. Ps. 121:7, 8, NIV

As Women and Children's Ministries director (of the East-Central Africa Division of our church), I was honored to be the main guest at a women's ministries congress in the West Congo from June 26 to 29, 2014. There were about three thousand women who came to attend those meetings and seminars supported, in part, by the provincial minister, not even a member of our denomination.

The meetings were successful and satisfying. However, there was an incident that happened to me one night during the congress.

On the second night as I was sleeping in a hotel, I felt as if there was a mosquito that had somehow gotten into my bedding. I had come to this conclusion because of slight but disturbing movement of the sheets down by my feet. The disturbance stopped for a while. Then, though sleeping fairly deeply, I felt that "something" again, this time climbing up and long my leg. Still very groggy, I dumped whatever it was on the floor and continued sleeping. After all, I was extremely tired from working hard at the congress all day when I'd had only five hours of sleep the previous night. After my devotional time the next morning, I decided to head toward the bathroom. But when I looked for my slippers by the side of the bed, I saw instead a scorpion trying to move along the floor, but it appeared it had been injured. I was so scared that I screamed loudly. Two hotel employees came running to find out what was wrong. When they knocked, I ran to open for them so that they could remove the scorpion as quickly as possible. No one knew where it had come from. Though I became frightened about sleeping in that room, Luke 10:19 came to my mind. God gave promises to those who obey Him: "I have given you authority to trample on . . . scorpions and to overcome . . . the power of the enemy; nothing will harm you" (NIV).

I was really amazed at realizing how God had protected me from being bitten by that scorpion. I believe He sent his angels to weaken it so that it wouldn't do anything to me all night, because I have dedicated myself to do His work with all my might knowing that He would take care of me. Have you dedicated *your* whole life to God and His work?

Debbie Maloba

A Lesson From the Snails

The great day of the LORD is near, it is near, and hasteth greatly.
Zeph. 1:14.

It was early morning on what promised to be a sizzling hot day. The sprinklers had been working all night, leaving the sidewalks, roadside grass, bushes, and flowers still dripping wet. I noticed hundreds of tiny snails crisscrossing the concrete walkways. But where were they going and why? The answer soon became obvious. They were avoiding danger as quickly as possible. As the temperature rose, the pavement became much too hot for their soft, little bodies and they were hurrying to reach the cool, wet haven beside the road. In their haven they would also avoid being stepped on by pedestrians going about their business. Then there were the birds, hungrily looking for breakfast. Danger was everywhere. The little snails had no time to lose.

It occurred to me that in some ways we are rather like these little snails. Our life journey has a destination so beautiful that we cannot even begin to imagine it. It's a place of safety from all the pain and heartache we so often experience, where we will enjoy life to the full, as God planned it to be, replete with everything that could possibly bring joy to a human heart.

The snails' journey is beset with danger. So is ours, fraught with temptations aimed at diverting us from reaching our destination. Time is running out for us too, whether it is life's candle burning low or the fact that quickly multiplying signs of Jesus' coming announce its imminence. We have no time to waste on useless pursuits that sap time, strength, and finances that could be better used to hasten His coming. Some are dazzled by ever-changing fashion, others clog their brains by indulgence in rich food or unhealthful drinks. Many of us, especially the youth, are enslaved by various electronic devices, while others spend and are spent on their idols of sports, politics, or entertainment. There is little time left for God. His Word is not as exciting as the newest, best-selling novel, and prayer too often becomes a meaningless routine. The opportunity for change remains, but for how much longer? Tomorrow just may be too late.

However, we are not snails, helpless midst difficult circumstances or voracious enemies. Help is always available so we can avoid spiritual danger and overcome even the most subtle temptation. All we have to do is ask God for strength to stay safe within His will—and to exercise a most precious gift—free choice—to His glory. Let's ask Him for help right now.

Revel Papaioannou

Living His Prayers

Prayer: an address (as a petition) to God . . . in word or thought.

Very early in the morning, while it was still dark, Jesus got up, left the house and went off to a solitary place, where he prayed.
Mark 1:35, NIV.

And whatsoever ye shall ask in my name, that will I do, that the Father may be glorified in the Son. John 14:13.

And pray in the Spirit on all occasions with all kinds of prayers and requests. With this in mind, be alert and always keep on praying for all the Lord's people. Eph. 6:18, NIV.

The prayers of Jesus sustained His personal mission and empowered Him to make right choices each day. Our prayers will do the same for us. Prayer changes circumstances. Prayer changes hearts. Prayer changes us.

And, oh, the creativity with which God responds to our prayers! Though always consistent—but never predictable—He answers through Scripture, through a rainbow, perhaps, or simply through His quiet presence in the midst of personal crisis.

Be blessed as you read the stories of God's involvement in the lives of His praying daughters. Be doubly blessed as these women share with you Heaven's amazing answers, wrapped in grace and showered upon those who love to spend time with Him.

Sweet Hour of Prayer

I cling to you; your right hand upholds me. Ps. 63:8, NIV.

When summer arrives there is only one thing that comes to mind: vacation. Vacation, whether it's to the mountains, the beach, or the woods. We make plans, set dates aside, and get all excited because we can take a break from school or work to relax and enjoy some precious time for ourselves. We can just unwind from all the stress.

But in the midst of all that vacation planning we sometimes forget that God wants us to have a *daily* vacation. God knows our needs and He has provided a daily "vacation" escape. It is during those sweet moments of communion through prayer when He comes near so that we can give Him our burdens and rest in Him.

So every day we can set aside some time to let go of the chores we have to do. During that time we can release the work that is piled up on our desks or on our "to do" lists and just enter into communion with our God. During that time of intimate fellowship we can spiritually slip away from all the bustle around us and the worry. Every day God is there, every day waiting for us, so that He can give our hearts and minds a place of rest. Prayer is that very special time when He "sits down" with us to have that morning's heart-to-heart chat. It is in that time when He shares His peace and love. It is in that sweet hour of prayer where we can pour out our hearts and souls to God so that He can fill us with His spirit and reassure us of His mercy and grace in our lives.

God gives us the opportunity to enjoy those special moments with Him every single day. He knows that we need help to do our work and chores. He knows that some days we just need someone to listen to us. That is why He gives us prayer so that we can carry our burdens to Him. Only He is capable of carrying the whole universe on His shoulders, yet He takes care of each person as if you or I were the only one in existence.

And indeed it is so sweet to feel God's peace and hope fill our souls as we pray to Him. Even though we cannot see Him face to face, these seasons of prayer with Him grant us a daily vacation from this world. Morning mini-vacations where we can experience refreshment and renewal and, in the process, catch a glimpse of Heaven.

Yvita Antonette Villalona Bacchus

Until the Morning

For the Lord . . . shall descend from heaven . . . and the dead in Christ shall rise first: Then we which are alive . . . shall be caught up together with them . . . to meet the Lord in the air. 1 Thess. 4:16, 17.

It was the end of a hot summer day. I was pregnant, weary, and apparently cranky, for three-year-old Teddy sagely commented, "I know a little girl who's tired and sleepy!" (Who could be cranky after that?) At bedtime we would lie down with him, Mom on one side, Dad Ted on the other, and sing "sleepy songs" to him, including "Go to Sleep, My Baby."

Little brother Tim arrived a few months later, and the rocking chair and new songs replaced the sleepy songs. All too soon both boys became adults, and we were left with an empty nest. Several years after retirement, Ted was diagnosed with prostate cancer yet, after aggressive treatment, got along well for a couple of years. Then the cancer returned, spread to his bones and spine, and he lost the battle. We were all devastated, but Teddy was a great comfort to me, calling every Sunday night from his home in Colorado to mine in North Carolina and sometimes in between. No matter how our day had been, we always found something to laugh about.

Less than two years after Ted died, Teddy learned that he also had cancer. A very private person and single, he didn't even want family or church friends to know. Finally he confided in me. When he became extremely sick, he agreed to let others in the family know. His cousin, Cathie, who also lived in Denver, took good food to him. Her sister, Annie, flew to Denver from Seattle to help. Tim and I flew to Colorado while Tim's family drove out. By now Teddy was hospitalized in the intensive care unit, the cancer having spread throughout his body.

The family gathered around his hospital bed, told him we loved him, sang hymns, and quoted precious Bible promises. With a tube in his mouth he couldn't speak, but he could hear and nod his head. We had prayed that he might recover, but I can imagine a loving Father saying, "I know a little boy who's tired and sleepy. Go to sleep, My child." Teddy is now sleeping until the trumpet sounds and the dead in Christ rise first. "Then we who are alive and remain shall be caught up together with them to meet the Lord in the air." Healing will happen then.

Good night, son. I'll see you in the morning!

Mary Jane Graves

Espresso Prayer

"Ask, and it will be given to you; seek, and you will find; knock, and it will be opened to you. For everyone who asks receives, and the one who seeks finds, and to the one who knocks it will be opened."
Matt. 7:7, 8, ESV.

First Thessalonians 5:17 tells us to "Pray without ceasing." *Well,* I thought, *this is what I've been doing. I've prayed and prayed and gotten even more weary and discouraged.*

Praying without ceasing can be very difficult for busy women. "My only quiet place," a busy young mother once told me, "is in the bathroom sitting on the toilet. But I can't stay there all day."

Then I discovered a little book entitled *Espresso Prayer. Espresso* (a Latin verb form meaning "to press out") is also the name of a strong-flavored coffee served in small cups. Though not interested in coffee, I found helpful the writer's comparison of prayer to espresso. The author of the book explained that, throughout the day, we can formulate short prayers, like espresso servings in smaller cups. God doesn't ask us to spend all day on the same long or "big" prayer. God asks us to pray "espresso" prayers throughout the day—short, strong, and aromatic. With God we can develop something like an SMS (short message service). We can do this by sending Him short, concentrated messages all day long. I have now started, besides my morning and evening prayer sessions, making espresso prayers a way of life.

When I see a mother in the supermarket struggling with a defiant child, I pray a short, intense prayer for her instead of judging her. *Please Lord, give this lady a special blessing for the day.* When I see a young man in the street, searching through waste in trash bins, I pray, *Dear Lord, help this young man find a shelter for the night.* In church, when I see an elderly person complaining about noisy children, instead of shaking my head, I pray, *Dear Lord, help this lady to find joy in the shiny and bright eyes of the little ones.* I now pray many espresso prayers during the day, sending God SMS "texts." And He has answered so many of these.

I would like to encourage every one of us to develop a SMS "culture" with our Creator. Espresso prayers will reach Heaven during those times when we can't be on our knees for hours. Unceasing prayer becomes a reality throughout the day as we develop new prayer habits. Prayer becomes a greater joy and a way of life that will bring you, as it has me, rich rewards.

Denise Hochstrasser

Seventy Percent Chance of Rain

And all things, whatsoever ye shall ask in prayer, believing, ye shall receive. Matt. 21:22.

Every summer an annual Fourth of July picnic is held in our back yard. My husband Norman loves to work outside, and his efforts reflect a green carpet of grass that gently slopes down to a little creek with perfectly maintained banks. Several shade trees invite visitors to relax and cool off. There are numerous shrubs, flower beds, and a vegetable garden, which are a treat to the eye. It is a very pleasant place to spend time, so we like to share it with our church family.

This year's plans had carefully been laid and executed. I had planned a picnic menu and purchased festive tablecloths and accessories. A program was planned, which included musical numbers, poems, a short patriotic talk by our pastor, and games. A hay ride down our country road was also planned. This was to be a very enjoyable day for all of us!

The day of the picnic dawned overcast, and my husband predicted rain after watching the forecast on the Weather Channel. "You might as well plan to move it inside; there is a seventy percent chance of rain," he advised. Last year we'd had to move inside, but isn't a Fourth of July picnic supposed to be outside?

The tent already stood dripping wet, the grass was damp, and the sky looked ominous. My spirits were not to be dampened though. "The Lord will send us the weather He wants us to have," I frequently commented. Noon revealed no clearing in the weather, and by three o'clock my husband was adamant that we plan for the picnic to be inside. At 4:00 P.M., a friend came over to help me, and I instructed her to take things outside. She looked at me with a question on her face but proceeded as I instructed her. As the 5:00 P.M., starting time approached, the sun began to peep through the clouds. Then the full sun appeared, quickly drying things off enough for our picnic to be held outside where I had planned and prayed it could be.

People began to arrive with their yard chairs and food, and my smiling husband directed them to a still damp back yard. We were all seated in a circle expectantly when Pastor Tom arrived. He glanced up at the bright sun and said, "Somebody's been praying; there is a seventy percent chance of rain today." I only smiled and said a silent *thank You* to God, who had answered my prayer of faith, changing the weather from rain to sunshine for our July 4 picnic!

Rose Neff Sikora

My Prayer Warrior!

"My servant Job will pray for you, and I will accept his prayer on your behalf." Job 42:8, NLT.

Last summer as I was traveling between Colorado and Minnesota, I stopped in North Platte, Nebraska, at the Walmart store to replenish my water bottle supply and other necessities. Much to my surprise I noticed my dear friend, Marie Harvard, coming down the aisle toward me. She is my prayer warrior! She has been praying for me every day since November 2005 when I left the United States to do ministry work in India.

Many people have prayed for me, but Marie is extraordinary.

During a visit at her home one Sabbath afternoon, I was impressed that this lady had a special relationship with God. She had the countenance of a peaceful, loving, and devoted servant. One who has taken hold of God's promises and prayed people around the world through their difficult and dangerous times.

We talked about many things that day, and I asked what her favorite Bible passages were. Without hesitation, she smiled and answered that there are many and she prays them over missionaries serving throughout the world. Praying the Psalms for them gives her the satisfaction that they are safe in God's loving arms no matter where they go. She feels Psalm 91 is like a gift from the Father, a gift of safety where we can walk outside in the dark knowing God's angels are with us.

During one of our conversations, Marie and I realized that she had been standing strong in prayer for me the day our mutual friend, Sheila, and I flew out of the Guwahati International Airport in India. The following day (which was our original departure date) the airport was bombed. God protected us by providing a mighty warrior who prayerfully stood in the gap for us.

It takes a special person with the diligence of a soldier to pray several times daily for those she may never meet on this earth. A prayer warrior who is willing to quietly and obediently call on God's promises to save those who are in the darkness and for safety for those who go to bring them the light. Marie is my prayer warrior. For whom are you a prayer warrior, helping fight their battles through prayer today—and every day?

Candace Zook

The Cure for Unhappiness

"Men of Galilee," they said, "why do you stand here looking into the sky? This same Jesus, who has been taken from you into heaven, will come back in the same way you have seen him go into heaven."
Acts 1:11, NIV.

U p to the point that we accept the outrageously beneficent loving sacrifice and abundant love of Jesus Christ, we cannot know real happiness. And if we experience His happiness now, already knowing that He has died to save us, imagine what our joy will be in Heaven when nothing from a sinful environment can taint our eternal happiness as we experience His visual presence. It will be as if awakening from a dream.

Those who know me best know that morning is not my forte. My children and family give me a ten- to twenty-minute grace period to get myself together.

Of course, I awaken with a list of things to do on my mind and start praying for help, guidance, and grace. I know my Lord hears.

Yet it is a bit later, in the car and during the first few hours of the day that I finally come to all my full "awakeness." I become fully aware of all the needs of the people I love, and those who have asked me to pray for them come to mind. This becomes my special time with the Lord to commune.

The time I experience my most complete happiness is when my heart and mind are totally on Jesus in prayer. I rely on Him to lead my steps before I take them. In fact, His leading me is always my prayer.

Though I long to do my best, I sometimes stumble; sometimes I even fall. My lack of heartfelt listening has allowed me to go astray even though I sometimes think I'm right. Leaving the path Jesus tries to guide me along takes me away from the joy and happiness He gives me to make it through successfully. But then I return to prayer.

Prayer is my cure for unhappiness.

"Show me your ways, LORD, teach me your paths" (Ps. 25:4, 5, NIV).

Daily, Lord, help me to stay close—ever closer to Your heart, Your will, Your guidance. Let prayer keep unhappiness from me. Keep me on Your path of happiness. Amen.

Sally J. Aken-Linke

Answered Prayer

"If you believe, you will receive whatever you ask for in prayer."
Matt. 21:22, NIV.

Here in my work, on the thirteenth floor, throughout the day, I hear the sound of cars passing by on the streets below. There are diverse sounds: honking, alarm sounds, ambulance, and police. I think about how life has been so hurried lately.

Amid such rushing and running, will people remember God as a maintainer, who sustains everything with His hands and who is ready with open arms to help us?

Ever since I was a child, my mother taught me to pray in the early morning. This habit follows me to this day. I am forty years old. Through prayer, meditation, and communion with God, I have learned many things—among them, the joy of being nice and always smiling. "A happy heart makes the face cheerful, but heartache crushes the spirit" (Prov. 15:13, NIV).

I talk to God and hear His voice speaking to my heart. He has answered my prayers, and I would like to share one of these answers with you.

I always took my husband to work and returned with the car to do my activities. He suggested I go with him to the gym and come back home, walking a distance of 2.5 kilometers. Walking home the first day, I stopped at a nearby supermarket, got excited, and bought some food. I left the supermarket with many heavy bags. I had forgotten that I was without the car. Thus, it would be impossible to walk carrying all that weight in my arms.

I prayed to God, "Lord, send someone to help me." I had walked only a block from the supermarket, when Brother Divino passed, recognized me, and stopped his car. Immediately, I told him that he was the angel God had sent to help me.

See, my beloved one, how God acts so that your prayers and mine are answered? Brother Divino told me that he was in his work and felt like going out to buy paint. He tried to refuse his insistent thought, for he would not need paint until the following week. He ended up leaving work to go buy paint right then without understanding his own actions. He traveled by a different route than he normally would have. And then he spotted me walking with heavy grocery bags!

When the Bible says that we can ask for anything, it is all right! It does not matter what it is—from a small, simple request, to a large, more complex one. Start your day with *God*!

Edna Ferreira de Souza

A Breakthrough

The LORD is my shepherd; I shall not want. . . . You prepare a table before me in the presence of my enemies; You anoint my head with oil; my cup runs over. Ps. 23:1, 5, NKJV.

My father died when I was only six, leaving also my four- and two-year-old brothers. Being a new Christian, my mother refused to follow the African custom of becoming my uncle's second wife. Consequently, she was driven from my father's family and forced to find employment in the city. My uncle, my late father's brother, refused to allow her to take us with her.

My aunt was a tough, hard-hearted woman who treated my little siblings and me as slaves. During rainy season she'd awaken us as early as 1:00 A.M. to go outside and till in her garden before we left for school. By the age of twelve, I was the cook and housekeeper for a family of nine—and never allowed to complain or ask for help. Whenever Mother visited, my aunt would not allow us to be alone with her, lest we reveal our ordeal. At the end of each visit Mother would sing and pray with us. That made a great impression on me. My favorite song that she sang was "More About Jesus." Whenever I felt overwhelmed by life's painful circumstances, this song—and the Jesus we sang about—became my comfort.

Political problems forced my uncle's family to move to the city, allowing me, though not my brothers, to finally live with my mother while Uncle paid my school expenses. My aunt assumed I'd never amount to anything. You can imagine her consternation when I passed all my classes, earning a certificate, while her daughter passed only one class. In rage, my aunt sent word that she'd soon force me to return to the country to be her gardener. I spent the whole night crying to God to set me free from this bondage. The next morning God's strong impression led me sixty kilometers away to a school district, looking for work as a nutrition teacher. I had only my grade card. Of the three applicants in line (the other two had certificates in hand) I was hired! When my aunt came looking to take me back to the country, she was infuriated to learn I was sixty kilometers away teaching. What a breakthrough from God! I would never be under her control again.

Does Satan have you in some type of bondage or "in the presence" of some enemy? Jesus is with you in your situation. Get to really know your Good Shepherd. In His time and in His ways, you will experience a breakthrough as He anoints your head with true freedom in Him.

Nokuthula Maphosa-Mutumhe

Wherever You Are, I'm There

"Your God will personally go ahead of you. He will neither fail you nor abandon you." Deut. 31:6, NLT.

I'm not one for collecting souvenirs. However, an automobile accident left me with a little memento—a bulge in my spine. While waiting for a procedure to help alleviate the pain, I was a bit apprehensive. There were no guarantees. Then I recalled the experience of one of my daughter's friends. That recollection brought me peace.

Jordan, a university student in Tennessee, worked at a daycare center. One morning he overslept, and he jumped out of bed only to trip over a shoe and cut himself shaving before rushing off to the cafeteria for breakfast. The only breakfast food left was grits, which he didn't like.

Arriving at the daycare center, Jordan met little Timmy, who was crying.

"What's the matter?" Jordan asked.

Through his tears Timmy cried, "My mommy left me here."

Jordan smiled. "Well, she'll come and pick you up later."

Timmy shook his head. "No, she won't."

"Of course, she will. Didn't your mommy pick you up yesterday?" Timmy nodded yes. "And didn't she pick you up the day before that?" Again Timmy nodded. "Then don't you think she'll pick you up today as well?" Timmy stopped crying, smiled a little smile, and everything was OK again.

After work Jordan hurried to his first class only to face an unexpected pop quiz. Later he ran into a former girlfriend whom he really didn't wish to meet. As he knelt by his bed that night, Jordan poured out his heart to God. "Lord," he said, "today has been terrible. Everything that happened was a disaster. Where were *You*?"

God seemed to respond, "Wasn't I with you yesterday—and the day before? Then don't you think I am with you today?" Jordan smiled a little smile. And everything was OK again.

Recalling this story, I, too, smiled and thanked the Lord that He would be with me during my procedure. Like Jordan, I knew that God, who was with me yesterday, would also be with me today—as well as be with me in all my tomorrows.

Marcia Mollenkopf

Wake Up and Pray!

I heard a voice of one that spake. Ezek. 1:28.

Pray for your dad." The voice was clear and distinct. It was three in the morning. I tried to ignore it and go to sleep, but sleep would not come. Praying for my dad at that time of the morning seemed absurd, but I recognized that Voice. I had heard Him before.

I slid off the bed as quietly as possible. It was urgent. I prayed earnestly for my dad. I interceded for him and asked God to intervene and deliver him from whatever the situation was. After about an hour of intercessory prayer, I went back to sleep.

The following morning I shared the unusual experience with my husband. In our family devotions that morning we again made Dad the subject of our prayer.

It was not long after that news came. My dad, an experienced seaman, had gone out on one of his regular fishing trips late one evening with my youngest brother. He was not only an outstanding seaman, but he could also accurately predict the weather. However, this time the weather suddenly became erratic and the sea had become very rough, whipped up by the fierce winds. The boat began to take in water faster than they could bail it out. They had to begin to make some life-saving decisions. To lighten the little ship they first threw overboard the evening catch of fish. The outboard motor was next to go overboard. Soon, however, the boat sank despite their best efforts. Dad and my brother clung to two buoys for dear life.

Back at home, our prayer meetings had been taking place because "Mr. Pank," as my dad was affectionately called, was the best seaman in the village. There had to be something wrong. Very wrong, because they had not returned from their trip. Police, with the help of two older brothers and friends, went in search of the missing seamen. After seven hours of searching they had to give up for the night. One of my brothers, however, refused to listen to these prophets of doom, continuing the search with another optimistic friend. He prayed as he resumed the search. At three that morning his flashlight caught sight of two persons floating on the waves: Dad and my younger brother—barely alive after more than twelve hours of battering by the rough sea.

The Holy Spirit had awakened me with, *Wake up and pray for your dad.* I thank God for that Voice that still speaks to us today. Let us each listen now for *Heaven's* prayer requests!

Claudette Garbutt-Harding

A Still, Small Voice

"My grace is sufficient for you, for My strength is made perfect in weakness." 2 Cor. 12:9, NKJV.

I began literature evangelism work at the age of sixteen though I didn't know much English. So the first couple of weeks were tough because to make sales you have to communicate. Yet I did not give up. Instead, I held on to the hands of God and made it through the ten-week program. Little did I know that would not be the only summer of literature evangelism for me.

I remember one hot summer day in Las Vegas, carrying a bag of fifteen books, which did not help me to cope with sales rejections for four hours straight. At one door I knocked for two minutes. No one answered. As I was stepping away, my feet got trapped by a wire in front of the door. Books flew everywhere as I fell on my arm. Blood stained my hands and skirt. I tried to call our team leader by walkie-talkie but soon realized the radio battery was dead. My mind went blank at that moment. I knew I could not sit on the side of the road until my leader eventually returned. So I decided to move on to the next house—where my sales pitch was rejected. Finally, my leader came by, picked me up, and quickly drove me to the hospital for a tetanus shot.

After the shot, I picked up my heavy book bag and continued working despite my sore arm. After another two hours of rejections, my level of joy was lower than empty. I stood at the beginning of a long uphill drive way and thought, *Why even bother to walk up there where I'll be rejected again?* However, I heard a still, small voice telling me to go. An older gentleman opened the door. After my introduction, I showed him couple of books. He left and soon returned with a check. Accepting the check, I started to cry my eyes out. I told the surprised gentleman what I'd gone through that morning, and he started to cry with me. He told me that his wife had just passed away a few weeks ago and that when he'd seen my books, he knew they would comfort him. Before I left, we prayed together.

Sometimes it is hard to believe in God's presence when we're going through trouble. However, God has ways of showing us His omnipresence. We must be patient, have faith, pray, and listen for His still, small voice. By falling we learn to stand. And through our honest testimonies, God will encourage others too. Don't be afraid to share your heart and blessings.

Vanya Hoyi Chan

Holding Back

Repent, and be baptized every one of you in the name of Jesus Christ
for the remission of sins, and ye shall receive the gift of the Holy Ghost.
For the promise is unto you, and to your children, and to all that are
afar off, even as many as the LORD our God shall call. Acts 2:38, 39.

I had a problem, a serious problem: I had lost the desire to live. In fact, I wanted to die, and suicide looked like the only way out.

For quite some time I refused to admit, even to myself, that there was a problem. Even when I finally came to the realization that I was in trouble, I would not acknowledge my need of help. Nor would I ask for it.

So for months I struggled on alone. Help was available, had I but the humility to admit my need of it. I see now that I could have greatly reduced my suffering by simply asking for help. Yet because of my pride, I thought I could fix the problem myself. And if, perchance, I couldn't, I would simply resign myself to my fate.

Each one of us suffers from two key problems: sin and its wages, death. Sin separates us from God, and death is its result.

In order to provide a solution to these problems, Christ came to this earth, lived a sinless life, and died on our behalf. His life takes the place of our sin-filled one, and His death replaces the death we all must die (see Rom. 5:10).

Help is there for us, and Christ is just waiting to give it to us. However, we must first realize our problem, acknowledge our need through prayer, and be willing to receive His help.

So often pride holds us back. We think it is below our dignity to ask for help, so we struggle on alone, trying to live a life that is beyond our power to live while we push the thought of death's inevitability far from our minds.

We cannot save ourselves. Without God in control of our daily lives, as we communicate with Him through prayer, we are beyond all other help. Yet when we come humbly to Him, repenting of our sin and acknowledging our need of a merciful Savior, it is then and only then that He can reconcile us to the Father, giving us the salvation we desperately need.

Ellen M. Corbett

The Recumbent Bike

You can be sure that God will take care of everything you need, his
generosity exceeding even yours in the glory that pours from Jesus.
Phil. 4:19, *The Message.*

Going to the gym was no longer safe because I have a neurological condition. My neurologist suggested that I buy a recumbent bike so I could continue to exercise in safety. Checking various online classifieds proved unfruitful, and as summer rolled around I forgot my quest.

Fast-forward to September. A friend and I were shopping at a Costco discount store when I noticed the store had recumbent bikes (a type of bicycle ridden in a recumbent position) for sale. Although they were quite expensive, I realized I still needed one. The following Monday I decided to check the on-line classifieds once again. Nothing. Then it dawned on me that God is interested even in the small details of our lives, so I prayed about it.

When I was running an errand later that morning I noticed a sporting goods consignment store that I had never seen. Should I stop or keep going? My illness requires expending a significant amount of energy to do basic things. I just wanted to go home. But with the words *go* and *stay* playing in my head, I noticed there was a place to park close to the door. I went in . . . and just about tripped over the recumbent bike that was just inside the door! The salesman said it had been brought in over the weekend—before I had even prayed! The bicycle was so perfect that I bought it on the spot.

Now, how could I get it home? I was so excited about my miracle that I went on Facebook (online social network) as soon as I got home—although I didn't say anything about needing to get the bike home. Within twenty minutes a friend called and asked, "Do you need help getting it home?" Her husband was home that day and could pick up the bike for me. Wow! He stopped at the church to pickup the pastor to help him (another miracle they were both available).

The two men picked up the bike and delivered it to my place within an hour of my purchase.

Sometimes we take only the big things to God in prayer. Yet He is interested in all aspects of our lives. We just need to remember to go to Him and not limit Him. There are many ways for Him to look after our needs. What needs can you take to Him today?

Jill Rhynard

I Know He Cares

He shall call upon me, and I will answer him: I will be with him in trouble; I will deliver him, and honour him. Ps. 91:15.

God has promised that He will answer even before we call. I experienced this first hand when we were on a trip visiting India. The train journey from Delhi to Pune seemed to take forever, but thankfully we were just one night away from reaching our destination. Everyone was busy doing their own thing. All of a sudden a passenger my parents had befriended noticed that the pouch my dad had around his wrist was missing. This wouldn't have been an issue except for the fact that this was the pouch that contained all our passports and traveler's checks.

My father pulled the chain to signal the train to slow down enough so he could jump off, followed by my brother. They both began running backwards. Within minutes the train started moving again leaving behind my dad and brother.

My mom and I were in tears, having no idea what to do or what was going to happen next if Dad and my brother couldn't find the missing pouch. We would not be able to leave the country if we did not have travel documents or even the personal ID documents that were also in the pouch.

We did the only thing we both knew we could, pray. We pleaded with God for the safety of our loved ones and for a miracle in their finding the pouch. The odds of my dad not finding the pouch were pretty strong. The stationmaster confirmed that as well when he directed us to the next large train station.

Having confidence that God could do everything, we continued to pray and trust Him. When our train pulled into the Pune station, we had a message waiting for us: not only were both my dad and brother safe, but the pouch had been found intact.

What a mighty God we serve! Not only had God used a stranger, at just the right time, to alert my dad that the pouch was missing, but against all the odds midst the teeming crowd and workers, God had kept that pouch safe and intact for my dad to find.

Many years have passed since this incident took place, but I am often reminded of this miracle and of the mighty God we serve. Tell someone today how He has answered *your* prayers.

Sharmila Rasanayagam-Osuri

The Heavenly Driver

Before they call I will answer; while they are still speaking I will hear.
Isa. 65:24, NIV.

Completing my education in the 1960s, while simultaneously working a part-time job and raising a family, I had to routinely travel between Washington, D.C.; Virginia; and Maryland. This schedule demanded a lot of daily driving time, physical energy expenditure, and alertness. One day as I left classes, I was extremely tired. Common sense told me to call my work contact, explaining I was exhausted and needed to go home to sleep. Yet I did not want to lose work time because I needed the income to support my family. So I headed to Virginia to work. Halfway through this leg of my commute, I found myself in the far left lane, dozing. I forced my eyes open and uttered a heartfelt prayer: *Dear God, please drive this car because I cannot.* Immediately, though unintentionally, I fell asleep. Seconds later a back-and-forth jostling abruptly awakened me. My car appeared to be literally jumping between other cars in the traffic, yet without hitting any.

My vehicle, now out of control, came to a stop on a grassy area to the right of the slow lane. Dazed, I saw that I was sitting in front of a house. Still in shock, I could not move. I don't know how long I sat, immobile, behind the steering wheel. Then I began to gather my senses. Feeling shaky, all I could breath was, *Thank You, God!* I wondered, *What do I do now?* I felt too scared to drive my car back up on the road. I looked at the house and felt impressed to seek help there. A man answered the door. I told him my name and what had just happened. Humbly, I requested that he please phone my workplace and inform them that I would not be at work that evening. When I told the man the name of my workplace, he said, "Really? My daughter also works there!"

"Who is your daughter?" I inquired. I actually knew his daughter from my workplace! This connection earned me that family's trust and help. How kind they were in allowing me to stay with them until my brother could arrive to pick me up and drive me home! Truly God had taken over the driving of my car when I'd fallen asleep due to my unwise decision to continue on to work. He had also "delivered" me to people with whom I would be safe.

What bumpy life commute are you experiencing right now? Do you need a heavenly Driver? If so, ask God to take the wheel, and then, in trust, watch Him get you safely home.

Joyce O'Garro

Praying Always

And pray in the Spirit on all occasions with all kinds
of prayers and requests. Eph. 6:18, NIV.

Have you ever tried to pray always—twenty-four hours a day, seven days a week? I'm not sure that this text means that we should be praying every second, but I do believe that Paul is encouraging us to live each day with a mind-set of prayer. Meaning that reaching out to God in prayer should come as naturally to us as breathing. It's easy to reach out to God when there is crisis in our lives or in the lives of persons we love or know. But living each day with a prayer mind-set no matter the situation, or the person, the event or the place, prayer should come to us naturally and easily.

Remember the story of Nehemiah, King Artaxerxes' cupbearer? Nehemiah 2 tells us that Nehemiah took wine to the king, but he was so sad by troubling news he had heard about Judah that the king noticed and asked him what was wrong: " 'Why does your face look so sad when you are not ill? This can be nothing but sadness of heart' " (Neh. 2:2, NIV). Nehemiah shared what was on his heart, and the king, who obviously favored Nehemiah, asked what he could do to help. Nehemiah's first response was *not* to share a list of concerns with the king but, rather, as verse 4 says, "Then I prayed to the God of heaven" (NIV). Amazing! Nehemiah had the ear of the king with which to share his troubled heart and mind. Yet, before he opened his mouth to answer the king, he prayed.

This is a perfect example of what it means to "pray in the Spirit on all occasions." Nehemiah lived with a mind-set of prayer; he had such a close relationship with God that turning to Him in prayer came easily.

So how do we apply this to our lives? For me it has taken practice. I've had to learn how to reach out to God in prayer at any time. To remind myself that God is the source of all wisdom, answers, comfort, strength, and so much more. So I memorized verses from the Bible on prayer. I placed small cards with verses on prayer on my bathroom mirror, my desk, and in my car. Doing this kept my mind focused on prayer, and I found myself praying about big and little things that happened each day.

We need to pray more. Not only in the morning, the evening, and before meals, but anytime, anywhere. Why? God is always ready to hear us, and He is Immanuel, God is with us.

Heather-Dawn Small

God's Artwork

"Do not be afraid or discouraged, for the LORD God, my God, is with you. He will not fail you or forsake you." 1 Chron. 28:20, NIV.

God has said, "Never will I leave you; never will I forsake you." Heb. 13:5, NIV.

One of our family's favorite vacation spots is Lake Powell. It's a place of stark contrasts; sometimes quiet, sometimes tumultuous, calm, then dramatic sky fire from electrical storms, often ending with a beautiful rainbow! How can one not marvel at the works of our God displaying His colorful and beautiful artwork! I am awed every time His paintbrush sweeps across the canvas of the sky with large, bold colors of every hue.

It is interesting that when we see God's artwork, it's usually after a rainstorm. When there are dark clouds, a rainbow is often reflected off an oil slick. During our times of tears, when days are dark and dreary, or when things just aren't what they are supposed to be, He will bring rainbows on the horizon of our lives if we continue to trust in Him.

Rainbows in our lives may come in unexpected ways, such as an unexpected, encouraging letter in the mail, a phone call, a touch on the arm, a hug, or a song that has a special meaning.

I remember a real rainbow day, a day when our sons were young. It had been a difficult day. The boys weren't obeying and were especially ornery. I prayed that God would give me wisdom and courage as a parent. Later that day as I was driving from our home to do some errands, I looked up toward Mount San Bernardino and there it was—a complete double rainbow! I had to stop and wipe tears from my eyes. I had no doubt that God had spoken to me that day through His artwork. He was assuring me that He was in control and had given a sign of His enduring love for me and my children.

I have sent many letters through the years to our dental patients, church members, and others who are going through difficult seasons in their lives. God gives me words of encouragement to pass on in what I call "the rainbow letter." Written on rainbow stationary, the rainbow reminds us that God always keeps His promise of the rainbow: "I will never leave you or forget you, and I love you very much."

I pray that when you see a rainbow in your sky, you will hear God speaking to you.

Bonnie R. Parker

After Midnight

"The LORD does not look at the things people look at. People look at
the outward appearance, but the LORD looks at the heart."
1 Sam. 16:7, NIV.

It will not get dark tonight," my son told me one July day in Alaska. "And with no restrictions set by the Fish and Game Department, we'll be able to fish all night." He and his wife, like so many Alaskans, looked forward to filling their freezer for the winter. And so, when we arrived at the beach at 11:00 P.M., they grabbed their twenty-foot-long dip nets and waded into the mouth of the tidal river.

My husband and I set up the tent, spread out the sleeping bags, and went down to the shore. Larry was in charge of assisting Garrick and Stephanie when they struggled to shore with a fish. My role was to hold Derion, our six-week-old grandson. The sun set around midnight, but daylight lingered in the sky until 2:00 A.M. when clouds moved in and it became harder to see our children in the water. I decided it was time to go to sleep so, with Derion still sleeping in the front pack, I walked over the sand to the steep metal bridge that protected a sand dune when thousands of feet moved from cars to the beach, from the beach to the washrooms and then to tents pitched on the beach. As I neared the end of the bridge, I saw that I would need to take a huge step to move onto the level ground.

Lord, what shall I do? I breathed. The flat light made it hard to judge distance, my balance was precarious because of the baby I was supporting, and chronic pain in my knees made me even more nervous. And then at the end of the bridge I saw him: long hair in a ponytail, a beard blowing in the light breeze; his leather jacket would have looked at home on a motorcycle. Tattoos emerged from his sleeves and snaked onto his hands. Multiple piercings decorated his face. I felt vulnerable and uncomfortable, a lone woman in the dark. But he saw my predicament, put his hand under my elbow and gently helped me down. With a quick, "God bless," he vanished from my sight. But not from my thoughts.

I had been quick to judge my benefactor based on the fact that he dressed and adorned himself in ways alien to me. But our brief encounter revealed a kind heart and a willingness to bear witness to the One who lived in his heart. I had come to false conclusions based on his outward appearance—and I needed to change my heart.

Denise Dick Herr

Who Am I?

And God said, Let us make man in our image. Gen. 1:26.

Dear God:
I have asked myself this question—oh, so many times: Who am I?

Though I come up with differing answers, they all have a common thread. That thread is You . . . at work in me.

Every time I seek a new answer to my "Who am I?" question, I receive more insight into what You are doing in my life: shaping, pruning, molding me, Jasmine Elaine, as I limp and shuffle along life's road. As I journey with You, entering more and more into Your likeness.

During my sixty-five years of life, I have at times fallen on my face in mud from hell. At other times, I've disappeared into potholes dug by the enemy of my soul. But my Lord and Savior has never failed to come searching for me, rescuing me without reproach. He, each time, accepts my feeble apology and helps me cast off my filthy garments. He washes me and anoints my bruised body with the oil of His Spirit.

Oh, how good and gracious is my Lord and Savior! He looks at me, sees who I am, and accepts me, anyhow. My Lord is not trying to make me into someone I am not. No, He's helping me mold and shape my life into what He intended me to be. My best—rather, His best. Jasmine Elaine, the person uniquely created by Him and distinct from every other person on this planet.

Oh, God, as I continue my life's journey, I train my eyes steadfastly on Christ. I yield myself to His Spirit because the work in me is not yet finished.

Who am I?

You, through John, have told me the truest answer in these words: "Beloved, now are we the sons of God, and it doth not yet appear what we shall be: but we know that, when he shall appear, we shall be like him; for we shall see him as he is" (1 John 3:2).

So, God, I don't need to worry or fret. As long as I yield myself to Your unfailing grace, I will complete my journey; for I am pressing "toward the mark for the prize of the high calling of God" (Phil. 3:14). It is only then I will behold who I am: a child of God made in His image. Thanks be to You, Father, for Your unfailing grace, faithfulness, and hope in Jesus Christ.

Jasmine E. Grant

The God Phone

But the Comforter, which is the Holy Ghost, whom the Father will send in my name, he shall teach you all things, and bring all things to your remembrance, whatsoever I have said unto you. John 14:26.

The office staff of my husband Bob was having a special potluck that day to celebrate their new building. Each staff member was supposed to bring a dish for six to eight people. The night before, I prepared my favorite salad for my husband to take with him to the potluck.

That morning Bob had left for work after a hug and a peck for me—but he forgot to take the salad.

I ran out to the street in my sweats, waving my arms frantically to see if I could catch him. I was too late, so I called his cell phone. It was off.

Suddenly the words, "bring all things to your remembrance," came to my mind. Oh yes! I could call on God! "Dear God, I'm sorry I always seem to call on You last, but could You please remind Bob of the salad and have him turn around?" I cried aloud apologetically.

Bob has a history of never turning around to get something left at home once he is on the road. I was afraid that even if he remembered the salad, he would shrug it off and not turn around. Besides, wasn't God too busy to bother with small things like a forgotten salad?

But I should not have been surprised when my husband came driving back into the driveway a few minutes later. I met him on the front porch with the salad and said, "I tried to wave you down on the street and I called you on the phone, but it was turned off. Finally, I prayed for you to remember and turn around."

Bob answered, "Well, it worked!"

"No, honey, God worked. Now go have fun at your potluck!"

Later, I had to laugh as I read John 14:26: "But the Comforter, which is the Holy Ghost, whom the Father will send in my name, he shall teach you all things, and bring all things to your remembrance, whatsoever I have said unto you."

God certainly can bring all things to our remembrance, even a potluck salad! That day my husband and I learned that it is better to call on God first, even before calling on the cell phone.

Mary Louis

God Surpasses Our Expectations

But as it is written, Eye hath not seen, nor ear heard, neither have entered into the heart of man, the things which God hath prepared for them that love him. 1 Cor. 2:9.

This was a new experience for me—house hunting! Work-related issues necessitated that my family and I relocate to another country. Consequently, I found myself searching for a house to rent. I was aware of my family's needs and requirements and tried my best to find a suitable house. This proved to be quite a challenge. Over a period of several weeks I was introduced to a number of properties, none of which seemed suitable.

Finally, I was shown a property that, in my mind, would be the perfect choice. The size, location, and price all fit into our needs. I took photos of the property and sent them to family still back in our homeland. They agreed that we should rent that one. I contacted the landlord and prepared to sign the lease and make the appropriate payments. "I rented it just yesterday," he informed me." How disappointing!

I informed my family, told my supportive coworker, and consoled myself that God must have a better plan. And I prayed.

During the next few days, my coworker and I took up the arduous task of house hunting again, but without success. One evening at about eleven-thirty, a friend of mine, whose hospital shift had ended half an hour earlier, came to my home to hand me a slip of paper bearing a telephone number. "The person at this number just posted information about a rental property on the hospital bulletin board," she informed me.

The next day I called the number. The person on the other end insisted that I come immediately to see the property. I asked my coworker to take me, and he agreed. We were pleasantly surprised at the quality, the location, and the rental fee for the property. The offer surpassed my family's expectations in every way! Indeed, God had a better plan.

Often we see palatial homes on this earth and admire them, knowing that we may never be able to afford such. We can take courage in Jesus' words "in my Father's house are many mansions." God has gone to prepare for us what "eye hath not seen." This earthly rental home exceeded my expectations. Our heavenly homes will exceed them so much more!

Gerene I. Joseph

Roxy

And all things, whatsoever ye shall ask in prayer, believing,
ye shall receive. Matt. 21:22.

"Mom, you've got to pray for Roxy!" My son's voice on the phone sounded frantic.

Concerned, I asked, "What's the matter?" Roxy was my granddaughter's new puppy, a tiny brown and white wiggly bundle of joy. And oh, how little Juliana loved her. In fact, we all loved her!

"Juliana was carrying some straight pins," Rich continued, "and dropped them on the floor. Roxy ran over and swallowed one before Juliana could pick it up. We rushed her to the vet. After taking an X-ray and finding the pin, she explained that Roxy had to have surgery or she would die."

My son continued, "There was one other option that the vet explained. We could take Roxy to an emergency vet clinic and perhaps that vet could reach down into her stomach with little pinchers at the end and pull the straight pin out. Madelin [my daughter-in-law] and Juliana took her there. Unfortunately, Roxy's stomach was full of food, so the pin was buried. The vet couldn't find it. Madelin and Juliana are on their way home. I can't afford three thousand dollars for the surgery, so we all need to pray."

I promised I would pray. And I did. "Dear God, please spare Roxy. Juliana is only eleven, and she loves Roxy with all her heart. I don't know how you'll do it, but please spare that little puppy's life." I must say that I had doubts. How could a straight pin possibly make its way through all those tightly wound puppy intestines without any damage?

About ten minutes later, the phone rang again. It was a jubilant Juliana.

She said, "On the way home, Mommy said, 'We forgot to pray to Jesus.' So we pulled over to the side of the road and prayed. Grandma, Roxy's not going to die. I prayed to Jesus and He told me she would be all right."

Four long, worrisome days later, a happy Juliana called again. "Grandma, Roxy passed the pin. She's going to be all right just like Jesus told me." Today Roxy is a healthy one-year-old pup and still a wiggly bundle of joy. So whatever you are facing in your day today, please remember the important lesson that a child taught me: nothing is too hard for God!

Dalores Broome Winget

July 23

He Hears and Answers Prayer

"Call upon Me in the day of trouble; I will deliver you, and you shall glorify Me." Ps. 50:15, NKJV.

Fourteen of us who had been on a week-long cruise (celebrating my friend Dee's and my birthdays) arrived back at port. We'd all had fun and felt relaxed after picking up luggage from the holding area. However, my suitcase did not appear on the conveyor belt. We searched all other nearby areas. "I can't find my suitcase," I told a baggage assistant.

"Then you need to fill out a lost luggage form at the office. We'll ship it to your address when we find it." I chose to remain calm and prayerful, leaving the lost suitcase in the hands of the Lord.

Two days later, I came home from doing some errands. There on my front porch was my lost suitcase! I thanked the Lord for two reasons. First, my suitcase had been found and sent to me. Second, this suitcase weighed fifty pounds, and I didn't have to load it into my car and then unload it. FedEx had done it for me!

But that wasn't the end of the cruise-related "losses." The week of my return I needed to pay a bill but couldn't find my checkbook. For two days I searched and prayed. That second night God brought to my mind what my sister, Joyce, had said to me before I'd left on the cruise: "Leave your checkbook and wallet in the guest bedroom dresser drawer here in my house." Though we'd both returned to her house after the cruise, we'd both forgotten about the items I'd left in the dresser. When we parted ways, I finished my long trip home, and Joyce had gone to visit in North Carolina.

Fortunately, my other sister Peg lives next door to Joyce. A quick long-distance phone call to Peg sent her quickly over to Joyce's, where she found my missing items—plus some others I'd forgotten leaving there. FedEx came in handy once again as my sister and her husband shipped my things to me.

Don't we serve a wonderful and caring God? We don't have to fret or worry but rather let "petitions and praises shape our worries into prayers " (Phil. 4:16, *The Message*). I had called upon God in my day of trouble, and He had "delivered" me—*and* my lost items.

Patricia Mulraney Kovalski

In God's Sight

Keep me as the apple of your eye; hide me in the shadow
of your wings. Ps. 17:8, NIV.

It was Friday, and my right eye was still red and uncomfortable. I worked
that evening but didn't feel well. Remembering that it is difficult to find
ophthalmologist help on weekends, I decided to leave work early and seek
medical attention.

I found a clinic online, but when I phoned, the receptionist said that the
doctors had already left. I decided to venture out. First, I drove to a clinic and
saw that the practice had moved.

Heartbroken, I prayed to God. I told Him, "Lord, I am not able to spend
the weekend with my eye hurting this way. Please, help me find a doctor able to
examine me."

I remembered the address of another clinic and went to this place next.
The very friendly receptionist pointed me to an ophthalmologist in one of the
commercial buildings near there. Sunset was approaching. Sabbath would soon
arrive. I still had not found a doctor.

I saw medical doctor signs on four different offices, but all were closed for the
weekend. At last I found a clinic one of the other floors.

The receptionist said no doctor could see me. I begged—but in vain. Then,
seeing my distress, she told me that there was a doctor in another tower, Dr.
Eduardo. Maybe he could see me.

I walked to the other tower, checked for the location of the office, and went
in.

The doctor kindly received me and examined my eye. He found an ulcer
of the cornea, explaining to me what it was and the best way to treat it. I was
delighted to have found help with this doctor.

Right there, I raised my grateful thoughts to God in prayer, thanking Him
for His care. Upon returning home, I was thinking about that situation and I
remembered the request of King David to the Lord, "Keep me as the apple of
your eye" (Ps. 17:8).

How uncomfortable and painful it was to have one of my eyes hurting! I
wondered what God feels when one of His daughters is afflicted, wounded,
asking for help. The Lord truly does keep us as the apple of His eye. If something
hurts it, He certainly feels it. He rushes to help, to give relief, to show how much
He loves us.

Janine Schwanz Ramos

Experiencing God's Presence in the Storm

"I will never leave you nor forsake you." Josh.1:5, NIV.

The Bible is filled with assurances that God is with us even in our times of greatest distress. We are taught that He walks with us through the storms of life—times of grief and loss, times of fear and anxiety. Yet most of us find that in our own personal storms, intellectual knowledge of God's goodness and faithfulness is not enough. Each of us must discover for ourselves that He truly is with us during those times and that He allows them for a purpose.

I have friends who are trying desperately to find God's promised Presence in their own furnaces of affliction. One has been diagnosed with cancer; another has lost a job because of vicious lies told about her by a church member; yet another friend has lost a beloved husband who was a faithful leader in the church. All three of these women of faith dedicated their lives long ago to serving Him and others, yet each of them has been haunted by the question, "Why did God allow this to happen to me/my loved one? Where was He when I needed Him most?"

Mary and Martha wondered the same things when Jesus didn't arrive in time to heal their brother, Lazarus. They loved and trusted Jesus as much as any of His followers, yet they still questioned why He arrived four days too late to save their brother. Soon, though, they understood. When Jesus called Lazarus from the tomb, they and everyone who witnessed the event realized that Jesus had the power of life over death and was, indeed, God incarnate.

In my own time of greatest loss, I was blessed to have godly friends who counseled me to seek God in the Scriptures and other inspired writings. As I read again about the final week of Jesus' life on earth and the unspeakable suffering He endured for *me,* I was convicted that I could never suffer as He did. While that conviction didn't immediately give me all the faith I needed to endure the furnace, it helped me focus on God's sovereignty and great love for me. I learned that as I clung to Him when I didn't understand, my faith was bolstered, and I received strength to endure, and eventually—unexpectedly—to thrive.

I experienced the truth of the words of poet John Greenleaf Whittier: "Nothing before, nothing behind; / The steps of faith / Fall on the seeming void, and find / The rock beneath."

As we cling to Jesus, we *will* experience the Rock beneath our faltering steps.

Carla Baker

Evidences of Divine Activity

Blessed is the one who does not walk in step with the wicked or stand in the way that sinners take or sit in the company of mockers, but whose delight is in the law of the LORD, and who meditates on his law day and night. Ps. 1:1, 2, NIV.

I've been impressed how the Holy Spirit leads the minds of mothers who put themselves in the hands of God to raise their children. In devotional books I read of experiences around the planet similar to mine—even though the writers and I don't know each other. But God knows us.

When I was born, my mother was already forty-two. So, in my teens, she was more of a grandmother than a mother. A simple woman. A widow. Yet she always had a deep relationship with God and was endowed with discernment and wisdom that could only come from the Holy Spirit leading in all things for her and her children, my two younger sisters and myself.

On one occasion, in the town where we lived, there was a party with performances of secular singers. My friends wanted me go. They were willing to request permission of my mother, but I decided to ask her myself. I asked my mother for permission to attend the concert with my friends. Instead of arguing with me, she simply asked me to read Psalm 1 and then to make my own decision. How wise she was with the wisdom of Heaven!

Today, as an educator, I know that there could be no wiser way than that to interact with a teenage girl. Although I had been baptized at the age of ten, that moment of conviction after advice from my mother was my real conversion. The responsibility for my choice was placed in my own hands. I had to decide which way to go. I know Mother was praying at that moment. For the words of the psalmist pierced my heart and weighed heavily on my mind. I had previously read the psalms as a child. But never had one held such meaning to me as at that moment of decision. Those words repeated themselves in my mind: *"having my delight in the law of the Lord . . . my delight shall be in the law of the Lord . . ."* That's it, I realized. My delight must be in the law of the Lord.

The Holy Spirit continues to work in the minds of pious mothers who cry for heavenly wisdom in the raising of their children. So, mothers and others, "If any of you lacks wisdom, you should ask God, who gives generously to all . . . and it will be given to you" (James 1:5, NIV).

Lidia Graepp Voos

Miracle at Nine

And they brought young children to him, that he should touch them: and his disciples rebuked those that brought them. But when Jesus saw it, he was much displeased, and said unto them, Suffer the little children to come unto me, and forbid them not: for of such is the kingdom of God. Verily I say unto you, Whosoever shall not receive the kingdom of God as a little child, he shall not enter therein.

Mark 10:13-15.

Waiting for my parents to come back from the party had become long and tiring. My seven-year-old sister, my five-year-old brother, and I (nine years old) had enjoyed an evening of play, but our nine-thirty bedtime was fast approaching. My aunt bundled us into our coats and tucked us into one of her beds, while she went downstairs to wait for my parents to come.

It was the first time I tried sleeping on my back, thinking that would be the best way to fit us all comfortably onto one bed. Both my sister and brother fell asleep quickly. It took me longer to get used to the foreign bed and nod off to sleep. Suddenly, my tongue slipped into my throat, causing my breathing to stop, and awaking me. I felt completely paralyzed while my siblings slept next to me and my auntie patiently waited downstairs for my parents. I could not call for help or move a finger. The only answer I had was God, as my parents had always taught us. I recalled all the stories at once, how He saved the Israelites from the Egyptians through the Red Sea and David from the giant Goliath. I mentally cried one of the shortest prayers of my life, *Lord, if I have no purpose in this life then let me die. If I have a purpose, please let me live.*

Just then, what felt like hands pushed on my back and flipped me over. My tongue fell out of my throat. I gasped for air—and finally breathed it in! Now fully awake, I looked around the room to see who had rescued me from death. No one else was in the room. My sister and brother were still asleep beside me and my aunt was still downstairs. It was then I realized that God had saved me in a miraculous way. I am still discovering my purpose in this life. The one thing that cannot be taken away from me is that night when God heard my prayer and loved me desperately enough to save me. This event helped shaped my character.

Lord, I thank You for my life and the people whom I have met along the way. Please refine me for Your kingdom. Amen.

Gail Frampton

The Attitude of Prayer

Be anxious for nothing, but in everything by prayer and supplication,
with thanksgiving, let your requests be made known to God.
Phil. 4:6, NKJV.

Have you noticed that sometimes it is easier to remain in the attitude of prayer if your day isn't going well. You may seem to be constantly saying, "please" and "thank you," to Him. I recently had one of those days. On Wednesday morning, I was notified that a friend of forty-four years had died. That evening, at church midweek service, some friends noticed my car's transmission fluid leaking. They determined that I could safely drive the short distance home but should drive no more until my car could be repaired. The following morning I was informed that my deceased friend's funeral service would be the coming Sunday. I immediately stressed out. I currently had no transportation and had previously promised to be in charge of a dinner for the large family of the deceased, as well as guests, following the funeral service. *Dear Lord,* I prayed, *we've got to have a serious talk. I need Your help.*

I rented a car Friday morning for a special weekend price, and, upon returning it, I found I had to pay only half of the previously quoted price.

The first thing on my list of errands was a stop at the bank's drive-thru window for some cash. Somehow, as I was putting the money-transfer tube back in the outside holder, with my driver's license and check in it, both fell out and disappeared. When I didn't find either my license or check in or under the car, I moved the vehicle forward and looked, again. No success. *Lord, please help me,* I prayed in desperation. Just after my heavenward plea, a lovely lady in the next drive-thru lane pulled her car over to help me look. Finally, we located the missing items.

As I tried to drive away from the bank, the steering wheel on my rental car locked so I couldn't drive. With a prayer, I called the rental agency. The right person was able to phone to talk me through the problem. Later, another "right" gentleman shared how I could add transmission fluid to an idling engine. It seemed as if angels were assisting me every step of the day. When I returned home, an unexpected card awaited from a friend that said she cares about me and considers me special. And so ended the day that began as a "poor me" day. I was surely reminded that a loving, prayer-hearing God honors an attitude of prayer throughout each day.

Dorothy Wainwright Carey

Three Laws of Prayer—Part 1

"Ask, and it will be given to you; seek, and you will find; knock, and it will be opened to you. For everyone who asks receives, and he who seeks finds, and to him who knocks it will be opened."
Matt. 7:7, 8, NASB.

Christ's use of three brief words introducing each law of prayer—ask, seek, knock—are not mere repetitions or redundancies. They might mean the same thing in some languages, but in this context of Christ's encouraging comment on our prayer life, they do not.

These commands denote a progressive movement toward the specific goal. They are like walking through the courts of the temple in the sanctuary that God instructed Moses and the people of Israel to build (Exod. 25:8). "Ask" represents the outer court. "Seek" is more than ask, for it leads one into the Holy Place. "Knock" is beyond them both, for it is an invitation into the Most Holy Place, where we may stand boldly before the throne of grace in the presence of God.

Law 1: Ask and it will be given to you. If anyone wants to test the validity of prayer, they must begin by asking. This, however, does not mean one gets anything or everything requested. Jesus did not promise or place the divine treasures and powers at the command of the immature, the irresponsible, and those who refuse to accept His call to join His family and be faithful to His Father.

This reminds me of a story about a physician who saw a woman praying by the bedside of her dying friend. Half contemptuously, he asked if she really thought there was any good in prayer. When she answered in the affirmative, he said "If I ask God for one hundred dollars, do you think I will get it?"

To his surprise, she said, "No!" Then she explained. "Do you know the President of the United States?"

"No," he answered."

"Would you ask him for one hundred dollars on a first introduction?"

"Of course not," said the doctor.

"Then why would you expect my Lord to give you one hundred dollars on a slight acquaintance?"

We can approach Christ and ask, because we know Him and are known of Him.

Hyveth Williams

Three Laws of Prayer—Part 2

"Seek, and you will find." Matt. 7:7, NASB.

In discussing the three laws of prayer, based on Matthew 7:7, 8, we have established that the first law is *ask.*

Yet there is more confusion in the average mind about unanswered prayers than most any other thing in Christianity.

Some complain saying, "Jesus said, 'Ask, and you will receive.' I have prayed and I have not received. Therefore, prayer doesn't work."

Yet, let's consider some of the reasons for the lack of answers.

Perhaps our human expectations differ significantly from the divine response.

Maybe, as James said, "You ask and do not receive, because you ask with wrong motives, so that you may spend it on your pleasures" (James 4:3, NASB). How many times have we asked God for things that afterwards we knew would not have been right for us?

What Jesus wants us to understand and have from this first law is the assurance that when we "ask," regardless of the outcome, there will be an answer (see Isa. 65:24).

Law 2: Seek and you will find. Seeking means persistence, and perseverance promises progress.

The one who asks and stops when there is no immediate answer is like some followers who were content to touch only the hem of Jesus' garments and never pursue His spiritual blessing, as did the woman with the issue of blood. Yet, through engaging her in dialogue about her need, Christ drew her to an intimate relationship with Him and then opened her spiritual understanding. Like such, many today are satisfied with just a touch of the fringes of the spiritual world now and again.

But the persistent seeker, who is willing to push past the apparent obstacles and come to the door of hope with great anticipation, will gain entrance—if not on the face of their faithfulness, then definitely on the fact of His sacrifice.

The one who merely asks discovers that there is something there. However, the one who *seeks* finds the treasure.

Hyveth Williams

Three Laws of Prayer—Part 3

"Knock, and it will be opened to you. For everyone who asks receives,
and he who seeks finds, and to him who knocks it will be opened."
Matt. 7:7, 8, NASB.

We are looking at three laws of prayer. The first two laws were to *ask* and to *seek*.

Law 3: Knock and the door will be opened to you. A knock is the moment of certainty. One has to be sure they want what they ask for. One must be specific about that which they are seeking, especially when their hand is raised in midair and about to rap on the door that is bound to open into the throne of grace. That personal certainty is mightier than anything we can imagine. Again James speaks to this issue: "Elijah was a man with a nature like ours, and he prayed earnestly that it would not rain, and it did not rain on the earth for three years and six months. Then he prayed again, and the sky poured rain and the earth produced its fruit" (James 5:17, 18, NASB).

Knock and you will see that the door swings open on earth for you to enter into heavenly places by faith. For some of us the door will not open very far on this side because we lack wisdom.

Let us hear again from James: "If any of you lacks wisdom, you should ask God, who gives generously to all without finding fault, and it will be given to you. *But when you ask, you must believe and not doubt, because the one who doubts is like a wave of the sea, blown and tossed by the wind.* That person should not expect to receive anything from the Lord. Such a person is double-minded and unstable in all they do" (James 1:5–8, NIV; italics added).

When we ask, it is given to us. When we go a few steps farther and seek, we discover to our delight that we also find what we are looking for and, sometimes, much more. If we persist, not giving up but proceeding with specificity to knock, God is always eager to open the doors of opportunity and grace to us.

If, for some reason, you are unable to apply any of these laws to your life and experience, take heart. God's grace is so magnanimous He has arranged it so that when other faithful souls open the door through prayer, glory spills out into the lives of those who didn't even ask.

Remember, the door is wide open to all. Just walk right in, boldly sit right down before the throne of grace, and say, "Abba, Father!"

Hyveth Williams

Living His Persistence

Persistence: the quality that allows someone to continue doing something or trying to do something even though it is difficult or opposed by other people.

And being in anguish, he prayed more earnestly, and his sweat was like drops of blood falling to the ground. Luke 22:44, NIV.

During the days of Jesus' life on earth, he offered up prayers and petitions with fervent cries and tears to the one who could save him from death. Heb. 5:7, NIV.

For the joy set before him he endured the cross, scorning its shame, and sat down at the right hand of the throne of God. Heb. 12:2, NIV.

Persistence is a steadfast courage that says, "I won't give up!" Words such as *earnestly*, *fervent*, and *endured* reveal this very quality in the life of Christ. Even today He is persistent in His pursuit of us and His patience with us.

This month's contributors have found evidence of God's persistence in many places—in the lingering fragrance of perfume or while watching a little bird build its nest. Others are learning persistence themselves. Dirty fingerprints on glass doors reminded one weary mother of God's patience with her and of her need to be patient with others. And then there's the brain surgery survivor, learning to walk again, who reaped the rewards of Heaven-empowered perseverance. As will we, when we live out His persistence.

And Still I Rise

Consider it pure joy, my brothers and sisters, whenever you face trials of many kinds, because you know that the testing of your faith produces perseverance. Let perseverance finish its work so that you may be mature and complete, not lacking anything. James 1:2-4, NIV.

By chance, or perhaps providence, I turned on the evening news. This was uncharacteristic of me in that my time is almost always totally consumed by travel and attention only to necessary projects during my few evenings enjoyed at home. However, for a fleeting moment this particular evening the news announcer caught my attention with a teaser for an upcoming report. After the commercial I was awestruck by an incredibly inspiring story.

The news story shared the special achievement of an eighteen-year-old high school graduate giving her valedictory speech in which she shared from the circumstances of her short life. She told the listeners how her father had died when she was only a year old and how she had lost her mother as well. She chronicled how she had come to live in an orphanage and throughout high school essentially lived in a homeless shelter and indeed was still living there.

Then, belying her brief eighteen years, she shared her advice—the wisdom of age—with her class and with the rest who were listening.

She reminded the listeners that we must not get caught up in temporary circumstances to the degree that we allow them to define us and dictate our outcomes in life. Like the apostle James she understood identity and perseverance and their importance in life. She reminded me of something I once learned: we must not confuse the journey for the destination.

Another perspective might be that we must never confuse the detour for the path. Life is full of pitfalls. At times we fall or are forced into one, but we must always get back up. We must climb up and out and restart on our course of calling. God always calls us out.

That's one reason I love some of the words from the poem and song, "Still I Rise" (1978). In her work, the late Maya Angelou described some terribly challenging circumstances of life and ended each scenario with the inspiring words, "still I rise." Her statement each time was a declarative, never wavering in strength and conviction.

This is the type of conviction we must have in the knowledge of our victory in Jesus.

Ella Louise Smith Simmons

God Is So Good!

God has said, "Never will I leave you; never will I forsake you."
Heb. 13:5, NIV.

By August of 1998 I'd been battling health problems for eighteen months. I'd been put under the care of a neurologist with whom I'd been discussing my severe headaches and nausea. I had lost weight and energy. I had lost my job. Finally, I'd also lost hope. Though only forty-two years old, I felt ready to die. A physical therapist ruled out vertigo and referred me to a chiropractor. He asked my neurologist to schedule me for an MRI.

I had the MRI procedure on Monday morning. It revealed a golfball-size mass in my brain. That very afternoon the medical partner of my neurologist (who was out of town) scheduled immediate surgery to remove it. I prayed for God's wisdom and notified my parents and oldest daughter that I was being admitted to the hospital. I was happy to finally have an explanation of the health problems I'd been having, but it was a tremendous shock for my family and friends. Many knew I'd been having problems, but hadn't known the severity. Family members came to support me and my daughters. Previous coworkers visited me in the hospital.

My family wondered how I could pay the medical bills following surgery. At times like this, all you can do is pray and ask God to help you hold on. Thanks to the earlier prompting of the Holy Spirit, I had continued my medical coverage, paying the premiums myself. After all of my medical treatments, I added up the bills. Out of a little over thirty thousand dollars paid out, I'd had to pay only about one thousand dollars. God is so good!

Friends and family helped me financially and provided twenty-four-hour care until I could be independent again. Coworkers from my recent work site brought meals for several weeks. Others drove me to my radiation treatment appointments. Though a challenge, I learned to walk again as surgery had impacted my nerves. God enabled my persistence—first, with a wheelchair; next, with a walker; and, finally, on my own two legs. When I thanked the chiropractor, five years later, for his earlier intervention, he suggested I "pay it forward" by helping others. I do that when I can. I want to do for others as God has done for me.

God is good! To me and to you! Right now, think about how He has blessed you, your family, and your friends. Then go out and pass it forward. Bless somebody else today.

Carol Jean Marino

Never Abandoned!

"Be strong and courageous. Do not fear or be in dread of them, for it is the LORD your God who goes with you. He will not leave you or forsake you." Deut. 31:6, ESV.

When my daddy was a little boy, his daddy (my grandfather) was abusive. Although Daddy feared his dad, he still loved him so much! When my father was eight years old, my grandpa abandoned the family.

Not too long ago my daddy was sharing stories with us, and with tears in his eyes he said, "I begged my dad to stay. When he left, I prayed every day that he would return. Despite my fervent prayer, he didn't come back."

The first time I met my grandpa, I was seven years old. Though with him for only a few moments, we all fell in love with our *"abuelito."* Shortly after I met him, Grandpa had a sudden heart attack.

The day of his funeral I clearly remember my cousins, my sister, and I crying so much. My daddy cried too. In my mind's eye, I can still see him hugging the coffin and saying, "Please, Dad . . . please don't go!"

I think that being abandoned as a little boy and then having his father back for such a short time was very difficult for my father. In fact, Daddy's heart grew cold. He would come to church from time to time but had such a hard time making a commitment.

Dad had prayed persistently for his own father; we now prayed and prayed for him. Then, after many years, one Sabbath after potluck, we got the wonderful news that Daddy had made his decision to surrender to the heavenly Father. The one who never left him and who always loved him with an everlasting love! On August 20, 2011, my husband had the privilege of baptizing my daddy. We were able to witness a miracle, a child reunited with His heavenly Father! "For this my son was dead, and is alive again; he was lost, and is found" (Luke 15:24). What a heavenly celebration!

Let us "be unceasing in prayer [praying perseveringly]" (1 Thess. 5:17, AMP) for our loved ones. Let's remember that our heavenly Father longs to spend time with us and embrace us when we run to His arms of love, fully trusting that He will never leave us nor forsake us.

Sayuri Ruiz Rodriguez

Dirty Fingerprints

In every thing give thanks: for this is the will of God in Christ Jesus concerning you. 1 Thess. 5:18.

After a late-night, weekly house-cleaning session, I felt irritated the following morning having to reclean tiny toddler prints from the slider door window—*again.* "Housework!" I grumbled to myself. "Why can't it just stay done for a day or two? I am so exasperated and discouraged from constantly doing the same chores. Lord, I am trying to be a good homemaker, but, honestly, I feel like a complete failure."

Wiping dirty, sticky fingers, I set my two toddler sons down for a favorite moment of reading together. Precious yet very active little boys, they had no idea of my mounting frustration in the area of housework. We pleasantly worked our way through Richard Scarry books, and too soon, kitchen duty necessitated my mopping up spilled juice on the floor—*again.*

Mrs. Tiggywinkle pawed at the slider door, and the boys were so excited, they signaled her with their little hands by patting them on the window pane. I groaned as I let kitty inside and reached for the window cleaner—*again.*

In my moment of resentment and discouragement with these repeating chores, I suddenly heard a distinct message, "Be happy you have children that can leave fingerprints on the windows." Wow, that was a unique thought this mommy needed to hear! As a speech and language pathologist, I had seen disabled children with severe disabilities, unable to do simple toddler tasks. I suddenly "got it." Ashamed, I prayed for forgiveness and, with humility, thanked God for His simple message of truth. My boys were healthy and active. They had the ability of making messes and leaving dirty fingerprints all over the house. I felt blessed, invigorated to take up the ongoing challenges of parenting.

I can't say I love housework, but I can honestly say I have never looked at dirty fingerprints in the same way—*again.* God gave me a major attitude adjustment and a fresh perspective. Today, as I wipe the smudgy windows, I thank God for grandchildren and great nieces and nephews that leave grimy fingerprints on doors and windows and lasting imprints of love on my heart.

Donna Reese

What's That Fragrance?

"You neglected the usual courtesy of olive oil to anoint my head, but she has covered my feet with rare perfume." Luke 7:46, TLB.

Science has discovered ways to put a fragrance on a little piece of paper for advertising purposes. These small scratch-and-sniff cards are then inserted into magazines to let people know what a new perfume smells like. By gently scratching an infused paper, one can release the fragrance within.

Though these small cards are meant to release their scent when you scratch them or pull the paper apart, they are often releasing fragrance even without being pulled apart. Since these scent cards are now being enclosed in our local newspaper, I can sometimes find my newspaper in the early morning light without being able to see it. I can smell it! I don't like scents that are so overpowering they make my eyes water and give me a headache. In etiquette classes we girls were taught to use perfume discreetly so, as one school chum said, we wouldn't be among those that could be smelled "both coming and going"—as one does a livestock feedlot.

The subject of fragrances reminds me of a long-ago banquet room where a young woman, Mary, quietly entered, unnoticed. She slipped behind Jesus and anointed Him with fragrant perfume of great value. Soon the sweet scent drifted through the air, and people began to notice what she had done. When onlookers criticized her, she persisted in her gesture of love. Jesus came to her defense and used her loving act as a teachable moment about the gratitude that follows Heaven's forgiveness (Luke 7:36–50). In anointing Christ, Mary also retained in her hair and on her hands the fragrance of her loving gift to Him.

I wonder, at times in our lives, how we portray the Savior we have accepted into our hearts. Do we impart the sweet, persistent scent of His love? Or do we brashly storm down life's road, impatient with those around us? We can live out Christ's attractiveness when we have spent time with Him in prayer and Bible study. During my worship time, He gently anoints me with the sweet ointment of patience and kindness. I want to be "fragrant" for Jesus all the time and every day. When people are around me, I want them to know not only that I have a relationship with Him, but also that I have been anointed with His love.

Mary E. Dunkin

The Test Before the Testimony

"Fear not, for I am with you; Be not dismayed, for I am your God. I will strengthen you, yes, I will help you, I will uphold you with My righteous right hand." Isa. 41:10, NKJV.

Because I have had a previous history of congestive heart failure (CHF), I recognized the symptoms of another event coming on, so on February 13, 2013, I prepared to enter the hospital. My concern was for my husband while I was hospitalized. God provided, for He alone knew what was ahead for me and my family. He knew the next seven weeks would be the most physically challenging of my life—most of which I do not remember. From mid-February until April 1, I suffered four or five congestive heart failures, spending most of my hospitalization time in the intensive care unit. At one point I was on a ventilator in an induced coma with my hands tied to the bedrails. I do not recall this phase either.

The one thing I do remember, however, is Dr. Renee Mobley, head chaplain at the hospital, saying to me, "It's up to you to choose whether you live or throw in the towel and give up. It's your choice." I knew nothing after that for several days. When I did become aware of my situation, which was grave, I was afraid to ask God, "Why?" I had had major surgery more than once before, including a triple heart bypass. Now, suddenly, within a week I was out of the hospital and on the mend.

I have come to understand that what happened to me was God's business. I could feebly "will" to live, but the outcome was really beyond my control. But not beyond God's. That's why I choose to consistently believe and trust in my heavenly Father. My Father, who loved me enough to send His only Son into this sin-sick world to rescue . . . *me*.

I've learned that persistent submission to God's will is such a sweet experience. Despite the fact that I have both chronic obstructive pulmonary disease (COPD) and CHF, I envision myself each night climbing upon the lap of Jesus and laying my head on my heavenly Father's shoulder as I go to sleep. No more anxiety falling asleep. Praise God!

I have learned to trust God no matter what the circumstances are; only He knows tomorrow. Each day He holds my life in His hands, and I couldn't be in better hands. Nor could you. Jesus saves, so why not let Him save us in the ways He knows are best for our salvation?

Jean Kelly

Lost Keys

"Rejoice with me; I have found my lost coin." Luke 15:9, NIV.

I have three small keys, two of which are for the cabinets at my work, and the last one is to unlock the "shopping cart" of the building where I live. As I used to constantly forget where I had left them, I decided to attach the three keys to the car keys. Sometime later, I decided to separate them from the car keys and put them on a heart-shaped keychain.

On Friday, when I needed a key to open the locked cabinets in my office, I realized that the heart-shaped keychain was not in the bag. I looked in the car, in the pockets of my coat, but I did not find them. I remembered that I could have forgotten them in the hospital where I worked two days before. I asked God to help me have my keys back.

The next week, when I returned to the hospital, I asked my colleagues if they had seen my keys. Unsure that I had even left them there, I asked two nurses if they had found my keys. One of them told me that a doctor had found them, taking them with her.

Finally, I got my three small keys back, and with them, I learned three lessons. The first lesson is that we must take care of what is of value to us, such as our children. Often, we realize that we have lost our children to this world but only when it is too late. It took two days for me to realize that I had lost the keys. Until then, I had the conviction that they were in the bag. Our children may even be going to church with us, but we pray that they develop a genuine relationship with God. Otherwise, when we least expect it, we'll discover they're as lost as my keys were.

The second lesson I learned is that God never gives up on us. I could have asked for new keys and could have forgotten those that were lost instead of waiting in hope to find my original keys. Likewise, God—after sin came into the Garden of Eden—could have destroyed us and made new creatures. But He would not give up and sent His own Son to "find" us.

And, finally, the third lesson I learned is that we must not give up on our neighbors either. We must persevere in prayer for those who are lost because one day the prodigal sons will return to the arms of the Father.

Thank You, my God, for the keys and the lessons that You taught me through them!

Adriza Santos Silva Barbosa

He Will Carry Me Through

But you, be strong and do not let your hands be weak, for your work shall be rewarded! 2 Chron. 15:7, NKJV.

One day after church, my pastor told me that Aysia, my nine-year-old stepdaughter, had requested baptism. I was surprised. She'd not said a thing about that to us. I remembered my own baptismal experience when my girlfriends had added my name to the baptismal list at the close of an evangelistic session. So I asked the minister a few questions: Had someone suggested to Aysia that it was time? He shook his head.

Driving Aysia home that afternoon, I asked her a pointed question. "Why do you want to get baptized? You are only nine years old." Her answer almost brought me to tears.

"Auntie Suzi," her voice was brighter than usual, "I would like to give my life to the Lord now while I am young because there are so many things in this world that can distract me and pull me away from Him. I know that if I give my life to Him now, He will guide me and carry me through. Then I, too, will be with Him in heaven."

I was dumbfounded. What had happened to my little girl? Before that day, she had never given me such a clear answer to any of the numerous spiritual questions I'd asked her during the six-year period she had been in my care. But today there was a marked difference. She was direct and very confident in her answers. At that moment I was convinced that she had made a personal decision to follow Jesus and He had already begun to make a change in her life.

That moving experience triggered several questions about my own spiritual journey. Where do *I* go for safety? Do *I* trust God enough to carry *me* through? King Asa's exhortation in today's text is excellent counsel for each of us. We all fight a war, not against flesh and blood, but against spiritual wickedness in high places (Eph. 6:12). That's why we need to "be strong" in the Lord (verse 10), keeping close to Him as our only safeguard.

You, too, can move to a safe spiritual place. It may be just a step away *from* your computer or telephone for a single day of seeking God and waiting patiently for His voice. Being strong in the Lord may call for a more radical move. Yet, I invite you to take one step today that would bring you closer to God. Trust Him. Be strong—in Him. And your work shall be rewarded.

Suzi-Ann Brown

Lovely Auntie Agnes

Gray hair is a crown of splendor; it is attained in the way of righteousness. Prov. 16:31, NIV.

Often we recall some of the thoughtful insights Auntie Agnes contributed to our lives. As she entered the ninetieth decade of her life, her sharp mind was ever thinking things through. Having learned frugality during the Great Depression years, she based her decision on whether she should buy new shoes on whether or not she would live long enough to wear them out.

Her cheerful attitude came through even during the years of her failing health. When she went to the doctor, her hearing loss made it difficult for her to hear everything he told her. She would always end her appointments by asking the doctor the same question: "Don't you think I am doing pretty well for my age?" When the doctor would say, "Yes" she would leave happy. Her answer when we would ask her what the doctor said was always, "I got a good report." Even during the months when her health was failing she gave the same answer. "I got a good report."

Auntie Agnes's influence in our lives and the lives of our children carries on today. Her ability and choice to remain cheerful and positive through every challenge she faced in her ninety-four years of life were an example for all. She experienced extremely sad times in her life when she lost both of her very young sons. Her personal sorrow served to give her an extra measure of love to others who went through similar experiences. Working with her husband, a mortician, she was a comforter to other parents who lost their children. Perhaps it was in triumphing over the negative times that she gained the strength and grace to be such a blessing to all she met. A quiet, unassuming lady, she gave so much to others. The heritage she left for us will not be forgotten.

Our family members are frequently heard repeating some of the same comments as Auntie. Our favorite comment when our children ask how our doctor's appointments went is to say, "I got a good report." Her memory lives on for each of us.

All have the privilege of developing a close relationship with beloved aunts and uncles. Their patient lives have much to teach us and will often be the ones to give us the uplift we need in our lives and create wonderful memories. Families who remember the special loved ones in their lives will draw strength and courage from this special legacy.

Evelyn Glass

Nest in the Heights

"Look at the birds of the air; they do not sow or reap or store away in barns, and yet your heavenly Father feeds them. Are you not much more valuable than they?" Matt. 6:26, NIV.

Our family has already received many demonstrations that God cares for us. We greatly appreciate creatures God has created, although we do not have any at home.

Once, my husband had the idea to buy two bird nests and put them on the balcony of our apartment. I inquired closely how a *bird* could find a nest there on the ninth floor of the building. Besides that, they'd have to find a way through the outside protective nets.

Yet I agreed to the purchase and accompanied my husband to the store for pet products. There we bought two kinds of bird nests: one of straw and another of wood. With great care, my husband attached them to the wall of the balcony. We looked like scientific researchers waiting for the moment in which a bird would enter our observation area and occupy one of the nests.

One, two, six, twelve months went by! Though we waited patiently, no bird came! Or had one come when we were away at work? But even on weekends, when we were at home all day long, we had never seen a feathery visitor. I thought my husband would remove the nests after all that time, but he did not do so.

What a surprise we had when, one day, a little bird—carrying sticks in its beak—landed on the wire netting. He stopped, looked around, and made his way to his chosen nest. This he did repeatedly. Behind the window glass were two joyful viewers watching his every move. We wanted a professional video camera to document this completely expected turn of events! We told many people, including our adult daughter, and they were astonished!

This episode made me think: it is not appropriate to give up on a goal even if its outcome seems impossible. Trust in God. *Perseverance* is one of the words describing a true Christian. Life lived with intentional perseverance rewards us with valuable lessons. Lessons from everyday life, from others, and from nature. And past blessings remembered bring us strength for the present. The same God who provided for us in the past is also with us today.

On our balcony God provided two nests for the little bird that needed a home. What are the needs about which you have been anxious? Are you not of much more value than the birds?

Queila Toledo Diniz de Andrade

Multiplied Blessings

"You shall eat in plenty and be satisfied, and praise the name of the LORD your God, who has dealt wondrously with you; and My people shall never be put to shame." Joel 2:26, NKJV.

One Friday in October 2010 I was devastated to receive a cell phone message that my mother in the Philippines had been hospitalized and was in critical condition. Within two hours I had booked a ticket with a travel agency. Coming home from church the next day, I received another message: Mother had passed away. After a long silence, I cried so much that I almost fainted. I recalled the last time I'd been with my mother two years earlier. She had seemed so happy. I remembered my mother had kept hugging and kissing me. How different this visit would be!

On the funeral day we did not expect a lot of people gathering in front of our house, but as we reached the church I saw a long line of "tricycles" (motorbike taxis) full of people who had come to pay their respects. I was touched beyond words as many told stories of how my mother had loved them and helped them in the past.

One of them said, "After your mother was taken to the hospital, some of us church members visited her and prayed for her. We asked her if she was willing to accept Jesus as her personal Savior and Lord. All she could do, as an affirmative response, was to slightly raise her foot, which she did. Then we asked if we could pray for her. Again she raised her foot and tears were rolling from her eyes. The prayer was a long one. As soon as we said 'Amen,' she stopped breathing." What hope this account gave me that my mother had surrendered her life to Jesus as her Redeemer and Savior!

During the burial service in the cemetery, one of the women whispered to me, "We didn't prepare enough food for the guests. We've planned food in paper bags for three hundred guests maximum. But over five hundred have shown up!" I bowed my head and began claiming promises, reminding God He'd fed over five thousand people once. I cited His promise, "Ask, and it shall be given you" (Matt. 7:7). So I asked and continued asking—and the Lord multiplied the paper bags of food!

Jesus is awesome and coming soon to wipe away every tear shed for our loved ones. I look forward to seeing my mother again.

Loida Gulaja Lehmann

My Daughter, My Teacher

But Jesus said, Suffer little children, and forbid them not, to come unto me: for of such is the kingdom of heaven. Matt. 19:14.

Life through the eyes of my daughter as a toddler was full of excitement and amazement. Running up and down the stairs (even when I had told her not do so) was like winning the marathon. Jumping in and out of the bed or the couch was like jumping in clouds similar to stories in nursery books. She found joy developing her artistic skills, even if it meant that I had to clean the walls of her crayon decorations. Her ability to remember words to songs and nursery rhymes not often told was very impressive. Her giggle and laughter were contagious.

Yet as with any other toddler her age (two and a half), standing still and waiting patiently were extremely difficult tasks to do, especially during prayer. I tried everything I could to get her to reverently stand for prayer. She didn't mind standing for maybe a minute, but anything longer and she would become fidgety and distracted. I also encouraged her to pray, even though I thought she had no idea what prayer was all about.

One day my best friend came to the house for a short visit. As usual, we talked and giggled about current events, family, and work. We hadn't noticed that the short visit had become longer than what my friend had planned to stay. Rushing to get home, my friend kissed us goodbye and ran out the door. My daughter didn't say anything but stood at the door, watching as if she were waiting for someone. Two minutes later my friend was knocking at the door; she had forgotten her package on the chair.

This time my daughter was not going to let my friend go. Holding on to her little brother's hand, my daughter insisted that we pray. After getting over the initial shock, my friend, my son, and I bowed our heads, and my daughter began to pray. I know that God was the only one who understood her prayer. Once she was done, she turned to my friend and said, "OK Auntie, bye-bye. See you later."

I was trying so hard to teach my daughter to stand still in prayer, and I didn't believe she even understood what prayer was. Yet she taught me that day: a good prayer wasn't necessarily about how you pray but that you prayed.

Diantha Hall-Smith

Standing Firm

"Stand firm, and you will win life." Luke 21:19, NIV.

While reading the Bible early one morning, I came across Isaiah 7:9. It states, "If you do not stand firm in your faith, you will not stand at all" (NIV). It doesn't say, "You *may* not stand." It says simply that you *will* not stand.

As I contemplated what it means to stand firm in the faith, I thought of my mother. My mother was married to someone who neither was a Christian nor had any interest whatsoever in spiritual things. Many times she stood firm in her convictions and never once gave in to my father's persuasive suggestions to do things she knew, from the Bible, were wrong. With Christ's help—and with kindness—she always stood firm. Eventually my dad became a Christian. Because of Mother's example, he, too, learned to stand firm for what he believed.

Other examples of "standing firm" come to mind. Daniel and his three friends resolved not to defile themselves (Dan. 1:8–17). In other words, they had made a decision to stand firm. Later God spared three of the Hebrews in the fiery furnace and Daniel in the lions' den.

For most of us, learning to stand firm is a process. It certainly was for Peter. Matthew 26:58 says, "But Peter followed him [Jesus] at a distance" (NIV). Not yet standing firm, Peter followed at a distance and ended up swearing he didn't know his Master! Fortunately, Peter repented with bitter tears and later wrote in his first letter, "Resist him [the devil], standing firm in the faith" (1 Pet. 5:9, NIV). What a transformation! Peter had learned that unless he stood firm in Jesus, he wouldn't stand at all.

Paul certainly understood the importance of standing firm. Throughout his letters to the early church, one can trace Paul's admonitions to remain spiritually strong. Paul told the Corinthians how they could stand firm: "it is by faith you stand firm" (2 Cor. 1:24, NIV).

Paul also shared that God blesses faith-based firmness. "Therefore, my dear brothers and sisters, stand firm. Let nothing move you. Always give yourselves fully to the work of the Lord, because you know that your labor in the Lord is not in vain" (1 Cor. 15:58, NIV). To His own disciples, Christ underlined the end result of standing firm: "the one who stands firm to the end will be saved" (Mark 13:13, NIV). Let's ask Jesus every day to make our steps firm (Ps. 37:23)!

Sharon Oster

Being More Than You Thought Possible

For we are God's handiwork, created in Christ Jesus to do good works, which God prepared in advance for us to do. Eph. 2:10, NIV.

My high school in Australia required that we girls take cooking and sewing classes, and boys, woodworking classes. Though I enjoyed cooking, sewing was another matter. The end-of-the-year project was to sew a dress. When all the other girls were busy making their dresses, I was still behind the sewing machine trying to sew a straight line on brown paper. Nor could I read the pattern well or make the sleeves lie flat. Somehow I finished my dress. Miss Lindsay was kind enough to give me a passing grade, probably because of the effort I had put into the dress that I never liked and never, ever wore. Sewing was not my interest nor my gift.

Though pastors' wives are often expected to play an instrument and work with the children's department, I don't play an instrument, but I loved working with kids. I also love being the background person for my husband. So I decided long ago that I would not focus on what I cannot do but rather on what I can do. I heard this story once. Two men were sent to Africa from a shoe factory to see if there was a possibility of opening a factory there. One man sent a message back that read, "This will never work because no one wears shoes here." The second man sent this message back: "There are great opportunities here. No one wears shoes." One saw possibilities where the other saw only failure. What do you see?

God has given each and every one of us a gift. But many times I look around and see women who are not willing to use their gifts because they feel inadequate or have low self-esteem. If only we would put our trust in God to lead us into what we can do! Ellen White wrote, "Not more surely is the place prepared for us in heavenly mansions than is the special place designated on earth where we are to work for God" (*Christ's Object Lessons,* p. 37).

What is it that you love to do? What gives you energy? Do you have a passion that you can use for God? Have others said things to you about what you are good at? Where do you feel God is leading you?

When you have answered these questions, pray that God will guide you into what you can do for Him and for others. Start seeing possibilities.

Clair Sanches-Schutte

Strength in Numbers

"Then I will ask the Father to send you the Holy Spirit who will help you
and always be with you." John 14:16, CEV.

As I was cleaning up after the breakfast I'd prepared, I found myself wishing
that I had someone to help me. I was thinking about the people in the
world who can afford that kind of pampering. It must be nice!

The phrase *strength in numbers* came to mind. I could not help but wonder
how blissful it would be to have a team of helpers—just twice a month—to do
a thorough cleaning of my home. I could handle the cooking, but sometimes
(most of the time) the laundry is backed up, the sink is full of dishes, and the dust
is noticeably settling on the surfaces of tables, chairs, fans, and more.

But then a realization came to my mind. I already have help. I really do. God
is all I need to help me keep my heart and my mind in order. "Create in me a
pure heart, oh, God, and renew your right Spirit within me" (Ps. 51:10, Aramaic
Bible in Plain English). Whose spirit? God's Spirit. I want to be renewed and
made clean by the Holy Spirit. The Spirit that Christ promised He'd request of
His Father for His followers after the Resurrection.

Hired helpers are certainly beneficial in a house that needs cleaning. Yet when
it comes to cleaning up the mess of this sinful world, there is only one Helper
that really matters. The following passages remind us not only who this helper is
but also what He does for us.

"Come to me, all you who are weary and burdened, and I will give you rest"
(Matt. 11:28, NIV). Not only can we rely on God to bear our burdens, but we
can trust Him to carry us as well.

"Cast your cares on the Lord and he will sustain you; he will never let the
righteous be shaken" (Ps. 55:22, NIV).

"Then I will ask the Father to send you the Holy Spirit who will help you and
always be with you" (John 14:16, CEV). What a wonderful promise! A divine
Helper *forever*! He wants to help with our burdens. Praise God that He will not
leave us alone to clean up our messes.

Now, about those dishes . . .

Joey Norwood Tolbert

Having Confidence

Having confidence of this very thing, that he who has begun in you a good work will complete it unto Jesus Christ's day. Phil. 1:6, DARBY.

When the new research teacher entered our classroom, I heard a voice whisper, "He will be your husband." I frowned. I felt uneasy. I looked around at my classmates; some were smiling, some were not. But when he introduced himself and boldly announced that he was single and definitely looking for a wife in the university, everybody giggled hilariously. I felt my heart flip-flop. A dear friend handed me a note: "Friend, you look good together." Sigh.

That night I talked to God in prayer. It was a heart-to-heart talk, bombarding God with questions and asking Him for assurance. I had been longing for a serious relationship; it seemed I always found myself heartbroken. About five months before, my sponsor had told me that the university was the best place to find a husband. And he seriously prayed for me. *Could this be the answer? Could this new instructor be the one?*

But there was a problem: he was my teacher. So I decided to avoid him, only to find out that was hard. We became friends within a circle of friends. We hung out, ate lunch, and spent time that helped us know each other better. I felt feelings begin to grow.

Then something went wrong. The administration was not pleased with our friendship, so we decided to avoid each other. I cried to God. Then the Spirit whispered to me in a Scripture song that reminded me that God, who had begun a "good work" in me, would be "faithful to complete it" in me. I kept this in my heart and sang it each time I felt doubtful and heartbroken.

Though my friendship with the teacher seemed to have ended, our mutual friends still believed God had plans for us. They kept on telling me, "The best is yet to come."

After my classes ended, I accepted a teaching invitation in Thailand. *This might be the chance to forget about him,* I reasoned. I was really wrong. I returned to Manila to attend graduation. To make a long story short, after a while, we eventually exchanged marriage vows.

God has plans for each of us—and a good work that He has begun in us. That "good work" will look different for each one of us, but God will complete it in His perfect time. We just have to wait in patience, in trust, and in prayer and listen for the Spirit's whispers of love.

Edna Buenaventura-Esguerra

Committed

The steps of a good man are ordered by the Lord, and He delights in his way. Ps. 37:23, NKJV.

I made a cup of tea in my favorite cup and took a seat at the kitchen table. As I felt the warmth of the beverage coat my throat, I reviewed the past week. I'd attended all of the regular church programs. Then I'd been involved in Food Pantry Distribution Day, women's ministries, and elders' meetings.

The community choir I sing in celebrated its twenty-fifth year anniversary with a three-day event that included a banquet, a musical, and a concert. *Whew,* I thought to myself, *it was a whirlwind and fun-filled week.* I couldn't help but marvel at the fact that I felt refreshed after getting six or seven hours of sleep on the previous night as opposed to four or five the other nights!

Oh, my, I thought to myself. *Have I reached a point of old age, or of dullness, that I'm excited over getting a couple extra hours of sleep?*

I chuckled to myself as I realized that I didn't *have* to do all those activities that had been squeezed into the previous week. I had done them—and all the others things I do for the church and the community—by choice. And I don't do what I do because I want to be saved, but rather because I am saved. I am a firm believer that God saves us to "serve" and not to "sit." "By this My Father is glorified, that you bear much fruit; so you will be My disciples" (John 15:8, NKJV). But what about the intensity with which I do these things? Instead of putting my all into everything, can't I just do them when I feel like it? Perhaps I can give a few hours here and there. After pondering those thoughts for a few moments I decided the answer is *No!* And my *No* can be attributed to one thing—*commitment!*

I've committed myself to several things. Not because I *have* to but because I *want* to. Not to gain points with the Lord but because I am a servant of the Lord. Yes, occasionally it seems I don't have adequate time to clean the house, watch television, sew, or read, but my commitments "call" me and humbly I respond, "Here I am, Lord. Use me for Your glory!"

That's me! I'm committed to serve Jesus in all the ways He directs me—no excuses.

"If they obey and serve Him, they shall spend their days in prosperity, and their years in pleasures" (Job 36:11, NKJV). My days are certainly pleasant. I hope yours are too.

Barbara J. Walker

Borders

And he brought them to the border of his sanctuary. Ps. 78:54.

Stenciling goes back to the eighteenth century when early American stencilry was designed and implemented by simple itinerant artists who traveled through the countryside. All an artist carried with him was a kit that held dry colors, brushes, measuring tools, a builder's cord, a piece of chalk, and stencils cut from thick paper. He would mix flat colors with skimmed milk and decorate white walls with flowers, leaves, and swags.

Effective stencilry demanded strong, lasting colors such as black, green, yellow, pink, and red. Blue was seldom used because it tended to fade. These colors were also used in prehistoric cave wall art and early church decoration. From 1778 until the first quarter of the eighteenth century, the same stencil motifs were used over and over to decorate homes.

When my daughter, Gail, and her husband, Douglas, were settled in Danville, Virginia, we stenciled over the chair rail (a type of moulding attached horizontally to a wall around a room's perimeter) of the mammoth foyer of their 1860 house. We stenciled around every corner and up the stairway to the second floor. My country house also has stenciling in several rooms.

Though still used today, the time-consuming and patience-demanding craft of stenciling is often replaced with the quicker application of wallpaper borders. This seems to work better for many people in this fast-paced age.

I once surprised my girls. When they came home from school one day, they discovered that Mother had painted daisies on one wall. What a surprise and delight this change was for them! God also delighted the children of Israel when He told them to build a beautiful sanctuary so He could dwell among them. He even commanded that they use certain colors, the same ones often used by early stencil artists, to decorate it. He gifted men and women to become artists who patiently crafted beautiful motifs that delighted them and enhanced their worship experience.

Today God has many other surprises in store for us as, with infinite patience, He brings us to the borders of his sanctuary, stenciling His beauty upon our characters. His love for us runs deep as He fills each day with His delights—whether that be a tiny forest flower, a golden sunset, or a renewed invitation to learn and patiently practice the artistry of His love.

Laurie McClanahan

August 19

Tongue-Tied

A tiny spark can set a great forest on fire. And the tongue is a flame of
fire. It is a whole world of wickedness, corrupting your entire body. It
can set your whole life on fire, for it is set on fire by hell itself.
James 3:5, 6, NLT.

Injustice always surprises me, although it shouldn't. It's part and parcel of
living on a fallen planet. You'd think the church would be an oasis of justice
in an insane and hurtful world, a place you could flee to for refuge. But more
often than not (at least in my experience) church is rife with injustice. It stings
when the world slaps your face; but when someone at church slaps it, the pain is
far more intense.

The worst thing about this is not the fact that it happens. After all, if Jesus'
church crucified Him, do you really think yours is going to treat you any better?
The worst thing about it is that nine times out of ten we miss the opportunity
to take advantage of witnessing opportunities that such circumstances provide—
because we can't see past the blinding pain.

When Satan can provoke a non-Christian to hurt someone, it's a win; but
when he can provoke one Christian to hurt another, it's a double win.

How many people do you know who have left the church or become
disillusioned with Christianity because they have seen one Christian rake another
over the coals or use a tongue to wound another in some way?

To misquote Shakespeare, "Though it be but little, it is fierce." Our tongues
are like little swords, cutting and slashing indiscriminately unless we rein them
in. But we are not strong enough for that. The most muscle-bound weight lifter
isn't strong enough to restrain a tongue bent on evil, and let's face it, left to their
own devices all tongues are bent on evil because we are all sinners.

If we want to use our tongues as God meant them to be used, we must allow
Him to control them. Otherwise they are the property of Satan, and everyone
knows how he will use them. The Bible tells us that "the words of the reckless
pierce like swords, but the tongue of the wise brings healing" (Prov. 12:18, NIV).

Commit your words to God today. Speak only the good ones.

Céleste Perrino-Walker

Small Things

The LORD is near to all who call on Him, to all who call on Him in truth.
Ps. 145:18, NKJV.

During many ten-hour, one-way trips from Colorado to Arizona to visit my aging mother, I would pass through mountainous regions. "Watch for Elk" signs were posted everywhere. I would indeed watch eagerly for elk but never saw any. Loving nature, I'd sometimes silently pray, *Lord, I'd* love *to see one of these elegant creatures in the wild. May I sometime?* Then I would feel guilty for asking because God has so many more important prayers to answer and problems to solve—besides just finding me an elk to look at. One day on the road I became persistent, restating my desire in a conversation with God. A short distance later, a muscular male elk, with a full rack of antlers, bounded up the high crest beside the roadway. Majestically, he stood there, shiny coat glistening in the sun—as if posing for me—before turning and disappearing down the mountainside. My heart swelled with gratitude to my all-powerful God who loves to make His children happy—even in the small things of life.

Another time, when I was visiting my sister in Florida, we went shelling on Sanibel Island. The hotel in which we were staying extended our checkout time as we searched the sand between waves. Talking to God, I silently shared, *Lord, I would so much like to find one of those rare little wentletrap shells* (also known as staircase shells, resembling a white spiral staircase). *Could You help me find one, please?* Once again I experienced guilt for taking such a minor request to such a busy God. So I quickly added, *Thy will be done,* and went on with my shelling. I'd all but forgotten my timid prayer request when, some time later, largely hidden by shore debris on the sand, I spotted the end of a white shell. Being careful not to break it, I removed surrounding debris and stared at the most unexpected, most exquisite little wentletrap shell I'd ever seen. My voice shouted the praise in my heart: "Thank You! Thank You, God!"

Many times, of course, we don't experience immediate answers to our prayers. Yet God knows us individually and intimately. He knows what we need and when we need it. He knows what we desire. He is good, wise, and powerful. Words from a song admonish that when we can't see God's hand at work, we can patiently trust His heart. We are safe faithfully trusting both the big things, as well as the small, to the One who loves us best—our heavenly Father.

Eileen Snell

Inseparable

Nothing in all creation will ever be able to separate us from the love of God that is revealed in Christ Jesus our Lord. Rom. 8:39, NLT.

My husband slides into our bed this morning and caresses the sickness from my face as he soothes my sleepy soul. "Why?" I audibly ask him. *Why me?* I think. This me of miserable head cold, stinky breath, and stuffy nose? This me of skipped shower last night because I was entirely exhausted? Me, worthy of unreserved love right now? Hardly! The sting of acceptance's opposite, rejection, wells up within me. My husband senses that this sickness is penetrating my spirit, and softly answers my soul's skepticisms, "I know you're feeling crummy, so I wanted to snuggle you." I try to comprehend the love of this man, a love that reaches through without regard to my condition. He wants to draw close to me, even though I'm miserably sick.

On some mornings I find myself questioning my Redeemer as He quietly slips into my heart and whispers, "Would you like for Me to restore your soul to health, My love?" *You want to spend time with me, God? This me of complaining about mismatched socks and a seemingly scattered future? This me with the reoccurring attitude of I'm-a-big-girl-I-can-do-it-all-by-myself-thank-you-but-no-thanks-Jesus?* Many a morning I have let my own weaknesses condemn me. On stuffy nose days, I am reminded that I am incapable of earning acceptance on any day—not from my spouse, not from my supervisor, and certainly not from my Savior. I've messed up in all of these relationships. Ticking off all the items on a "to do" list to please others doesn't garner true acceptance. However heartfelt, well-considered plans and desires are often trumped by shortcomings—others' or my own.

Due to sin, we are all spiritually sick. Our sickness is our sinfulness, and yet Christ does not reject us. Our sins have separated us from God, but Christ's desire to be with us forever compelled Him to bear at the cross those same feelings of rejection and separation from the Father—on our behalf. Although the disease-perpetrator attempts to infect us in every way, the Cross assures us that nothing can separate us from the love of God in Christ Jesus.

Today, I try to comprehend the determined love of my Christ, a love that keeps reaching through without regard to my sinful condition. He wants to be with me. Inseparable.

Charity Stone

She Was Faithful to the End

Charm is deceptive, and beauty is fleeting; but a woman who fears the Lord is to be praised. Prov. 31:30, NIV.

Long ago, the wise Solomon wrote that the fear of the Lord is the beginning of wisdom. How much truth we find in those words! So did Catharina. She was a poor girl, almost with no schooling, who faced the vicissitudes of life without losing sight of the fear of the Lord. This blessed fear of the Lord made her a strong and tough woman. She bravely faced the struggles and difficulties that life had for her.

Married to a man of a different religious background, Catharina prayed for him throughout her lifetime. She raised her children in the ways of the Lord, faithfully admonishing them—often with tears. However, her efforts were not in vain. At church, Catharina did not seem to know the expression "I can't." She always found ways to help people. Her clear, smooth soprano voice could always be heard praising the Creator as her active hands stitched clothing for the needy or gave injections to the sick. Her children's evangelism efforts blessed the lives of many children, especially mine, as she lifted up the blessed hope of the soon appearing of the Lord Jesus.

When Catharina died, some of the young people to whom she had ministered sought out others who had turned away from the ways of God, inviting them to their former teacher's funeral. Together they followed her coffin to the grave, singing the song she had taught them: "I will wear a crown when I go to heaven." A number of the backslidden youth returned to the ways of the Lord.

Catharina. Blessed daughter of God, who put the fear of God ahead of everything else in her life! And now I cannot hide this fact anymore: Catharina was my mother! She taught me to pray and to walk in the fear of the Lord. I hope to see her in that great day.

Friend, let me share what my mother tirelessly taught me. Do not be afraid if the waves of difficulties and struggles of each day come whipping the boat of your life. Do not lose sight of the fear of the Lord. Cling tightly to Jesus. He will firmly hold your hand so you are not lost. He will help you enter the gates of the Holy City. I hope to meet you there.

Maria de Lourdes I. M. Castanho

Listening Skills 101

Let the wise listen and add to their learning, and let the discerning get guidance. Prov. 1:5, NIV.

Many things that we consider as one item are often composed of other smaller parts. Although I'd never thought about it before, prayer could fall into that category because it has at least two parts; talking and listening. I have trouble with the second part. I'm sure this is true for many of us. Talking to God comes rather easily for me. When it comes to listening to what He has to say, I'm afraid I don't do very well. Listening takes patience. That was especially true when it came to my car. My two daughters let me know—gently, of course—that it was time for me to buy a newer car. Every so often one of them would casually say, "You know, it's hard to get parts for an older car." Another would drop a hint, mentioning that the car was so old that perhaps it wasn't safe to drive. I would tell them that this automobile had been a faithful friend for twenty-four years, and I couldn't see why it would let me down in the future.

So finally, mostly to prove my point, I told the Lord what He already knew. *Lord,* I said, *I don't want a different car. If You want me to have a new car, You'll have to show me.* Since I was certain He felt the same about my car as I did, I didn't take time to listen and considered the matter closed. One evening, a few days after that prayer, I drove Old Faithful to a women's ministries meeting at church. I'd almost arrived when I noticed the dashboard lights went off. My headlights weren't working either. I pulled over just before the engine died. Since I didn't own a cell phone, I borrowed a phone from a nearby business and called a tow truck.

The mechanic called me the next day and said, "Your car is now working." I assumed God wanted me to keep the car. He didn't. I just wasn't paying attention. Because I had my mind fixed on my agenda, I wasn't listening to what the Lord was telling me. I needed to take God's course, Listening Skill 101. The car quit working two more times that week before I finally got the message—and a different car.

As God says in Psalms, "My people, hear my teaching; listen to the words of my mouth" (Ps. 78:1, NIV). I'm patiently working hard on my listening skills now. And I'm so glad that my gracious Lord is still patiently working on me.

Marcia Mollenkopf

The New Proverbs 31 Woman: A Call to Virtue

Who can find a virtuous woman? For her price is far above rubies.
Prov. 31:10.

Growing up in the 1950s, I was supposed to be "pure" until marriage. Then the 1960s influenced me, until I met Christ. Now I would like to revive an old-fashioned character trait—one that is highlighted in Proverbs 31, the biblical chapter that still stands as a template for the modern woman, although for some the Proverbs 31 woman has been used as a model for the twenty-first century *superwoman:* businesswoman, wife, and mother.

The chapter begins with a mother's warning to her son: "Give not thy strength unto women, nor thy ways to that which destroyeth kings" (verse 3). We remember the failure of Samson, David, and Solomon to follow this advice. The mother describes the virtuous woman—the kind, apparently, that her son should marry. Talented and accomplished, this godly woman will be a good wife and mother. According to verse 30, she puts fear of the Lord above all else.

There are still virtuous women around, and we'd expect to find them in church, since good character is a Christian ideal. Sometimes manner of dress and comportment, though, belie their testimony. Therefore, in Christian circles the question, "Who can find a virtuous woman?" is even more relevant.

Virtue seems often out of style these days. In the nineteenth century, women were warned to be virtuous or pure—meaning to remain sexually pure, virgins until marriage. But after the 1960s rolled around, it seemed to me that many virgins "disappeared" as virtue flew out the window. Until then literature had told stories of knights fighting for virtuous women. Virtue was a quality to be treasured. That's why Joseph worried when Mary became pregnant before marriage. It's also the reason that the Catholic Church exalts Mary as the virgin.

Mothers have traditionally been seen as virtuous because motherhood has a way of refining character. Mothers are called upon to put aside self in order to sacrifice for their children. This pure love reflects the character of Christ: selfless, loving, thoughtful, modest, loyal, kind, willing to forgive, patient. In short, virtuous. Christ's character reflects God, who is love. Pure love. Mothers or not, shouldn't this be our renewed calling as Christian women—to reflect the virtue and purity of the Proverbs 31 woman—who reflected the virtue of Christ?

Mary McIntosh

Dedication

Always be zealous for the fear of the Lord. Prov. 23:17, NIV.

The temperature hovered at a humid 105 degrees Fahrenheit (40.5 Celsius) in Little Rock, Arkansas, that summer day. So why were we sitting in the unshaded sun on such a sweltering afternoon? Because Skeeter, grandson number three, was playing in the Arkansas Little League All-Star Baseball Tournament. We were there to support him, along with his teammates, both male and female. The hitting, running, and fielding skills of these young players amazed us. Though we agreed that all the children there were champions, it was, nonetheless, *our* grandson who was the center of our attention—and, in our opinion, the best in the state, especially when he literally dove through the air to catch a fast-flying ball.

And with what passion the children played! Three games in that heat with only fifteen-minute breaks between games. They ran. They threw. They hit. They caught the ball. All without complaining. What zeal! What dedication!

Watching all this focused and passionate gamesmanship made me ponder a question. *What would happen if Christians put as much dedication into witnessing for Jesus as these little guys and gals put into baseball? Would not the world be better prepared for Jesus to come?* Then I got personal—with myself. *When it comes to outreach activities,* I had to ask myself, *do I let myself off the hook because it's too hot . . . too cold . . . too, well, out-of-my-comfort-zone? I mean, what would I do if someone asked me a question for which I didn't have the answer?*

Or, *My neighbors already belong to (fill in the blank) church, so they won't want to hear what I have to say.* Or, *I've tried witnessing before, but no one wants to listen—or accept literature.*

Ellen White once wrote, "Earnest, persevering effort must be made for the salvation of those in whose hearts an interest is awakened. Many can be reached only through acts of disinterested kindness. . . . As they see evidence of our unselfish love, it will be easier for them to believe in the love of Christ" (*Christian Service,* p. 114).

So now I ask myself, *How hard is it to be zealous in performing "acts of disinterested kindness"?* Friends, why can't we learn from our children? Using just one-tenth of the zeal of these young ball players, as God directs, we could move the world for Jesus. It's about time.

Barbara Lankford

Free Transit

"Raise your staff and stretch out your hand over the sea to divide the
water so that the Israelites can go through the sea on dry ground."
Exod. 14:16, NIV.

Every day in the morning my husband takes our baby, Bianca, to school. In
the afternoon, my mother takes her from school. In the evening I pick her
up from my mother's house and bring her home. This has been our routine
since the end of maternity leave.

To meet our rush hour needs getting to work, we depend on public
transportation, the bus. But to travel from home to school and back again, we
use our bike fitted with a chair for our baby, making the daily commute a little
easier. Besides, it's free transit. However, for safety's sake, I try to go slow and am
very careful to always observe the crossings. That time of day the streets are busy
with students and workers returning home after work and school. Many of them
travel at high speeds in order to get home more quickly.

One evening, following our routine, I took Bianca from Grandma's house and
headed towards home. Something about the traffic in the quickly approaching
intersection suddenly frightened me. To slow our approach to the intersection, I
pressed the brake of the bike.

Without warning, it broke! I had no way to stop the bike! Prior to that moment,
the brake had been working just fine. In fact, we had changed brake pads not
long before. Now, with the bike rolling onto the asphalt of the intersection, all
I could do was scream, "No!" I had no time to think of an alternate plan to save
my little girl and myself, it was all happening so fast. And then we were safely
across! I stopped, took a deep breath, and looked back at the intersection—with
eyes of gratitude.

Our Savior, who opened a way across the Red Sea for Israel to pass through,
had made a way for us through the fast-moving cars, buses, motorcycles, bicycles,
and pedestrians. We had crossed in safety!

Now every time I cross that intersection, I like Miriam of old, break into a
song of praise and gratitude from my heart for God's protection and deliverance.
I renew my commitment to trust His guiding hand, the free transit He provides,
to lead us all into full and eternal safety.

Thank You, Lord, my God!

Luciana Barbosa Freitas da Silva

God Will Surprise You

"For I know the plans I have for you," declares the LORD, "plans to prosper you and not to harm you, plans to give you hope and a future." Jer. 29:11, NIV.

My plan was to become a lawyer and work for a successful law firm. There were times when I thought about working with children but never really saw any job that struck me. Then law school never worked out. I prayed for discernment about my life direction, often becoming frustrated or discouraged because I did not see evidence of God leading me.

After graduating from college, I had a job that I didn't find very fulfilling. Then one day a close friend mentioned a job opening in the Children's Ministries Department of my church's world headquarters. She encouraged me to apply. Is this what God had in mind for me?

I sent in my resume, went in for an interview, and two weeks later found myself working in that administrative assistant position, where I helped plan projects through which children could understand the gospel and be empowered for ministry at the same time. God had truly surprised me in His answer to my years of prayer. Two years later, I received a letter in the mail from a university seminary about a master's degree being offered in children and family ministry. I had applied to many grad schools before, but nothing had ever worked out.

I discussed this master's degree program with my boss and my parents. Then I applied, leaving the result in God's hands. A few months later, I received a phone call as well as an acceptance letter into the program! I cried with joy and was astonished at God's latest miraculous surprise in my life. Not only was I working for children's ministries at my church's world headquarters, but now God had provided me an opportunity to pursue a master's degree in a ministry I so loved doing.

All along, God had had a plan for my life. I just had to be patient and wait for His perfect timing. Everything *I* had planned had fallen apart. But *God's* plans surprised me in ways I never could have imagined!

When you feel discouraged about your career, education, or any other personal issue, remember that God is still with you working behind the scenes. Hold on. Keep praying. Never lose faith in the fact that He will surprise you!

Tanya Muganda

Delivered

The angel of the LORD encampeth round about them that fear him,
and delivereth them. Ps. 34:7.

The day started out early for us at 5:00 A.M. And it was beautiful. We were going to the Feast of the First Fruit, which is celebrated each year in Mamborê-Sítio-Paraná.

The trip was uneventful. Because it was very early, the passengers slept. I was dozing and listening to some people quietly talking in the background. Then I heard something strange; was I sleeping? I felt like it was a dream, but I heard somebody say, "It will be close, it will be close!" Unintentionally, I opened my eyes and turned my head to the right side of the minibus. I could only see a truck with two trailers loaded with sugar cane crossing a track, and I saw it like in a movie. The back trailer came ripping through the side of our bus, and it pushed the entire bus onto the shoulder of the road. I was completely mute, and so was everyone else. *Is this a nightmare?* I wondered. *No, it's real.*

The bus stopped. We were in Mandaguari, alive, and without severe wounds. People who were on the side of the bus that took the strike felt the blow, and some were a bit sore, but it was so apparent that our God fulfilled once again His promise presented in Psalm 34:7, today's text. God sent His angel and He protected us. I know that it was God Himself who stood between us and the trailer. It was God Himself who did not allow us to be killed or more severely injured. Thanks to Him, His children were still alive!

We had to wait three hours before our pastor, Dário Gonçalves, came to our rescue. After the conventional adjustments had been made, another bus was sent, and we were able to continue on our journey. Our God honored our faith. We missed the morning program because it was noon before we finally arrived at the church. However, as firstfruits of God, rededicated to Him, we didn't lose our lives.

Dear friends, in the same way, our dear Jesus stood between us and the devil on the cross of Calvary. And in our day, He has been—and will continue to be—our shield, our protection, the One who camps around us and delivers us from danger. And if sometimes we take some blows, we shall not despair because "the LORD is good, a refuge in times of trouble. He cares tirelessly for those who trust in him" (Nah. 1:7, NIV).

Mònica Magali Bandeira

Running Aimlessly

Everyone who competes in the games goes into strict training. They do it to get a crown that will not last, but we do it to get a crown that will last forever. Therefore I do not run like someone running aimlessly . . . so that after I have preached to others, I myself will not be disqualified for the prize. 1 Cor. 9:25-27, NIV.

This August the 2016 Summer Olympic Games will take place in Rio de Janeiro, Brazil. Four years ago the 2012 Olympic Games were held in London, England, just thirty miles (forty-eight kilometers) from where I live. A bit over two weeks before the start of the London games, the Olympic torch relay was to pass through my town. My daughter, Sarah, was singing in the concert to celebrate the arrival of the torch in our town and had given me a ticket to get in. The venue was a park just one mile from my home. I'd bragged to quite a few people that I would be there to see the torch arrive at 6:00 P.M. At 11:05 A.M., we left the house. A few minutes later, Sarah hopped out of the car and waved goodbye. I had planned to walk the dog, cook dinner, do some laundry, and pop into Dunelm for much-needed curtains before returning to the park by 6:00 P.M. in order to see the Olympic torch carried through.

By 2:30 P.M. dinner was ready. I ate and set off for the shops. At 4:20 P.M., I was still looking at curtains when an announcement through the overhead speaker informed shoppers that the store would close in ten minutes. I rushed to the checkout counter. My phone beeped. Sarah had sent a text message: "Torch arriving later." I decided to run some more errands. Sarah's next message at 6:15 read, "Torch is on its way from Hemel Hempstead." I figured it would take at least an hour before the torch arrived in Luton. That would be enough time for me to do some ironing. At Sarah texted again: "Torch is at Mill Street . . . I'm with the aunties."

My, that was quick! I thought. A moment later Sarah's next text read, "It's coming." In fact, it had arrived—and I was ironing.

Because I'd continued "running aimlessly" all day and losing sight of my goal—planning so I'd be ready to see the Olympic torch arrive in town—I had missed it! In my spiritual journey, Christ wants me to keep the true goal in sight: staying in touch with Him, which prepares me for His soon coming, instead of running aimlessly.

Avery Davis

To Create Beauty

My strength is made perfect in weakness. 2 Cor. 12:9.

When I was leaving the beautiful Tahitian island of Huahini after a blessed women's congress, one of the local women gave me a pearl as a gift. A pearl? I could not believe it! Pearls are so beautiful and valuable that I thought I did not deserve such a gift.

The birth of a pearl is truly a miraculous event. A natural pearl begins its life as a foreign object, such as a parasite or piece of shell that accidentally lodges itself in an oyster's soft inner body, where it cannot be expelled. To ease this irritant, the oyster's body takes defensive action. The oyster begins to secrete a smooth, hard crystalline substance around the irritant in order to protect itself. This substance is called "nacre." As long as the irritant remains within its body, the oyster will continue to secrete nacre around it, layer upon layer. Over time, the irritant will be completely encased by the silky crystalline coatings. And the result, ultimately, is the lovely and lustrous gem called a pearl. Amazing process! This makes a good metaphor for spiritual strength. God uses intense outside forces to rid us of impurities and to perfect His strength *in* us.

God's strength is made perfect in our weakness, says the apostle Paul. I wish this verse were not true because I don't like to see many women around the world weak, without strength due to poverty, lack of education, and health problems. At this moment as I write this devotional I have a friend dying from cancer. And I've met women in India who were abandoned by their husbands. Widows in Nigeria who were left with nothing. Young women in Thailand fighting for education in order to fly beyond prostitution. But the good news is that God still works in us, though us, and for us where we are. And He works through our weakness. He promises to make us strong through our difficulties and trials.

Maybe this is your day to look at your life, look up, and claim this promise: "Lord, I am weak, but I know through You I can be strong and beautiful as the pearl." Ultimately God's loving purpose is to make us strong as we continually depend upon Him.

Lord, thank You for giving us the strength to live today's challenges. Help us to remember that You can take the most painful hurts in our lives and turn them into something beautiful.

Raquel Queiroz da Costa Arrais

Daring and Undaunted

"Our Father knows the things you have need of before you ask Him."
Matt. 6:8, NKJV.

On any given, customary Sunday morning most people are curled up or sleeping in late. Therefore, on this particular Sunday morning, this warm gathering was an exception. A dedicated, committed group of six volunteers refused to be lulled by the hypnotizing raindrops. The group, guided by their soft-spoken leader, Lucien Ambo, took the challenge and the eight-hour round-trip from Port Saint Lucie to a Hawthorne campsite to help with the enormous task of changing the face of the campground.

The extent of the job at hand was unclear as the energetic and undaunted crew made their way to the red GMC Envoy with water bottles and fruit snacks in tow. The able and capable driver, young Ambo, took up his charge, and the group left Port Saint Lucie at 6:45 A.M. The rest of the neighborhood slept as the group embarked on the adventure to work in God's vineyard.

After two circuitous detours, with the brain overtaking the GPS (global positioning system), we arrived at the campground in the midst of a downpour. The sight of Pastor Mack and the volunteers working in the rain gave buoyancy to our spirits. This needed shower of blessings was replaced with clear skies. We were enthusiastic about the tasks of repairing the landscape at Blue Motel and the first aid station. The strength of the men on the team was displayed during the removal of tenacious shrubs that required the transfer and the replacement of breath-taking red and pink rose foliage and crepe myrtle that created a serene and kaleidoscopic design. The ladies, Sisters Ambo, Lola, and "J," were not to be outdone. Their wisdom, organization, and designing creativity were put on display. "Good job," "Nice work," and the invitation to the lunch were welcome and delightful distractions and rewards for persistent, unselfish service.

The amazing finale of the day was its clarity. We were exhilarated and exhausted but would not have changed anything about the day. Our heavenly Father would prefer our trusting Him before life's many trips rather than just at the end of the journey. He already knows the end from the beginning and knew we would be delighted with the results. Proof of this is found in Jeremiah 29:11: "For I know the plans I have for you . . . plans to prosper you" (NIV).

I know that He will prosper your faithful efforts for Him as He did ours.

Marjorie Gray-Johnson

Living His Balance

Balance: the state of having your weight spread equally so that you do not fall; a state in which different things . . . have an equal or proper amount of importance.

There is a time for everything, and a season for every activity under the heavens. Eccles. 3:1, NIV.

At daybreak, Jesus went out to a solitary place. The people were looking for him and when they came to where he was, they tried to keep him from leaving them. But he said, "I must proclaim the good news of the kingdom of God to the other towns also, because that is why I was sent." And he kept on preaching in the synagogues of Judea. Luke 4:42-44, NIV.

Let your moderation be known unto all men. The Lord is at hand. Phil. 4:5.

What woman doesn't struggle with maintaining personal balance in her fast-paced life? Yet Jesus lived a purposeful, balanced life, all aspects in perfect harmony. In order to maintain balance, He sometimes had to say no—even to doing more good things. Once, when a group of people begged Him to minister where *they* thought He should, He declined, stated His priorities, and moved on. To stay vertical in an off-kilter world, we need to live Christ's balance.

This month's authors share their struggles in dealing with stressors such as impatience, sleep deprivation, boredom, overwork, interrupted plans, and early life trauma. They also share their secrets for getting back in balance: humor, a healthy lifestyle, and reliance on God.

Finding Balance

There is a time for everything, and a season for every activity
under the heavens. Eccles. 3:1, NIV.

One of the greatest challenges I face is finding balance in life. Like many of you, I face a heavy daily schedule, with full-time graduate studies and research, a full-time job that requires frequent travel, a part-time job in the clinic seeing patients, managing a home, and serving at church, among other things. It is a challenge to prioritize what is really important.

Sometimes when I feel overwhelmed, a picture of my grandmother Lourdes comes to mind. During each summer, my brothers and I'd spent several enjoyable weeks with our grandparents. Grandma was in charge of us plus the cooking, the house, her volunteer work at church, her Bible studies, feeding the many pets on the ranch (with our help), and much more. Yet she had the habit of getting up one hour before us to read her Bible and pray in her quiet place. Sometimes when I got up early I would see her, and that example is still with me. From there she rose up with a cheerful smile and much energy for the day. She brought us much joy!

She reminded me of Jesus. After being baptized, Jesus entered into a very intense ministry. Multitudes flocked to hear Him and be healed by Him. He always had time for the important things. Like my grandma, Jesus started His day with prayer and communion. While there, God impressed His mind and choices. He followed His Father's impression and plan throughout the day on what to say *yes* to, and what to say *no* to. This was His secret!

In my search for finding balance I came across an insightful book, titled *Too Busy Not to Pray*. I was reminded that prayer can help busy people be more efficient and do more in less time. Too often we take on too much while we neglect physical exercise, rest, or time with the family—all in the name of serving God or helping others. Yet by habitually keeping late hours, gratifying appetite at the expense of health, neglecting physical exercise, or overworking mind or body, we unbalance our nervous system, perhaps even shortening our lives. Imbalance can hurt relationships and render us less able to serve God due to disease and even death.

As Solomon said, there is time for every activity under the sun. Jesus lived by that principle. May we choose to place our time with Him first, and then follow His counsel as we find balance each day.

Katia Garcia Reinert

Dull Days

Isn't it obvious that God deliberately chose . . . women that the culture overlooks . . . , chose these "nobodies" to expose the hollow pretensions of the "somebodies"? . . . Everything that we have—right thinking and right living, a clean slate and a fresh start—comes from God by way of Jesus Christ. 1 Cor. 1:27, 28, 30, *The Message.*

I woke this morning, like many industrious women, dreading to step on the bathroom scale, worrying today's choices and tomorrow's schedule, and loathing my self-imposed routine. Instantly depressed by the dullness of my life, I let my mind wander into memories where perhaps I could cheer up. Memories of travel, exploration, schooling, independence, parties, and possibilities. Like short-lived fireworks, they quickly burned off as I gazed into the still dark sky outside my window and dropped back into bed, where I stared at the red numbers on my alarm clock. What had happened to me? Back in my days of being twenty-something, I knew what I wanted and I made things happen. I was strong. I was energetic. I was confident.

Lord, I pleaded silently, *how did I become so ordinary, so boring? Don't You have anything unique left for me, to give my dull existence meaning?*

Then I remembered Joan, a friendly acquaintance from my West Virginia childhood church, once confiding, "I was watching you one day at church when you were maybe sixteen. I can't remember if you were offering prayer or singing. I just was so thrilled to see a young woman participating in the worship service with such poise of character. Then," she continued, "I remember hoping my thirteen-year-old daughter would be like you some day."

How could this woman have seen through my adolescent struggles with an eating disorder, poor self-esteem, fatigue from working so hard to earn my school tuition, and worries about which color lip gloss to wear? Yet somehow Joan had seen past my exterior and admired me for the simple act of worshiping God!

So, refreshed, I thanked God for reminding me that nothing we do is mundane. It's not what we've done that matters most. What matters most, especially on dull days, is who we are—daughters of God. He uses our commonness, our simplicity, to inspire righteous aspirations in others. Praise God for the commonness of life—may He use your dull day to inspire others.

Wendy Williams

September 3

My Delight

Delight yourself also in the LORD, and He shall give you the desires of your heart. Ps. 37:4, NKJV.

Your commandments are my delights. Ps. 119:143, NKJV.

Blessed is the [wo]man who fears the LORD, who delights greatly in His commandments. Ps. 112:1, NKJV.

Since I was a little girl I have loved music, especially pianos. We had no piano at home, but some of my friends did, and when we were together, supposedly to play, I would escape to their pianos and "play." Mom noticed my interest and sent me to a private piano teacher. I did not stop studying until I received my degree at a conservatory, the same month I also graduated from university.

All those years and endless hours of piano practicing should have a purpose. And God's purpose for my "delight" in music continues to be fulfilled. Over the years, in different countries and cultures, and midst peoples speaking languages different from my own, I have had the delightful privilege of directing church music. God knew His purpose for me and prepared me to fulfill that purpose. He even gave me a husband who is a musician!

Later on I had the privilege of learning to play the organ. With my teacher's help I learned several famous pieces, such as Bach's Toccata and Fugue in D Minor and Widor's Toccata. Eventually I was able to play them in an enormous European cathedral. The huge organ huge pipes at my back boomed powerfully, sounds rising in perfect acoustics to every corner of the high-vaulted cathedral, as I pulled out all the stops. This experience was beyond my wildest dreams. Visitors sat and enjoyed. My teacher was pleased. I was too. But most important of all, my Father in heaven was pleased that I had worked with Him in developing the musical gift He had given me. After all, a God-given delight brings balance and joy to our lives, especially when we offer it back in praise to the Lord for His goodness and great love to us.

Where there is abiding love for Him, there is always delight and desire, determination, decision, dependence, and development!

What delight in your life can God use to fulfill His purposes for you—and bless others?

Marli Ritter-Hein

What Is Your Story?

"You are blessed because you believed that the Lord would do what he said." Luke 1:45, NLT.

"For he took notice of his lowly servant girl, and from now on all generations will call me blessed." Luke 1:48, NLT.

Recently I attended a women's retreat where the theme was "The Story of My Life." As I was handed the program my mind immediately reflected on the song, "The Story of My Life," which was made popular by Neil Diamond. I thought about once-upon-a-time stories; stories that warmed my heart and always had happy endings. As the women's sessions continued I was forced to think about my personal stories. Stories of failures but also of triumphs, stories of hate but also love, stories of confusion, hurts, brokenness, but now of peace.

Some of us have stories of deep, dark, painful hurts. Stories of being brokenhearted, stories of battles with illnesses that have left ugly scars or worse. Then there are the stories of immoralities, which we repress in the recesses of our minds, hoping that no one finds out. Stories that keep us stuck in our past, forcing us to live our lives behind closed doors like prisoners. Stories that bring fear. Fear of trusting and being open to love and being loved.

The keynote speaker admonished us to allow Jesus to rewrite our stories.

Christ's mother, Mary (in today's texts), is an example of a woman whose life was changed forever because she allowed Jesus to change her story. She chose to believe the angel and was blessed because of her faith. This was a promise from God, and whatever He promises, that He will do.

We, too, need to believe. John tells us we can be confident that God will listen to whatever we ask in harmony with His will; furthermore, if we know He listens to us, then we have the petitions we desire of Him (1 John 5:14, 15).

There are several stories in the Bible of women (some anonymous) whose lives were changed in positive ways because they allowed Jesus to make the difference. We can reflect on the woman with the infirmity (Luke 13:10–13), the woman with the issue of blood (Mark 5:24–29), the woman who was a prostitute (Luke 7:37–48). Jesus wants to change your story, too, so that your story can be one of praise and of having the blessed assurance that He is yours forever.

Tamar Boswell

Dreams Deferred

Hope deferred makes the heart sick, but when the desire comes, it is a tree of life. Prov. 13:12, NKJV.

In his poem "A Dream Deferred," Langston Hughes asks a question that is essential in life. What happens to dreams deferred? So many people, especially women, have a storehouse of deferred dreams locked away inside them. As a young girl I loved science and dreamed of becoming a scientist. Then an unfortunate incident occurred that deterred me from pursuing that cherished dream, even mentally. The dream that had once energized me now dried up like a raisin in the sun, as the poem says, and died. What the poem doesn't ask is what becomes of the dreamers when the dreams are deferred or die? In my case, I continued to love science but never considered its professional pursuit again. For years I floundered, thinking I had no talents God could use, though raised a Christian and later becoming a Seventh-day Adventist. Though excelling academically and developing socially, I still felt I had no true identity.

Without much ado I chose another path, education, which I loved almost as much as research science. Education was exciting, rewarding in a quieter sort of way, yet still invigorating and something God could use in ministry. Now nearing the end of a career in educational ministry, I still love it but still also wonder, What if I had taken the scientific journey?

I also wonder what has happened to so many others who had dreams deferred. Did they fester and die along with their dream? What makes a difference in this regard in the individual life? For me, the difference was a mother who beat the odds of naysayers and succeeded professionally and never ceased to encourage me even to this day. Let us always exercise the gifts of encouragement. Without encouragement many girls and women, whose dreams are routinely deferred, will never use their God-given gifts and talents to further His cause.

God wants and needs us all in His vineyard. If He equips us, God calls us; and He has equipped us all. "We have different gifts, according to the grace given to each of us. If your gift is prophesying, then prophesy in accordance with your faith; if it is serving, then serve; if it is teaching, then teach; if it is to encourage, then give encouragement; if it is giving, then give generously; if it is to lead, do it diligently; if it is to show mercy, do it cheerfully" (Rom. 12:6–8, NKJV).

Ella Louise Smith Simmons

The Beauty of Nature

Behold the fowls of the air: for they sow not, neither do they reap, nor gather into barns; yet your heavenly Father feedeth them. Are ye not much better than they? Matt. 6:26.

As I sit here I am not only humbled by the blessings of the past week but I am truly thankful to God for His never-ending love, mercies, and continued grace. I am thankful to be greeted almost every new day by rays of sunshine cascading through the room of my parents' hilltop home. I am also thankful for the scenic view that gently extends from my bedroom window to the lush vegetation of our Caribbean island home.

On typical weekday mornings, I often find myself in fits of hurry getting ready to head out to work. On those busy days I sometimes forget to give God thanks for the many ways He daily and unfailingly reveals Himself to me through nature. Today in particular, as I have some spare time on my hands, I've decided to write about what I'm experiencing. Writing about my scenic and prayerful meditation is a form of devotional therapy for me.

From the vantage point of my bedroom window, I can often see a variety of birds visiting the various fruit trees stretching forth on the outside of my heavenly Father's garden. What a variety: grass birds and a few ground doves. I can often see these little creatures feeding or collecting straw from nearby trees to build their nests. To say the least, I find myself in awe as I watch these beautiful little creatures go about their tasks without a care in the world, a humbling contrast to my own sinful, murmuring state. Too often I murmur instead of remembering to thank God for His very own promise to take care of me.

As I sit here the beauty of nature refreshes my mind, body, and soul. It restores my balance. These reminders draw my thoughts to the Bible. In particular, I think of what Jesus said: "Behold the fowls of the air. . . . Are ye not much better than they?"

I can tell you that not only do these visible sights do wonders for my senses but God's Biblical reminders that come to mind offer me hope that He—who cares so much about those tiny birds—also cares for me. I'm reminded He sends the Holy Spirit as a Comforter to guide me when I am tempted and distressed by worldly cares. God calms me through the beauty of nature. With a thankful heart I sit, watch, and praise God who also created—and cares for—me!

Samantha Bullock

Two Strokes in One Month

Men and women don't live by bread only; we live by every word that comes from God's mouth. Deut. 8:3, *The Message*.

I walked into the hospital where I am a volunteer chaplain assistant. The plan was to have a cerebral angiogram and go home after six to eight hours. I'd been dizzy, experiencing right-side head pain. A previous artery biopsy had supposedly ruled out temporal arteritis. A follow-up CAT scan showed the appearance of a mild aneurysm. So, here I was for another test.

During the test, two strokes (a neurologist subsequently told me) completely erased my motor skills. I couldn't type, drive, work, vacuum, cook, or even think straight. Among other things, I'd have to learn to walk again.

I'd been working fifteen-hour days as accountants do during income-tax filing season. I was sleep deprived and spiritually undernourished. My personal time with God was a quick read from a devotional book each morning while my evening prayers often ended with me sound asleep almost as soon as my prayers started.

I tried to find the silver lining in this double-whammy stroke setback. For starters, it made me a better chaplain. When my minister and the paid hospital chaplain came to visit and pray, all I could do was open my eyes, look at them, and close my eyes again. Now, when I enter patients' rooms and they make no response, I realize it doesn't mean that they don't want me there or they don't love God. They are just very sick!

Second, I learned better relationship management. Angry and sad that close family members ignored me, I consulted a Christian counselor and learned that I'd allowed people into my inner circle who did not belong there. People I knew the best weren't there for me. Yet people I hardly knew came to my rescue. I learned to readjust relationships according to reality. After a month in physical therapy, I abandoned the walker and quad cane. I saw everything in a different light as though I had another chance at life. I couldn't walk and now I can!

You don't need to have two strokes in February to profit from the lessons that I learned. If you are spiritually deprived (and physically overtaxed), you cannot be a blessing to others. Look at your nutrition from a spiritual viewpoint—and adjust according to reality.

Patricia Hook Rhyndress Bodi

Who Is in Charge?

We plan the way we want to live, but only God makes us able to live it.
Prov. 16:9, *The Message*.

Life is a challenge! As women we often feel we must do *everything* and do it *perfectly*! It's wearying, overwhelming, and discouraging to live with such unrealistic expectations. I'm so glad today's text takes the pressure off and the gives opportunity to appreciate the *here* and *now*.

If you have listened to the news or walked past the bookstore magazine racks, you have heard this message: "You *can* have it all!" Christian women need to define what "all" is! It is important to know what our priorities are and who sets them for us. The world would have us believe priorities are the corner office, a palatial home, a fine car, and a job that provides at least a six-figure income. We struggle with not being a failure.

On the other hand, the Lord tells us, "My kingdom is not of this world!" Christian women have a responsibility to live a life with balance. Our witness— when we are always tired, frazzled, and irritable—does not reflect God's kingdom. It also diminishes any testimony we may have. Listen to the Word: "Be well balanced (temperate, sober of mind), be vigilant and cautious at all times; for that enemy of yours, the devil, roams around like a lion roaring (in fierce hunger), seeking someone to seize upon and devour" (1 Pet. 5:8, AMP).

As the wife of a pastor, I have often found myself in situations where I felt all eyes were on me! It used to terrify me—certainly I would stumble, make a mistake, have crumbs on my face, whatever! I was *so* relieved when I found out it wasn't about me! God has a plan for my life, and I just have to walk where He says walk and do what He tells me to do. I learned I did not have to explain, excuse, or apologize for following *His* leading. Yes, at times, that has made others uncomfortable. However, I can move with confidence and smile because *God's got it!*

Christian women, it's time to remember Christ's words to Martha when she was overwhelmed with serving: "Martha, dear Martha, you're fussing far too much and getting yourself worked up over nothing. One thing only is essential, and Mary has chosen it—it's the main course, and won't be taken from her" (Luke 10:42, *The Message*). If we sit at the feet of the Master and hear His voice guiding, directing our lives, we will take better care of ourselves and show how our confidence comes from His guidance and love. This will be our witness.

Wilma Kirk Lee

Brokenness

The LORD is close to the *brokenhearted* and saves those who are crushed in spirit. Ps. 34:18, NIV; italics added.

I lay there on the concrete staring at my hand. In disbelief I looked at the deformed wrist as it jutted out in a direction it shouldn't have. Just a moment earlier I was upright and carefree. What a difference a few seconds can make! During my one-hour lunch break I'd been running errands. One of these stops was to fill up the gas tank of my car. As I removed the gas tank nozzle, I noticed the hose tangled in a loop and frozen into place by the cold weather. With the wind whipping about me, I was determined to get back into the warmth of my van. I placed the nozzle in my tank and then noticed I needed to step over the hose to open the driver's door.

That's when the accident happened. And in a split second. The tip of my boot caught on the gas hose, which became a launching pad for me before I hit the ground, smashing my wrist. With my arm in a cast nearly halfway up my shoulder, there was no denying that I had an injury. Subsequently, I jokingly told my coworkers how I'd wrestled with alligators, but the story didn't fly. It just sounded more heroic than what had actually occurred. But no one could see the jigsaw of emotions that my spirit held in check.

Brokenness. We live with it every day. It is much easier to see physical brokenness than it is the spiritual. The Bible demonstrates to us that Jesus saw the physical needs of those He healed—the blindness, leprosy, bleeding, crippled arms and legs. But He also saw the spiritual. Gently leading the Samaritan woman in conversation, He uncovered the layers of spiritual brokenness that had imprisoned her life year after year. His questions revealed her issues with prejudice, ancestry, and apostate beliefs stemming from cultural differences. He also told Nicodemus that he must be born again. And that had to do with the Holy Spirit at work within. It also has to do with letting God heal the damage caused by sin and wrong life choices.

My broken arm is doing much better now, thanks to a great hand surgeon, a protective cast, and time. My choice of a spiritual Surgeon is, of course, an easy one. He's the One who came to heal the brokenhearted and the crushed in spirit. In fact, He became brokenness for me. My surgeon of choice is Jesus. Make Him your choice today as well.

Karen Phillips

In Pursuit of Perfect Beauty

Instead, your beauty should consist of your true inner self, the ageless beauty of a gentle and quiet spirit, which is of the greatest value in God's sight. 1 Pet. 3:4, GNT.

While browsing through a teen magazine, I saw pictures of young women whose appearances were enhanced by colorful makeup, tinted and perfectly shaped eyebrows, curled eyelashes, rosy-blush cheeks, and glossy pink lips. The glamour of these beautiful women was accentuated by the trendy, fashionable clothes and accessories they wore. One glance at their flawless skin, perfect eyes, and confident poses could beat down any insecure girl.

So I had to ask myself, is true beauty composed of perfectly placed makeup, the latest fashions, and stylish shoes? Is true beauty having a willowy body that appears to be on a continual diet? The world honors outward beauty through beauty pageants, modeling shows, and the attractive women seen in magazine advertisements and on television shows. But I've taken a closer look at what real beauty is and have arrived at the following conclusions.

First, real beauty is nurturing a relationship with the Creator. God created us to be wonderful creatures as declared by David (Ps. 139:14). And because God is our Creator, we are privileged to have a deep and growing relationship with Him as we read His Word, pray, and follow the guidance of His Holy Spirit. In this intimate relationship we find our true worth.

Second, real beauty is acknowledging God's wonderful unique creation of you. Accept yourself for who you are—unique and one-of-a-kind, created for a purpose only you can fulfill.

Third, real beauty is discovering your purpose in life. Focus on what you can do instead of on what you can't do. A beautiful woman is an industrious woman, ready to fulfill God's mission for her, no matter what season of life she is in.

Finally, real beauty is seeing and bringing out the beauty in others. Real beauty is caring, loving, sympathetic, and helpful. A beautiful woman shares with others what she knows about Jesus—as did Mary Magdalene after Jesus made her whole again. A woman's true beauty comes from within, reflecting God's character, and seeing the worth of each soul she encounters.

Forget the world's standard of beauty, for "charm is deceptive and beauty disappears, but a woman who honors the Lord should be praised" (Prov. 31:30, GNT).

Grachienne L. Banuag

Reconciliation

For the LORD watches over the way of the righteous, but the way of the wicked leads to destruction. Ps. 1:6, NIV.

Paul sends a message to two women, faithful and important workers in the church, who apparently were not getting along. They were under the leadership of the Holy Spirit and were well known. Though we don't know the reason for the quarrel, we do know that Paul asked a third person to intervene and work toward resolution, adding. "I plead with Euodia and I plead with Syntyche to be of the same mind in the Lord" (Phil. 4:2). The early church could not continue growing when there was not agreement of thought and union among brethren. Quarrels, whatever the reasons, would divide the members and consequently damage the work.

Euodia and Syntyche were women like you and me. We are dreamers, dedicated workers in the cause of God, but unfortunately liable to imperfections. Many responsibilities can leave us tired and vulnerable to irritation. Frictions can lead to heartbreak. Sometimes, as in this New Testament experience, a third party needs to help resolve the situation and bring reconciliation. Reconciliation restores balance to our relationships. Though we don't know how the Bible story ended, we want to believe that these two women made peace and continued the work of ministry.

God's counsel through Paul (Phil. 4:2) remains the same today. Reconciliation needs to be one of the ingredients in our "daily bread," for it is the key to the success of any institution or interpersonal relationship. The world is made up of different people with different opinions and behaviors. To this mixture, stir in the stress of everyday life and physical exhaustion from demands put on us. Sooner or later, this all becomes a recipe for frayed nerves and vulnerable egos. Disagreement then becomes almost inevitable. Fortunately, we can add the ingredient of forgiveness, and that makes a miracle out of any disagreement.

Following close behind forgiveness is reconciliation, which restores relationship again. Both forgiveness and reconciliation involve the breaking of self-pride. This too is possible if we invite Jesus to be the "third party" that helps resolve a disagreement and bring reconciliation.

Dear friend, if today brings something into your heart that you need to resolve with someone, do so without delay. Call Jesus to bless and strengthen you. He will be right there!

Sueli da Silva Pereira

Jesus Laughs

The joy of the LORD is your strength. Neh. 8:10, NIV.

Some time ago, Dorrett, a friend of mine, forwarded an e-mail to me with pictures and entitled "Jesus Laughs." As I viewed the seven images in the forward, I was immediately flabbergasted by the painter's portrayal of Christ laughing.

The first frame portrayed Jesus bending over and holding the hand of a toddler as He walked. The next image showed Jesus seated and playing with a child in his lap, as another leaned on His back looking over His right shoulder, watching. The third pictured the Savior tenderly hugging a little girl, while the fourth portrayed Christ holding a little girl in his arms, the child's mother looking on with joy. The fifth picture featured Jesus in a joyful small-group discussion with two young women. The sixth portrayed Christ smiling over a small baby that He was gently rocking to sleep.

The last picture, which is my favorite, showed the Savior smiling up at a baby He was holding up in the air as the baby giggles with delight. Looking at these images drew me to a simple, yet captivating, characteristic of our Savior—He is joyful. I immediately saved the forward to "My Documents" on the computer. The pictures reminded me that a Christian woman, who is whole in Christ, is also a joyful woman.

Later that same day, as I was preparing for our family's evening worship, Crystal (one of my daughters) unexpectedly asked, "Mommy, how does Jesus laugh?" I was a taken aback by her question and wasn't sure how to answer her. Then, like a lightning bolt, the memory of that day's e-mail forward came to my mind. I smiled broadly, realizing that my God of joy had already made provision for the answer to my daughter's question.

"Crissy," I responded, "I will show later you some pictures of Jesus laughing." She smiled at my promise. My heart was at ease, knowing that God answers all our prayers—even the simple ones—and often before we even pray them. Later the entire family all enjoyed the pictures together, animatedly discussing the details of Jesus laughing in each frame. The details of a God who has assured us that not only is His joy our strength, but also that He—as the pictures portrayed—rejoices over us (Zeph. 3:17).

Thamer Cassandra Smikle

Praise Prescription

Praise the LORD, my soul. Ps. 103:1, NIV.

My daughter was diagnosed with kidney failure in April of 2002. This harsh reality destined her for dialysis treatments the rest of her life—unless a match could be found for a transplant. Upon hearing the news, I collapsed to the floor, crying and praying. My sister-in-law, Esther, heard the news. She called and told me that a ninety-year-old retired minister suggested I read Psalm 103 three times a day in order to cope. That sounded like a prescription. Distraught, I decided to try it. Doing so turned out to be such a blessing as I praised God three times a day.

Thus began my love affair with God and my new spiritual exercise of praising. In fact, I memorized the entire chapter of Psalm 103 so I can still praise God when away from my Bible.

On my newfound praise journey I have experienced what some people refer to as the ABCs of prayer. ABC stands for ask, believe, and claim—all within the context of praise.

It was in praise that God helped me understand that my desired way and timing of answered prayer are not always His way and His timing. Praising God led me to trusting Him more deeply—and gave me patience in my wait on Him. I learned that praise is a wonderful counterbalance to pain. Three and a half years after diagnosis, God provided a kidney transplant for my daughter and a new life, which she still enjoys today. And I still continue to praise God through Psalm 103. Three times a day! It's still a good prescription that has sustained me through my husband's heart attack in 2006 and my own incurable, though treatable, illnesses.

One morning I was impressed to "rewrite" Psalm 103 in words as if God were speaking to me personally. I prayed, asking for His anointing, and sat down to write. What an awesome experience! I can't even describe it. It was difficult to pull myself away from this inspired time in order to prepare for the rest of my day.

God inhabits our praises (Ps. 22:3). As long as I have my breath I will lift my voice in praise to my awesome and amazing God as a balance to life's trials. And I can't wait to share our praise stories when we meet at our first heavenly praise celebration.

My sisters, with what Bible passage can you intentionally praise God—three times—today? I invite you try the "praise prescription" and experience the difference it will make.

Harriet Breach

Housekeeping

What? Know ye not that your body is the temple of the Holy Ghost which is in you . . . . and ye are not your own? 1 Cor. 6:19.

I used to think that if I chose to overindulge in anything—say junk food or TV—the indulgence wouldn't affect anyone except me. Oh sure, I'd practice moderation—sort of.

This careless mind-set changed, however, when, as a young missionary wife, I learned I was pregnant. While carrying this child in his first "house," my womb, I grew very careful about, well, housekeeping. I drank enough water for both of us. And napped and exercised and breathed fresh air. I was careful about what I let, or didn't let, into my mind. I had read that how a mommy-to-be treats herself is how she treats the child in her womb. Suddenly I felt very responsible for childcare even before I ever saw the child about whom I now cared so deeply.

The baby arrived safely despite the unseasonal rains that washed out a bridge necessitating his being born in a Congolese jungle clinic instead of in a real hospital in Uganda.

The process was quite casual, actually, as I birthed in my street clothes assisted by two dedicated missionary nuns. French was our mutual language of communication. Sometime during my fourteenth hour of labor, around sundown, the generator at the little clinic gave out. Two hours later—ta-da!—my son arrived. A natural childbirth in every sense of the word, his entrance onto life's stage was illuminated by the underwhelming glow of a kerosene lantern and a flashlight. Though five weeks premature, the five-pound, two-ounce baby boy was healthy and soon gaining weight like nobody's business.

I was glad I'd taken good care of him by taking good care of me.

Years later, while reflecting on the in utero experience, I wondered if a mother's "self-care" of her unborn baby might also have a spiritual application. After all, the Bible shares that my body is "the temple of the Holy Ghost"—for it houses the very Helper who Jesus promised would indwell His followers and be with them forever (John 14:16). So my physical being still houses Another. My choices still—and always will—matter. More than ever, I want to be a purposeful, attentive housekeeper. I wouldn't want poor choices that hurt me to hurt Him too.

God, help me ever be mindful that You dwell in me and will empower my best for You.

Carolyn Rathbun Sutton

September 15

My Healing Garden

And the LORD God planted a garden . . . Gen. 2:8.

I like paging through garden magazines and also admiring people's gardens. I love flowers, but my late husband did all the gardening. That is, until he fell ill in October 2010 before passing away on September 17 of the following year. Though I was grieving, it became clear to me that the house and garden needed attention. And all the responsibility now fell on me.

First, I trimmed all hedges, which had overgrown, before purchasing pretty plants to grace the front driveway. On one side of the driveway I planted two shades each of marigolds and begonias with assorted pansies. On the opposite side of the driveway, I planted more pansies and mesemfryanthemum (*bokbaai-vygie*). The latter are bright, colorful, shiny flowers that open in the full sun. Everyone passing by or visiting admires their beauty.

However, my marigolds and pansies soon began to disappear because of snails munching on them for a midnight snack! So I bought more pansies and begonias to fill in where snails had eaten marigolds—roots and all. The hot sun and strong wind withered the vygies and pansies, although I watered them every day. The more challenges I had, the more I became interested in gardening. Soon I was investing in more plants, bulbs, and seed packets.

I chose and planted seeds from which sprung alyssum, zinnia, petunia, gazania, gladioli, and cornflower. They all grew well. When I bought the amaryllis, I also bought zantedeschia (yellow arum lilly) and poliantes (the pearl). I thought the poliantes was never going to show signs of life and gave up hope. I thought all fifteen bulbs had died. But now, after so many months, they all have leaves and one plant is sprouting buds.

My beautiful garden has attracted bees, butterflies, and *kwiksterjies* too (a very friendly bird), which visits every day to keep me company.

My garden blesses me three ways, in particular. First, it constantly teaches me patience and makes me so glad that God doesn't give up on me. Second, it is living proof that without God's hand being involved, nothing in me can grow. Finally, this beautiful garden brings healing because it takes my mind off of sorrow and loneliness.

Loving Creator God, give us hearts receptive to Your beauty and healing. Amen.

Priscilla Adonis

A Star, Car, and Bunny Rabbit

Fear thou not: for I am with thee: be not dismayed: for I am thy God:
I will strengthen thee; yea, I will help thee: yea, I will uphold thee with
the right hand of my righteousness. Isa. 41:10.

The wide-open landscape and roads of Stillwater County, Montana, with its high terrain, mountains, tree-dotted hills, and rolling plains punctuated with grazing cows and horses envelopes one with awe and solitude. It reminds us of how small and seemingly insignificant we are in comparison to the grandeur and expanse of nature and its Creator God. How beautiful and inspiring this sight is during the day; how dreadfully dark and formidable its replica at night.

I traveled through Montana with my daughter in October to help her relocate for her new job. Eventually the time came for me to return home. My flight departure time was 7:00 A.M., which meant leaving in the dark. Unsubsiding fear began to grip my thoughts despite the successful test drive on the previous day. I arose early the next morning and prayed with my daughter, asking God to be with her. *But wait, did I even hear and understand the prayer I uttered for my daughter? Did not I even trust God to be with me?* Not really. As I began my journey, I was in tears, all alone and frightened. Then it happened. I looked up, and there in the utter darkness was one lone star that brightened the sky. My heart leaped for joy and I thanked God for His guiding light, the star. This star led me for the next ten minutes. Then the star was gone. But before I could become fearful again, I spotted a little red car directly ahead of me that I knew God had sent to guide me on my way. And it did guide until the exit just before my turn-off exit to the airport. Wow! All I could do was to praise God and begin trusting Him more.

After my airport arrival, I had to drive past the airport's lighted entrance to park in the distant, dark parking lot. Fear defined me as I began the long walk in the dark back to the airport's entrance. Then suddenly right in front of me hopped a bunny rabbit. I couldn't believe it. Once again, I knew that God was with me and that there was no need to fear. This bunny rabbit stayed in its position until I walked into the airport. I was ecstatic! Despite my wavering faith in God, God never left me nor forsook me.

Friends, God lovingly reminds us: "Fear thou not: for I am with thee . . . I will help thee" (Isa. 41:10). And His sure presence always brings peace.

Cynthia Best-Goring

Peace Be to This House

"When you enter a house, first say, 'Peace to this house.' "
Luke 10:5, NIV.

The evangelist, Luke, relates an episode when Jesus sent out seventy disciples to preach the gospel. Jesus gave them various instructions for the success of their missionary labor. In one of His recommendations He tells them that the first thing they must do when they enter a house is to say: "Peace to this house."

This is a wonderful way of greeting as you enter a home. Various important things could be noted in this blessing for homes today.

First, Jesus knows that homes need peace. It is sad to listen to the news and observe with sorrow what is happening in families today. Violence of all kinds in the family circle is bringing destruction to many homes.

Second, Jesus knows that there can be peace in homes. No matter how critical things are in the home, its members should not lose hope of a happy solution. On occasion you hear people say: "My home is like hell." Jesus wants to tell these households to believe that it is possible to change these homes from places where Satan reigns to a home where God and holy angels live.

Third, Jesus wants every family member and, in general, all the children to seek the peace that only He can give: "Peace I leave with you; my peace I give you. I do not give to you as the world gives" (John 14:27, NIV). Ellen G. White explains how we can receive this peace that Christ offers: "This peace is not something that He gives apart from Himself. It is in Christ, and we can receive it only by receiving Him" (*The Ministry of Healing*, p. 247). Jesus does not desire that this peace comes sporadically to your personal life, but that you should seek it daily. It is within our reach if we only ask for it first thing as we begin each day.

Fourth, the peace that Jesus brings to our personal life will be noticed in the kind of relationships we have with others, especially with those of our own family. Fathers, mothers, husbands, wives, sons, and daughters will be filled with the peace of Christ.

Peace be to this house.

Christ is willing for this desire to be fulfilled in every life and in every home every day, if only we ask for it.

Cecilia Moreno de Iglesias

Being a Light

"You are the light of the world. A city set on a hill cannot be hidden. Nor do people light a lamp and put it under a basket, but on a stand, and it gives light to all in the house. In the same way, let your light shine before others, so that they may see your good works and give glory to your Father who is in heaven." Matt. 5:14-16, ESV.

Knowingly or unknowingly, parents practice discipleship in rearing and shaping the future of their children. Their beliefs, perspectives, and practices shape their children's worldviews, perception of life, and future. When I was a sickly girl of eight, my father desired that I become a nurse. I had very little understanding of what a nurse was except that they wore a white cap on their heads, a crisp white uniform, and spotless white shoes. It was my dream.

Educating his children was the impetus for my father's hard work. He valued Christian education in spite of greater financial obligations. I grew up as a Christian and attended a Protestant high school. My going to a Christian nursing school was my dad's obsession that led him to Philippine Union College (PUC). Was that God's leading so I could know about Jesus and the Sabbath? My father went to visit the campus.

The student guard at the PUC gate welcomed my father and escorted him to the administration building. He ensured that Dad's questions were answered to his satisfaction. My father could not resist the leading of the Holy Spirit evidenced by the beauty and character of the people at the school. He then declared PUC was the right school for his daughter's nursing training. While there, I accepted the Bible teachings and also the Sabbath, finished nursing, joined the PUC nursing faculty, became involved in missions, and received scholarships to advance my career. God blessed Dad's quest for Christian education and the guard's kindness.

My father's vision for Christian education was a virtue and a legacy passed from his generation to the next. He demonstrated that efforts made for others bring souls to the feet of Jesus and give glory to our Father in heaven. My father went to rest in Jesus before his eighty-ninth birthday.

As for the student guard who let his light shine, may we each emulate him so that we may make an difference in someone else's life.

Edna Bacate Domingo

Regenerated Résumés for the Chronologically Gifted

I will guide thee with mine eye. Ps. 32:8.

It was 839 months down and one to go before the headlights of age seventy coming toward me on the train track would smack. Not that I minded, for with every birthday I've crowed, "One more year down, one year closer to heaven with one year less on earth—and the devil don't got me yet." Each year I gratefully take inventory that my body parts remain present and in working order. And after the many vegetables I've diced, I still have five digits on each hand. But this time a warm glow of anticipation was added to my crowing.

A sudden awareness washed over me of all the time-busters God had cleared from my "to do" docket in the last year. I had already checked off on my retirement fun-list those that had beckoned me. I was available for new adventures at this season of life! I was excited!

I had some things I still wanted to do, and God had me prepared for this moment! All that heretofore had been "work" in my word-processing livelihood would now be an adventure with God alone as my Boss! I had my Bibles, concordances, commentaries, and more. I was ready!

So what does this have to do with a devotional message? Here is a quote that has helped me to know what God wants me to do for my current résumé: "If we consent, He will so identify Himself with our thoughts and aims, so blend our hearts and minds into conformity to His will, that when obeying Him we shall be but *carrying out our own impulses*" (*The Desire of Ages,* p. 608; emphasis supplied).

Does it work? I am now fifteen days into my seventieth year. One project is organized on the dining room table, another on the daybed in the spare bedroom. *Oh, the temptation to get with the next two before these two yield their space!* But I did have to stop and share this in the event that another sister might be energized to realize her "own impulses" as God's plan. My friends, too, are following their God-given impulses. One prayed her way through her fiftieth birthday and the next thing I knew, she was going on mission trips! Another found her passion volunteering at the kitty-cat shelter, and another as the hospital information desk receptionist, where she thrived. We needn't write up our résumé for senior years—God already has. He can't wait for us to read it!

Janet Lankheet

Even What Seems Impossible Happens

"Even on my servants, both men and women, I will pour out my Spirit in those days." Joel 2:29, NIV.

When we finished arranging the things in our new home, I looked out the window and imagined what our new neighbors might be like. Would they welcome us? How would we relate to them, and how could we influence them through our testimony?

I talked about it with Rutinha, my faithful servant, who, more than a simple servant, is a prayer partner, a trusted friend with whom I can share concerns.

A few days later, I had to make a trip. When I returned, Rutinha's smile surely meant something. "You seem very happy," I said, and with a broad smile she told me that she was studying the Bible with Dr. Carlos. "Who is Dr. Carlos?" I asked. I also asked myself, *How could a semiliterate person explain the Bible to a doctor?*

Rutinha then told me that the doctor was our neighbor who lived across the street. "One day," she told me, "because of the heat, I was in the kitchen with the door open, when suddenly a man entered, breathlessly, asking for help to hide because his wife wanted to kill him." After Rutinha offered him a glass of water, he told her the sad reality of his marriage. Then Rutinha invited him to pray, ensuring that God could help him in solving his problems. With simple words, but full of faith, Rutinha took that problem to God, certain that God would act in that situation. Dr. Carlos, calmer now, but very embarrassed, apologized for the inconvenience, but Rutinha said it had been a privilege to pray with him and then invited him to study the Bible. She told him that through the study of God's Word, he and his wife could find peace.

Rutinha and I started studying the Bible with that dear couple, and over time we could see the transformation that God was carrying out. Eventually, when problems arose, even professional ones, Dr. Carlos would come to me and asked permission to pray with Rutinha. And when they prayed, he left more comforted and in peace.

It makes me understand what the writer Ellen White wrote, "There is no limit to the usefulness of one who, by putting self aside, makes room for the working of the Holy Spirit upon [her] heart, and lives a life wholly consecrated to God" (*The Desire of Ages,* pp. 250, 251).

Eunice Michiles Malty

Outward

And, behold, there came a leper and worshipped him, saying, Lord, if thou wilt, thou canst make me clean. Matt. 8:2.

So when they continued asking him, he lifted up himself, and said unto them, He that is without sin among you, let him first cast a stone at her. John 8:7.

"Man looks at the outward appearance, but the Lord looks at the heart." 1 Sam. 16:7, NIV.

Recently, while preparing dinner, I needed an onion. I knew that I had two left. While I looked in the refrigerator, my granddaughter Makenzi told me the onions were in the trash because they were spoiled. I looked at the top of the trash and there they were. Upon close examination, the outside of the onion was very spoiled to look at; however, I laid it on the cutting board and cut it in half.

Upon cutting the onion, I noticed that only two or three layers of the outer skin were spoiled—the inner onion was pure white, like new. I tasted it and it was sweet as all Vidalia onions are. Therefore, I cut away the outsides of the onions and discarded them and what was left was beautiful. I began to chop and dice the onion into what I needed.

When the people saw the leper in Bible days, he was considered unclean and had to be cast away from the multitude of people. As today's first text says, he asked Jesus to make him clean once again. When Jesus saw him, He saw from a different perspective; He looked at his heart and told him he was now whole.

When people in the city found the woman caught in sin, she was unclean and they wanted to stone her; the men who assisted in her "uncleanliness" were soon lost in the crowd after the Lord wrote in the dust. "So when they continued asking him, he lifted up himself, and said unto them, He that is without sin among you, let him first cast a stone at her." The Lord had looked at her heart and saw that she was not what people projected that she was. She had outward dysfunctions; He went for the heart as only the Lord could do.

Cleansing from the inside out is better than an outside-only cleansing. People look at us and judge us by our outward appearance; however, we have a merciful Lord who looks at our hearts, and performs His works within us. If that were not the case, we would all be lost.

Betty Glover Perry

Are You OK With Being Just OK?

Whatever you do, work at it with all your heart, as working for the Lord, not for human masters. Col. 3:23, NIV.

Many of us are employed and, therefore, blessed to have a job. While you may dread heading out the door to face another day of work, there are many who long for employment.

We often view work as negative, counting the days until the weekend or our next vacation. We put in our time, but our efforts are halfhearted at best. In our lackluster approach to work, we settle for mediocrity instead of pursuing excellence. We settle for "good enough." But are we OK with being just OK?

Truly believing our scripture for today will change one's perspective. Seeing our work as "for the Lord" generates new purpose and brings meaning into our tasks. Each part of our work becomes an opportunity to bless others. Even the smallest deed is done in love. As we work "for the Lord," our halfhearted efforts end as we become convicted of their God-dishonoring impact. For paid employees, the bonus outcome of this shift in thinking is that we become highly valued workers, an indispensable part of an organization.

But you may argue, "My job is not at all related to ministry or service. How can I be working for God in this job?" The interesting thing about the context of Colossians 3:23 is that Paul is speaking to slaves, people with very little say or control over their lives. People with every reason in the world to believe that they were not working for the Lord. And yet, this is exactly how Paul is challenging them to view their slave labor.

Every job, paid or unpaid, can be done with honor and purpose, as "to the Lord." I am inspired by the idea captured in this quote: "There is something very beautiful in work which is well and precisely done. It is participation in the activity of God, who makes all things well and wisely, beautiful to the last detail" (Jean Vanier, *Community and Growth*, p. 300).

Praise God that He can change attitudes and hearts! Our work becomes a source of joy and purpose when we look for God's activity and leading. If you struggle to be thankful for work or lack drive and passion for it—whether at home caring for little ones or in paid employment—ask God to change your attitude. He will be pleased to help you not be OK with being just OK.

Nancy A. Gerard

God: Chief Administrator

And lo, I am with you always, even unto the end of the world. Amen.
Matt. 28:20.

Life was closing in on me. Two staff members were leaving. As staff separation procedures demanded, I needed to pass on completed paperwork. If they were to be paid their final salary that day, their files needed to be completed and turned in before the bank closed. Driving to work that morning I'd suddenly remembered, "Tax returns are due today." I was stunned. I had absolutely forgotten. The consequences of late tax returns are costly, as I'd experienced. When tempted to go into a tailspin because of stress, I started prayerfully listening for the voice of my Chief Administrator: God. A solution for the paperwork deadline came into my mind: "Let the ladies come in next week to sign off, hand over all their documents, and collect their packages." I sighed in relief. God, my Administrator, was already at work today.

I had scheduled orientation of new staff for Monday, January 2, a public holiday that year. However, the resident doctor advised me that morning he would only be in the office on Sunday, January 1. Unsure how this late change would be received by the recruits, I was prompted to "Call now!" The recruits graciously consented to the appointment changes despite the late notice. Thank You, Chief Administrator! He knows how to make all things right.

During the late afternoon I again felt overwhelmed as the end of the day, week, month, and year responsibilities hung heavy over me. My busy work day ended. Walking to my car, I suddenly remembered that my good friend was having a birthday that very day. And another friend was celebrating hers the very next day. Yet here I was, "remembering" in time to contact both of them with my good wishes. I would have cried had I forgotten these birthdays again.

As with me, many women struggle with daily responsibilities and often feel alone in their struggle to complete them. They also struggle with hearing the guiding voice of their Chief Administrator. The same One who created and manages deep oceans, lofty mountains, and heavenly bodies suspended in space. This same Administrator also wants to help us manage tax returns, birthday greetings, and the tiniest details of our lives. I cannot imagine surviving one day without God's administration in my life. With unblinking attentiveness, He watches over us.

Before we even know solutions to the day's challenges, He is already present with us.

Keisha D. Sterling

Genetically Modified Truth

Test everything that is said to be sure it is true, and if it is,
then accept it. 1 Thess. 5:21, TLB.

I started my early morning jog at the usual spot. About a half kilometer later I sighted a beautiful garden of cabbage. The biggest heads of cabbage I had ever seen! Then I remembered how, the previous day, a market vendor had tried to sell me some pak choi (a variant of bok choy). The vendor declared that this cabbage variant had been organically grown right from a garden at the school where I live. But I was skeptical because of concerns I have about genetically modified seeds being used to grow the produce. I wondered which part of the plant the vendor considered to be organic. Did he simply *assume* it was organic because it had been grown by someone I might know at the school? Did he *really* know that no quick-grow "miracle" (chemical) fertilizer had been used by the gardener to produce fresh produce earlier than its normal growth?

I consider myself a "fruitarian" because I love fruit so much. Yet I'm never sure if the fruit I purchase is organic. *Truly* organic, that is. It feels as if I take a risk when purchasing fresh produce because I don't know if it's been genetically modified or not. In fact, one can't be certain of produce these days unless one knows the origin of the seeds used.

My GMO dilemma with produce, carried into the spiritual realm, makes me wonder if we Christians don't sometimes ingest genetically modified truth. Do we take the necessary time to examine the source of doctrines we hear in order to verify that they've sprung from the fertile soil of balanced biblical principles? Sometimes produce vendors take advantage of shoppers' naiveté by calling their product "organic" when it's not. Unfortunately, some bearers of "truth" do the same. In fact, the apostle Paul warned Timothy that "the time will come when people will not put up with sound doctrine. Instead, to suit their own desires, they will gather around them a great number of teachers to say what their itching ears want to hear" (2 Tim. 4:3, NIV).

We can often recognize nongenetically modified fruit by cutting it open to see if it still contains seeds for reproduction. Likewise, we can recognize non-genetically modified truth when we find the seeds [principles] of God's Word firmly rooted in any given doctrine (Isa. 8:20). A sound rule of thumb for each of us would be to examine before you ingest!

Nadine A. Joseph

September 25

Patience for Warm Bread

The Lord is . . . patient with you. 2 Pet. 3:9, NIV.

A light breeze rustled leaves that hung languorously over the deck. Orchid sprays of every hue dipped gracefully over curving branches. Brightly plumed birds sang and played hide-and-seek in the trees. Melissa was so busy drinking in her surroundings she had forgotten to eat. Almost. Glancing at her plate piled with tropical fruits, nuts, and dates, Melissa asked suddenly, "Where's the toast?" *Yes, where indeed?* Quite frankly, I had been surprised to discover that our tiny beachfront thatched cottage even had a toaster oven. A full twenty-five minutes ago, Melissa had placed slices of bread on sagging metal racks and turned the *on* button to toast. I suggested she check. Almost immediately a wail emanated from the direction of the toaster. Returning to the deck, Melissa stood legs apart, arms akimbo, and the very picture of vibrating impatience. "The bread hasn't offered to get brown!" she shrieked. "I'm *very* tired of waiting! Aren't you upset?"

"It is what it is," I said, shaking my head and munching on my last slice of dragon fruit, marveling at both its appearance and taste. "I'm on vacation and choose to avoid wasting any energy getting upset about a toaster oven that is most likely working up to its capability." A rather long pause ensued before Melissa quietly admitted she might have overreacted a bit.

"Can you figure out what triggered your overreaction?" I asked.

"Expectations," Melissa replied promptly. "I let my expectations lead me to exhibit behaviors that resulted in negative outcomes." I chuckled at her word-for-word rendition of one of my seminar comments. "I expected a toaster in another country to work just like the one I have at home and—I chose to be impatient." She smiled wryly.

Good girl, I thought. *You figured it out for yourself.* Aloud I said, "You can eat *warm* bread or wait 'til this little toaster huffs and puffs its way to crisper bread—I doubt it will ever produce the brown toast you're accustomed to back home."

"Warm bread it is," Melissa said, moving toward the kitchenette and muttering under her breath, "How ridiculous to be impatient with a toaster!"

The Lord is patient with you. How ridiculous for you to be impatient—not with an ancient toaster but with yourself and others.

Arlene R. Taylor

Things That Will Last

I will establish his line forever, his throne as long
as the heavens endure. Ps. 89:29, NIV.

Whenever my husband invites me to go to our small farm, I hesitate because it does not have running water or electricity; we have to leave the comforts of the city: telephones, the Internet, and so on. However, the truth is that whenever I accept his invitation, I never regret my decision. When I am there, with nothing but nature surrounding me, I can see life from a different point of view. There I find peace. There, the sun warms me and replenishes me with vitamin D. My eyes rest upon the natural beauties and upon the green fields and the different hues of the flowers. I feel rejuvenated, I feel like walking and gardening. I wake up earlier, to the soft singing of birds. I breathe better because the air is purer, and I eat and sleep peacefully. I also feel like reading, praying, and meditating more often. I even try to write and sing (two talents I do not possess). When it is time to return to the city, I often go back sad and unwilling to leave the country but always with renewed vigor.

This also happens when we close ourselves inside our world of sadness and pain. We may not feel like going to church; however, when we decide to go, it is a blessing! There is always a song that uplifts the spirit, or we hear a sermon directed to us that fills us with hope, and we go back home refreshed and ready to win the battles of life.

In this world so many things seem to capture our attention. Sometimes, these things that charm the spirit make us want to stay on this earth a little longer. Sometimes we just want to escape. Many times, we get so involved in the things of this world that we forget about the spiritual beauty, the treasure to be cultivated.

Everything here will finish, everything will have an end. Why don't we turn our eyes on Jesus now? Feel His love for us, His sacrifice on the cross, His forgiveness, His character, His choices, His words, His look, and His voice. To know that He intercedes for us before our Father is very comforting. Remember the beautiful words that we find in 1 John 2:1: "My dear children, I write this to you so that you will not sin. But if anybody does sin, we have an advocate with the Father—Jesus Christ, the Righteous One" (NIV).

Let us look for and enjoy now the things that will really last.

Lourdes S. de Oliveira

September 27

Michal

But now thus saith the LORD that created thee, O Jacob, and he that
formed thee, O Israel, Fear not: for I have redeemed thee, I have
called thee by thy name; thou art mine. Isa. 43:1.

Michal, the daughter of King Saul, was of royal blood and the first wife of
David. Her love for him was real. In response to her, David delivered a
high-priced, life-costing dowry to King Saul. David was not forced upon
her; she loved him; he was her choice. She was the daughter of a king marrying a
future king. The future was bright as they both shared mutual love.

Yet what caused Michal to despise David later? Unfortunately, most women
at that time of history did not have much control over their lives—even women
of royal birth. After David's abrupt departure to save his own life, King Saul gave
Michal to another man. When David eventually returned, he reclaimed Michal
as his wife, breaking the heart of Michal's new husband. Was Michal angry,
feeling David had abandoned and neglected her soon after they were married?
Or was she distressed over his handling of her second marriage?

From David's point of view, he probably wanted to redeem Michal from
another man because she was his first love. Although their lives together did not
begin under ideal circumstances, now as king he wanted her with him to solidify
his position. But Michal was not grateful. She did not seek to return his love. She
became critical. Most likely she felt trapped, causing her to vent her frustrations
in open sarcasm when David "danced before the Lord with all his might" (2 Sam.
6:14, TLB). Her criticism of David's jubilance was met with stinging rebuke.
Poor Michal. Having lost her first love, she now lashed out at her king.

As God's chosen, we sometimes find ourselves in Michal's predicament.
We lose that fervent, dedicated, passionate love we once had for Him when
circumstances change or challenges come. But just as David did not forget
Michal and sought to redeem and restore her to her honored position as first
wife, so God seeks to restore us from our fallen position as sinners and to instate
us as princesses of the King.

During times when we don't understand why life seems so out of control,
how will we respond to His gestures of love? The choice is ours. And that choice
can make a difference between a blessing and a curse. May we let God help us
make the choice to return His love.

Maureen Thomas Pierre

Do Your Best

One thing I know, that, whereas I was blind, now I see. John 9:25.

Trust in the LORD . . . and he shall give thee the desires of thine heart.
Ps. 37:3, 4.

One Friday night over twelve years ago, Nial was involved in an automobile accident while traveling home. In addition to other injuries, shards of shattered windshield glass had pierced his eyes. In the hospital the doctor frantically attempted to save Nial's eyesight. But vision in the right eye was gone, with his left eye vision greatly impaired. Despite this setback, Nial determined to continue working for the Lord. In 2008 he spoke at an evangelistic series using key words and texts which Juanita, his wife, had written out for him in large, bold letters. Though always hopeful of regaining sight in his right eye, his vision worsened. Soon Nial had to allow family members to guide him when he walked from place to place

When doctors in Cuba (2010) and then in Trinidad (2011) couldn't help his vision, Nial and his wife determined to seek medical help in the United States. After raising money for transportation and medical expenses, they traveled to Miami, Florida. By now Juanita was expecting their third child. To complicate matters, she knew she'd have to have the baby delivered by caesarean section. Nial found a doctor who said he might be able to help with his eyesight through a surgical procedure. When Nial learned that his eye surgery was scheduled for the same day as Juanita's caesarian section, he rescheduled his long-awaited eye surgery.

By now Nial and Juanita's funds were nearly depleted because all the preoperation medical tests had eaten up the monies they had. The little church they'd begun attending in Florida began to pray for them. After much prayer, the couple watched God provide for their financial needs, and Nial's surgery was rescheduled.

"I can't promise any guarantees," the doctor told him, "but I'll do my best."

Nial responded, "All I want is for you to do your best, and I believe God will take care of the rest. I did not come this far to experience failure. I am trusting that I will see better again." An exclamation of "I can see!" were Nial's first words after the completion of the eye procedure. Eighty percent of the vision in his right eye had been restored.

Today, why not resolve to do *your* best and then trust God to take care of the rest?

Ruby H. Enniss-Alleyne

Completely Misinformed

Who can understand his errors? Cleanse thou me from secret faults.
Ps. 19:12.

I was born in Michigan. When I was two years old our family moved out to California, where I grew up.

When I was a sophomore at Hoover High School in Glendale, I was always interested in sports. I used to watch all the football games.

Now, most all the high schools in Southern California were built in front of large hills, so each high school could place its school's initial (often using large white rocks) into the hill for all to see. Hoover, of course, had an H on their hill. One night after a game someone climbed the hill and turned the H into a B. Since we had played Burbank the night before, we decided that Burbank High School must have done the mischief. Under cover of night, some of the Hoover players went over to Burbank High School's hill and changed that B into an H.

Since Burbank High had just played a game with Hollywood High School, Burbank students thought Hollywood students had played the prank on them. They went over to the hill behind Hollywood High School and changed the H into a B. Naturally, students from Hollywood High School thought the Beverly Hills students had done this and returned the "favor," changing the Beverly Hills B into an H.

Talk about making big mistakes on misinformed conclusions! Many students had acted on assumption and appearance instead of on a balanced overview that bore out all the facts.

After football coaches from all four schools got together and sorted out the details, they discovered that students from Beverly Hills High School—not Burbank—had actually started the pranks. All the coaches made their football team members return to the sites of their "crimes" and restore the original initials on the hills.

I'm wondering if we sometimes don't make the same type of mistake as these students when we *think* we know who caused some issue. Yet we don't have all the facts. Misinformed conclusions and unbalanced points of view are the best reasons never to seek revenge. I am so glad that the Lord looks on the heart and knows the whole story of our lives. Since we can only see what's on the outside, let's remember not to judge so that we "be not judged" (Matt. 7:1).

Anne Elaine Nelson

Night Journey

Brothers and sisters, think about the things that are good and worthy of praise. Think about the things that are true and honorable and right and pure and beautiful and respected. Phil. 4:8, NCV.

Restlessly, I turned over in my bed. It was just 3:00 A.M. I knew I needed to go back to sleep, but I was waking up every few minutes. So I thought to myself, *I'll take a pillow trip,* remembering the many times I had followed my memories to some delightful place I'd called home.

In the past I would always fall asleep before I reached my "destination," but this time it didn't work. Minutes unfolded seemingly into hours, and then I felt God saying, *"Think of something beautiful!"* I pondered various things—my dear friend's new grandbaby, the colorful garden outside my bedroom window that I had so often captured on camera. But right then everything seemed dull.

Then God put a tune in my head: "Something Beautiful." I couldn't quite remember all the words, so in the darkness, I raised my hand to trace the meaning, pondering the strange scene, if discovered, of my hand raised above my pillow and moving in mysterious circles.

Then the words of that beloved Bill and Gloria Gaither song unfolded in my head as God led me through it. I mouthed the words in the stillness to keep my journey going.

Minutes passed as I was stuck in the middle of those lyrics, and then they tumbled out like a confession. It's true that "brokenness and strife" is all I had to present to God. It's also true that He did do beautiful things with my life. I mulled over the thought that He had made me beautiful in His sight. A big smile of relief spread across my face.

My sweet heavenly Friend had taken a sleepless night to remind me that I am beautiful, perfect, and whole in His sight. Right there in the darkness when sleep had eluded me, God had also brought me straight to His throne of grace to remind me that He is faithful.

I rolled over and wrapped my blankets tightly around me and relaxed into sleep, knowing who—and where—I really was.

Beautiful. And in His arms!

Are you there too?

Nancy Ann (Neuharth) Troyer

Living His Compassion

Compassion: sympathetic consciousness of others' distress together with a desire to alleviate it.

And Jesus went forth, and saw a great multitude, and was moved with compassion toward them, and he healed their sick. Matt. 14:14.

Finally, all of you, be like-minded, be sympathetic, love one another, be compassionate and humble. 1 Pet. 3:8, NIV.

Christ's kindness to others was a result of His compassion for them. This month's devotionals share every day stories of compassion, both human and divine. Always God notices the details of our needs and desires, as in the story of a red shoe "discovery" during a life crisis.

God's compassion in our lives shows us how to extend it to others, as in the unusual women's outreach that began when the neighborhood drunk (a woman) made a ludicrous birthday request.

A quiet theme running through these stories reminds us that we can turn the pain from our own broken dreams into compassion that penetrates hurting hearts around us, hearts that need God's love, understanding, and acceptance.

Firsthand. Through us.

In the Palms of My Hands

For the LORD . . . will have compassion on his afflicted ones. . . . "See, I have engraved you on the palms of my hands; your walls are ever before me." Isa. 49:13, 16, NIV.

Relationships are fragile treasures. They can fail for different reasons. Sometimes misunderstandings tear relationships apart. Sometimes unresolvable conflicts explode between people. Sometimes fears learned in earlier relationships undermine new investments in intimacy. Sometimes a person harms a relationship by cheating or deceit. For these and many other reasons, friendships, business partnerships, marriages, and family relationships break apart.

Working with women in different cultures helped me to understand how they face brokenness from many painful experiences and how healing takes place in their lives when they accept the fact that they can use their pain and brokenness to bless other women. I learned that when a significant relationship fails, a part of us dies with it. When our relationships break, our hearts also break. We grieve. We search for ways to understand what happened. We want to know what went wrong. And we long to find healing for our broken hearts.

Part of the healing we need as we recover from a broken relationship is to experience God's compassions and faithfulness to us. "They are new every morning; great is your faithfulness" (Lam. 3:23). God will not leave us or forget us. When our losses overwhelm us, we can turn to God for comfort and compassion. God promises never to forget us. "See, I have engraved you on the palms of my hands; your walls are ever before me" (Isa. 49:16). I like the words "your walls are ever before me." Walls here represented the walls of Jerusalem that were completely destroyed in Isaiah's time. In order to affirm the people with words of hope, God said even their walls—their pain, losses, fear, brokenness, worry, suffering—were before Him. What a powerful promise. God sees our walls. God knows. God cares.

Since we have this good news, how can we share it with the broken women around us? We can reach out to them with compassion and understanding. Perhaps the next time a broken woman comes into our church doorway or ministry, she will feel our compassion, our understanding, and the warm welcome Jesus is giving her. It's my dream that as we grow in His grace, we will make it our *ministry* to reflect His love and compassion to those around us.

Raquel Queiroz da Costa Arrais

Nature's Contrast

To every thing there is a season, and a time to every purpose under the heaven. Eccles. 3:1.

Due to a lack of water, landscapes turned brown and our beautiful bush areas became a potential fire hazard. Whole townships were razed by roaring infernos, with many perishing tragically, disasters vividly remembered. In South Australia our main water supply comes from the Murray River, with its origins many hundreds of kilometers up stream in another state. The level of the river had dropped dramatically, leaving dry, crumbling banks of dirt and exposing islands midstream never before seen. Citrus-growing industries relying on the river could not survive; therefore, orchards were left to die. Lakes supporting dairy farming dried up, forcing farmers to sell their cows. As debt and despair increased, sadly, suicide numbers rose. Water restrictions were enforced on everyone, with concern affecting all, as we learned to respect each drop of water used. The mouth of the Murray River had silted up completely and, in essence, was dying.

The country could not support the animals, and stock died in great numbers. Wild animals such as kangaroo, dingo, fox, and feral camel, which normally live away from civilization, ventured near town areas in search of food and water.

It was a blessing when a few showers fell mid-2010, but little did we know that deluge after deluge would be coming. As I write in September 2010, dams are overflowing, with creeks and rivers bursting their banks. Storms have left damage to roads. Whole towns are flooded, with homes having to be evacuated. The mighty Lake Eyre in northern South Australia is usually a dry salt pan, but now it has become a flooded sea, attracting thousands of birds and crowds of intrigued tourists visiting this natural wonder. However, with flooded rivers up north, many have become stranded by washed out roads and bogged vehicles.

Nature has burst to life, and the land is completely changing. Dry has turned to wet and renewal has begun. What great contrasts people face, and it's not always the ideal we would desire. In a world of continual disaster, we must trust our heavenly Father, for He is coming soon. "For he doth not afflict willingly nor grieve the children of men" (Lam. 3:33). There will be no destruction by fire or flood in heaven. Praise God.

Lyn Welk-Sandy

People Need Our Hands

Your thoughts—how rare, how beautiful! God, I'll never comprehend them! Ps. 139:17, *The Message*.

Noreen is a drunk. This has not always been her lifestyle. In the city where we live she once used to belong to the "jet set" crowd along with her husband. I first met her while volunteering at a homeless shelter. When her mind and body are not ravaged by alcohol, Noreen is helpful—cleaning the counter during breakfast and telling the resident men not to put their knives in the peanut butter and then into the jam jar. Often she will appear in the morning with a couple of fresh flowers for me and another staff member. We suspect she has helped herself to those flowers in the park across the street. She loves to give and receive hugs.

In my retirement years I thought that I would spend time helping the hospital auxiliary. It's safe there, with people who are more "like" me. My husband was already volunteering at the shelter, though, making breakfasts when another worker went on vacation. I said I would try filling the temporary need even though that meant my days would have to start at 5:30 A.M. I soon learned that I love interacting with the homeless "residents"—most of whom are men struggling with alcoholism, addictions, or mental illness. Yet all are people who need a touch of love, and their responses have been rewarding.

Right after I met Noreen she kept talking about her sixtieth birthday that was approaching and that she would like to have an English high tea. Obviously, that was not something our shelter provided or funded. A few weeks after hearing Noreen express her birthday wish, I had a thought that I believe came from God: I should be the one to plan a birthday high tea for Noreen. I phoned the shelter asking permission to have the tea in their dining room for a few people. A few friends from church agreed to attend, though I warned them that Noreen might not show up. Even if she did, she might be drunk. Noreen, surprisingly, did show up and was astounded by our loving support, the beautifully decorated table, and her delicious birthday meal.

Since that day Noreen has made no major observable lifestyle changes. However, she has not forgotten how God used us to be His caring and loving hands on her sixtieth birthday.

As God's hands, how will you cheer, encourage, and help someone today?

Carol Stickle

Let the Son Shine In

"The LORD make His face shine upon you, and be gracious to you; the
LORD lift up His countenance upon you, and give you peace."
Num. 6:25, 26, NKJV.

The World Health Organization (WHO) reported in 2012 that globally around 350 million people of all ages are affected by depression. I have suffered with clinical depression since 1998 after a series of life-changing events in my life. When I began to work with my sisters around the world in women's ministries in 2001, I began to realize that the problem of depression is a problem that need to be addressed.

As I look back at my journey with depression, there were many dark days. Days when I thought the sun would never shine. Many times when I felt no one understood and no one cared. But God has been good to me. So good I cannot help but give Him the praise and glory. The text today is one that speaks to my heart because in my dark days, when I could not feel the presence of God, I knew He was with me and looking at me. I knew that the face of God saw my face, my pain, my struggle.

As women we often tend to deal with life based on feelings. What we eat, the clothes we wear, the people we relate to, the decisions we make each day, so much of that is based on feelings. But in my spiritual journey I have learnt to put my feelings aside. Feelings can deceive. And so instead, I have learnt to focus on what I know to be true, even if I cannot feel or sense it. In my dark days when I cannot feel or sense the presence of God, I remember these words of Jesus, "And surely I am with you always, to the end of the age" (Matt. 28:20).

When I cannot feel God or sense Him, I turn to what I know to be true. He is with me. He sees me. He cares. He loves me. He shares my burden and my pain.

So what about you? Have you been disappointed in God because He did not seem to hear your cries? Dear sister, don't depend on what you feel or sense; depend on what you know is true. Turn to the Word of God and claim the promises, such as Psalm 27:10, Isaiah 41:10, John 14:1, and 1 Peter 5:7. Memorize them so that when Satan comes against you with negative thoughts, the Holy Spirit can remind us of positive promises from the Word.

Remember, you are not alone or without help. God's face is shining on you.

Heather-Dawn Small

Awesome Answer to Prayer

And we know that all things work together for good to them that love God, to them who are the called according to his purpose. Rom. 8:28.

Today I went for my routine mammogram, and when a medical technician asked if I had any concerns I said, "Well, I wonder if I've been feeling a lump. It seems to come and go."

"Then this isn't a routine breast scan," said the technician. "We must change the mammogram order to Diagnostic instead of Routine. I'll have to contact your doctor to change this order."

Fifteen minutes later the test proceeded. The report itself looked fine, yet because of my question, they would follow up with an ultrasound test. Since I wasn't scheduled for one, the office would have to "fit me" into their schedule.

About that time a lady came into the waiting room. She was quietly sobbing. I went over to her and put my arms around her. She opened her gown and pointed to her breast. She was from Ecuador and knew very limited English. So I tried my best to comfort her, offering her tissues to blow her nose and asking if she wanted to pray. She nodded yes.

Just then a technician came along. I said to her, "We are going to pray. Do you want to pray with us?" She replied that she prays all day long for every patient she sees, that I was an angel, but she was hurrying to care for her next patient. What a comfort to know there are such caring individuals working in the health care.

So I prayed in English. My new Ecuadorean friend prayed in Spanish. Then we sat silently holding hands. I recalled how, in my devotional this morning, I had actually prayed for God to use me in some way today. What an awesome answer to my prayer! I know that God used me for His purpose that day, and it felt truly exciting to be a part of His plan.

Three hours later the examining doctor declared that all my breast tissue was healthy. She smiled when I said, "Thank You, Lord!" I quickly followed up with "Thank you, doctor, and thank you, technician!"

I wonder how many opportunities we miss to reach out to others with God's love. How about you? Just now, will you ask Him to open your spiritual eyes to His work, the work of sharing His love and showing His compassion to those who cross your path?

Patricia Buxton Flores

The Mushroom Farm

Then He took the five loaves and the two fish, and looking up to heaven, He blessed and broke them, and gave them to the disciples to set before the multitude. So they all ate and were filled, and twelve baskets of the leftover fragments were taken up by them.
Luke 9:16, 17, NKJV.

ook what I've got!" my husband held up something about the size of a grocery bag with "dirt" in it. I attempted to paint a look of interest on my face. "Soon there'll be a bunch of Teddy Bear mushrooms growing in it." He likes to try out new things. I lean toward the tried and true. Sure enough, in a week or so, tiny little reddish brown mushrooms started to appear. They grew at record speed, and before we knew it they were massive and Hubby had to pitch them.

"They'll grow again," he assured me. "You can do this several times before they fizzle out." He was right. But we lost interest and eventually he just dumped the whole mess, minus the plastic bag, into the woods back of our property. A few days of rain and then it happened.

Multitudinous mushrooms blanketed the lawn between our garden and the woods. They even took "root" in the garden. We set out to pick them, hopefully before the spores developed. We picked and we picked and dumped them into garbage bags to be left at the curb. The pesky things kept returning all summer. We started joking about our "mushroom farm" and getting a contract with a soup factory!

Oh well. A cold Canadian winter would surely take care of them. But the next year they were back again with a vengeance. As I write, it's October and we've picked, chopped, and smashed mushrooms all summer. We didn't dare eat any as wild mushrooms had soon made friends with them. Kind of reminds me of the time when the compassionate Savior blessed the loaves and fishes and they ended up feeding over five thousand men plus women and kids! I often wonder just how it happened. Did they multiply when He placed the pieces into the baskets, or when the disciples passed them around? Did anyone actually see it happen? I doubt it. Like the mushrooms, perhaps the pieces just kept coming and coming and coming!

Sort of like faith. If we even have a grain so small as a mustard seed, it will grow and grow like a tree, providing shade, protection, and rest for others. *Hmm.* In addition to the patience we developed during our mushroom farm experience, a good lesson grew from it as well.

Dawna Beausoleil

The Right Color Shoe

And we know that all that happens to us is working for our good if we love God and are fitting into his plans. Rom. 8:28, TLB.

In April 2011 a friend and I visited Barcelona, Spain, for a short vacation. I had a wonderful time discovering the many beautiful sights and phenomenal buildings and architecture, including the famous Antonio Gaudi's La Sagrada Familia Basilica.

With all the walking, I needed a new pair of comfortable black flat shoes. I particularly like Spanish and Italian shoes, due to the soft leather used to make them. So we went shoe shopping. I tried on a lot of shoes, but none were very comfortable. The only pair of shoes that met my criteria were red, not black! However, my friend persuaded me to purchase them because they were different and unusual and not like what I would normally buy.

Back home, three months later, I ruptured my left Achilles tendon while running at a church Fun Day. I had to wear a plaster cast on my foot for six weeks, which made it very difficult getting around. I am a busy woman and always on the run. Yet, in His compassion, God knew that I needed some time to be still. During this period of my being laid up, God allowed me quiet time to study His Word more intensely, to pray and intercede for others, and to be able to write and learn more life lessons.

When my plaster cast came off, I had to wear a special air cast boot. When I first saw the boot I'd have to wear, I could not stop laughing. The doctor kept looking at me as if I were mad. But I knew what God had done for me—because He cares so much for me.

When I went to church the following Sabbath I had a matching red air cast boot *and* red flat shoes! People thought that I had gone out and bought the shoes to match the boot and kept complimenting me on dressing so stylishly despite my injury. I knew that God had seen into my future and had ordained that the right color flat shoes that I needed should be red and not black! I was able to testify about His goodness and how He cares about even the little things in our lives. He must have a wonderful sense of humor as He provides for our needs, even before we ask. He takes care of His daughters in so many wonderful ways. Every day I have to thank Him for providing for my needs, even down to the red flat shoes!

Sandra Golding

The Mountain Ahead

The Lord is my Shepherd. Ps. 23:1, NKJV.

On any given afternoon you will find Jenny and Megan sitting together in the Pediatric Oncology Hospital playroom. The playroom has toys and many other items for precious children to spend time away from their hospital beds. Today, Jenny and Megan sit on a table with large pieces of drawing paper and a bucket of crayons. They are best friends. They both have cancer. They are both only eight years old. I have seen Jenny sneak out of her hospital bed to check on Megan after Megan's radiation treatment. I have seen Megan help Jenny drink water because Jenny is too weak. Today, during family time at the play room, Jenny and Megan sit across the table from one another, drawing, enjoying a moment of peace. I hear them laugh and talk. But then all goes silent. I watch as Jenny stands up and looks at Megan's picture.

"What are you drawing?" she asks.

"It's a mountain," says Megan. "It's bigger than the other ones."

Jenny sits next to her friend and asks about the mountain. Megan explains she will have to stay in the hospital a little longer. She overheard the doctors talking to her mom. The doctor said, "It's just another mountain to climb." So Megan is drawing what the mountain must look like. It is a tall, brown mountain with a little bit of green grass and many jagged rocks.

"I am too tired to keep climbing mountains," says Megan.

Jenny begins to draw on Megan's picture. As she draws, Jenny assures Megan the mountain is not *that* tall and they will *both* climb it together, they just need a guide. I hear them laugh as they finish the drawing and then watch them leave with their parents, back to their hospital beds. The drawing is left on the table.

Curious, I walk towards the drawing. There is a mountain, and at the foot of the mountain are two sheep, both pink, and each one has a name: Jenny, Megan. Next to the sheep is a man pointing at the mountain, holding a rod: *the shepherd*. The drawing is of two little sheep, two little girls, about to climb a mountain together with the Lord.

Heavenly Father, when we lose strength to climb the mountains ahead, thank You for being our Shepherd. Thank You for carrying us through the mountainous terrain.

Dixil L. Rodriguez

Mysterious Ways

Trust in the LORD with all your heart, and lean not on your own understanding; in all your ways acknowledge Him, and He shall direct your paths. Prov. 3:5, 6, NKJV.

G oodbye!" I yelled to my two friends, walking backwards and waving. Turning quickly, I proceeded to make my way up the escalator to security. Finally heading home after a year of medical missionary training in Honduras, I was anxious to be on my way. But entering my first checkpoint, a security woman took my passport and residency. "How old are you?"

"Twenty," I replied confidently.

"I'm sorry, you're underage. You may not leave the country without a stamp saying your parents gave you permission," she replied with a proud look in her eyes.

"Ma'am, I'm returning to my own country," I tried to explain; but she would not budge or let me pass without that stamp. "You have to go back downstairs and talk to immigration."

I spun around, hurried back downstairs, frantically found my two friends, and explained my difficult situation. I then followed them to immigration.

"You cannot leave until we see the documents with your parents' signature." Those words hit me like a stone wall. What was I to do?

Again I fought to explain, "I'm returning to my country and to my parents." Cutting me off, the immigration officer spat out, "Because you hold your residency here, you are a minor and have to follow the laws of Honduras." I dropped my backpack, defeated.

I struggled with what to do. Then a thought entered my mind: *My earthly parents might not be here, but I have a loving heavenly Parent always watching over me.* With hope in my heart I sent up a silent prayer, *Lord, I'm in a tight situation. I can't miss my flight. Please help!*

Just then the officer left, saying something about going to talk to the boss. I looked up, and my friends and I waited. Upon returning, the officer did not look happy. I held my breath as he took my passport, opened it, and stamped inside my key out of the country. He did not do this, though, without making it clear that next time I better have my parents' permission.

Thanking him, I took my passport and again I said my goodbye to my two friends. No matter what happens in our lives, if we allow Him, the Lord will work. Trust.

Haleigh Van Allen

A Love Story

The Lord appeared to us in the past, saying: "I have loved you with an everlasting love; I have drawn you with unfailing kindness."
Jer. 31:3, NIV.

I was born into a Christian home in 1948. I lost my mother when I was only seven days old. My father remarried, having two more daughters and two sons. When I learned to read, it became my favorite hobby, although my grandmother, a Christian, did not support my reading. So at night I read secretly by moonlight or by the light of a nearby street lamp. My stepmother, however, encouraged me to study. I became a teacher. When I was around twenty years of age, a young Christian man wrote, asking me to date him. I did not answer the letter because I thought a more serious commitment would be premature at that time.

In 1986, I met and eventually married a widower gentleman. In 1993, however, I became a widow. For two years, I suffered with grief over the loss of my husband. A sister of the church suggested I remember the good times we spent together. Her advice helped me. Then in 2000 the same man who had asked me to date him back in 1968 searched for me. He shared that in 1975 he had married another young woman. Together they had had four children. Now he was a widower and was full of love to give me. We got married in 2001, at the farm of his parents, where the civil and religious weddings were held out in nature.

Interestingly enough, my new husband, Ivaldo, had written four books, his first being his autobiography entitled, *Three Loves—Happy Ending*. He describes first the love we share with God, the love we have for our neighbors, and then the love for ourselves. This book also mentions our earlier brief history and also an account of how God miraculously saved him from death several times.

I praise God for His care in providing someone to make me happy. Together we await the Great Hope, the return of Jesus. We begin our days with worship, song, prayer, and wishing each other a happy day. Together, through missionary work, we have won two families to Christ. "God never leads His children otherwise than they would choose to be led, if they could see the end from the beginning and discern the glory of the purpose which they are fulfilling as co-workers with Him" (Ellen G. White, *Our Father Cares*, March 5 entry). Praise God!

Neide de Sá Soares

Godisnowhere?

And Joseph said unto them, Fear not: for am I in the place of God? But as for you, ye thought evil against me; but God meant it unto good, to bring to pass, as it is this day, to save much people alive. Now therefore fear ye not: I will nourish you, and your little ones. And he comforted them, and spake kindly unto them. Gen. 50:19-21.

What is your understanding or perception of this brainteaser: *Godisnowhere?* Did you perceive it as "God is nowhere" or as "God is now here"? In a sense, how we perceive God can determine our behaviors and the outcome of our lives.

Take Cain, for example. He chose to believe that his way to bring an offering to God was better than God's way (Gen. 4). When God refused to accept Cain's offering by not sending down holy fire to consume it, Cain felt angry and rejected. Behaving as if God was nowhere around, he—in his human pride and jealousy—murdered his brother, Abel.

Lucifer (whose name became Satan) sometime earlier started perceiving himself as equal in worthiness with Christ (see Isa. 14:11–15). Warfare in heaven caused Lucifer and his angelic followers to be cast out of that holy place. In both Lucifer's and Cain's situations, even words of life from the divine lips of God didn't change their hearts!

Joseph, on the other hand, perceived God rightly as always being "now here"—ever present with him. Because of Joseph's correct perspective, he was able to navigate through life's challenges wisely. Joseph's perceptions were formed by faith, and this resulted in his living a life that honored God and benefited others. Therefore, when tempted by his master's wife to commit an immoral act, Joseph refused, saying, "How can I commit this sin against God?" Joseph's perceptions of God enabled him to perceive others as worthy of his help, kindness, and faithfulness. How different from the end results of Cain's choices were Joseph's!

Both Cain's perspective and Joseph's perspectives exist today. Because of the Cains, some churches are full of wounded worshipers and hurting families. The Josephs, however—like Christ did—bind up wounds and remind people that "God is now here" with them, bringing hope and healing. Let's ask God to us see others from His ever-present perspective of mercy, grace, justice, and love. Choose God's perspective, be blessed, and be a blessing to others.

Tamara Brown

Animal Story

A while back I heard a sermon by my former pastor which was entitled, "Two Cows, a Fish, Two Birds, and a Donkey." The pastor, who hailed from Jamaica, talked about the two cows of 1 Samuel 5, the fish of Jonah 1, the birds mentioned in 1 Kings 17, and the donkey in Numbers 22. As I sat, enjoying the sermon, it dawned on me that I, too, had an animal story to tell showing how God, in His lovingkindness, gives protective instincts to animals.

When I was a little girl, we raised a few head of cattle, one of which was a young heifer named Pemya. In those days the cattle stayed in the pasture, some returning home in the evening if they chose to. We visited the cattle out in the pasture a few times a week, taking them treats such as plantain, other vegetable skins, and a high protein drink to supplement their grass diet.

When we discovered that Pemya was carrying a calf, we were concerned as to how this first-time mother-to-be would handle it because she always opted to stay in the pasture. The full moon was approaching, and my own mother knew that the calf was due at any time. With no new developments, however, my mother left for church. Midway through the sermon someone came to the door and said that a pacing, mooing cow was in the churchyard. When my mother heard about it, she knew at once that it was Pemya. Our church was more than a mile away from our house in the opposite direction from the pasture, yet Pemya, who never came to the house, "knew" that it was Sabbath and that we were at church. My mother then got one of the young men to help. Pemya led them to her calf, which they brought home. Neighbors said Pemya had come to the house a few times bellowing and returned to the pasture. The last time they saw her, though, she was trotting towards town.

If God cares about sparrows and gave the instinct for survival to a first-time animal mother, a cow, think how much He wants to give us a plan for our lives if we ask Him. We need to trust the One who asked Job "Where were you when I laid the foundations of the earth?" (Job 38:4). God is faithful to all His creation. And His creation includes you and me.

Vashti Hinds-Vanier

Your Blessing Is Not Always About You

"Blessed are the merciful, for they will be shown mercy." Matt. 5:7, NIV.

One Saturday evening I was driving from a girlfriend's house in Queens, New York, to Long Island. Along the way, I heard a clicking sound coming from the rear passenger side of my vehicle. Early the next morning God impressed me to get up and take my vehicle to the shop to get the tires checked. The mechanic looked at my 2007 Lexus IS250 with 163,000 miles and informed me that my rear axle needed to be replaced—immediately! He was surprised that my car had lasted this many miles without a rear axle replacement. He suggested keeping the car at the shop because my vehicle was not safe to drive. I asked, "How am I going to get home?" When he told me he'd drive me home, I said, "Praise the Lord!"

The next day a phone call from the mechanic informed me his shop couldn't fix my vehicle. I needed to go directly to the dealership. Immediately I got a taxi (very difficult in Long Island) in order to retrieve my car from the mechanic. I phoned the Lexus dealership about the situation and was told to bring my car in. They'd give me a loaner car. And they did—a brand-new 2013 Lexus GS350! I drove it home. The next day the dealership informed me that repairs on my car would cost more than $3,000 (US)! The news devastated me. Now I was torn between repairing my vehicle or purchasing another. I needed a day to pray about this situation.

I'd owned my car for seven years. In prayer God told me it was time to get another vehicle. The next day I started the process of purchasing a new vehicle on a trade-in. However, I couldn't find the title to my current car! I requested a replacement title online. The process would take five to seven days. In the meantime, I wouldn't have a working vehicle. Then the Lexus dealership unexpectedly allowed me to continue driving the loaner until my replacement title arrived. Who allows you to drive a loaner vehicle for over a week if you are not receiving repairs? Only *God*! Here's the kicker: Two people (one in Queens and the other in Brooklyn) contacted me the next day asking for rides to Connecticut. Guess who picked them up in the loaner vehicle driving from Long Island? Me. God gave me a blessing—so I could bless others.

Moral of the story: your blessing is not always about *you*. Let's continue to use God's blessings to bless others on this journey we call "life"!

Andrea D. Hicks

October 14

Dreams and God's Leadings

"But He knows the way that I take; when He has tested me, I shall come forth as gold." Job 23:10, NKJV.

When I saw you in church, a dream I had three years ago popped into my mind," Norval said. Later, he shared that he'd noted the dream on a pad of paper. The dream came after he'd become a widower. He also shared he'd appreciated the help of an attractive young neighbor (one of two women proffering help) in meeting the needs of his now orphaned children: a ten-year-old son and a twelve-year-old daughter. However, the young neighbor had declined to attend church with him and the family.

I had not known any of this because I had been working in Hinsdale, Illinois, in the hospital's medical records. When the current department head shared she would be retiring, the hospital administrator suggested I work to qualify for the position. This required my taking coursework in Danville, a smaller, nearby town. After I was accepted, the school director helped me find weekday lodging at the local YWCA. For months I'd return to Hinsdale to attend my church and be able to work my Saturday night and Sunday shifts before returning to school.

One day Mrs. McDole, the medical records department director, encouraged me to attend church in Danville. "A small church. They'll welcome you," she said. So on Friday I stayed put at the YWCA. Early that Sabbath morning, I took the bus to the Danville church.

Following the services, many members welcomed me. Among them was Norval A. Jackson and his two children. He helped me with transportation. Later, he shared with me about his dream and said he believed me to be the fulfillment of his dream as his new spouse and mother to his children.

One Sabbath our local church minister preached on Esther's obedience to God's leadings. He read Esther 4:14: "Who knoweth whether thou art come into the kingdom for such a time as this?" He repeatedly incorporated the verse in his sermon, reaching my heart.

Norval's family helped plan the wedding, and my physician brother flew from California to give me away. Esther 4:14 had become my favorite Bible verse. Throughout the ensuing years, the message became a source of comfort to me. How has God's Word comforted you?

Consuelo Roda Jackson

A Willing Vessel

But the Lord said unto him, Go thy way: for he is a chosen vessel unto me, to bear my name before the Gentiles, and kings, and the children of Israel. Acts 9:15.

Our lives are not our own. It is a powerful blessing to be chosen by God to be used by Him to speak to another person for His purposes. When we have a relationship with Him and allow Him to put His love in our hearts, He can then shine through us. When He shines through, people stop seeing us, and they see the beauty of the Lord. It is lifesaving and life-changing.

One day I was in the bank and the lady behind me was talking about how humid it was outside. I smiled and agreed. Then she mentioned that she really liked my hair. Our small talk turned to "hair talk." During the exchange, she mentioned how happy she was that she still had her hair despite the chemotherapy treatments she'd recently had to start.

I said, "Well, that is such a blessing!" Then I was moved to ask her name, which was Gwen. "Gwen," I said, "you will be in my prayers." She thanked me and we continued with my banking business. When my transaction was complete, I reminded her, "Now remember, Gwen, I will be praying for you."

"Thank you," she said. "Let me give you a hug." I blinked back tears on the walk back to my car. You see, I was the one who really needed a hug that day. Yes, I truly believe God had me speak to Gwen in order to encourage her in the fight for her life against cancer. Yet, in turn, God blessed me through my exchange with her. The memory still brings tears to my eyes.

Tears because God used me—this often unworthy, wayward, rebellious girl— to say "I will pray for you" to a woman in need of spiritual support. Yet, knowing my needs, God used Gwen to give me a reassuring hug as well.

I still pray for Gwen. And Mike. And Pat. And perhaps even you, if you've asked me to. I'm a firm believer that prayer changes things: weeping turns to joy, death to life, mourning to dancing, chaos to peace, and confusion to understanding. I want to be God's vessel—increasingly emptied of self and filled with His love that will bless someone else.

I challenge you to invite Him into your heart today. Be willing to let Him shine through you. You won't regret it, for you will be blessed as well.

Kelli Rai Collins

Divine Protection

The LORD will watch over your coming and going both now and forever more. Ps. 121:8, NIV.

It was Sunday, October 16, 2011, a typical Caribbean day with beautiful sunshine. My husband, the principal of the St. Thomas/St. John Seventh-day Adventist School, left home around 7:00 A.M. for the school, which is only a six-minute drive from home. He was going to help some high school seniors erect canopies for their food sale.

As my husband left home, I settled down to the usual Sunday chores. About eight minutes later, the telephone rang. It was a coworker calling to say that my husband had encountered an accident as he was waiting to turn in to the school's entrance. A sports utility van had slammed into the back of his 2000 Toyota Corolla car. The coworker said that he was coming to get me because my husband would be taken by ambulance to the hospital.

My heart started to race as I hurriedly changed my clothes and waited to be picked up. When I arrived at the accident scene, I saw that the back of the car was severely damaged. The ambulance had arrived, and my husband was being strapped onto a stretcher before being lifted into the ambulance. I accompanied him to the hospital.

I have been to the emergency room several times, but each experience is different. My husband had to stay in bed and be waited upon. Medical technicians ran tests on him, and doctors prescribed medication for whiplash pain and to help him relax.

With God's help, the accident's effects were not as bad as they could have been. My husband didn't experience the normal intensity of pain one can have with a whiplash injury. He was back to work on Tuesday as if nothing had happened.

The insurance company wanted to write off the car, but we did not wish to because it was in very good shape before the accident and could be repaired. In conferring with our mechanic, he suggested that we ask the insurance company to keep the car. We were allowed to retain the car. It was repaired and continues to provide us with great service.

This experience serves to remind us that we serve a compassionate God who is interested in every aspect of our lives. He made and sustains us. This accident reminds me that we can trust God whatever the situation—He has promised to take care of us.

Janice Fleming-Williams

Will You Pass the Test of Faith Today?

Trust in the Lord with all your heart, and do not lean on your own understanding. Prov. 3:5, NASB.

As long as we live on this earth, circumstances, issues, and problems will come our way. How we respond to them and with what, will determine our well-being and our health. God does not promise us a problem-free life. He promises us His Divine power, not human power, if we trust Him.

The story of Peter (Matt. 14:28–33), among many others, drives home the point that God can reach us anywhere as long as we trust Him. Peter was walking on the water towards Jesus when he saw the effects of the stormy wind and was afraid. He lost sight of who had called him. Consequently, Peter saw the challenges only. Experiencing fear, Peter began to sink. But, praise God, Peter responded appropriately and effectively after coming to his senses by shouting, "Lord, save me!" Immediately, Jesus reached out and rescued Peter from drowning.

We are not told in the story how far or near Jesus was from Peter. The important fact is that Jesus can save us wherever we are, and under any circumstance, if we put our trust in Him. No distance, barrier, or situation can stand in the way of Jesus when we call on Him in our time of need. Let us trust Him implicitly because His unfailing love is always available to be poured out on us without measure. Let us not believe the devil's lie that God is punitive and vindictive. Love is the character of God, and God can never be anything that reflects otherwise.

Sara Young, in her devotional book *Jesus Calling* (January 26), writes that God's light shines most brightly when believers trust Him "in the dark." She says that God is less interested in right circumstances than in right responses to whatever comes our way.

May we, like Peter in the hour of weakness, give the right response: "Jesus, save me!" The psalmist David, who learned from experience how important it is to put his trust in God, writes in Psalm 112:4 that even in the darkness, "Light arises . . . for the upright; He is gracious and compassionate and righteous" (NASB).

May God's unfathomable love envelope us all as we trust Him to honor our faith in Him and to direct our paths.

Kera Gwebu

A God of Deliverances

God is to us a God of deliverances *and* salvation; and to God the Lord belongs escape from death [setting us free]. Ps. 68:20, AMP.

It was late afternoon one work day when I got a phone text from my husband, Will, suggesting that I take Old Columbia Pike home rather than Route 29—Columbia Pike, a major highway many use to get to and from work. A four-car accident early afternoon had Route 29 northbound blocked. Various traffic Web sites verified this accident, showed an overturned car, and indicated that a young woman with life-threatening injuries had been taken to a hospital. The reports also said that police needed assistance from eyewitnesses to the accident. My heart sank momentarily as I imagined the trauma this woman probably suffered.

As the end of the work day approached, I monitored the heavy traffic from a nearby window. Traffic on Old Columbia Pike was bumper-to-bumper, cars barely moving. All the streets nearby were the same. It would take an hour to get home instead of my usual fifteen minutes! Despite the thunder and lightning of an impending storm, I returned to my desk. An hour and a half later, the roads looked a bit better, and the storm hadn't materialized. I headed home.

At five-forty the next morning, an overhead helicopter awakened us. My husband suggested there was either a search on for an escaped prisoner or a traffic accident nearby. News reports soon delivered late breaking news: "Accident on Route 29-Columbia Pike." A very short distance from the accident the previous evening and involving another overturned vehicle. I couldn't believe it! *Lord,* I thought, *what is going on? Two accidents in less than twenty-four hours on the same road—the road I take to work! Will I have a long commute again?* Before I further pursued selfish thoughts, my mind immediately envisioned another person or persons, gravely injured perhaps, in the overturned vehicle. I whispered a prayer for those involved. On my drive to work I saw no evidence of any accident. Later I was relieved but amazed to hear there had been no injuries. As I recall these accidents today, I am reminded of God's promise of deliverances for us. Although the evil one has every unimaginable threat, accident, or ill-intended adversity waiting to cause us worry, anxiety, sadness, suffering, or death, God in His infinite wisdom can bring us through.

Let us entrust our lives to His keeping and be thankful for His love and power to save.

Iris L. Kitching

Lessons From Nature

"Look at the birds of the air; they do not sow or reap or store away in barns, and yet your heavenly Father feeds them. Are you not much more valuable than they?" Matt. 6:26, NIV.

Once my husband called me because the dogs were euphoric in the yard after they had caught some small animal. When I went to see what was happening, I realized they were disputing over a baby bird that had fallen from its nest. I was sad because the little animal was already badly hurt. It did not open its eyes.

Some people said, "It will agonize to death." Others said, "The bird has to be sacrificed because it is suffering."

However, I decided to take care of it. I gave it some medicine, and I let it rest. Later, I offered water, and the bird accepted. I noticed its eyes were opened.

After another day, the little creature already rehearsed some flights inside the house, but I still could not release it because it was not strong enough to fly for any distance. At times it fluttered away from me, following its natural instincts.

What happened with the injured bird made me reflect on the following: How many times are we bruised and wounded in the grip of evil, feeling weak and helpless? The answer is often. Some may look on our helplessness and say, "There is no way out. The end has already come for you."

People around us do not always seem to care about our sufferings. Yet a Father of love leaves everything to care for us, our wounds, and our scars. He sustains us and protects us and promises that all will be well.

However, our natural (sinful) instincts cause us to be stubborn and ungrateful. We want to turn away from God. We insist on trying to fly away, but we cannot bear the weight of our own injuries and weakness. However, God is so merciful, always willing to take care of us, and to carry our burdens.

Our loving Savior asks only one thing—that we trust His love and compassion for us.

The bird did not resist much because it was too injured. However, God offers us a chance to be healed of our wounds and receive His new life. What will be your response?

Tamara Lemes Marins Silva

The Gift of Compassion

Finally, be ye all of one mind, having compassion one of another.
1 Pet. 3:8.

I could sense that something terrible had happened or was about to. I felt an urgency to leave this lunchtime birthday party and go back home! I called to Jonathan, my three-year-old, who surprisingly and unprotestingly left his friends, calmly collected his birthday party favors, and got into the car seat by himself. Across town, I turned into our driveway to find friends, Allan and Shirley (my son's godparents), parked there. Shirley's face told me something was wrong.

I sat down on the front stoop of our house, waiting for the silence to break amid the "hellos" and "how are yous." Allan walked with Jonathan toward the small creek behind our house as if to create a distraction so that Shirley could share whatever news she had come to bring. "Gail," she started, tears welling up in her eyes, "we got a call from your dad this morning. Gail, it's your mom . . . your mother passed away this morning and . . ." I could not make sense of the rest of her sentence. "Gail?" I felt my friend's arms around me, but I could not respond. "Come home with us—you shouldn't be alone."

I screamed a scream I have not screamed since! My body shook, my heart pounded, and my mind raced. I had just spoken to Mommy! It was our custom on Sunday morning; we spoke every Sunday! She lived in New York and I lived in Nashville. She loved and adored her grandchildren, Shellie and Jonathan! Tears mixed with snot ran down my face onto my shirt.

Then I felt this gentle, tiny hand on my shoulder: it was Jonathan patting my shoulder. He was attempting to make sense of my tears as I had so often done for him when he fell at play or was having a day of being told No more often than Yes. He was trying to assure me that everything was going to be all right. "Mommy, don't cry," he pleaded again and again. He disappeared into the house and then reappeared leaving a bathroom-to-front door toilet tissue trail behind him. No time to tear off a piece of tissue. He just wanted to comfort his mommy as he had been comforted so many times by her. His unexpected compassion soothed and settled me.

Though now an adult—and an accomplished producer, songwriter, and recording artist living in South Africa—my Jonathan's heart still beats with kindness and compassion for so many others. The same gift of compassion he showed to his mother the day she lost hers.

Gail Masondo

In His Wisdom

"For your Father knows the things you have need of before you ask Him." Matt. 6:8, NKJV.

The living and omnipotent God we serve is really awe-inspiring! Words are inadequate to praise Him and tell of the wondrous things He does for His people. I know how true this is because He has done many great things for me.

Very recently a former student of mine, of thirty-some years ago, sent me an e-mail to tell me that he and his classmates would like to pay me a visit and also see the college where I was involved in teaching English as a second language. Since my husband and I were winding up our two years of volunteer service, we were happy that we could show Mission College to these former students. We sent e-mails back and forth to each other and came to an agreement that January 22 would probably be the best for everyone. However, the weekend before January 22 my former student e-mailed and said that there would be complications with this date since the Chinese New Year was closer to that date. So would it be possible to move our get-together to January 15? We agreed and prepared, looking forward to the students' arrival.

They came early enough for us to show them the college campus and the different places where the various schools were located before we had our lunch. We had a beautiful visit, reminiscing about those bygone days when they had been in high school. For the classmates who weren't able to come, we were told that they were all doing well except one who had an accident and another who had passed away. The students who came were driving Mercedes cars, which showed me they truly had done well in their chosen professions, as they assured me they had.

A week later—on the Sunday they were originally to visit me—I came down with a very bad cold, a cough, and a recurrence of my back problem. I could hardly walk because of my herniated disk. As I lay in bed, I thanked God over and over, for He had known what would transpire that weekend. So He had made the arrangement that my get-together with the former students would take place a week earlier. What a great God we serve! Our Almighty God certainly knew my future plight, and He made a better plan. Aren't His plans always the best?

My prayer is that God will help us to trust Him implicitly all the time. Though we sometimes think our plans are good, His ways are always best.

Ofelia A. Pangan

Cat-itude

Let this mind be in you, which was also in Christ Jesus. Phil. 2:5.

We have two cats, a female named Alaska and a male named Rascal. During a recent move, Alaska became quite grumpy. In fact, she caught some cat-itude! The first couple of days in our new home, she was irritable and would run after Rascal for no reason. Seriously, he would be minding his own business when she would, without cause or warning, run across the room, hiss and growl at him and bite him. He looked at her like, *What did I do?* She had a really bad case of cat-itude! Fortunately, it subsided after a few days and life returned to normal. I am thankful cats can adjust rather quickly to new surroundings.

This experience led me to think about the attitude—or cat-itude—we sometimes get as well. It's easy to be grumpy when you don't feel well. Have you ever witnessed a child throwing a tantrum and discovered the reason for the meltdown is because he or she wasn't feeling well? Adults can be like that too. Whether we are sick or pressed down on every side with trials and temptations of life, when there's more money going out than coming in, or even just when someone says or does something that we don't like, we can develop an attitude. If we look around long enough (honestly, it probably wouldn't take that long!), we will see something about which to be unhappy or grumpy.

But is that the attitude Jesus wants us to have? No, certainly not! Philippians 2:5 tells us to "let this mind be in you, which was also in Christ Jesus." Jesus was never grumpy or harsh due to His circumstances. His spirit and demeanor were always filled with grace, compassion, love, and dignity. He desires for us to have His same sweet spirit in us, even during the difficult times.

How can we have that same sweet spirit that Christ has? Ephesians 4:23 tells us that we can be renewed in our minds, our attitudes. And 2 Corinthians 5:17 tells us that we are new creatures in Christ and our old behavior has passed away. Then 2 Corinthians 3:18 states, "But we all, with open face beholding as in a glass the glory of the Lord, are changed into the same image from glory to glory, even as by the Spirit of the Lord." That's the key! We must behold Jesus in His Word and be transformed into His image, His attitude, instead of cat-itude.

Samantha Nelson

God's Tender Care

"But the very hairs of your head are all numbered. Do not fear
therefore, you are of more value than many sparrows."
Luke 12:7, NKJV.

My co-teacher had recently been diagnosed with cancer. My thoughts were gloomy. The slow-motion Walmart cashier had no seeming concern about my tardiness for an appointment. Then purple tulips in the floral case near my cart caught my attention. Too bad I didn't have time to take cheery flowers to my friend. Shifting from one foot to the other, I wondered, *Why in the world did I pick this line?* Finally, in desperation, I started to walk to a shorter line.

The tulips once again grabbed my attention, reminding me of the poem in my purse. One that I'd clipped and saved for my cancer-diagnosed friend. Funny, but the poem was a conversation between a tulip and God. To God the tulip complained that, being winter and all, "she" could not bloom. So what was God going to do about her uselessness?

God, in the poem, replies that she's been placed exactly where it's best for her, where she'll soon unfurl her "fragile petals" for everyone to see. But for now, the responsibility of the tulip was to trust God and obey Him.

Maybe this poem will strengthen Marsha to deal with the difficult path ahead, I thought. Then I snatched the tulips from the floral case, discovering a shorter line in the process. I felt the unseasonal flowers were not a coincidence.

I seemed to hear God's whisper in my ear, "Today Marsha needs both the poem and the flowers."

While I was paying for my purchases, someone caught my attention out of the corner of my eye. I turned and spied Marsha standing right by my grocery cart! Due to her ordeal with chemotherapy, I barely recognized her. She looked at me. I handed her the flowers. *God, You have perfect timing!* With a hug and a smile, my friend gave me a look of loving gratitude.

I mentally thanked God for reminding me how much He cares about everything. In all situations, whether small or great, ordinary or life threatening, God assures us that He is always by our side. I thought of the Bible text that says He knows the very number of hairs on our heads. God's tender love assures us that He cares—even when hair is missing.

Juli Hamilton

A Visit From Sandy

Thy words were found, and I did eat them; and thy word was unto me the joy and rejoicing of mine heart. Jer. 15:16.

On Tuesday, October 23, 2012, Jamaica started receiving warnings that Hurricane Sandy might be visiting. As usual I did not know exactly how to pray. When we had prayed previously for protection, hurricanes had passed us, usually at the expense of Haiti or Cuba. Anyway, I prayed to "Him that is able to do exceeding abundantly above all that we ask or think" (Eph. 3:20).

By Wednesday morning we knew Sandy was coming. I made basic survival plans and asked the Lord to protect my property, as He declares, "I know the plans I have for you; plans to prosper you and not to harm you" (Jer. 29:11). During Sandy's passage I saw big trees next to my home sway wildly as the winds and rain increased their force. Yet I felt peace. "Be anxious for nothing," God had said, "but in everything by prayer and supplication, and with thanksgiving, let your requests be made known to God, and the peace of God, which surpasses all understanding, will guard your hearts and minds through Christ Jesus" (Phil. 4:6, 7, NKJV).

Worrying never makes the storm go away; God gave us promises to claim. Sad to say, I stand guilty of worrying sometimes instead of exercising my faith. Guilty of not letting go and simply watching Him bring the calm. Hurricane Sandy calmed by nightfall. On inspection, my roof appeared intact, and no water had leaked in elsewhere. All my utilities were operating, though 70 percent of the island was without electricity, and many were without piped water.

As I watched the footage on television of the devastation that hundreds of citizens had experienced, I saw many faces of despair. Personal possessions were destroyed. Homes were demolished by the winds, surging waters, and fallen trees. In two instances, boulders had crashed into homes. Though deeply saddened by what I saw, I was grateful that no more than one person had perished in the storm.

I had memorized the promises (cited above), repeating them every morning in my devotions, and then I'd claimed them on October 24, 2012.

Then came my prayers of thanksgiving. I felt blessed and highly favored. Do you?

Cecelia Grant

Compassed With Favor

"Never will I leave you; never will I forsake you." Heb. 13:5, NIV.

In addition to a good teaching job, I also accepted the job of after-school care at the school where I taught. After just a week I was told I would be doing after-school care at another school. "But I do not drive," I told my supervisor, "and I can't depend on the public bus to get me there in a timely manner."

"I'm sorry," she said, "but someone else—someone who's worked here longer than you have—insists she should have the after-school care job instead of you, a newcomer. So you will have to do after-care at another school or lose that job."

Truly I was disturbed. I had been asked—and accepted the job—before she did. Also, she drives, so why couldn't she, with reliable transportation, do her after-school care at the other school site instead of me? However, I did not argue or persist. I would do my best to work at the other school after teaching here during the day. Besides, I needed the extra income.

With a heavy heart I did what it took to work my second challenging job for the next five months. I had to jump from bus to bus in order to do so. As winter became colder and days grew shorter, my lot grew more difficult, especially when it snowed. Yet I never complained. I just prayed and waited for God's help.

Then came February when educational inspectors visited the schools and wrote reports on their findings. One report suggested that I should carry out my after-school care responsibilities at my own school—and that the other lady should work at the other school. This time my coworker could not argue or refuse because the inspectors themselves had evaluated the need of an experienced person doing the job at the other school. They also advised that a special education teacher, as she was, should be sent to that school. They were also surprised that I had been able to handle the children for four months without special help.

I knew that my God would not forsake me. That is why I had held to my faith in Him and hoped He would act in His way and His perfect timing. I still do after-school work and in peace.

God promised never to leave nor forsake His children no matter what. He looks on and compasses them with favor. This is His promise to me and to you.

Mabel Kwei

October 26

A Smile Is Friendly Magic

A merry heart maketh a cheerful countenance: but by sorrow of the heart the spirit is broken. Prov. 15:13.

I remember going to my room with a frown on my face when I didn't get the beautiful flowered dress I'd wanted to wear to a birthday party. Within minutes, Mother came into my room. I looked up, expecting to see a frown on her face too. Instead, she gave me a hug and said, "Here's my beautiful daughter! Jesus loves smiles and wants His children to smile." Upon hearing my mother's words and seeing her smiling face, my sadness turned to joy and gladness.

Working with children during my adult years as a teacher, I have experienced children with sad faces. Some willingly chose to listen to God's words found in Proverbs 15:13 reminding me that a merry heart maketh a cheerful countenance but by sorrow of the heart the spirit is broken. Daily I resolved to bring a smile to some child's face, including my own.

One day, I was putting newly purchased groceries into my car when I saw a woman getting out of hers. Looking at her, I smiled and said, "Have a good day." Surprisingly, before I drove away, she came over saying, "Excuse me, miss, but I needed your smile." Words began pouring from her heart. I listened, feeling sorry for her plight. God gave me words to say as she, in turn, listened attentively. With tears she shook my hand saying that I had been a blessing to her with my words and my smile.

On my way home the thought came to mind that I had not even asked the woman for her name. But I put her on my prayer list anyway.

God has done miraculous things for us, including His creating us with the ability to smile. He loves our smiles, and the world needs them. Families need smiles. Coworkers need smiles. Those we meet and greet need smiles. I've decided that a smile is friendly magic. A smile uses less facial muscles than a frown. It costs nothing to smile, yet its benefits are great. The disheartened find encouragement. The sad experience joy. Smiles last for only a moment, but often memories of a smile will be kept or remembered for years to come. Maybe forever.

Join with me today, and each day, in the choice to keep smiling. For a genuine smile can be as friendly as a warm hello.

Annie B. Best

Answered Prayer

"It shall come to pass that before they call, I will answer; and while they are still speaking, I will hear." Isa. 65:24, NKJV.

During my life I have experienced numerous incidents of God's handiwork in my life and the lives of others. I want to share two of those incidents.

Once I was in the Secret Santa Club at work. With our names, we were asked to write three things on a slip of paper for our wish list. The person's name I picked included a devotional book on her wish list. I was acquainted with the devotional book ministry at our church and was impressed to purchase the book entitled *Love Out Loud* (a copy of which I already had) for my Secret Santa gift. The day arrived for the clinic staff Christmas luncheon. We enjoyed the meal and fellowship. It was time to pass out the Secret Santa gifts. When my time came, my coworker was not in the room. After the luncheon, I took the gift bag to her. Sometime later, she came looking for me. After looking in her bag, she was amazed to find the very book she wanted. She had seen the book in another place and had wanted to purchase it.

I was thrilled to know that God had both of us in mind and led me to purchase that book. We were blessed by that experience. I am glad that God used me, through the workings of the Holy Spirit, to bring cheer and to satisfy my coworker's desire.

In another incident, my time to be a greeter and hostess at our church was coming up, and I needed an inspirational thought to read after welcoming visitors to our church. I prayed a short prayer in my mind for God to give me special words to say. I searched the Internet for a spiritual thought and couldn't find one that touched my heart. The next morning, during my devotion and prayer time, the Holy Spirit led me to words in my devotional book. I received God's answer! I needed to speak on God's love and peace to the congregation. I was satisfied, and when I read the spiritual words from that book, I believed that others would be blessed.

God's way is the best way. The Lord wants us to "seek Him with all your heart and with all your soul" (Deut. 4:29, NKJV). He knows our needs and desires and is waiting for us to ask.

After all, He has promised, "And my God shall supply all your need according to His riches in glory by Christ Jesus" (Phil. 4:19, NKJV).

Carolyn Venice Marcus

Love

And we have known and believed the love that God hath to us. God is
love; and he that dwelleth in love dwelleth in God, and God in him.
1 John 4:16.

I believe there are three kinds of love: first, God's love for us; second, our love to
God; and, finally, our love to others shown through our acts of compassion.

God's great love for us was expressed at the cross. Romans 5:8 says, "But
God commendeth his love toward us, in that, while we were yet sinners, Christ
died for us." In the Garden of Eden mankind had fallen into sin, but Jesus Christ,
who is the only Son of God, died on the cross to save us from sin. And it shows
His love to us. Furthermore, 1 John 4:10 says, "Herein is love, not that we loved
God, but that he loved us, and sent his Son to be the propitiation for our sins."

Now, when God shows His love to us, then it is our responsibility to love
Him also. Matthew 22:37 says, "Jesus said unto him, Thou shalt love the Lord
thy God with all thy heart, and with all thy soul, and with all thy mind." When
we love God, we will want to obey His words and commandments. John 14:15
says, "If ye love me, keep my commandments."

Finally, we can show our love for Jesus Christ by treating others with His
compassion. The Bible says, "Verily I say unto you, Inasmuch as ye have done
it unto one of the least of these my brethren, ye have done it unto me" (Matt.
25:40).

So when we help needy person or listen with love to someone's problems,
then God also helps us according to our need. Additionally, John 13:34 says, "A
new commandment I give unto you, that ye love one another; as I have loved
you, that ye also love one another."

The Bible is about God's love to us and to others, through us. "Greater love
hath no man than this," the Bible tells us, "that a man lay down his life for his
friends." There are so many ways we can express God's love for others, and the
overwhelming needs are all around us. We probably will not be asked to die for
someone, yet we can do many things to improve their lives.

There are many creative ways to show God's love to others, especially those
times of year when we are celebrating His love to us. "God is love, and all who
live in love live in God, and God lives in them" (1 John 4:16, NLT). Who will
you love today—and how?

Mahuya Roy

Voice of Victory

In October 1999, I was privileged to join ministries with the Quiet Hour and travel to Papua New Guinea to participate in an evangelistic crusade. Upon arrival I definitely experienced culture shock! It was like being in a different world. A world that included pain and poverty that I had not dreamed possible. In spite of, or maybe because of this, I witnessed a people with a tremendous hunger for the truth and hope. And once accepted, full of tremendous faith and devotion to God.

One evening while the director/speaker for the Quiet Hour, Bill Tucker, was preaching, it began to rain in torrents. The rain was so loud and so strong it was very difficult to even hear his voice. In very short order, the ground was so wet people could not sit down. They stood there in the pouring rain listening to every word of hope they could catch. Realizing the rain was not going to stop, Elder Tucker asked the audience, "Do you want me to quit?" In unison you could hear the crowd, twenty thousand in number, say, "*No!*" In spite of the torrential downpour and ankle deep water, no one left!

The next day, I came down with a terrible cough. By the next evening I was coughing every few seconds and, at times, uncontrollably. As the time of the meeting approached I prayed, "Lord, I know You didn't bring me around the world just to watch. I want to sing for Your glory!" Just before the meeting began, the local pastors gathered around me and prayed some mighty prayers of faith.

In faith, I joined the team leaders on the platform. Not a single cough came out of my mouth the entire time I was up there. As soon as I stepped off the platform I began to cough profusely. This miracle happened for several successive nights until I gained full recovery. This was tangible evidence for me and everyone else to see that God, who hears our prayers and who cares, was miraculously at work for His glory.

Remember how the Israelites had to step into the water first before God parted the Red Sea? In your own life today, take a greater step of faith—go ahead. He is waiting for you!

Vonda Beerman

Stranger in the Parking Lot

"For I was hungry and you gave me something to eat, I was thirsty and you gave me something to drink, I was a stranger and you invited me in, I needed clothes and you clothed me, I was sick and you looked after me, I was in prison and you came to visit me."
Matt. 25:35, 36, NIV.

on't go outside into that parking lot and talk to that stranger—even if it is in the church parking lot!" one of the teachers advised me. We'd been watching a bedraggled man warming coffee over a can of Sterno heat. I'd just stopped by the church preschool to drop something off.

"Should we call the police?" the third adult present wondered aloud. "We want to keep our children safe here, but they, too, saw him ride up and park his bicycle before warming his hands over that Sterno flame."

"I am suddenly feeling impressed to offer him food from the kitchenette," I said.

"Then I'll go with you for safety reasons," offered Alisha.

"Do I need to leave the premises?" asked the stranger as we approached. We responded that we'd come with food and an offer of help.

The man began to tell his story. "I've been estranged from my father for twenty years. I'm trying to ride the final sixty miles to Colorado Springs to see if we can have reconciliation before he dies. I'm on my final stretch, but it's hard riding in this cold weather."

"May we pray for you?" I asked the man.

"Yes, please," he responded. As I lifted up this struggling man in prayer to God, the man began to weep. He then thanked us for our kindness, packed up his things, and rode off. I am thankful that I listened to the Holy Spirit, who gave me courage to walk those few feet in order to minister to this homeless person—and receive a blessing myself in the process of this holy encounter. When I drove away from the school a few minutes later, I was a changed person who had a deeper trust in God and a bigger love in my heart for hurting humanity.

As we listen and obey our Savior, He will transform us, helping us truly love as He loves. We need not fear any stranger when God calls us to act and gives us the discernment to know a dangerous situation from one of true need. The important thing to remember is we need to be ever listening for His voice with a heart that is willing to obey it.

Lee Lee Dart

Oh Yes! He Cares!

Casting the whole of your care [all your anxieties, all your worries, all your concerns, once and for all] on Him, for He cares for you affectionately and cares about you watchfully. 1 Pet. 5:7, AMP.

As Mom lay in the intensive care unit I held her hand, gently explaining the dreadful truth that her cancer mass hadn't been removed. This was hard news. Her brother just went through cancer treatment: radiation, weakness, and the sickness. Absorbing it all, she looked at me thoughtfully and asked, "Will I go good?" I smoothed her hair and caressed her face, assuring her that she wouldn't be alone and the doctors would see she wouldn't be in pain.

Mom, not a professed Christian, had recently begun listening to the old hymns again. But when a Salvation Army officer walked by and Mom said, "I want one of them," I was puzzled. "What is it, Mom, that you want?"

"Them," she said with an odd little grin, again pointing to the woman. By the time I figured out that she wanted to speak with the Salvation Army officer, the lady had disappeared into another room. She settled and soon fell off into a deep sleep.

That would be our last conversation. After a couple of days of unconsciousness, Mom passed away.

Three weeks later, about four o'clock on a Sunday morning, I woke up with a start! The realization of what Mom was asking swept over me. Had reaching out to that officer been Mom's way of reaching out to God? Her question, "Will I go good?" had nothing to do with whether she would have pain or if her family would be near. Mom was wondering if God would accept her! I could have helped her make her peace with God but missed the opportunity.

Getting out of bed, I paced the kitchen floor, holding my sides, tears streaming down my face. My heart hurt. I kept shaking my head in disbelief at my stupidity. "Oh God, I missed it! I missed it!" And then, I heard Him! That still, small Voice, *Yes, but I didn't.*

Jesus had been there. He saw Mom reaching out and was there ministering to her. I missed the opportunity, but my precious Jesus didn't. His sweet peace calmed. New tears flowed. Oh yes, He cares! I know He cares! He cared for Mom, He cares for me. And He cares for you.

Diane Burns

Living His Thanksgiving

Thanksgiving: the act of giving thanks; a prayer expressing gratitude.

As he was going into a village, ten men who had leprosy met him.
They stood at a distance and called out in a loud voice, "Jesus, Master,
have pity on us!" When he saw them, he said, "Go, show yourselves to
the priests." And as they went, they were cleansed. One of them, when
he saw he was healed, came back, praising God in a loud voice. He
threw himself at Jesus' feet and thanked him—and he was a Samaritan.
Jesus asked, "Were not all ten cleansed? Where are the other nine?"
Luke 17:12-17, NIV.

The Bible tells us to "give thanks in all circumstances" (1 Thess. 5:18, NIV). "In all circumstances" means just that. *All* circumstances. Not just the pleasant ones.

That's what this month's authors have learned to do. Give thanks. Turn their faces toward Jesus to say "thank you" one more time—despite inclement weather, lost prizes, accidents, and earaches. They have learned that giving thanks "is God's will for [them] in Christ Jesus."

Jesus publicly pointed out the gratitude of the one healed leper.

Likewise today, the unchanging Savior still takes note of—and delights in—our heartfelt expressions of thanksgiving to Him.

Singing in the Rain

You have collected all my tears and preserved them in your bottle. You have recorded each one in your book. Ps. 56:8, NLT.

Many years ago, circumstances brought about by my own wrong choices had led me to the brink of despair. I cried from morning until night—or so it seemed. It was all I could do to put one foot in front of the other in order to keep going.

While standing, one day, at the kitchen sink washing dishes, I felt deep within my soul that I was dishonoring my heavenly Father by my constant sadness and despair. Even in all of my distress, God had been so good to me. So how could I not thank Him for still claiming me as His precious child?

Perhaps I couldn't change my situation, but I could change my response to it. I decided I wanted to let God and all of heaven know that I wasn't yet ready to throw in the towel. Even though I was hurting so terribly, I wanted to sing a song of praise to God. I would sing it with all my heart.

So, with my hands still in the dishwater and with tears pouring down my cheeks, I lifted my face toward heaven and began to sing in a small, shaky voice. "Hallelujah. Hallelujah. Hallelujah. Praise the Lord."

Trying to sing while weeping at the same time is not the most lovely sound you'll ever hear! As I listened to the off-key, squeaky tones coming out of my mouth, I wondered how in the world this kind of ghastly music could be pleasing to God. Yet I was not going to stop. Over and over I sang that little chorus until I began to feel that Heaven was accepting my worship, and I was comforted.

When your day has been long and exhausting, when a life crisis has brought everything to a standstill, when you are sick and tired of being at the end of your rope, there is always still room for a song. We offer thanksgiving in personal prayer. Why not in personal song? Lift your face to heaven. Never mind if the tears start to flow. If you can't think of anything to sing, praise Him with the words of that children's song, "Jesus loves me. This I know." Sing it over and over until you feel His peace and are covered with His presence.

Terry Wilson Robinson

Having God's Joy—Regardless

A merry heart does good, like medicine, but a broken spirit dries the bones. Prov. 17:22, NKJV.

It was a beautiful Sabbath morning; I could feel an extra spring in my steps powered by the warmth of the sunshine, the blue skies, the fresh air, and the peaceful environment around me. My heart was praising God for His many blessings. I stood in front of the congregation as I led out in the praise and worship service. We were singing the beautiful songs that pointed to Zion, songs of hope and cheer to lift our eyes and thoughts beyond the cares of this life. But as I looked at the faces of the majority of the congregants, it struck me that many were not in the same happy frame of mind as I was. They were singing but their faces looked sad and blank as if no one cared, as if no one loved them, as if no one understood their unhappiness.

I stopped midsong and shared with them what I had just observed. I reminded them that the joy of the Lord is our strength, so we should leave our burdens with Jesus, and savor the blessings of this beautiful Sabbath day—and sing with thanksgiving in our hearts.

After the service I continued to reflect on the lack of joy and laughter that many of us experience. I read an article once that stated babies laugh approximately four hundred times a day, compared to adults who laugh, on the average fifteen times a day. No wonder Jesus said that unless we become as little children, we cannot enter the kingdom of heaven or into its joy and thanksgiving. "Then our mouth was filled with laughter and our tongue with singing. . . . The LORD has done great things for us, and we are glad" (Ps. 126:2, 3, NKJV).

Not so long ago, after a severe bout of illness, I was sitting in a wheelchair at the airport awaiting my turn to be transported to the plane. It was my first time using this mode of transportation. Suddenly, the tears began to flow as I thought of how much of my mobility I had lost. I felt frustrated at having to depend on someone. Would I ever regain full mobility? This was another cross added to the many crosses I already carried. Then right there God spoke to me, *Sonia, my grace is sufficient for thee, be thankful for the wheelchair.* I dried my tears and thanked and praised Him for His many blessings. Ever since then I have been encouraging others to be more joyful in the Lord regardless of the circumstances. Yes! I still need a wheelchair when I travel—praise the Lord! For what are you grateful and for what can you praise Him today?

Sonia Kennedy-Brown

Do I Trust God?

"Come to Me, all you who labor and are heavy laden, and I will give you rest. Take My yoke upon you and learn of Me, for I am gentle and lowly in heart, and you will find rest for your souls. For My yoke is easy and My burden is light." Matt. 11:28–30, NKJV.

It was evening. Before retiring, I did something that I should never have done—I checked my e-mail. One of the e-mails sent my blood pressure up, increased my heart rate, and made me extremely upset. Yes, sleep evaded me as a flood of negative thoughts raced through my mind. After tossing and turning for more than an hour, I told the Lord that I needed to rest as I had a full day of appointments ahead of me.

So I took out my lavender oil, a soothing balm to induce sleep, and got on my knees. Resolutely, I focused on God, and He sent several thoughts into my overactive mind. *Why are you so flustered? Don't you trust Me enough? Don't you believe that even the king's heart is in My hands and that I can turn it wherever I want it to go (Prov. 21:1)? Are you not convinced that I am in perfect control of this entire universe?*

God whispered Matthew 11:28–30 to me. *"Come to Me, all you who labor and are heavy laden, and I will give you rest. Take My yoke upon you and learn from Me, for I am gentle and lowly in heart, and you will find rest for your souls. For My yoke is easy and My burden is light" (NKJV).*

As these soothing words penetrated my very soul, I chose to listen, and believe, and gradually my body relaxed. Within a few minutes, I was lulled into a deep slumber by our loving heavenly Father.

As I wakened refreshed and revived to face a new day, God again reminded me of the lessons learned from the previous night of restlessness. I asked for forgiveness for not trusting Him fully. I realized that what I did was in the wrong sequence. As soon as the e-mail started to fluster me, my first thought should have been to pray, even thank Him for His blessings, instead of allowing my thoughts to run wild.

In addition, I resolved never to look at e-mails again just before retiring for the night. Rather, a better option should be to turn to God's Word that never fails to bring restfulness and peace to any soul. I suspect doing this will help you sleep better too.

Sally Lam-Phoon

November 4

The Priceless Gift

Thanks be to God for his indescribable gift! 2 Cor. 9:15, NIV.

Despite nearly a decade of missionary work in Africa, we'd never seen a Maasai village. Exhausted from emotional farewells before departing Rwanda, we were trying to slip from missionary mode into tourist mode for a couple days, sight-seeing in Kenya on our trip home to the U.S. But my heart was still back in the Interior. In riotous, high-jumping welcome, colorfully clad dancers—adults and children—encircled our tour bus. Tourists spilled out. Cameras clicked. An ochre-decorated tribesman approached. "Pay before pictures," he gently scolded. The bouncing beaded bib-necklace and excited eyes of a little dancer caught my attention as the circle of dancers melded into a band of curio hawkers. Swatting flies, tourists and tribesmen haggled over prices of the intricately beaded jewelry. I felt alone. I belonged to neither world.

A gentle pull on the front of my jacket startled me. I looked down. The little dancer stood in front of me. Uncharacteristically close. She was, maybe, ten. Too young yet—by perhaps a year or so—for female circumcision and marriage. Liquid brown eyes stared up into my blue ones. Feeling a tug at my heart, I returned her infectious smile. Then, pinched between thumb and forefinger, she held up a small, crudely crafted ring.

Probably leftover wire and discarded beads, I thought. *She's trying to make a few cents.* But when I opened my purse, the child shook her head. Small grimy hands encased one of mine. On my palm she placed the ring and folded my fingers over it. She pointed to her heart—and then to mine. Her loving gesture rendered me speechless. She had just given me all she had—for free. "Thank you," I stammered as the tour guide barked, "Time to go!" His earlier cultural lecture had shared that the life expectancy of a Maasai woman is forty-five. And that red in their jewelry symbolizes blood and courage while white denotes peace. My beaded ring was red and white.

Through the van window—and flowing tears—I frantically waved more thanks to the little dancer. With the other hand, I clutched my rusty-wired, and priceless, circle of beads.

Jesus, I can't give her the courage she'll need to face a life of pain. Nor the peace. But You can. So thank You for however it is You plan to let her know that Your crimson blood flowed for her and a white robe awaits her. Thank You for Your priceless gift to her. To all of us.

Carolyn Rathbun Sutton

329

In the Midst of It All

While they were telling these things, He Himself stood in their midst.
Luke 24:36, NASB.

It was another damp, wintry morning. Leaving home for work before the sunrise, I decided to turn off the car radio and talk to the Lord. You see, my spirit was in a wintry state as well. Depression had gripped me. Pray as I might, it would not let me go. My heart was heavy and full of sorrow. I could not see how God could use me in the midst of brokenness.

As I drove down the South Shore Road, Devonshire, I became overwhelmed with emotion as I emptied myself before the Lord. With tears pouring down my face, I could no longer see to drive and pulled over in the entrance of the botanical gardens. Between sobs, I looked up to see if any passing drivers saw my state of being. Gazing across the street at the open expanse of grassland, the scene paralleled my state of mind. The morning's cool temperatures and damp air caused a dense mist to hang just above the ground, the thick gray blanket blocking any view beyond.

After drying my tears and putting the car in gear to continue on to work, God unfolded a most amazing sight. The sun began to make its grand entrance upon this gloomy scene. As it peeked up over the row of homes perched on the bank that forms the backdrop for this grassy area, the rays burst through the mist. As the warmth of the sun caused the fog to lift, I saw something it had been concealing. There, in the middle of the grassy expanse, stood a lone duck—on one leg—peacefully sleeping. God had created this scene for me at this very moment!

Although completely shrouded from view by the weight of the earlier gray mist, evidences of peace and serenity were present as God unwrapped this visual gift. Like the healing balm of Gilead, *His* peace and serenity began to flow through me. God used this scene to serve as a vivid reminder that no matter how weighted down I was feeling, His Son was still there with me. At just the right moment He made His grand entrance known, causing the mists of gloom in my heart to evaporate. I was so grateful.

When you cannot see through the gloom, surrender your cares to Him. He will lift the mist of this sinful world so you can see who you are in His eyes—His daughter filled with the sunshine of His peace and presence. For He is there in the midst of it all.

Luann Wainwright-Dill

November 6

Before You Call

Commit thy way unto the LORD, trust also in him; and he will bring it to pass. Ps. 37:5.

My husband called from school one Friday morning, asking me to deliver something of urgency to an individual about to board an international flight. I had only twenty minutes in which to find this person before he left his office for the airport. My day was already crammed full because I wanted to get my work done before the Sabbath hours that evening. Reluctantly, I told my husband, "Yes," though I knew I couldn't lose even one of those twenty minutes if I were to make the contact. And I also might not be able to finish all the work I'd planned to do that day.

I quickly got into my car and hurried down the road. Oh, no! The section of the drawbridge I needed to cross was up in the air to accommodate boats passing through the channel. There was nothing I could do but wait. The few minutes of delay seemed like an hour. I had no control over what was happening, so I just sat, impatiently, and waited.

Finally, the elevated portion of the drawbridge lowered. Again I pressed the gas pedal and drove off toward my destination—the office of the individual leaving for his international flight. Ten minutes later I was in front of the office.

Hurriedly I turned my car into an officially designated parking space, telling myself I would be right back, before any authorized driver showed up. As soon as I stepped from my car, I saw the frame of a male figure. His back was turned toward me; he seemed to be in a hurry too. He was attempting to overtake another gentleman, ahead of him, whose attention he was trying to attract. I could hardly believe my eyes. This tall gentleman with his back to me was the very person my husband had asked me to endeavor to contact!

My heart turned in grateful thanks to God who had planned so well for me: the drawbridge delay; the man outside the office at just this moment; the timely contact with him—and delivery to him—just before his departure. I thanked the Lord silently and then aloud. God had somehow helped me avoid losing the precious time it would have taken for me to go through the office security guard, the office receptionist, and the office secretary.

I had not audibly asked for God's help, but He had arranged it all. I praised Him all the way home. And I will continue my praise until I reach my eternal destination, heaven.

Quilvie G. Mills

330

The Accident

In all their affliction he was afflicted, and the angel of his presence saved them: in his love and in his pity he redeemed them; and he bare them, and carried them all the days of old. Isa. 63:9.

Bike riding is my favorite form of exercise. The sunshine, the fresh air, and the physical motion blend in a symphony of praise that uplifts my mood and draws me to prayer. My husband and I often ride together for recreation. In fact, he gave me a new bike in 2012. On it I pedaled over four thousand miles that year, one thousand more than the previous year. I decided to try for one thousand additional miles during the remaining two months of the cycling season.

Then it happened, the accident! I didn't see the bale of wire jutting out into the roadway that cold December day and collided with it. Thrown off my bike and onto the pavement, I hit my hip, back, and head—thankfully, protected by my helmet. Shock is a wonderful thing sometimes. But after a hot shower back home, I decided a doctor should examine my right thumb, which I couldn't move—not good for a piano teacher. Waiting in the radiology department, my shock-induced anesthesia wore off. Waves of pain, overwhelming pain, swept through my body. I could hardly move due to my aching back. More comprehensive X-rays revealed a bruised back, broken hip bursa, and a displaced fracture in my thumb bones necessitating surgery. I was laid up for months. The forced inactivity due to my injuries was a real trial for me. Although I tried to pray and count my blessings, I hated feeling so helpless, weak, sore, and depressed.

In retrospect, I've learned though that pain is a great teacher. Her lessons are unforgettable. Here are just a few of the ones she taught me.

- God did not cause the accident nor was He punishing me. "As a father has compassion on his children, so the LORD has compassion on those who fear Him" (Ps. 103:13, NIV).
- Satan was trying to immobilize me, but healing came through the resulting rest. "The thief comes only to steal and kill and destroy" (John. 10:10). "In repentance and rest is your salvation, in quietness and trust is your strength" (Isa. 30:15, NIV).
- God was with me all the time. "In all their affliction He was afflicted" (Isa. 63:9).

I'm back on my bike again and thankful to God for every ride. No, I didn't achieve five thousand miles, yet I reached the goal Christ had for me: renewed enthusiasm for His purposes in my life.

Antoinette Franke

You Are My Miracle

"You will seek me and find me when you seek me with all your heart."
Jer. 29:13, NIV.

OK, My daughter. Do not despair. I am with you. In the twenty-fourth week of pregnancy, I was told by my doctor that I had toxoplasmosis. He asked me some questions and explained about the disease and its causes. He told me that my baby could be born blind, with a brain disease, or with a heart problem. I said, "But, Doctor, I have made it to the twenty-fourth week of pregnancy. This is just happening now?" He said he would prescribe an antibiotic and "I will be with you."

I left the room with my heart bruised and said to God, *Lord, take action.* Without strength of my own, I remembered that the Eternal God had chosen and trained me last year to lead the Women's Ministries Department at our church and given me the honor of having a team of wonderful women friends of prayer. Dagmar, Maria de Fátima, and Carmem were women full of faith and the Holy Spirit.

Extremely sensitive and tearful, I told my husband, "Call my friends of prayer." Without strength to pray, I told Dagmar and Carmem to pray for me for three months, and I explained the reason. They cried and sought God wholeheartedly.

I took all my medicine. I had a morphological ultrasound, and I could hear the heartbeat of my baby. The little body was perfect. The doctor told me everything was fine, but we didn't know if the sight was good, because we could verify that only after birth. The child within was a girl. Joy bloomed in my heart. I already had little John Wesley. Now Ellen was on her way. And I was trustful because my friends were interceding on my behalf.

During my last prenatal consultation, the doctor was unavailable. A very young, friendly lady doctor saw me instead. She told me that I would be admitted to the hospital, for I would soon go into labor because I was already losing fluid. My daughter came into the world, thanks to God and to the intercession of my friends. The next morning the ophthalmologist ran detailed tests on the baby. "Mother, your daughter is healthy. Be at peace," he said.

Oh, merciful God! Blessed be Your holy name! Everyone who asks, receives. He who seeks, finds. What a joy! Now I tell my child, "Daughter, you are my miracle." *Thank You, Lord! I am so grateful for Your response to intercession.*

Edna Soares da Cruz

The Last Race

Surely you know that many runners take part in a race, but only one of them wins the prize. Run, then, in such a way as to win the prize. Every athlete in training submits to strict discipline, in order to be crowned with a wreath that will not last; but we do it for one that will last forever.
1 Cor. 9:24, 25.

Secretariat was a strong and beautiful three-year-old colt when he won the Kentucky Derby, the Preakness, and Belmont Stakes all in record time. The year was 1973, and this was the first time in twenty-five years that a horse had won the Triple Crown.

On the day of the Belmont, Secretariat would compete against four other horses. Only Sham, who had finished second in the Derby and Preakness, was given any chance by punters.

The stadium was packed with 67,605 persons. There was an air of expectancy as the crowd anticipated that something spectacular was about to happen. Finally the horses were at the starting point. The gates flew open. Out they came, and off they went. Ron Turcotte, Secretariat's jockey, was in control and rode with wisdom and understanding. Down the track the horses galloped, furlong after furlong, Secretariat and Sham neck and neck for the first six furlongs. For many the horses disappeared around a bend. With bated breath the spectators watched as Secretariat burst forth like a bullet. The crowd was electrified. Spectators clapped and cheered. Secretariat neared the finish line, raced to the post, and won by thirty-one lengths.

The stadium of life is jam-packed. The race for the destiny of the human race is on; the most stupendous race to the final post is about to unfold. Very soon the eastern gate will be flung open, and we'll behold the Master Jockey coming with a retinue of angels. We are in the last furlong. For some, the view is hidden by wars, famine, love of money, violence, and materialism. Alas! Others have fallen off their horses or have galloped into doubt, discouragement, and fear. The saints, with steady effort, watch and wait to see Jesus Christ burst through the eastern sky. Those who have endured the race to the end will experience victory and a crown of glory.

Secretariat was the horse of the decade, but Jesus Christ is the Savior of the ages! Won't you run the race to receive the prize: the eternal crown—which will testify that we have overcome by the blood of the Lamb (see Rev. 12:11)?

Bula Rose Haughton Thompson

Look Up!

And it shall come to pass, when I bring a cloud over the earth, that the bow shall be seen in the cloud: And I will remember my covenant, which is between me and you. Gen. 9:14, 15.

You've experienced, haven't you, that quick intake of breath when you catch your first glimpse of a rainbow at the end of a dark storm? Seeing a double rainbow is an even more spectacular sight. I remember once flying through a turbulent storm, miles above earth's surface. The strong gusts of wind battered our aircraft as boiling black clouds enveloped it. I silently, fearfully cried out to my Creator for safety. Then I happened to look out the window at the dark clouds below. Moving across their rolling billows was the shadow of our airplane! Staring more intently, I recognized a rainbow that appeared to encircle the shadow of our plane! I emitted a peaceful sigh. Only God makes rainbows. He said, "I do set my bow in the clouds" (Gen. 9:13).

Seeing that rainbow surrounding the shadow of our storm-tossed plane dissipated my fear of the turbulence pounding our aircraft. Even life burdens on my heart seemed to melt away as I stared intently and gratefully at the splendor of the majestic rainbow just below us. I recalled that a rainbow represents God's promised presence with us. The Bible portrays a rainbow overarching the throne of the living God, our Creator of heaven and earth (Rev. 4:3). He promised, "Fear thou not for I am with thee: be not dismayed; for I am thy God: I will strengthen thee; yea, I will help thee; yea, I will uphold thee with the right hand of my righteousness" (Isa. 41:10). God's rainbow promise not only concerns the promise of no earth-wide flood but also extends to the protection of His children when the enemy of our souls "comes in like a flood" (Isa. 59:19).

In times past God didn't speak through the sun shining in blue skies. He spoke through a cloudy pillar (Ps. 99:7). And brilliant clouds will one day surround Him as He returns for His children to take them home (Acts 1:9–11). Yes, a cloudless sky makes for a beautiful day. Yet few sights in nature are more spectacular than the near-blinding, light-diffusing clouds that surround a multi-colored sunset painted from the Creator's own palette of numberless hues.

So look up! Do you see clouds in your life? Take heart, for somewhere—in those dark billowing clouds of trial, sorrow, despair, loss, and suffering—is tucked the beautiful rainbow reminder of God's faithful love. And it's surrounding *you* right now!

Naomi Naylor Lokko

Instant Miracle

And it shall come to pass, that before they call, I will answer; and while they are yet speaking, I will hear. Isa. 65:24.

Since becoming a mother, I had heard other mothers talk about "the dreadful earache," and I prayed and hoped my kids never got it. My first child was now nineteen years old, and I was very grateful she didn't get the dreadful earache.

My next child was now five years old, and I was hoping and praying again, so can you imagine the fear in me when one night as we were returning home, I heard my little daughter say, "Mummy, my ear is hurting me." All my fears came flooding down, but then I noticed she wasn't crying, so I calmly asked, "Is it hurting bad?" and she replied, No. I then breathed a sigh of relief. After reaching home she went straight to sleep; I kissed her goodnight and went to bed myself. About 11:00 P.M., I was awakened by loud screaming. Both my husband and I ran to our five-year-old's side and asked what was wrong. She yelled, "My ears, my ears!" We immediately started rushing around, getting ready to go to the hospital.

With her screaming so loudly, I became very confused and felt weak and helpless. Somehow I told myself, *You need to get some appropriate clothes on.* So I hurried to the closet, and as I touched the door she screamed so hard that it stopped me in my tracks. With tears in my eyes, I lifted my head to heaven and cried, "Lord, have mercy on my child!" And then all I heard was a sigh and the screaming stopped. *Oh, Father, she is dead,* I thought as I rushed to where she was. To my amazement, she was just sleeping peacefully. I could not believe my eyes! God had answered my prayer instantly! All I could do was praise Him and thank Him; and I still thank Him today for that miracle.

I had asked God to keep my children from getting the dreadful earache, but it took an ear-splitting earache for me to experience the power and joy of an instant miracle. We serve an awesome God; He is worthy to be praised. I have learned over the years to give thanks for everything just as the text tells us: "In every thing give thanks: for this is the will of God in Christ Jesus concerning you" (1 Thess. 5:18). First Chronicles 16:34 says it all: "O give thanks unto the LORD; for he is good; for his mercy endureth for ever."

Pauline Sinclair

This Beautiful Day

This is the day which the LORD hath made; we will rejoice and be glad in it. Ps. 118:24.

Beautiful days are not only those days aglow with bright sunshine, blue skies, gentle breezes, and singing birds. Rainy days have their beauty as well. Imagine that you are a flower. Would you complain about the weather if gray clouds replaced the sunshine? Or would you be thankful for rainy days as well?

Just as flowers need all kinds of days to grow, we need a variety of "weather" factors in order to mature into the Christlike beauty He intended for us.

Of course, we usually have no problem with the "sunny" days in our lives, when life events are moving along smoothly. But what about the other days? Days when we must push through the clouds of despair and the darkness of physical, emotional, or relational pain? Days when we must struggle to remember that the Light of the world—the Sun of righteousness—has the answers to our needs and perplexities? Days when we *must* remember that the light of His love is *always* shining through life's storms? Rainy days can grow us into a faith and trust that too many sunny days never would.

When we sink our roots deeply into the rich soil of God's Word and accept the "rain" that falls upon us, we can be certain we are growing in grace, sheltered in His arms of love. In fact, Jesus told His followers that "rainy" days—days with problems, trials, and sorrow—would be part of their earthly growth in grace. "These things I have spoken unto you," Jesus said, "that in me you might have peace. In the world ye shall have tribulation: but be of good cheer; I have overcome the world" (John 16:33). Through Paul He assured us that we can make it through anything because of Christ's strength in us (see Phil. 4:13).

Rain or shine, God bestows his loving care upon each of us, His "flowers." And the beauty of any day lies in our ability to understand that He will take care of us and continue to grow us into His grace and truth—regardless of the "weather."

Dear Lord, thank You for the gift of this beautiful day. Help me appreciate its new beginnings and endless possibilities. Help me gain victories and grow closer to You. Help me trust that You love and care for me. May I know that—with You—there's nothing I can't handle.

Rhodi Alers de López

Emily

Train up a child in the way [she] should go: and when [she] is old, she will not depart from it. Prov. 22:6.

Emily was just a toddler when she came to live with her new mother and her aunt and started attending the children's classes in our church in Palm Bay. Everyone was excited to meet this beautiful toddler, but we could not get past her constant crying. Each time any one of us greeted her, she would cry.

Her new mother was the Adventurer leader [similar to Cub Scouts], so Emily started in the club at a very early age. The third Sabbath of each month the Adventurers would go to a nursing home, where they would sing, read Bible passages, and greet the residents of the home. Young Emily went with them.

One Sabbath when she was about six years old she visited the nursing home and declared, "I would like to sing a song from the hymnal." Surprised, we questioned each other, "Can she really do it?" Not only was the little girl very shy, but we had never heard her sing a solo before. But she took a hymnal, opened it to hymn number 305, and sang, "Give Me Jesus."

At seven years of age, Emily asked for Bibles studies. I did not take her request seriously. I let it go for a while, but each time she saw me she asked, "When can I start Bible studies?" Finally, I agreed to have Bible studies with her. She was given a folder in which to keep her lessons. She never left that folder at home but took it with her to church every time she went. She kept her tattered folder until it fell apart and had to be given a new one.

During those months of Bible studies and instruction in church beliefs, Emily continued being focused on growing in Jesus, never once wavering. Toward the end of the studies, she announced. "I want to get baptized." Again I hesitated and told her to talk to her mom. When I saw her next, Emily was happy to report that her mom had agreed she could be baptized. Emily, like other children who have gone through Bible classes with me, has taught me a valuable lesson. When I make any decision for the Lord, I need to stand firm like she did.

On October 12, 2013, along with three others, Emily was baptized. My grateful heart sang, *To God be the glory!*

Gloria P. Hutchinson

God's Love for Me

The Lord . . . is patient with you, not wanting anyone to perish, but everyone to come to repentance. 2 Pet. 3:9, NIV.

Someone very close to me was making dangerous choices by habitually breaking local traffic laws. Over the years I had reasoned and begged, prayed and begged, warned and begged, but to no avail. As the offenses multiplied, the courts meted out the fines and punishments. I often helped, intervened, and cried. But my precious one just would not yield to the laws.

One night, as yet another harsh penalty was leveled, I sat down with this individual to review, on paper, the record of lawlessness. Together we looked at this person's past choices and the resulting consequences. The outlook seemed hopeless. Out of desperation, my dear one looked at me, confused and befuddled, groaning, "What are we going to do, Rose?"

Speechless, I contemplated the question and in my silent sorrow, I remembered God. I caught a spiritual glimpse of His longsuffering, of His unyielding patience and of His incomprehensible love for me. I understood then, in a small way, how God feels when I fail to heed His loving voice and warnings through His laws. How sad He must be to watch me face the results of my disobedience!

You see, many times, I have ignored or doubted God's Word and have forged ahead like a stubborn child intent on having my own way. Often God has pled with me through His words, His servants, and His providences. Yet, I move ahead full force until justice crosses the path of my rebellion and demands that I pay the consequences. When my offenses yield dire results, I throw my hands up and wail, "What are *we* going to do, Lord?" Yet whether or not His mercy deletes the sad results of my sins, the grace of His presence comforts, guides, and restores me.

My sins hurt Him. He cannot bear to see me face the price of my unfortunate actions any more than I can stand to see my dear one hurt as a result of breaking so many traffic laws.

So in response to my dear one's question, I said, "I'm here with you. I have stayed close to help, guide, and alleviate just like God, for Christ's sake, does for me."

Dear God, thank You for not abandoning me when I go astray. Please give me a heart that listens and obeys. In trust and obedience I will find happiness in Jesus. Amen.

Rose Joseph Thomas

When God Turns the Impossible Into Possibilities

Ye shall not need to fight in this battle: set yourselves, stand ye still, and see the salvation of the LORD with you, O Judah and Jerusalem: fear not, nor be dismayed; to morrow go out against them: for the LORD will be with you. 2 Chron. 20:17.

I was a third year student at Valley View University in Ghana when my mother retired. It was then very difficult for her to take care of my tuition because the process for her to access her retirement benefits was taking too long. Mom and I did not know where to get the money for my rent and registration for the semester. But we kept on praying seriously.

Before leaving my country (Côte d'Ivoire) for school, we decided to intensify our prayers, pleading with God to work out a miracle. Thus I returned to school without anything except faith. After praying again and again, I decided to go meet the university financial officer to ask permission to register. At his office, I met many students seeking the same thing without success. After whispering a few words of prayer, I walked in and explained my predicament, still praying silently in my heart. Miraculously—and to my amazement—he allowed me to register.

I was then allowed to attend classes till the end of the semester even though no money had yet been paid into my account. But then the exam period approached, and I still didn't have the money. Apparently, the devil had hardened the heart of the people who were supposed to process my mother's retirement benefit. But God still showed Himself ever victorious in my life. Two days before the examination period, I felt the urge to go see the university treasurer. On my way, I felt unusual peace, and this gave me the assurance that God was about to act again. And true to my conviction, God did it again. Before entering the treasurer's office, I was inspired to go print a copy of my account to show him that since I started school I had never owed until now when my mom was facing financial challenges. The man looked at me and said: "I will help you be able to write your exams after obtaining the necessary exam permit. But you will have to raise the money and pay as soon as possible." Then I received a Women's Ministries scholarship!

God had turned the impossible into an unexpected possibility again. In God's words to Israel of old, He still commands us today, even in the face of great obstacles, "Go . . . for the LORD will be with you."

Linda-Luiselle B. Yapi

The Right Word at the Right Time

And a word spoken in due season, how good it is! Prov. 15:23, NKJV.

Tommy was the kind of guy who'd slam the door in your face, kick his cat, and knock over the neighbor's bike—all in ten seconds. He had a scowl on his face and a chip on his shoulder, and my girls were scared to death of him.

Our family lived in the upstairs of the duplex, and he, his mom, and his three-year-old brother lived downstairs. His mom and I spoke pleasantly as we passed one another going in and out of the house, but twelve-year-old Tommy was a different matter. We advised our kids to stay out of his way, but in reality, none of us could avoid him. That he was big and tough for his age made it even worse.

Then one afternoon I saw Tommy's little brother playing alone in the back, yard. He was throwing leaves and playing with sticks as little boys will do. Minutes later I heard a shrill voice screaming angry, vile words. Tommy's mother was calling Little Brother into the house. Aha! Now I understood Tommy a bit better, but that didn't solve our problem.

One evening Tommy's mom called and told me that the plastic ware I'd ordered from her home party had arrived. When I went down to pick it up, she invited me in. The kitchen was to the left of the front door, and I saw Tommy standing at the stove frying something in a large skillet. "Tommy, I bet your mom loves it when you help fix supper," I told him. "I'm always glad when my girls help me."

Tommy forked a chunk of meat from the sizzling oil and held it toward me. "Here, have a taste," he said. Now, I had been a vegetarian for decades, but there was no way I was going to hurt that boy's feelings.

"Thank you," I told him. "You've got it so nice and brown." And he did. Then, speaking around the mouthful, I said goodbye and hurried upstairs—where I spit it out.

The next afternoon Tommy was lounging around the front yard as usual, but this time he held the door open for me with a big smile. And I'd be lying if I didn't tell you that around us Tommy was a changed kid. In small ways he was helpful with our girls, and he always had a big smile for me. Kindness can have that effect on people. It's funny like that.

Penny Estes Wheeler

9-1-1

Before they call I will answer, while they are yet speaking I will hear.
Isa. 65:24, RSV.

Years ago, long before iPhones, I waded through deep snow, across the frozen lake, to walk in the silent woods. But I when I reached the far shore, I was not alone. Laughter filled the air as three teenage girls on a sled hurtled down a nearby steep slope. And suddenly laughter turned to cries as one girl spilled from the sled. When she sobbed that it hurt from her neck to her waist, I told her two friends, "Keep her still and as warm as possible. I'll call for help." I strode home to dial the three powerful numbers: 9-1-1.

Just four minutes later, an ambulance stopped in front of my house, and I directed the two emergency medical technicians (EMTs) to the accident site. One man jogged down the hill and across the lake while the other made a phone call before he followed.

By the time I arrived, one EMT was assessing Melissa's physical state; the other was putting a neck brace on her. Then I saw more activity. Five firefighters were speeding across the frozen lake on a quad.

Soon capable hands were lifting Melissa onto the backboard, placing foam blocks on either side of her neck, strapping her carefully so she wouldn't slip as she was lifted her from the ground and carried to the quad. One EMT removed the jacket that Melissa's friend had used to cover her. Instantly, knowing that Melissa was suffering cold and shock, a fireman and the ambulance driver removed their jackets to warm her.

Twenty minutes after I punched in the three numbers—9-1-1—Melissa was on her way to the hospital. I had thought she was in an inaccessible location, but I didn't know the resources available when I called. Not only was there an ambulance and two strong, trained experts, but there was a quad for driving over the snow and ice and through the fields, and five more skilled professionals. People whose caring and competence—and whose warm, jacket-sharing hearts—had them ready for action as soon as they were called.

I am grateful to be able to be part of such a community. But even more, I rejoice to be part of God's family. I don't have to phone for help. It doesn't take twenty minutes—or even four minutes—for my Father to be beside me. He is there even before I call.

Denise Dick Herr

Angel to the Rescue

The angel of the LORD encamps around those who fear him, and he delivers them. Ps. 34:7, NIV.

My oldest daughter, Lillian, and I headed to the Orlando International Airport. It was the Friday before Thanksgiving, and Lillian was flying by herself to New York to meet my cousin, Hope. From there, they would board a flight for England, ultimately ending their trip in Paris, France.

During the hour and a half drive, Lillian talked about what she and Auntie Hope planned to do on this vacation. Lillian had been dreaming of this day for many years. We'd also been saving money for this trip, which would be an early celebration of Lillian's fifteenth birthday.

I was a little surprised by Lillian's demeanor. I had expected her to be a little nervous about traveling by herself. Yet she wasn't. A few months ago, when Lillian and her sister Cassandra had flown to Boston, Massachusetts, to spend some time with my brother and his wife (Peter and Connie), she'd seemed anxious when boarding the plane. Maybe she'd felt reticent about having the responsibility of her little sister. In fact, as soon as she could, Lillian had texted me stating that she was concerned about the trip.

Today, however, I didn't see that same child. Instead I saw a confident young woman who was ready to step out on her own—at least temporarily. Inwardly, I was the typical concerned parent but outwardly I was relaxed. I wasn't worried about Hope taking care of Lillian. I was concerned about Lillian's flying alone to New York. Allowing Lillian to travel by herself to LaGuardia Airport was rather daunting for me. But God knew my concerns. Suddenly in the airport crowd I spotted a vaguely familiar face.

Yes, I did know him. He'd been one of my childhood friends. Today he was traveling with his wife to New York for vacation. Without Lillian's noticing, I was able to greet them and ask if they'd keep a protective eye on her during the flight. They assured me that they would also make sure she'd connected with Hope before continuing on their way.

God had arranged for this couple to watch over Lillian. The name of my friend? Angel. How thankful I was that Lillian had her own guardian Angel on that flight. God is amazing!

Tamara Marquez de Smith

White Grape Juice

How sweet are your words to my taste, sweeter than honey to my mouth! I gain understanding from your precepts; therefore I hate every wrong path. Ps. 119:103, 104, NIV.

rowsing through a beloved book one morning, I paused after reading a powerful passage. "Many are the ways in which God is seeking to make Himself known to us and bring us into communion with Him. Nature speaks to our senses without ceasing" (Ellen G. White, *Steps to Christ,* p. 85). Mulling over that last sentence, I asked, *Are You trying to tell me something, Lord?* His answer came at breakfast the next morning as I reached for the apple juice and took a sip.

"Something's wrong with this juice," I complained, lifting the glass to examine the pale gold nectar more closely.

"That's not apple juice," Mom said, laughing. "That's white grape juice." Nonplussed, I sampled it again. But this time with a different fruit "label" in my thoughts. She was right. Now my taste buds had different expectations and the juice tasted very good.

That incident made such an impact on my thinking that I sought to find allusions to "labeling" in other areas of my life. On a psychosocial level, I noted how our skewed—often erroneous—expectations can cause us problems in terms of how we "classify" other people. We sometimes respond negatively to them until we give ourselves the chance to truly know them.

On a spiritual level, I remembered Christ's parable of the wheat and the tares as recorded in Mathew's Gospel. The farmer told his workers to let them both grow together until the harvest when he would have his reapers separate them, burning the tares and storing the wheat in his barn (see Matt. 13:30). We are not to judge who are wheat and who are tares. For God often sends into our lives the very individuals we might be too quick to "label"—and reject—as being unsuitable to our "taste." Maybe we need to take more time to get to know others personally and to appreciate the unique "flavor" they would bring to enrich our lives. Besides, if we're daily "tasting" the goodness of the Lord (see Ps. 34:8), we'll appreciate and love others as He does.

What lessons I have learned from that simple sip of white grape juice that morning!

Thank You, Lord, for the five senses that bring us closer to You—and to others.

Glenda-mae Greene

November 20

God's Will Is Best

Cast your cares on the LORD and he will sustain you. Ps. 55:22, NIV.

I was in a quandary. My daughter and I, who can no longer live alone, were going to lose our helper. She was leaving us to further her education—a venture I've always applauded. How could we find a new attendant, one who can work and meet our multitask needs? One with whom we are mutually compatible?

My daughter is virtually bedbound, and I have the abundance of ailments that descend on octogenarians like me. I need extra eyes and working legs. Without that help we couldn't stay at home.

I talked over the situation with my son one evening, unwittingly sharing my deep distress. Then another voice piped up. It was my granddaughter.

"Grandma, just remember this: 'We have nothing to fear for the future, except as we shall forget the way the Lord has led us.' " I was moved. I didn't even realize that she knew the precious passage (Ellen G. White, *Life Sketches,* p. 196). God had stepped in and delivered His message to me through a nineteen-year-old.

Reflecting on that incident I asked myself, *Why did I worry despite the fact that I knew that God was in control? Why couldn't I just have trusted Him in faith and prayed for the best?*

Then I turned to something else Mrs. White had written more than an hundred years ago. I smiled as its relevance to my own situation became clear.

"Though we can not see the definite outcome of affairs, or discern the purpose of God's providences, we are not to cast away our confidence. Remembering the tender mercies of the Lord, we should cast our care upon Him, and with patience wait for His salvation" (*Christ's Object Lessons,* p. 61).

When the new aide came, she was tentative at first but soon became a helpful member of our household.

God's promises are true!

Sisters of the world, let us confidently wait on Him. God will work out all things for our good. When we lean on His tender mercies, it makes all the difference!

Carol J. Greene

Holding On

Let us hold fast the confession of our hope without wavering; for He who promised is faithful. Heb. 10:23, NKJV.

Glancing out of my study window, I noted my daily "inspirational" leaf on a nearby tree. Spring's gentle warmth had unfolded its tight curl. Summer's heat slowly moved in. "My" leaf matured as its rich spring green faded slightly from excessive heat. Yet warbling birds brought more "color" to the tree branches during this season.

With autumn's arrival came cooler temperatures. Rain pelted my leaf, turning it round and round. Would it be twisted or blown off the branch? No, it just kept holding on!

Winter came early; the chilling north winds were brutal. They blasted the now-gray, discolored leaf, twirling it more than autumn's rain had—round and round and round. Would it separate from the branch? Amazingly, it did not let go. It hung on! Through all four seasons. My leaf reminded me of my own earthly journey. My personal spring had lightly touched me with laughter and much love. Life had been good and there was happiness. The summer of my life had brought its share of challenges, but youthful enthusiasm and courage had overcome them. No worries. Autumn had introduced coldness that pierced my soul and caused tears to fall. Heartaches followed. And now winter has come. Its blasts have been pummeling me and causing me to wonder,

Does God really know and care about me?

Does He know that I am hurting?

Does He have solutions to my problems?

Yet my little leaf has taught me I need to keep holding on—holding on to my Father's hand. Although I cannot see the future, that is the only answer I have. Life can never be relived, so I must continue to trust. He has guided me through these many, many years. I must continue to claim His promises "and be content with such things as ye have: for he hath said, I will never leave thee, nor forsake thee" (Heb. 13:5).

Help me, Lord, to treasure Your care during this season and the ones to come. Holding on to Your powerful hand, may I look for joy and contentment in each new day. Amen.

Muriel Heppel

Kennedy—Part 1

There is no longer Jew or Greek, there is no longer slave or free, there is no longer male and female; for all of you are one. Gal. 3:28, NRSV.

As the nation recently remembered John F. Kennedy on the fiftieth anniversary of his death on a fateful day in November, I couldn't help but remember where I was when the news came to me.

I had just arrived at River Plate College (now the Plata Adventist University) to spend an academic year taking theology and religion courses to polish up my skills in Spanish and experience another culture. It was a new adventure that filled me with fear and excitement all at the same time.

As I walked down the stairs from my dorm room to the lobby of the women's dormitory, the women's dean, Señorita Bellido, stopped me and looked at me in the strangest way.

"What's the matter?" I asked still trying to decipher that look.

"Haven't you heard? Your president is dead. They just killed President Kennedy."

"My president?" I repeated in a stupor, trying to take in what was inconceivable.

My president? I suddenly had a perspective on myself that I hadn't had until that moment: I was an American, and this president who had just been assassinated was *my* president. In my country I had previously thought of myself as an outsider, a "Hispanic" with strong roots in Puerto Rican–Venezuelan and Mexican-American cultures and customs. Now, suddenly, I was given a picture of myself that summarized who I was in one word: American.

On the one hand, I felt cheated out of my Hispanic heritage that would link me in some way to the Argentine people. On the other, I was grateful to be forced into understanding who I was through the eyes of another people and seeing myself as truly belonging to my own country.

It was a revelation that was life-changing.

In many ways, "my" president, President John F. Kennedy, had embarked the entire nation on an adventure of self-discovery when he took a stand to define "American" as multiethnic, multiracial, and multilingual.

And now I knew I was part of that adventure as well.

Though not always an easy journey, self-discovery is an essential one each must travel.

Lourdes Morales-Gudmundsson

Kennedy—Part 2

But let justice roll down like waters, and righteousness like an ever-flowing stream. Amos 5:24, NRSV.

The circumstances that set President Kennedy before a precedent-setting, life-and-death decision were created by the then-governor of Alabama, George Wallace, who saw himself as the preserver of a long tradition of black-white apartheid. Mr. Wallace had come to believe that his position on segregation was a matter of principle and conscience. He was willing to stand up to a law that had passed in 1954—*Brown v. Board of Education*—declaring segregation unconstitutional and even stand up to the president of the United States for a way of life that had benefited one group of people to the detriment of another. Kennedy's definition of "American" Mr. Wallace could not accept, though justice and mercy, righteousness and grace demanded it.

What struck me as I recently watched Robert Drew's amazing documentary on their confrontation was that the President had to use force to implement a just law. It did not matter what an individual or even a group of individuals felt was just or right—the nation through its highest court had already adjudicated on the matter—segregation by race went against the spirit and truth of the Thirteenth, Fourteenth, and Fifteenth Amendments against slavery. It was easy for the Alabama governor to "say" that his fight for segregation was a moral issue; in fact, the opposite was true. Truth over custom must determine what is a matter of conscience.

That is what God was saying to His people through the prophet Amos: search your conscience to see if you have been just with Me and with your brother and sister. You who "turn justice to wormwood and bring righteousness to the ground!" (Amos 5:7), seek the Lord and seek life. God did not use force to bring His people to their senses but appealed to their sense of justice and mercy. God's harsh evaluation and condemnation of His people was not based on failure to observe rites and rituals, but on their moral failures to Him and to one another: "They . . . abhor the one who speaks the truth" (verse 10). God's call to truth was a call to soul searching, to find the roots of injustice and unrighteousness, not so much in their society, but in each human heart. In mercy, God daily calls each of us to break the heart's hardness, allowing justice and righteousness to tumble into the lives of those with whom we come in contact.

Lourdes Morales-Gudmundsson

The Lost Art

Give thanks to the LORD, for he is good; His love endures forever.
1 Chron. 16:34, NIV.

I made a special trip to the bank and got a crisp brand-new bill. It wasn't a huge amount, but it was large for my budget. At home again I happily tucked the money in the birthday card and got it in the mail to my out-of-state friend.

Days passed, weeks passed. The card was not returned although my home address was on the envelope. No phone call, no letter, no text, no comment when I saw her in person. I was disappointed. I certainly felt less inclined to repeat the gift. I didn't want a lot. Just two words—thank you.

I've gotten gifts (even from my husband!) that would not have been my first choice. And I know I've given gifts that the recipient didn't especially like. However, if we try to understand the intention of the giver, it's easier to be gracious and appreciate the gift. Appreciation needs to be sincere and not come across as phony. Salt is a small ingredient in tasty bread. Appreciation is a small ingredient in good friendships.

God's divine heart doesn't need my praise and appreciation to be happy, but I have to believe He likes it, and a thankful heart does a lot for my attitude!

An unbelievable story of praising God and acknowledging His greatness comes from Job. After Job had been given the devastating report of losing his oxen, donkeys, sheep, camels, servants, and then all of his children, do you know what he did? He praised, blessed, and magnified the name of the Lord. (Job 1:21). Now, can you imagine keeping things in perspective well enough to thank God in that kind of adversity?! What an example of a great attitude of trust even during tragedy!

It's easy to make a long list of things God provides that we can be thankful for—things in nature, the satisfaction of basic needs, the intricate balance of the human body, spiritual blessings—things we take for granted. God must be disappointed that we get so busy even with good things that we don't have a grateful heart that whispers "Thank You" often. The simple expression of appreciation seems to be coming more of a lost art even among people and certainly to our Creator! And Redeemer! And Giver of every good gift!

Roxy Hoehn

Saved by a Stranger

The angel of the LORD encamps around those who fear him, and he delivers them. Ps. 34:7, NIV.

Howard (my four-year-old brother) and I (the oldest of nine children and sixteen at the time) almost drowned on the island of Bermuda. One summer afternoon in 1945 my mother decided to take her nine children for a swim at a place called Spithead in the Parish of Warwick. We lived within walking distance from the shore, and I helped my mother with the younger children.

Upon arriving, my four older brothers immediately headed to the springboard from which they liked to jump. My mom and I were with my four younger siblings. After helping her settle them in a shallow part of the water, I decided to go for a swim farther out, so I jumped into the water and swam toward a gentleman who was in his boat fishing.

Suddenly, as I was swimming I heard a man's voice shout, "Look at the boy!" I turned around and saw that it was my youngest brother, Howard. He had followed me without my knowledge, had lost strength, and was drowning! I got to him just in time. However, he grabbed me around my neck and we both went under the water. As I came up for air, I yelled for help and then under the water we went again.

I felt a stronger hand than mine grab my brother and pull him out of the water. Then the man pulled me out.

Later we learned that the man who saved us was Mr. Corbel, a United States Naval officer. He said he was passing by and noticed my mother with her nine children and decided to stop and watch us. He sat on the wall beside the water not far from us and had been close enough to rescue us from drowning. My father, who was in the Navy, was so grateful that he wrote a letter to his commanding officer thanking him for saving us. I know that God used Mr. Corbel to save us and that we were saved for a purpose.

Today, my brother Howard is seventy-three years old, is married with three children and eight grandchildren. He is an active member of his church in several capacities. As of this writing, I will be eighty-five years old on my next birthday. I know my purpose at this point in my life is to share my faith with my family and with the residents here at the rehab center where I now live. I thank God for saving us that unforgettable day long ago. Remember to thank Him for saving you.

Violet Crockwell Wilson

New Fears

"When you pass through the waters, I will be with you; and when you pass through the rivers, they will not sweep over you." Isa. 43:2, NIV.

My husband and I were still in college. When vacations came, we sold books in order to pay for our studies. This time we were to go to Palmas, Tocantins, 1,118 miles (1,800 kilometers) away from our home in São Paulo. We were taking a couple of friends with us and hoped to develop a successful sales season. The proposal seemed good, and so we invested what we had in having our old 1986 Manza checked before traveling.

It took two days to travel to our sales field; then troubles and difficulties began. A sudden illness caused my husband to spend seven days in bed. Our struggles were softened by angels that God sent in the form of the Helfenstens family, who offered us their home, their resources, and their prayers.

Two months later we headed home, tired and frustrated, with only debts. Between Tocantins and Goiás, the traffic stopped and I noticed water flooding over the road. It was then that I discovered a new fear that I was unaware of: a fear of floods! The car doors were not locking properly, and the rusted-out floor allowed water to enter. *After all we've been through this holiday, there is there still more that can go wrong?* My husband stopped the car. If he went ahead, we could be washed away. If we stayed there, the water might rise and it could be worse. I was sweating cold drops of fear. Suddenly, I saw a new, high car with a wheel pulled off because it had fallen into a hole in the dark water. A 4x4 truck passed with difficulty, bumping along. Failure was certain, but my husband said, "Pray, because we're going to try to go through." I prayed, "Lord, please watch over us!" I had barely completed my prayer when my husband started to cross that river. We crossed smoothly as I watched out the window. Amazingly, not a drop of water leaked into the car. Everything was dry when we checked.

I felt that God was with me, not to give me what I wanted, but to protect me and tell me that He would provide the means to sustain me and my family. And that is what He has been doing ever since. If today you are desperate, in trouble, and needing assurance, trust—because the impossible is God's specialty. What a wonderful thing for which we can be thankful!

Daniela Santos de Oliveira

The Umbrella

He ruleth by his power for ever. Ps. 66:7.

God performs miracles today as He did in days of old. We just don't take time to think about all the things we take for granted that God does for us by His power.

To be alive after seventy years, to have a sane mind, to be able to walk, to drive, and to have good vision are all miracles. A child born without defect of body or mind is a miracle. But the most beautiful miracle of all is when a sinner is converted.

The Bible instructs us to think on God's power, His love, and His protection day and night and to always give Him praise. When the powers of darkness sometimes come up against us, God steps in and takes control, especially when we acknowledge His power and give Him control of our lives. The following incident is a good example of God's control and power.

My brother had driven me and two of my sisters in his van to Cedar Lake Academy, a Christian boarding high school, to attend our niece's eighth-grade graduation.

One of my nieces had given me a beautiful, multicolored umbrella, which I had taken with me to Cedar Lake. When we prepared to leave the reception hall after the graduation, I made sure my umbrella was hanging on my arm by its strap. My purse hung over the umbrella. This was to make sure I wouldn't lose the umbrella. What happened next is unbelievable.

I helped my niece load some of the items she was taking home from school into her parents' van, making sure all the time the umbrella was safe on my arm. When I left my niece's van and walked to my brother's van, which was only about twenty feet away, I discovered my umbrella was gone. My first thought was that the strap had broken and the umbrella had fallen to the ground, but it was nowhere to be found.

Returning home, I thought seriously about what had happened, and I prayed, *Lord, I know You are all-powerful; if it is Your will, please return my umbrella. In Jesus' name I pray.*

Two weeks later my brother was cleaning out his van and there underneath the back seat, strap intact, was my umbrella. I can't imagine what actually happened in this situation. What I do know for sure is God answered my prayer and He returned my umbrella.

We serve an exalted, all-knowing, powerful God! He deserves our praise—always.

Moselle Slaten Blackwell

He Never Fails

A man who has friends must himself be friendly, but there is a friend who sticks closer than a brother. Prov. 18:24, NKJV.

Relationships of various kinds go through periods of highs and lows. And during these ebbs and flows, the dynamics of a person's life can change such that sometimes these relationships grow stronger while, at other times, they may weaken or fall apart completely. But, many times, God places people in our lives who are there for us through thick and thin. These persons would be considered our bona fide friends or relatives. They are always there to support us, pray for us, or give us a listening ear. They find time to celebrate those special moments with us. You will find them on your solemn wedding day or by your side after the birth of that long-awaited child. They take time to observe those yearly birthdays and anniversaries and are excited about finding every opportunity to celebrate with you.

And even when things become dismal, they are still there for you. They sacrifice their personal means, their time, their talent, and their financial resources to help you and others. Without a doubt, you know that you can count on these persons to come through for you or to simply be there for you. Can you think of such a friend or relative? Well, even if you have had some curve balls along the way regarding relationships, or you have not found that really close friend yet, remember that Jesus is always there for you. He is there for you through the good times and the bad times, and He always has your best interest at heart.

As the key text says, "there is a friend who sticks closer than a brother." Jesus is that friend who has been and will always be there for you. Sometimes you may feel as if He is far away, but always remember that He loves you with an everlasting love. A love so pure and true that He sacrificed His life to save you and me from sin. He truly loves us, and His love and friendship will never fail. The words of an age-old hymn say, "What a friend we have in Jesus, All our sins and griefs to bear. What a privilege to carry everything to God in prayer."

Won't you take some time to talk to your Maker and Friend, Jesus? Ask Him to show you how to make your relationship with Him better. Thank Him for wanting to be your closest Friend and for always waiting to listen and talk to you.

Taniesha Robertson-Brown

Deception

Rather, we have renounced secret and shameful ways; we do not use deception, nor do we distort the word of God. On the contrary, by setting forth the truth plainly we commend ourselves to everyone's conscience in the sight of God. 2 Cor. 4:2, NIV.

As soon as I saw the e-mail pop up, even without opening it, I knew it was a scam. But just looking at the scammer's name made me laugh. In fact, I thought it was so funny that I left it in my inbox for a week because it brought a smile to my face.

It was one of those swindles that you may have received as well: someone had a lot of money in a bank, but they died. The writer claimed, "I have the opportunity of making you the beneficiary to his deposited funds with our bank. I have all the details and required information." And the scammer's name? Rachael Goodluck.

Good luck. Sure. Much better than Rachael Toughluck. Or Rachael Tofoolyou. Would someone really be influenced by contacting someone named Goodluck?

But even more, I thought about Rachael. Although the biblical woman's name is spelled a little differently, she certainly brought deception to my mind. Rachel was a member of a family of deceivers: her husband Jacob's name even meant "he grasps the heel" or "he deceives" (footnote on Gen. 25:26, NIV). And he certainly deceived his father and even his brother Esau. And Rachel's father Laban deceived Jacob by substituting Leah for Rachel, and even cheated Jacob from his wages (Gen. 31:7). And Rachel herself deceived her father by stealing the household idols and sitting on them, telling a lie as to why she could not stand up (verse 35). It was a family you really could not trust, not one with whom you would want to do business.

So, someone named Rachael Goodluck wanted me to trust her with my personal identification and access to what money I might have. Oh, that all deceptions would be so obvious! The fact is that the devil has untold ways to deceive us, and so many of them look so attractive, so innocent, so full of potential for wealth and happiness—even good luck. Sometimes we ourselves are not even honest in or about our Christian walk. Today would be a good time to take today's text as a pledge and join Job in promising, "my lips will not speak wickedness, and my tongue will whisper no deceit" (Job 27:4, ESV).

Ardis Dick Stenbakken

Get Ready, Stay Ready, Be Ready!

Death and life are in the power of the tongue. Prov. 18:21.

As often as I can, I "preach" what I call my sermon to anyone who is willing to listen. So to you I now preach my sermon that says "Get ready, stay ready, be ready, and help someone else to get ready to meet Jesus. Even if Jesus takes one thousand years before coming back to this earth, you and I are only ensured for this moment." Let us use our time well. Jesus has given us the power of choice. He is always waiting at the door ready to come in to guide us in making the right decisions. All we have to do is open the door and let Him in. He defeated Satan at Calvary. With our hand in the hand of Jesus, we can never be defeated.

At times we find ourselves resorting to worry. Corrie ten Boom reportedly said, "Worry does not empty tomorrow of its sorrow, it empties today of its strength." When you find yourself tending to worry, sing the song "Why worry when you can pray? Trust Jesus . . ." (If you don't know this song, create your own tune.)

Quite recently I witnessed, on a Web site, one of the photographs from the Hubble Telescope. I was amazed at how small this earth is compared to our solar system. I was even more amazed to learn that there are numberless universes in existence. This made me think about how large the created universe is, yet how awesome God is—this God who is concerned with the small details of the lives of everyone on this planet. It's beyond my comprehension.

I can't forget the time when I needed to find an article that I had not used for months. I had no clue where to find it. I needed it. I told myself that I wouldn't bother the Lord this time. I put my head on my pillow, and immediately He told me where to find it. It was right where He said it was.

Life on this earth is smaller than a speck when compared with what life will be like in the new earth that Jesus is preparing for you and me. Yet to think that He became a human being for our sake, died for us, and is willing to take us home to live with Him in the new earth is beyond comprehension. Let's stay ready and be ready to enjoy life in the new earth with Him and with one another. Time on this earth is limited. I plan to be in the new earth. Please join me there!

Have a blessed day!

Jean A. (Lloyd) Blake

Living His Hope

Hope: a feeling that something good will happen or be true;
someone or something that gives you a reason for hoping.

But now, LORD, what do I look for? My hope is in you. Ps. 39:7, NIV.

She gave thanks to God and spoke about the child to all who were
looking forward to the redemption of Jerusalem. Luke 2:38, NIV.

We wait for the blessed hope—the appearing of the glory of our great
God and Savior, Jesus Christ. Titus 2:13, NIV.

Hope is not an expectation that we renew only at the Christmas season. Rather, hope—along with its many blessings—is ours for the choosing all year through.

We can find hope anywhere as this month's authors point out: through our children, in a women's devotional book, tucked into our own words of faith and courage, and—most of all—in Mary's little Lamb. That's why hope is an anchor for the soul (Heb. 6:19), a reminder that God has our backs (Jer. 29:11), and a harbinger of peace regarding the future of our children (Jer. 31:17).

During this holy season, may the God of hope fill you with His joy and peace (Rom. 15:13, NIV).

Hope Is Not a Dream—It Is Real

Now the God of hope fill you with all joy and peace in believing, that
ye may abound in hope, through the power of the Holy Ghost.
Rom. 15:13.

If you ever had a trip longer than thirty minutes, with ten-year-old child, you know that you have to be prepared to listen to two questions: How much longer? And, are we there yet? "Mom, how much more? Dad, are we there yet?" Four years ago, my husband, our little daughter, and I were traveling from Bellingham, Washington, to Sacramento, California. My husband and I had big expectations for this trip, hoping to relax during the sixteen-hour drive. Our daughter had hopes as well—to be in Sacramento within sixteen minutes after departing. The evening before our trip, my husband and I made a decision. We woke up very early and said to our daughter: "Honey, when you see the sun set tonight, only then can you ask us, 'Are we there yet?' And when it grows so dark outside you can't see anything, that means we're close to Sacramento. At that point you may ask, 'How much longer?' " Well, our entire hoped-for peaceful trip was punctuated with two questions: "When will the sun go down?" and "When will it be dark?" We had different hopes.

Hope is something deeply rooted in every human being. One old Latin proverb says *Dum Spiro Spero,* which means "While I breathe, I hope." Human beings, regardless of education, cultural background, or profession, all have hope. Sometimes what human beings hope is just wishful thinking. But God offers us real hope.

Through His prophet, God says, "I alone know the plans I have for you, plans to bring you prosperity and not disaster, plans to bring about the future you hope for" (Jer. 29:11, GNT). When the Bible talks about hope, it is not wishful thinking. The biblical definition of hope is to have a confident expectation. We *expect* God to make good on His promises. They aren't dreams—they're real.

Sometimes on our life journeys we face disappointments or failing expectations. In those moments we sometimes show up with the same questions as my daughter: "How much longer? Are we there yet?" God may tell us we'll have to wait a little longer and that, no, we're not there quite yet. However, our expectation in His promises can remain confident. For He will bring us safely to the final destination. After all, He has plans to give us a future and, always, hope.

Aleksandra Tanurdzic

Oh, Very Young

And a word spoken in due season, how good is it! Prov. 15:23.

Cat Stevens, a.k.a. Yusaf Islam, the seventies singer/songwriter who converted to the Muslim religion after a near-drowning accident, had a way with a musical phrase. One of his most plaintive songs asks, "Oh, very young, what will you leave us this time? You're only dancing on this earth for a short while." In tune and lyric he captured both the glory and the fragility of youth.

Last week a young person from my extended religious community died in his sleep. I have no idea how he died, and I didn't know him personally. But his death triggered memories. I've known many glorious, fragile young people, some very dearly. And some danced off the earth in a very short time.

I remember one conversation in which I pled with a young woman, "Just live. That's all I'm asking." She understood my plea perfectly because the will to live lay at the foundation of all her struggles. Thankfully, she said Yes.

But another young person I know took his own life. He struggled with the will to live and said No. Suicide, whether intended, accidental, gradual, or sudden, leaves us with a deeper hole in our hearts than death. It pushes us into our own will to live. It forces us to face our own life disappointments. And beyond this, we just miss these precious souls and think of what might have been.

When a young person dies, we mourn more than just the loss. We mourn the lost *future*. That unrealized future sits on the desk of the heart, a check never cashed, a ticket never used.

Let's do what we can to prevent this. Let's come around the families of young people. Let's support them and pray for them. Let's take off the mask of "everything's fine" and admit that life can be harshly tragic.

And when we see a struggling young person, let's deal ruthlessly with our inner Pharisee. Let's stretch out our souls and speak to their souls, offering them hope.

Let's love them sincerely.

After all, what if they do dance away? What will we wish we'd done?

Jennifer Jill Schwirzer

Daily Reading

Guard your heart above all else, for it determines the course of
your life. Prov. 4:23, NLT.

Each morning as I enter the building where I work, I pick up the newspaper that has been delivered to our company. After getting settled at my desk, I'll eventually get up and take the paper to our company kitchen. There I place it on the table for anyone to read. On most days someone will soon enter the kitchen and head straight for the paper.

They aren't checking out the headlines to see what happened while they were sleeping. No, the page of greatest importance to a number of my coworkers is the horoscope page. I have actually heard some say they have to read it before starting their work day so they will know what kind of day they're going to have.

One day I was delayed at my desk for a while and didn't get the paper to the kitchen first thing. A coworker actually came to my desk asking for the paper and wanting to know what the horoscope predicted for that day.

Really? You'll govern your day by how your horoscope reads? I silently mused when seeing several people poring over the horoscope page. Evidently that's where they look for hope.

My morning starts differently. I don't just look for hope—I find it as I begin each day with prayer, a reading of that day's devotional from my women's devotional book, and some Bible study with our church's weekly Bible study lessons. As my work day begins, my prayers continue as well because I want God to be in charge of my day.

In these last days of earth's history we must guard our hearts and minds. Let's take care to fill our hearts and minds with the truth, hope, and guidance of God's Word. Let's commune with Him through ongoing prayer on a daily basis throughout each day.

Let's meditate on what we've read each morning in the Bible so that we can have His discernment for our daily lives—no matter what we're experiencing.

We can also share the richness of our spiritual walk with others. In fact, I've recently had a thought: maybe I should swap the morning newspaper at work for a Bible. I could place it on the company kitchen table. And who knows? Maybe some of my coworkers would gather around it and begin to read it at the start of their work day. Best of all, maybe they would find hope.

Angèle Peterson

Hope

And she said, "Let your maidservant find favor in your sight." So the
woman went her way and ate, and her face was no longer sad.
1 Sam. 1:18, NKJV.

In the beginning it had been easy. Easy to dream. To hope. To wish. To want.
She was so sure God would answer. Why wouldn't He? They were good
people. They loved each other. They loved Him.

But month after month it got harder to hope. Months turned to years. Years
turned into hopelessness. Why didn't God answer? Had she done something
wrong? Had her husband? What else could she do? She had tried everything
anyone suggested.

People whispered. They said God had cursed her. That she had done something
horrible. It was her fault. She avoided the marketplace and social events as often
as she could. Their words and distance or their pity was too hard for her already
broken heart.

Eventually, they had given up hope. Elkanah had taken another wife. A
young wife. One who had gotten pregnant quickly. And often. And never let her
forget it. Her home became a place of tension and hurt. Mean words. Sarcastic
comments. The pain drove her to such depth that she wept and did not eat.
Many women eat when they're hurting, but this pain was so deep that even
chocolate couldn't touch it. Yet she could never quite completely give up.

Finally, she poured out her bitterness to God. Prayed and wept. It wasn't pretty,
but it was honest and true. It was her heart. Her hurt. Her hope. Her doubt. Her
despair. Her dependence on the only One who could heal and provide. And
when her heart was empty of the hurt and despair and her tears were spent,
she found hope again. She walked away, believing God would answer. "So the
woman went her way and ate, and her face was no longer sad." Her hope was
based on her trust in God. She believed He had heard her. She believed He would
respond. She believed He loved her. And she lived like it. Her face and actions
reflected her trust.

I want to hope and trust in God like Hannah did. I want my face and actions
to reflect a trust and hope that brings peace—even in the moments that are
the hardest and most painful. A hope that is found by pouring out our hearts
honestly to God, believing He loves us, and living—expecting Him to respond.

Tamyra Horst

Treasures of the Snow

"Though your sins are as scarlet, they will be as white as snow; though they are red like crimson, they will be like wool." Isa. 1:18, NASB.

As a child I would stand at the window and look at the very first snowflakes of the winter. There were four things I liked about winter.

First of all, I would look forward to its arrival, from the falling of the leaves and then the turning of the weather into cold chilly nights. With anticipation I would watch my mother get out mittens and snowsuits. This made it seem closer. I'd watch my father and brothers chop the wood and pile it into rows of dullness. Only the approach of Christmas and the beautiful carols and decorating the tree could liberate me from the dreariness of winter.

Another winter treasure was the snow angel. My family members would create them by lying on our backs in fresh snow, then moving our arms and legs back and forth. We created masterpieces. We'd get up carefully to gaze upon the impressions that looked like flying angels.

Third, I treasured the snowflakes individually. My teacher told me to wear dark colored mittens when it snowed because when the white flakes landed on your hands, you could see the design of each flake. I also found the whiteness of the snow to be a treasure. It sparkled in the morning sun and painted a landscape as lovely as any great artist.

Now that I don't make snow angels any more, I must rely upon my memories of these snow treasures. My reflections often cause me to think of my Creator. For every angel I remember swishing into the snow as a child, I think of ten thousand angels traveling between earth and heaven. One of them is my very own. And thinking about snowflakes landing on my gloves reminds me that God has created us all with a unique diversity of talents and abilities.

I fondly remember the white blankets of snow covering the dull winter landscape with feathery brilliance. Such alabaster memories remind me that "though your sins be as scarlet, they shall be as white as snow." This is truly the greatest treasure of all—that the landscapes of our sinful lives could ever be as brilliant as a field of snow sparkling in the sun.

As I anticipate snow, I also anticipate, with longing, the Second Coming. I desire, as do you, to catch that first glimpse of Jesus descending to set us free from the doldrums of sin.

Vidella McClellan

On Birthdays

But it was you, a man my equal, my companion, and my acquaintance.
Ps. 55:13, NKJV.

irthdays are becoming more meaningful as I age. My most recent birthday promised to be no exception. I got a very complimentary e-card that day from my very busy sister. There was also a card from the neighbor lady, along with a shimmering scarf with a matching barrette in the envelope too. *Oh, what a special day my fifty-first will be,* I thought as I donned the new apparel in front of the mirror. Some good friends had invited my husband and me to come for dinner (which I joyfully anticipated) the Saturday after my birthday—and in honor of it.

The morning of my birthday the receptionist at work greeted me with a "From all of us" card and a festively packaged bottle of sparkling grape juice. Both my voicemail boxes had "Happy Birthday to You" sung beautifully by a favorite friend. Facebook was shouting my praises, primarily my daughter's post. All of this excitement reminded me how good it is to love and be loved. There was one person, however, from whom I was especially desirous of hearing before the shadows lengthened that day. My husband of twenty-one and a half years. I was hopeful!

By nightfall—which isn't that late during winter months in Maine—I hadn't heard from him. Nor from my mother. Even though it was the first birthday in my life my mom had forgotten, it didn't bother me nearly as much as my husband's forgetting. I began phoning him incessantly until he finally picked up. Angrily I stated, "I would have thought that you would have at least called to see how my day was going. Did you forget it was my birthday?"

My husband responded apologetically. He had been at work, had watched our sons play basketball, and had in no wise intended not to acknowledge my birthday. He had just neglected to communicate. Though I have forgiven him, there will always be a wound in my heart.

And so I experienced what David was talking about in Psalm 55 when his hopes were disappointed by someone close to him. "But it was you, a man my equal, my companion and my acquaintance. We took sweet counsel together, and walked to the house of God" (verses 13, 14). As a believer who believes that all things do work together for good (Rom. 8:28), this birthday experience reminds me that while it is important to let people know our expectations, it is equally important for us not to disappoint their hopes by how we treat them.

Kristin McGuire

The Power of Influence

Charm is deceitful, and beauty is passing, but a woman who fears the LORD, she shall be praised. Prov. 31:30, NKJV.

In our world today many women are abused, molested, and marginalized. Yet they possess a strong power of influence—either for good or for bad. A woman, consciously or unconsciously, exercises an influence on her children, husband, and other family members. The Creator endowed woman with this unique power. As a woman seeks God and His will, she gradually develops the fear of God that governs her life. With the help of the indwelling Spirit of God, she casts a positive influence upon members of her household. She gives good counsel to her husband and children. Relying upon God for wisdom through prayer and Bible study, she can discern the assaults of the devil and influence her family to walk in the right path.

Reflecting on this reality, an inspired writer wrote, "Woman, if she wisely improves her time and her faculties, relying upon God for wisdom and strength, may stand on equality with her husband as adviser, counselor, companion, and coworker, and yet lose none of her womanly grace or modesty. She may elevate her own character, and just as she does this she is elevating and ennobling the characters of her family, and exerting a powerful though unconscious influence upon others around her" (Ellen G. White, *Good Health,* June 1888).

We read in the Bible about how women used their power of influence. Many times women are unconscious of the power of influence they possess, and they ignorantly go about misusing it. The author of the above quote continues, "Satan knows that women have a power of influence for good or for evil; therefore he seeks to enlist them in his cause."

Eve, the mother of all, unwittingly became an instrument in the devil's hand to influence her husband to disobey God, Adam also sinned and brought unspeakable woe to the human race.

Dear woman of value, do you recognize the power of influence—a unique gift from God—that you possess? You are responsible for the kind of influence you exert upon others.

Our beauty and charm are not sufficient to positively influence our household for God, but the fear of God, an everlasting principle, is what is needed to make it happen.

Lord, help me love and fear You so that I may exert a positive influence upon others around me. Amen.

Omobonike Sessou

Hearing the Call—Part 1

"Give ear and come to me; listen, that you may live." Isa. 55:3, NIV.

If you know me well, you know that I hate to drive. When I was seventeen years old I moved to California from Miami to obtain California residency in order to be able to get the Cal Grant Scholarship to pay for my college education. It was something I didn't even think twice about. However, if I had known what would happen my senior year, I suspect I would have never moved to California. The day after I turned eighteen, I was involved in a head-on collision on my way to high school. I suffered major injuries, was airlifted to a hospital, bedridden for several months, and had to go through extremely painful and intense therapy to be able to walk again.

Now you can see why I dread driving. In fact, I get slightly nervous and am very paranoid whenever I am behind the wheel. But this paranoia, fear, and anxiety completely leave when my husband takes over the wheel. When he drives—and by far is he is not the best driver out there (I love you, honey)—I breathe a sigh of relief. My seat is no longer straight; it is slightly leaned back. I enjoy the scenery and sometimes even doze (in between dealing with my two children in the backseat). I don't have to worry about how we will get where we are going. I know the driver will figure out the way. I don't have to watch for street signs, freeway exit signs, other cars, or even the speedometer. I can relax, not because he is the safest driver, but because I trust him. I know my husband cares about our children and me, and he always has us in mind.

If only life were so easy, right? If only we could have a driver taking us where we need to go, and we could just sit back and enjoy the scenery. "That's impossible," we grumble. "Not with our schedules, the children's needs, our jobs, our bills, and our problems. Sitting back is not an option. We have to drive through this life, full speed, anxiety and fear within us, trying to make it to our destination. A frenzied, sometimes hopeless, cycle."

Yet what if I told you we *do* have a designated driver? What if I told you that street signs and exit signs or road rage are not things we have to worry about any longer? And they aren't— because Christ, our driver, is waiting for you and me behind the wheel. All we have to do is open the passenger door and get in.

He calls: "Give ear and come to me; hear me that your soul may live" (Isa. 55:3).

Raquel Carrera

Hearing the Call—Part 2

And we know that in all things God works for the good of those who love him. Rom. 8:28, NIV.

With Jesus as our driver, we get into the vehicle by saying, "Yes, I will follow You, Lord. Yes, I love You, Lord." But the difficult part comes when the engine starts and we hit the road. Instead of relinquishing all control of our lives to Jesus, we become passenger-drivers. You know how we get—pointing at other cars, making suggestions to our own Driver, and stepping on our imaginary brakes. In times of stress or when we can't see the end from the beginning, why do we suddenly want to be in control of the vehicle, charting out our own route? Why do we second-guess the GPS, feeling we know the way, even though we've never been "there" before?

"God," we grumble, "why won't You tell me what will happen next and what I'm supposed to do? I need to know!" God shakes his head and points to the Bible. "Read it and you will know. 'For my thoughts are not your thoughts, neither are my ways your ways' " (Isa. 55:8).

I think back now to my car accident so many years ago. I have no regrets, despite the pain, as that experience grew my faith and prepared me to witness and minister to other college students through a campus ministry. I have no idea how many lives God has touched through mine as many people, often in tears, come to me at the end of a service thanking me when I've shared my testimony. How ironic, though, that I had to hear God's call through so much pain. Had I known ahead of time what the journey would be like, I would have thrown away my airplane ticket and stayed in Miami. Yet, never would I have been so blessed as I am now.

Noah heard God's call. "Build an ark, a flood will come." Noah obeyed. But maybe, just maybe, if Noah hadn't experienced the ridicule and long, painful, intense labor that it took to build the ark, would he have had faith to step with his family into that ark full of wild animals? With God as His driver, Noah had a long, wild ride—even before they "hit the road." Yet through it all, God knew that Noah was being blessed, along with his family.

So whether you are ministering as a result of your pain, are being ridiculed for heeding God's call, or are still waiting to hear the call, don't lose heart. Hope lies ahead. Your Driver will take you where you need to go. Sit back, have faith, and remember God uses "all things."

Raquel Carrera

The Lost Prize

Pray without ceasing. 1 Thess. 5:17.

We were in first grade, eager to learn to read, write, draw, sing, memorize Bible verses, and play. At this stage, I had already memorized the Lord's Prayer, the Shepherd's Psalm, and the Lord's Promise. One day our teacher asked us, one by one, to stand in front of the class and recite from memory our favorite Bible verse. Whoever recited a verse perfectly would win a brand-new notebook. This prize was precious to the children and, for that matter, to parents. World War II was not over yet; parents did not talk to children about their hardships during the war. Yet in our one-room elementary school, our paper was a green banana leaf. Our pencil was a sharp-ended bamboo stick. If you pressed the leaf too hard when writing, the leaf shredded into strips, and if not enough pressure was applied, the markings or letters would not show. So you can understand that receiving the notebook would be winning a precious, coveted prize.

Of the children, only my cousin Arile and I were ready to recite by memory in front of the class. I stood first and I recited: "The Lord's Promise: Let not your heart be troubled: ye believe in God, believe also in me. In my Father's house are many mansions: if it were not so, I would have told you. I go to prepare a place for you. I will come again and receive you unto myself; that where I am, there ye may be also." I bowed and sat down. Arile smiled at me before he arose to say his verse: "Pray without ceasing." He made a slight bow and sat down. I said, "That's it?" The teacher gave him the notebook. I put my head down to hide my shame and my tears of sadness. The teacher came to me and whispered, "Rose, you missed part of the verse that says, "and if I go to prepare a place for you." I nodded my head; I had forgotten to say it. *This is not fair. Arile's verse was only three words.*

That night, I looked in the Bible, and sure enough, it is a perfectly complete verse. Arile and I remained friends; but every time we see each other and he tells me, "Pray without ceasing," I always want to cry. His mother advised me to not show him I feel bad about it. "Treat it as a reminder from him to pray without ceasing." And I also don't want to forget the Lord's Promise: "I go to prepare a place for you. And if I go and prepare a place for you, I will come again, and receive you unto myself, that where I am, there ye may be also." That's the real prize!

Rose Eva Bana Constantino

Thinking Out Loud

Meanwhile, all the other people live however they wish, picking and choosing their gods. But we live honoring God, and we're loyal to our God forever and ever. "On that great day," God says, "I will round up all the hurt and homeless, everyone I have bruised or banished. I will transform the battered into a company of the elite. I will make a strong nation out of the long lost, a showcase exhibit of God's rule in action."
Mic. 4:5-7, *The Message*.

I've been thinking a lot about the times we're living in. It seems the times get increasingly more difficult. The world is so topsy-turvy, unstable, and volatile.

I remember when my husband, Mel, lost his job and was out of work for two and a half years. It was a time when engineers were out of work across the country. We literally had to start over again. That's not easy to do in midlife when, under normal circumstances, one would begin to slow down toward retirement. He became discouraged to the point of thinking suicide was the answer. Thankfully, God did a miracle and the attempt was unsuccessful. It wasn't too long after that that he got a job—and continued working till retirement some fifteen years later.

Now we see so many who have lost their jobs, homes, and savings. People who are trying to survive from one week to the next.

When God tried to get Israel's attention in the latter part of the Old Testament, we see how He brought famines and troubles to the land, but His children refused to turn from their evil ways. They had been sucked into idol worship, forsaking the mighty God who created this earth.

Time after time God sent them into captivity because they would not listen to Him. Even though some of the people did not forsake God and were true to Him, they also were subject to these trials and taken into captivity. Remember Daniel and his friends, and Nehemiah, Ezekiel, Esther, and Mordecai, among others? These also suffered the consequences of Israel's evil doing.

Even though they also suffered, God was with them in their captivity and trials. He gave them continual encouragement and helped them one day at a time. So we can be assured today, despite losses we suffer or trials we endure, that God is with us, giving us strength to go through.

May each one of us, today, lean on our everlasting God as He carries us through the tough times.

Peggy Curtice Harris

The Comfort of My Children

Every good gift and every perfect gift is from above, and comes down from the Father of lights, with whom there is no variation or shadow of turning. James 1:17, NKJV.

They are grown, my three young adults. All over thirty, they are mature, reasonably independent, self-directed, and legal! I indulge myself in reverie, remembering their "baby days," the time when they required total care—attending their night-time crying, feeding them, and changing diapers. The days seemed endless when they were toddlers, then came elementary school and, finally, academy (high school) years. Certainly we struggled with finances, rules, and the consequences of poor decisions. We also enjoyed growing-up experiences, roller-skating, amusement park rides, summer vacations.

Then, one by one, they went off to college. I feared I would undergo the proverbial "empty nest syndrome," grieving my loss as they experienced more and more autonomy. Surely I missed them each, and I treated myself to a good cry after safely leaving them in their new campus homes. But my journeys home were filled, too, with joy and pride in their progress.

Perhaps these changes were made easier because, as they grew, our relationship grew as well. Yes, that's the joy. Certainly they do not need me for the things they needed during the younger times, but they need me, nonetheless. They need to share their experiences and bounce ideas off of me, and (alas!) they still need resources.

Oh yes, and I need them too. I appreciate their perspectives, I want approval and affirmation, and I thrive on their love and confidence in me. My greatest joy, perhaps, is that they frequently call simply to pray with me. They want me to accompany them as they boldly go to the throne of grace. This need, this activity, this connection, is my greatest comfort.

My relationship as a parent with my children reminds me of my relationship with my heavenly Parent. I hope I am growing in grace. Yet as I grow I continue to need Him. I need His guidance, His intervention, His correction, and His constant love.

The Bible says that God wants me to glorify Him (Isa. 42:12). This is my relationship with Him. Knowing I am His child comforts me as my parenting comforts my children.

Lord, thank You for all your gifts—especially the gift of our relationship. Amen.

Elizabeth Darby Watson

A Sister's Gentle Solution

A soft answer turneth away wrath: but grievous words stir up anger.
Prov. 15:1.

The day of our dad's funeral was sad beyond belief. Dad, my safe place, my tenderhearted cowboy-hero, was gone.

The circumstances of his death were so overwhelming we had a hard time coming to terms with it. Just ten days earlier, we had gathered as a family at our parents' house to celebrate our sister Margaret's birthday. She came out of the house saying something was very wrong with Mom, and indeed there was. We rushed her to the hospital, where for three weeks the doctors couldn't tell us what was wrong. On the sixth day, when I picked Dad up to take him to see her, he was having a major heart attack—yet another in a series of them. But this time his trip to the hospital ended with this dear old cowboy dying. Surrounded by all his children and grandchildren, we quietly sang old cowboy songs to him, our hearts breaking.

Before we even knew that Mom had contracted two diseases that gave her brain damage, we had to arrange the funeral for her beloved husband, whom she would never know was now gone from her side.

We arrived at the cemetery to lay Dad to rest, everything carefully pre-planned by our parents so we would have nothing to worry about. But what was *this*? Imagine my horror—and anger—when relatives and friends gathered, only to discover that workers had forgotten to dig the grave! Dan, our brother, and I were ready to tear into someone. Our sister, seeing what could create a bad scene, said, "Let me handle this." Knowing in our hearts that this was a better idea, we relented. She walked to the office and came back with a plan.

The cemetery workers felt badly about this terrible mistake, so she wrangled a deal out of them that served a good purpose. They arranged for a year's worth of flowers on the grave, a tree planted beside it, and a bench in the location where we could sit when we visited. "A soft answer" was so much more prudent than angry words. God's gentle ways are the best. My sister was so right when she said that day, "You know, Dad would have thought this was funny."

And you know what else? I have the hope that someday Dad, too, will get a good chuckle out of all that happened.

Kathy Peterson

Hope Beyond Trauma

Blessed are those whose strength is in you, whose hearts are set on pilgrimage. As they pass through the Valley of Baka, they make it a place of springs. Ps. 84:5, 6, NIV.

ife on this earth can bring painful experiences. Traumatic events may come at a very young age through child abuse, parental divorce, a disability, or loss. For others, these may occur later in life, perhaps with the loss of loved ones. The reality of trauma is inevitable in a world that is center stage of a great conflict between good and evil. There is no question that no matter when they did occur, these traumatic events can have lasting negative effects on one's physical, mental, emotional, and spiritual well-being. Many of us go through life carrying the pain and brokenness of such trauma. That is a fact, but the Bible tells us it does not have to be that way. There is hope even after the worst possible trauma a person may have experienced.

One day, as I searched God's Word for encouragement for a personal traumatic experience, I came across a healing passage that brought me hope. It talked about the Valley of Baka. I learned that Baka is a valley in Palestine, also known as Dry Valley. The primitive Hebrew word from which Baka originates means to weep, complain, lament, or mourn. The passage brought me hope, for in it God promises, to those in pain who seek strength in Him, that our Valley of Weeping (Baka) and sorrow can turn into a spring—a source, the origin, or the beginning of life in a dry place. What a beautiful promise! The passage says we can have a new beginning, a rebirth in a dry place, and that our weeping will turn into a spring of life! Believe His promise! This new life of joy and peace is possible when you and I embrace daily the virtues of forgiveness and gratitude. It is sometimes difficult to let go of the pain we experienced when those we loved chose to turn their back on us. Like many reading today, I, too, have experienced that pain.

But when I turn to God and seek His strength, He lovingly reminds me of the many times He suffered betrayal and pain from those He came to die for. He reminds me of the many times I betrayed Him, and how He still embraced me with an unfailing love and compassion. How can I not do the same? And when I forgive as He did, with gratitude in my heart, healing occurs and hope is born. May you, too, see your Valley of Baka be transformed into a spring today.

Katia Garcia Reinert

They're There!

If ye have faith as a grain of mustard seed, ye shall say unto this mountain, remove hence to yonder place; and it shall remove; and nothing shall be impossible unto you. Matt. 17:20.

We lived in Pune, India. For Christmas one year, we decided to go to Hosur. To get there, my husband, Gordon; our son, Gerald; and I had to travel by train. A few days before Christmas, a friend drove us to the train depot. When we stepped onto the platform, the train started to move away. Our friend quickly shoved us toward a train door, exclaiming, "That's your train! Quick, get on! Here's your luggage!" We pulled our luggage into the general compartment, where the most impoverished citizens travel.

Gordon and I wondered why our train was leaving earlier than its scheduled time. Inside the moving train, he inquired of someone, "Is this the train going to Mangalore?" No, the man replied, it was headed to Coimbatore. We were advised to get off at the next big station where, we were told, we'd be able to switch over to the right train. But "our" train wasn't there. So we reboarded the first train's general compartment.

We got off at another big station and waited for our train. We worried that the sleeping berths we'd reserved for our family had been canceled. On trains in India a ticket collector usually checks tickets of boarding passengers at every station. Berths reserved by passengers who don't show up are reassigned to people who do not have berths.

Our incoming train slowed to a stop with the right door of the right carriage just in front of where we stood on the platform. Gerald led the way inside and disappeared momentarily. Reappearing through the crowd, he exclaimed, "They're *there*! The berths we reserved are *there*! Empty and waiting for us!" Evidently, the ticket collector had not come through on the most recent leg of the train's journey, so our empty berths had not yet been reassigned.

"How did you know our berths were still there waiting for us?" Gordon asked our son.

"Because I prayed they would be," Gerald replied. "I asked God to have the train stop with our car's door right in front of us if the berths were still open." I'd wondered all day why God had allowed these inconveniences into our lives. To experience the kindness of the poor in that general compartment? Yes. And maybe also to strengthen the faith of a teenager—my son!

Rosenita Christo

I Believe in Miracles!

God also bearing them witness, with signs and wonders, and with divers miracles, and gifts of the Holy Ghost. Heb. 2:4.

Over the years I have heard and read wonderful stories of people who experienced miracles. I believe that sometimes, just when we need an extra dose of hope, God does something special for us. I can think of several events in my own life. Once I accidentally dropped my pair of glasses at a beach. I did not know that they had fallen in the water till I saw and retrieved them. I was mighty glad to have them back, because it's hard for me to go without them!

My God-fearing parents also shared special things God did. God once protected my mother from being bitten by a poisonous snake when I was still in her womb. My father, who conducted evangelistic meetings, told how God had saved my life when I underwent a tonsillectomy. I had been given an amount of anesthesia that was too strong for me at such a young age. I stopped breathing on the operating table. I know now that God was in the operating room that day. The experienced missionary doctor was able to revive me. In heaven I want to meet her to say thank-you. Then just recently I learned I don't have thyroid cancer, which is an answer to many prayers that were ascending on my behalf around the globe.

Now retired, I look back over the years and see how God has been with me and had a purpose for my life. Many times I got discouraged, didn't have much hope, and was not bringing God any glory. God knew I had to learn some lessons like Moses did in the wilderness. God led me through some very trying experiences. I survived because He was with me all along. I learned to trust Him more and more and to pray like I need to pray. It would be impossible for me to list all the things God has done for me because He cares for me. He cares so much for you and me He sent His own Son to suffer and die on the cruel cross to set us free.

I am so glad that God woke me up from the lukewarm spiritual condition in which I lived for so long. He showed me that I am His ambassador and must share with others about His great love as shown through His miracles in my life. God is truly a God of miracles. He has a plan for each one of us. A close connection with our Father, through prayer, will help us recognize His miracles in our lives. Let us be encouraged and live lives that honor Him.

Rose Muthiah Davy

A Friend Like Jesus

"I have called you friends." John 15:15, NIV.

On the first day of 2003 we left all family and friends to attend the inauguration of a boat. The shipwright who had built this boat was my brother, Almarindo, who has been working on boats since the age of eleven. This was the first boat of his that would be inaugurated.

We sailed near the mouth of a river near a place that attracted people who used the area as a resort—to eat, drink, and swim. Along with some others I went ashore to relax while the boat remained out in a deeper part of the river. The rest of our party stayed on the boat.

After a while, some of the people with me on the shore decided to swim out to the boat.

I could do that too, I thought. *The boat isn't that far away.* I waded into the water to begin my swim. I swam, fairly comfortably, some distance away from shore. Suddenly I became tired. It was hard to catch my breath. I soon realized that, due to lack of practice and the necessary degree of physical fitness, I might not reach the boat after all. In fact, I soon felt absolutely powerless.

Then I heard a voice that said, "Let's go, Mary. You will make it!" That voice, which spoke so hopefully, seemed to give me a surge of strength. I was able to swim hard and finally reached the ladder of the boat. The "voice," as it turned out, was that of a good friend of ours from Rio de Janeiro. He was spending the holidays with us and was one of those who had gone ashore. The encouraging words of a friend gave me power just when I needed it.

That experience brought to mind another friend who is with us at all times: Jesus. The Bible says that His eyes are always upon us. He promised, "I will . . . teach you in the way you should go; I will counsel you with my loving eye on you" (Ps. 32:8, NIV). How good to know that when we are tired, discouraged, and powerless to fight, we have a constant Friend who gives strength to the weary (Isa. 40:31).

As the calendar points us to the end of this year and toward the beginning of a new year, the One who calls us His friends (John 15:15) wants to see us reach the safe haven of heaven just as I reached the ladder of that boat. His voice tells us not to fear. For He will strengthen, help, and uphold us (Isa. 41:10). He says, "Let's go! You will make it!"

Marialva Vasconcelos Monteiro Chaussé

Pain With a Purpose

Weeping may endure for a night, but joy comes in the morning.
Ps. 30:5, NKJV.

Recently my friend, Bea, was hospitalized with severe abdominal pain. She had had the pain for several weeks but kept hoping it would go away. When the pain reached a level that she described as worse than childbirth, she finally told her family she needed to go to the emergency room at the local hospital—right away! At the hospital doctors discovered that Bea had an almost complete intestinal blockage. She needed surgery. Since her pain was still intense, she willingly agreed to surgery. During the surgery, which lasted several hours, the doctors discovered the cause of Bea's pain—a cancerous growth in her colon, which they removed.

Afterward, Bea praised God for the pain that forced her to seek medical treatment. Because of the unrelenting pain, the cancer was found early, and she didn't even need chemotherapy or radiation. To Bea, the pain became a blessing and a cause for rejoicing.

Bea's story reminds me of my favorite Bible character, Joseph, the favorite son of Jacob. Joseph could not understand why his brothers hated him and sold him into slavery. He could not understand why God allowed him to be imprisoned unjustly because of the lies told by Potiphar's wife. Then, in prison, he couldn't understand why the cupbearer forgot all about him after he correctly interpreted the cupbearer's dream as well as the baker's. Joseph languished in prison another two years before Pharaoh had a dream, and the cupbearer remembered—at exactly the right moment—that there was someone who could interpret dreams.

When Joseph correctly interpreted Pharaoh's dream, Pharaoh recognized Joseph's godly wisdom and elevated him prime minister of Egypt, second only to him. *Then* Joseph understood how his suffering had been part of God's plan to save his entire family from the famine. Because he saw God's unmistakable hand in his suffering, he was able to forgive his brothers' treachery. And best of all, he was reunited with his beloved father and younger brother Benjamin.

When you and I inevitably experience pain and suffering, we can be sure that God has a purpose for allowing it. We can come through each trial victoriously if we trust God and remain faithful, as Joseph did. Never forget that we serve a God who can take any evil and use it for His glory, our own growth, and the good of others.

Carla Baker

What I Learned With My Babies

Know that the LORD is God. It is he who made us, and we are his; we are his people, the sheep of his pasture. Ps. 100:3, NIV.

It happened when I nursed my youngest daughter, Eliane. Suddenly, she looked at me like babies look at their mothers, enchanted. I realized that she had long eyelashes like a doll.

When I was a girl, I dreamed of a doll with hair. I always had plastic dolls, whose hair was just a brown paint on the head. The eyes were also painted and were always open, obviously. But there were those dolls that looked like real babies. They closed their little eyes and had quite long eyelashes. Their hair was implanted and could be combed. I always dreamed of a doll like that, but I never had one.

But now, looking at my beautiful baby, I realized that here was my childhood doll, but much better because she was a living and beautiful little girl. God had given me a little doll with hair, a real baby. At that moment I thanked Him for His goodness to satisfy a request of my childhood. It took so long, but it was better than I could have ever imagined.

Whenever we have a baby, we think it is ours because it depends on us for everything. We think that we are its only means of survival and that we control its entire life. One day I discovered that things are not quite like that. And I made this discovery through a very simple reality of life, and it reminded me that all things are in the hands of the Lord. In fact, everything belongs to Him. My children belong to Him.

What was this simple occurrence? When the first milk tooth fell out of my older daughter's mouth. The time had come for Eliete's baby teeth to be replaced with permanent ones. I had fed, taught, and protected her. I had thought that everything depended on me. But behold, one tooth told me that Someone Else was monitoring the phases of her life. Someone commanded the teeth to start falling to make way for stronger, permanent ones. Yes, the Lord God was watching and taking care of details that I could not control. At that moment, with that tooth in hand, I realized that my daughter did not belong to me. She and her sister belonged to the One who could really take care of them in every detail.

We do not belong to ourselves. We belong to the Lord, who gives us life and love.

Het Jane Silva Carvalho

No Impossibilities With God

I can do all things through Christ who strengthens me.
Phil. 4:13, NKJV.

Before I pursued higher education, I worked in an HIV/AIDS clinic for about seven years in western Uganda. I worked with many patients. Among them were women prisoners and their babies from a nearby prison. I was touched especially by the children and could only imagine the conditions they were living in. Finally I came up with the idea of collecting needed items from willing donors to help better the welfare of these patients.

One Sabbath afternoon my friend, Betty, and I went to the prison with the items we had collected. We did this for several weekends in a row. On most of these visits, Betty would preach on a topic that encouraged the women or I would give a health talk. However, I was shy about speaking in public to large gatherings. I began quietly sharing with God a hope I had in my heart—that one day He would give me the confidence to speak to the prisoners like Betty was able to do so freely.

A few months later Betty was transferred to another hospital far away. Without her, I stopped visiting the prison. One of the reasons I stopped going was that I did not know what I should say to the women there. I was still very shy. At the same time I had become so busy at work that I no longer had time to collect items to give to the inmates. The prison officers even called several times to find out why we were no longer coming to minister to the prisoners.

One day I sat down and thought about my purpose in this world. I remembered all the blessings around me. I prayed to God, read my Bible and other inspirational books in search of answers. *How could I contribute to the salvation of God's people?* Then, with the help of fellow church members, I was able to resume my prison ministry. I realized that one does not need only material things to be able to reach out to other people (Luke 4:4). Just listening, sharing, and being a shoulder to lean on can make a big difference in the lives of many others. I discovered that I have a gift of listening, and this has created a strong relationship with my prisoner-patients.

I can now stand confidently in Christ to preach. My prayer is that, as a result, God will bring hope into the lives of the women prisoners.

Just give God what you have (Acts 3:6). He will use it to save souls for His kingdom.

Ruth Mbabazi

December 21

Waiting at the Window

"Here I am! I stand at the door and knock. If anyone hears my voice and opens the door, I will come in and eat with that person, and they with me." Rev. 3:20, NIV.

ast year's Scottish winter was the coldest for decades. For two months the temperatures stayed below freezing and deep snow crusted the ground. Every day a black and white cat called Lovey came and sat on my kitchen window ledge, looking into my cozy kitchen. We didn't have the heart to leave him out there all day while his owner was at work. So after a few weeks my son let him in. The little furry bundle soon made himself at home, and we gave him an old pillow next to the radiator. Lovey came regularly. Sometimes he was there before dawn or waiting for us to come home again. Always he waited quietly and patiently. Whenever we opened the door for him, he uttered a delighted meow of thanks. Once indoors he was happiest sitting close to us, laying his paw on our lap, just wanting to be near us. If he wanted water, milk, or to be let out, he just stroked the floor softly with his left paw until we figured out what he needed. Occasionally, he left special presents for us, the best he could offer—limp, cold mice. One day he came and lay down weakly on our doorstep—he wasn't strong enough to jump up to the window. When I opened the door I found him bleeding and torn from a battle with a rat. He'd lost so much blood I thought he would die. It was two months before his neck was healed completely. We realized he'd been protecting us from rats ever since we moved in, and we hadn't even noticed.

I came downstairs very early one day last week, and Lovey was already waiting at the window. As I let him in out of the bitter frost, I was reminded how God waits so patiently for me to let Him in to my life each day. He doesn't make a fuss or push His way in—He just stands at the door and waits. When I open the door of my heart, He's delighted to come in and make Himself at home. He wants to be as close to me as possible, so I can feel His loving hand in my life. And Jesus suffered, bled, and even died to keep me safe from something much more dangerous and life-threatening than rats.

Father God, thank You for being there at my door each day. Thank You for the gifts of Your sacrifice and protection. May I never leave You out in the cold. Amen.

Karen Holford

376

Austin's Snake

In the end it bites like a snake and poisons like a viper. Prov. 23:32, NIV.

Christmas is my favorite time of year. I am called "Gigi-Claus" by my three grandchildren. They sing, "You better watch out, you better not cry, you better not pout, I'm tellin' you why: Gigi-Claus is coming to town!" The reason they gave me this nickname is that each Christmas I try to buy them *everything* on their wish list. (I know, I *know*. Skip the lecture!)

Surprisingly, the family learned last Christmas that even Gigi-Claus has her limits when the oldest grandson, Austin, put a python snake (for $120) on his wish list. His friend had one, and Austin begged for one also. For the first time in his twelve-year Christmas history with Gigi-Claus, she said, "Not in a million years! The snake will get loose in your house. You have to purchase frozen baby mice, heat them in the microwave, and feed them to the snake every three days. Yuck! No!"

Since Gigi-Claus refused to change her mind, Austin pleaded until his mother gave in and took him to purchase the snake with his own Christmas money. It came with a tank and a locked lid. Sure enough, while feeding the snake a few months later, Austin unlocked the lid to fill the water container. Zing! The snake was out and under the bathroom cupboard somewhere.

A snake finder service was called ($200) but failed to find the snake. Sticky paper was put on the bathroom floor, and the bathroom door secured with tape. To no avail! The snake has yet to be seen again. But somewhere—in the house—is a snake on the loose.

I couldn't help but think that sin is a lot like Austin's snake. Others engage in activities that seem enticing ("our friends have one"), and we don't want to be left out so we "buy the snake." We're positive we can manage it because "we're Christians," we say with confidence, and Jesus Christ is our "lock." But often in the crush of life our time is consumed by immediate needs, and we fail to pay attention to our "lock" through prayer and Bible study. We distractedly hurry through our days; and sin, like Austin's snake, escapes into our lives when least expected.

God is fully aware of our weakness and propensity for "buying the snake" and believing we can contain it. May He help us this day to stay focused *totally* on Him, recognizing that we, of our own strength, are incapable of handling the sin Satan is so anxious to let loose in our lives.

Ellie Postlewait Green

Unto Us a Child Is Born

"I prayed for this child, and the LORD has granted me
what I asked of him." 1 Sam. 1:27, NIV.

A h, September. The month of sapphires and forget-me-nots—and the birth of my first child. No baby was ever anticipated with more joy and wonder as he lay there, right under my heart. Of course I didn't *know* the baby was "he." In 1968, there were no sonograms or fetal Dopplers to herald his presence.

At each visit I hung on the doctor's every word, eager for any detail about this developing miracle that made me want to sing and laugh, run in the streets and shout! I washed tiny clothes and hung them in the New England sunshine to dry, happy advertisements to the world. Then I folded them and put them in the white four-drawer chest, handmade by a friend and decorated with teddy bear decals.

My baby was supposed to come on September 21, but he didn't. Even though it had been an "educated guess," I was so disappointed. I threw myself into a whirl of church and social activities, filling the days. Then the following Wednesday evening it became apparent that something was going to happen. I should go to the hospital early the next morning, the doctor said. *The next morning?* I couldn't believe it. Sure, I'd been waiting for nine months, and my suitcase was packed—but look at the house! The kitchen floor should be mopped, the bathrooms cleaned—I better make bread! (I forgot to put in salt.) Somehow I dropped the pickle jar, spilling sticky juice all over the floor. On hands and knees and reaching under the frig and around the kitchen chairs (and my enormous belly), I had to wash it again.

At the hospital I was assigned to a ward filled with women in varying stages of labor and all that pertains thereto. In those days there was also no such thing as birthing suites, and the four birthing classes I'd attended didn't begin to cover this reality. Nevertheless, whispering a non-stop mantra of "women have been doing this since Eve," and keeping a white-knuckled grip on the bedrail, I got through the next six hours.

And then he was born, wide-eyed and quiet, turning his head to take in this new place. Breathtakingly beautiful and perfect he was as he lay on my heart. The joy of Sarah and Hannah—and Mary—overwhelmed me. I wanted to sing and laugh, run in the street and shout.

Jeannette Busby Johnson

The Christmas Lamb

The next day John saw Jesus coming toward him and said, "Look! The Lamb of God who takes away the sin of the world!" John 1:29 NLT.

The church was beautiful in readiness for Christmas. That Sabbath morning everything in the worship program pointed to the joy in the birth of Jesus. The sweet sound of the singer filled the air with the familiar words, "The virgin Mary had a baby boy." My three-year-old granddaughter was playing quietly on the pew next to me, watching and listening. Again the words came, "The virgin Mary had a baby boy." Suddenly, Ashley called in words that could be heard clearly through most of the sanctuary, "I thought Mary had a little lamb!"

Though she didn't know it, Ashley had spoken a great truth that morning. The Christmas baby truly was a lamb. But not just "a lamb" but "the Lamb," as He was called by His cousin, John the Baptist when he said, "Look! The Lamb of God" (John 1:29 NLT).

When Mary held her baby close, traced the line of His little cheeks, laughed at the sweet baby sounds coming from her little one, I wonder if she ever called Him "my little lamb!" without ever thinking of what the future held. When she saw the lambs being led to the temple, did she ever think of her little lamb as the Lamb of God? Or did she simply enjoy His baby days as all mothers do? Did she hide His future from her heart?

The Lamb of God! What a picture of sweet innocence!

How Mary must have enjoyed her boy. She watched Him grow with that sweet innocence in His heart. She nurtured His love for God and taught Him to love scripture. Worship for God the Father grew in His heart as His mother must have role-modeled her own worship of the God she loved and served.

The home of Mary and Joseph was hand picked as a safe place for the little Lamb of God to grow into the sacrificial Lamb of God.

There came a day when the time was right and the Lamb was grown.

Once again Mary was there to watch her Lamb.

This time there was no joy. Perhaps the only peace that could quiet her heart was found in the words of her nephew John, "Look! The Lamb of God who takes away the sin of the world!"

Ginny Allen

The Biggest News

But the angel said to them, "Do not be afraid. I bring you good news
that will cause great joy for all the people. Today in the town of David a
Savior has been born to you; he is the Messiah, the Lord."
Luke 2:10, 11, NIV.

The Christmas the world celebrates today does not have the same meaning
that it has in the Bible story, because of all the hype around Santa Claus,
gifts, dinners, and trade of yielding profits without measure. Yet that does
not take away the brightness and the importance of the first coming of Jesus
Christ.

The text above describes the night when a delegation from heaven comes to
earth to bring the biggest news: the birth of the man-God, Jesus.

It was an ordinary night, when shepherds were working at their routine of
caring for sheep, without the notion that an important event for all humanity was
taking place. As they witnessed the supernatural, they were afraid, even terrified.

The angel's message went straight to the point. It held great joy for those
receiving it in the city of David—and for all men and women of all ages who do
the same—the Savior is born.

And His mission had a philanthropic, donor, sacrificial, and substitutive sense.
All the expression of the divine love (philanthropic, sacrificial, substitutionary)
was manifested in Christ, showing His grace in making us beloved children of
the Father. Forgiven children . . . because of Jesus' blood shed on the cross of
Calvary. If Jesus had not come, our story would have been hopeless. We'd not
have the confident expectation of heaven nor our names written in the Lamb's
book of life. At Christmas, though we are unworthy and undeserving, we well
know this Gift, offered so freely.

Christmas is the greatest news that you can have on a night full of darkness
and uncertainty. It is a message of hope sent from above, pointing to a Savior
who wants to be born not only in a manger, but also in the hearts of everybody
who knows the story of God's love for lost humanity, separated from the heavenly
gates. Of Himself Jesus said, "I am the way and the truth and the life. No one
comes to the Father except through me" (John 14:6).

Open your heart to Jesus on this special day, and experience the true joy of
heaven!

Maria Raimunda Lopes Costa

New Plans

"For I know the plans I have for you," declares the LORD, "plans to prosper you and not harm you, plans to give you hope and a future."
Jer. 29:11, NIV.

Less than two weeks after my thirty-third birthday, my husband announced that he wanted a divorce. At the time I was a stay-at-home mom who worked only two days a week. As I faced the heartache of divorce and the fear of not being able to find full-time employment to support myself and my three-year-old daughter, my mother read Jeremiah 29:11 to me. God had plans for me.

As I began to apply for jobs and send out résumés that received no response, I struggled not to panic. When the panic seemed like it was about to win, a close friend sent Jeremiah 29:11 to me in a text message. Ah, yes. God still had plans. A few days later I received a call from a hospital two hours from my home that wanted to interview me for a full-time job. It was the only employer to respond to any of my applications. The salary they offered was exactly the amount that I needed to make! I accepted the job offer.

My next challenge was handling the logistics of being a single mom with a two-hour commute to work (each way) and still meet the needs of my daughter. My new job was to begin January 2. On New Year's Day, still feeling overwhelmed, I began reading a new devotional book I'd received for Christmas. The opening verse for January 1 was Jeremiah 29:11! By this time I began to notice a pattern. When I'd become discouraged, that particular verse would be brought to my attention, one way or another—for God has plans.

Two years have passed since my thirty-third birthday, and Jeremiah 29:11 still keeps "showing up" just when I need it. I recently suffered a broken relationship, leaving me with sadness and discouragement. While waiting to meet a friend for dinner, I decided to browse through a nearby bookstore. I picked up a daily calendar with Bible promises to find a word of encouragement. Of the 365 promises that I could have opened to, the calendar fell open to a midyear date—the one bearing Jeremiah 29:11.

I'm still on my journey, yet God gently reminds me when I most need it that He is being faithful to the plans He has for me—plans to prosper me, give me hope, and a future.

Angelina Vandiver

Words Matter—Part 1

What you say can preserve life or destroy it; so you must accept the consequences of your words. Prov. 18:21, GNT.

In *Raise a Leader* (p. 27), I tell the story of an accomplished professional who confided in me by sharing the trauma and the resulting low self-esteem that his parents caused him to suffer when they pointed to his best friend and said, "Why can't you get good grades like Richard? Now, he looks like a leader." The message of this story is this—parental words matter! What we say to our children makes a lasting impression. We are their trusted heroines. Therefore, our words define their world; we tell them who they are and forecast what they will become. Parents write the script. What script are you writing?

Then, there is the story of Dick Hoyt and his disabled son, Rick, a spastic quadriplegic. Rick could not speak, but working with engineers, his parents gave Rick a voice. Rick selects letters on a computer screen to form words and sentences. At the age of thirteen, Rick "tells" his dad he wanted to "run" in a race. After the benefit run, with Dick pushing his son's wheelchair, Rick tells his dad that when he "runs" he feels like his disability disappears. Rick's parents saw their son's disabilities, but knowing his intelligence they encouraged his dreams and looked for ways to make Rick's dreams a reality. A script of success was written for Rick by his parents.

According to our text, words either kill or give life! And we get to choose. *We choose whether we will be agents of life or the bearers of death.* Today is a new day; new opportunities await us. What words will we choose to use—to use in our homes, to use in the workplace; or with your coworkers or supervisors? What words will you choose when talking with your child or spouse? If a coworker is rude, what words will you choose? And if you have the "boss from hell," what words will you use?

Even words spoken carelessly come back to haunt *us*. Words are powerful; take them seriously. Words can make a positive impression. Words can also condemn. Words matter. Telling your child they are bad, impossible, naughty, and so on, sends the message that he or she is bad. To that child, doing good things won't change that *label*. The impression has been made.

Help me today to speak words that inspire, encourage, and bring out the best in others.

Prudence LaBeach Pollard

Words Matter—Part 2

"For by your words you will be acquitted, and by your words you will be condemned." Matt. 12:37, NIV.

Words have the ability to empower or to condemn others, especially children. Instead of telling your child he is bad or naughty, tell him instead that the behavior is unacceptable and that you know he can do better because he is a good boy. Your child will not feel condemned but will learn that he can control his actions and change the negative behavior. Words can either build confidence and faith in your child or condemn and tear them down. Watch closely which words you choose to use today, because words matter. We want to speak words that will inspire, encourage, and bring out the best in others.

We also want to take care how we think about others. What I think influences what I say, and what I say affects how I think. *Words react on the character.* Words are just as powerful as the "sticks and stones" that can break our bones. As a little child I learned to repeat, to chant this familiar phrase: *Sticks and stones may break my bones, but words will never hurt me.*

With that phrase I was no longer a victim of the schoolyard bully's taunt. Saying those words made me feel powerful, assertive, and invincible. Speaking strength made me feel strong.

The bravado may have provided short-term strength but in reality, *sticks and stones may break my bones, but words may break my spirit.*

Words are powerful; use them wisely today. Positive words have constructive effects, and negative words have damaging effects. Positive words motivate while negative words interrupt the action of the brain. When you hear angry words, your initial response is likely to be defensive, emotional, and not well thought out.

Children who are raised in a positive environment, where words of affirmation and motivation are common, are more likely to develop into resilient, initiative-taking adults. However, the child from the negative, condemning environment will be reactive, demonstrate poor use of logic and reasoning abilities, and is less likely to succeed.

Lord, help me today to speak words of affirmation.

Prudence LaBeach Pollard

Words Matter—Part 3

Why are you cast down, O my soul? And why are you disquieted within me? Hope in God; for I shall yet praise Him, the help of my countenance and my God. Ps. 43:5, NKJV.

Because words matter, we choose whether we will be agents of life or the bearers of death.

Because words matter, they react on the character. Our thoughts influence our words. Our words influence ourselves and others. Children who are raised in a positive environment, where words of affirmation and motivation are common, are more likely to develop into resilient, initiative-taking adults. However, the child from the negative, condemning environment will be reactive, demonstrate poor use of logic and reasoning abilities, and is less likely to succeed.

I have a daily practice that helps me to manage my mind and my mouth. I spend ten minutes concentrating on positive words before my day begins. *Words Can Change Your Brain* by Newberg and Waldman (2012) reminds us that it takes only a few seconds to prove the neurological fact that words can heal or hurt.

My focused attentiveness to the positive coupled with vocalizing my positivity builds a more resilient and motivated brain. During the day I am more likely to think positive thoughts about myself and people I interact with at home, work, or elsewhere.

The next time your boss, spouse, colleague, or child says or does something negative, instead of just counting to ten, try the following: Take hold of your reaction and replace it with positive words. While the person is talking, hold the positive words in your mind.

For example, your work colleague is accusing you unjustly, and your desire is to cut her off and defend yourself. Instead you say to yourself, *This is a child of God; Lord, please help me to represent You even in this difficult moment.* You may even have to repeat it a couple of times. You are now training your brain. Words affect our reality, and when we use positive words to train our thoughts and feelings, our behaviors will be positive.

Words really do matter. Life and death are in the tongue (Prov. 18:21), and we rise to the level of our confession; therefore, "Let the weak say I am strong" (Joel 3:10).

Lord, please help me today to think positive thoughts even about the most difficult person.

Prudence LaBeach Pollard

A Surprise Gift

Though you have made me see troubles, many and bitter, you will restore my life again; from the depth of the earth you will bring me up. You will increase my honor and comfort me once more. Ps. 71: 20, 21.

The devotional book *Love Out Loud* came as a surprise gift. I never expected to receive a copy of my denomination's annual women's ministries devotional book that year. Yet one afternoon I got a surprise delivery from the postman. I considered the book heaven-sent because it came at the very time I was feeling down. In fact, I was about to give up on a ministry that I had loved for a very long time.

The year 2011 brought me a lot of trials and suffering at work. There was never a day when I came home and didn't tell my mother that I was going to quit my job. Every morning I dragged my feet going to work. Every day I wished the day would end quickly. I lost all the enthusiasm and interest I used to have. Though I wanted to resign, I could not. Being the head of my family, I had to work in order to provide for our needs. So it was with a very heavy heart that I had to face my trials day by day.

Then the devotional book arrived unexpectedly.

I browsed through the articles. Then I noticed in one story this line: "In her distress and pain God did not forsake Hagar." I stopped reading for a moment. Like Hagar, I also was in distress. Since God would not forsake me either, I had renewed hope.

God knew I needed encouragement, so He had sent me that book and that line inspired me to go on. Through that book God spoke to me and told me not to give up. Through that book, He told me to continue working where I was because He would see me through all the troubles I was facing. And indeed, God's promise came true. My troubles ended. Every problem I had was resolved, and more blessings came my way. I emerged stronger, wiser, and more trusting of God. Through the stormy situation in the workplace, I have experienced God!

Dear Lord, thank You for the ladies who share their stories of faith. Truly they are Your instruments to make people realize that there is hope in You. You see us, Your children, and You are always there to comfort, love, and care.

Minerva M. Alinaya

Singing a New Song

He hath put a new song in my mouth, even praise unto our God: many shall see it . . . and shall trust in the LORD. Ps. 40:3.

It is New Year's Eve, and I am thinking of how I might be a better person during the coming year. I've heard how important attitude is for happiness and good health. Since I believe that to be true, I resolve, with God's help, to be a more positive person. The problem is, How do I get through the tough days when it seems that nothing is going well?

In the last couple of months, a dear friend of ours was given the news that his condition had reached a place where the doctors could do nothing more. We were all devastated to know that we would lose him. End of life is something we all expect at some point, but it is never a happy thought, and our tears were not tears of joy.

After several weeks of vacation, we arrived back home to discover that water had worked its way through the stucco walls and had ruined our beautiful new hardwood floors! You guessed right. I didn't feel like "whistling a happy tune." It was one of those dark hours of life like Paul and Silas experienced in a Macedonian jail. We know the story well. Hopeless as it may have seemed, they would not let their situation get them down. Instead, as the Rodney Griffin song puts it, the two prisoners chose to lift their voices in praise, trusting God come what may.

It seems almost abnormal to respond to trying circumstances with, "God is good. He's good all the time" or "Praise the Lord!" I have met some who often express that "Pollyanna" attitude. I'm amazed and, at the same time, very disappointed in myself! I may never reach that level of perfection. I know that God wants the best for me, and I'm usually a cheerful recipient of His good gifts, but when life comes crashing 'round me, is God disappointed with the way I react? What is the appropriate Christian response to disappointment and difficulties? Rodney Griffin, in his song, "God Wants to Hear You Sing," suggests that even when things go badly, God wants to hear us sing—He wants us to trust Him! In fact, it is at times like these, writes Griffin, that we truly "bless the Father's heart."

The song has become a favorite and will continue to inspire me in the months ahead. What an awesome thought that I could be a blessing to my heavenly Father!

Bernadine Delafield

2016 Biographies

Betty J. Adams, a retired teacher and wife for 60 years, enjoys her children and their families. She is a published writer, is active in Community Services, and lives in California. **Apr. 9**

Taiwo Adenekan is a teacher and a women ministries leader. She is married to a church elder and has four children. She currently resides in the Gambia, West Africa. **Apr. 19**

Priscilla Adonis writes from Cape Town, South Africa. She likes writing and flower gardening. She has two daughters and two grandsons and, as a widow, is thankful for God's care. **Sept. 15**

Shelley Agrey is a university English teacher in Thailand and works as a neonatal ICU nurse in Canada. She and husband, Loren, enjoy their four children along with their families. **June 19**

Sally J. Aken-Linke lives in Norfolk, Nebraska, where she maintains a Web site and is active in a music ministry with husband, John. They have five children and nine grandchildren. **July 6**

Mofoluke Akoja is happily married to Olalekan. They have a 15-month old daughter, Esther. She is church clerk and works at Babcock University in Nigeria. She loves to inspire. **May 23**

Minerva M. Alinaya is an assistant research director and full-time faculty member of Imus Institute. She is an elder and Sabbath School teacher at her church in Binakayan. **May 14, Dec. 30**

Ginny Allen, a retired school nurse, lives with her pastor husband, David, in Vancouver, Washington. This international speaker/writer is committed to God's will for her life. **Dec. 24**

Queila Toledo Diniz de Andrade, a native of Brazil, taught for six years and has a degree in medicine. She likes to travel with her husband and daughter and enjoys the piano. **Aug. 10**

Raquel Queiroz da Costa Arrais, a minister's wife, is associate director of the General Conference Women's Ministries Department and enjoys music. Previously an educator for 20 years, she has two adult sons, two daughters-in-law, and adored grandson, Benjamin. **Jan. 3, Apr. 15, Aug. 30, Oct. 1**

Edna Bacate Domingo, PhD, MSN, RN, and mother of three grown daughters, lives in Loma Linda, California, where she is an associate professor at National University. **Sept. 18**

Yvita Antonette Villalona Bacchus writes from the Dominican Republic, where she serves as a music director and violinist for her church. She loves reading and writing devotionals. **July 1**

Taylor Bajic met her now pastor husband, Filip, at Newbold College in England. After living in the UK for six more years, they have moved back to Chattanooga, Tennessee. **Mar. 13**

Carla Baker, the Women's Ministries director of the North American Division of Seventh-day Adventists, loves flower gardening, traveling, and being with her grandchildren. **July 25, Dec. 18**

Jennifer M. Baldwin works in risk management at Sydney Adventist Hospital in Australia. She enjoys family, church, and word games and has written for these books for over 16 years. **May 29**

Mônica Magali Bandeira lives with her mother in Londrina, PR/Brazil. This dressmaker is director of Stewardship in her Quadra Norte church. She likes books and word games. **Aug. 28**

Grachienne L. Banuag writes from Adventist University of the Philippines, where she is a medical laboratory science student. She plays guitar, writes poetry, and scrapbooks. **Sept. 10**

Adriza Santos Silva Barbosa, a pediatrician in Brazil, has two treasures: her husband and her beautiful daughter. She likes being with family, hiking, and intercessory prayer ministry. **Aug. 7**

Carol Barron is Mom to three fantastic adult children and a son-in-Christ. She writes from Silver Spring, Maryland, and is looking forward to meeting Jesus face-to-face. **June 16**

Dana M. Bean, an educator from Bermuda, loves God and enjoys working in various areas of church ministry, including being Adventurer Club leader. She caught the photography bug from her father. **June 17**

Dawna Beausoleil and her husband, John, live in a tiny town in rural northern Ontario, Canada. A retired teacher, she enjoys reading, singing, painting, and writing for publications. **Oct. 6**

Vonda Beerman is an inspirational, much-traveled vocalist, considered by some to be today's sweetest voice in Christian music. She is married, has four children, and lives in Oregon. **Mar. 21, Mar. 22, Oct. 29**

Xoli Belgrave writes from North West London, England. She is married to best friend, Antonio, and has two children. She is a training professional in the pharmaceutical industry. **Apr. 12**

Sylvia Giles Bennett lives in Suffolk, Virginia, with husband, Richard. She loves camping and personal ministry. She has two adult children and three adoring grandchildren. **May 25**

Annie B. Best is a retired teacher in Washington, D.C. A widow, she has two adult children and three grandchildren and composed a song published in *Let's Sing Sabbath Songs.* **Oct. 26**

Cynthia Best-Goring is the principal of a pre-K–6 elementary school in Maryland. Her passion is helping children learn, teachers teach, and all to become acquainted with our Father. **Sept. 16**

Moselle Slaten Blackwell is a retired widow living in Detroit, Michigan. She has two adult children and one granddaughter. She is involved in her church and loves religious music. **Nov. 27**

Jean A. (Lloyd) Blake, PhD, taught mathematics at the high school and university levels in Jamaica and in Alabama before retiring. She is a wife, mother, and grandmother. **Nov. 30**

Julie Bocock-Bliss lives in Hawaii with her husband. She is an active member of the Honolulu Japanese Seventh-Day Adventist Church in Manoa. She is "mommy" to three cats. **June 11**

Patricia Hook Rhyndress Bodi, a long-distance student at Andrews University (completing the theology degree she started in 1956), is active in women's ministries and loves to travel. **Sept. 7**

Fulori Sususewa Bola is a Fijian working in Papua, New Guinea, as senior lecturer with the School of Education at Pacific Adventist University. She has two adult children. **Mar. 8**

Evelyn Greenwade Boltwood is the mother of two young adults and grandmother to two grandsons. Active in a wide variety of ministries, she also raises scholarship funds. **Apr. 3**

Tamar Boswell, from Loma Linda, California, is a registered nurse who leads church prayer ministries, is involved in outreach programs, experiments with vegan recipes, and travels. **Sept. 4**

Althea Y. Boxx, MPH, is a Jamaican registered nurse who has authored a motivational devotional entitled *Fuel for the Journey.* She enjoys traveling, writing, and photography. **Feb. 15**

Harriet Breach, a retired geriatric nurse and interior design consultant with husband, Ted, has five adult children, grandchildren, and church children. Huntsville, Alabama, is home. **Sept. 13**

Alison Brook, a Michigan-based singer/songwriter, studied religion and music at Andrews University and is currently working on her second album. She just got married! **May 15**

Suzi-Ann Brown, a native Jamaican, writes from central Florida, where she currently resides with her family. She enjoys singing and spends her free time singing in nursing homes. **Aug. 8**

Tamara Brown is a native of Cleveland, Ohio, and a U.S. Army veteran. Married to Robert and mother of Robert II, she loves writing, church ministries, and reflecting on 1 John 1:9. **Oct. 11**

Edna Buenaventura-Esguerra writes from the Philippines. An English teacher by profession, she chooses to stay home with her son, Horez, and to be a full-time wife to Teofilo. **Aug. 16**

Samantha Bullock lives on the Caribbean island of St. Vincent and the Grenadines. This professional economist is actively involved in church ministries. She enjoys writing. **Sept. 6**

Diane Burns lives with husband, Lawrence, in beautiful Corner Brook, Newfoundland, Canada. She leads a women's small group Bible study about Jesus and loves to walk and laugh. **Oct. 31**

Elizabeth Ida Cain is administrative assistant at a motor vehicle dealership. Active in women's ministries at her church in St. John, she also teaches floral arranging art design. **Mar. 1**

Hyacinth V. Caleb, raised in the West Indies, presently resides in St. Thomas, (U.S. Virgin Islands). University educated in Trinidad and Jamaica, she now teaches high school. **Feb. 24**

Florence E. Callender is an author, speaker, speech-language pathologist, and president of DaySpring Life Options. She has a teenage daughter and works and lives in New York. **Jan. 15**

Laura A. Canning, born in Surrey, England, is the mother of three who "led" her into children's ministries during their growing-up years. She enjoys country life, people, and her pets. **June 2**

Dorothy Wainwright Carey, widowed after a blessed 48-year marriage, writes from Ocala, Florida. Her son and grandson bring joy to her life as do writing, traveling, and friends. **July 28**

Eveythe Kennedy Cargill, wife of Stafford for 42 years, moved from Jamaica to Huntsville, Alabama.

She teaches college and serves on the board of elders at the Oakwood University Church. **Jan. 14**

Raquel Carrera attends church in Calimesa, California, and is married to Obed. They have two children, Samuel and Leila. Her passions are for serving God and education. **Dec. 8, Dec. 9**

Het Jane Silva Carvalho earned degrees in the human sciences from two universities in Brazil. She has taught at the university level. Her favorite activity is sharing Christian literature. **Dec. 19**

Camilla E. Cassell writes from Manchester, Pennsylvania. A retired postal employee, she attends Berea Temple Seventh-day Adventist Church and treasures her great-granddaughter. **Mar. 19**

Maria de Lourdes I. M. Castanho lives in Brazil with her husband, five sons, three daughters-in-law, and her granddaughters, Julia and Luisa. She loves children's ministry and reading. **Aug. 22**

Vanya Hoyi Chan, originally from Hong Kong, is in her first year of pharmacy school. She has sold religious books to help fund her education and writes from San Marcos, California. **July 11**

Marialva Vasconcelos Monteiro Chaussé is thirty-nine, is married, and serves as church music director. She likes art, especially painting, and lives in Canavieiras in the State of Bahia, Brazil. **Dec. 17**

Suhana Benny Prasad Chikatla is an online consultant/trainer at Wallace State and a part-time adjunct professor at Auburn University, Alabama, and is married to Royce Sutton. **Jan. 8**

Caroline Chola, the director of Children's and Women's Ministries for the Southern Africa–Indian Ocean Division, is married to Habson Chola, has five adult sons, and is proud of her two grandchildren. **Mar. 18**

Rosenita Christo is the Shepherdess and Secretarial Management coordinator for Southern Asia Division, India. She and her husband, Gordon, wrote an adult Bible study guide. A church choir director, she loves singing. **Dec. 15**

Rosemarie Clardy writes from Candler, North Carolina, where she and her husband enjoy country living, their three teenage sons, pets, and volunteering at church and school. **Mar. 5**

Kelli Raí Collins works as a receptionist and is earning a degree in English. She lives in Suitland, Maryland, with her husband and three children. She enjoys writing poetry. **Oct. 15**

Dana Connell is currently studying at Andrew's University Seminary in Berrien Springs Michigan. Her favorite things in life are divine appointments with people of various backgrounds. **May 7**

Rose Eva Bana Constantino is associate professor at University of Pittsburgh School of Nursing. Married to Abraham, this mother of three teaches nursing and practices law. **Dec. 10**

Sandi B. Cook is married to Tim and has a daughter and granddaughter. She lives on a farm, works as an occupational health nurse for 3M, and is church clerk. She loves to help people. **Mar. 11**

Ellen M. Corbett lives in British Columbia and attends Canadian Union College. Her interests include canoeing, music, languages, ham radios, and following Jesus wherever He leads. **July 12**

Maria Raimunda Lopes Costa, residing in Bacabal, Maranhão, Brazil, is a poet and teacher involved in missionary work. She has a published book, *Vivências* (Experiences). **Jan. 1, Dec. 25**

Patricia Cove from Ontario, Canada, has just published two books. She is a semiretired teacher who enjoys all outdoor pursuits (especially sailing and hiking) and church ministry. **Apr. 2**

Edna Soares da Cruz writes from São Paulo, Brazil. Secretary for the Department of Women's Ministries and a mother of two, she works at a school and is earning a degree. **Nov. 8**

Lee Lee Dart is a pastor at the Adventure Seventh-day Adventist Church in Windsor, Colorado. This wife and mother of two is passionate about being a conduit of God's love to others. **Oct. 30**

Jean Dozier Davey and her husband, Steven, live in the mountains of North Carolina. A retired computer programmer, she enjoys family, cooking, walking, and encouraging others. **Feb. 9**

Avery Davis lives in England. She has a passion for women's ministries. She considers it a privilege to share these stories and thanks God for her husband's and children's support. **Aug. 29**

Rose Muthiah Davy, originally from India, is a retired nurse who is settled down in Hendersonville, Tennessee. She enjoys sewing, natural remedies, and her grandchildren. **Dec. 16**

Jennifer Day and pastor husband, Sean, reside in northwest Alabama with their three small children, who never cease to give them a glimpse into the mind and heart of God. **May 2**

Bernadine Delafield writes from Apopka, Florida, where she retired after 21 years of service at the General Conference and North American Division. She has three grandchildren. **Dec. 31**

Kerstin Dorn is married and has two children. At the moment she is in charge of a book project. Her dearest wish is for the salvation of others to the glory of God. She lives in Germany. **June 5**

Cheryl Doss directs the General Conference Institute of World Mission. She holds a PhD in Christian Education and Intercultural Studies. All her family are involved in missions. **May 8**

Louise Driver, now retired, lives in Idaho where her three sons and four grandchildren also live. A part-time elementary school librarian, her hobbies include singing and traveling. **Mar. 26**

Mable C. Dunbar, PhD, wife of Pastor C. A. Dunbar, mother of three, and president/CEO of Women's Healing and Empowerment Network (whenetwork.com), is a licensed counselor in Washington State. Her book *The Truth About Us* deals with abuse issues. **May 6**

Mary E. Dunkin loves to create fun stuff like prickly pear truffles. Serving in church ministries, she also travels with her husband, Al. She has one small dog named Colt Magnus. **Aug. 5**

Pauline A. Dwyer-Kerr, a native of Jamaica, resides in Florida and serves her church in various capacities. She holds a doctorate degree and is currently a professor. She enjoys travel. **June 7**

Peggy S. Rusike Edden is a mother of three and a grandmother to lovely little girl. In 2014 she married Robert Edden. She attends the Redditch Adventist church in England. **May 21**

Ruby H. Enniss-Alleyne works in the Treasury Department of her church conference in Guyana. She lost her spouse in 2011 and is active at her home church, Mt. Carmel. **Sept. 28**

Doreen Evans-Yorke is a Jamaican-Canadian mother, educator, and certified child life specialist who currently lives in Montreal. She enjoys playing various instruments. **Mar. 16**

Melinda Ferguson lives in Plainfield, Wisconsin, where she works as a registered nurse. She enjoys church involvement, assisting with family, reading, and catching up with friends. **June 9**

Vera Lúcia F. S. Ferrari lives in Pederneiras, in the state of São Paulo, Brazil. She is married to Luiz and has three children: Jonatan, Wilson, and Júlia. She likes puzzles and knitting. **Feb. 2**

Carol Joy Fider, a retired educator, writes from Mandeville, Jamaica, where she is an elder, Family Ministries director, and teacher in her church. She and husband, Ezra, have two adult daughters. **June 14**

Thaiane Firmino is from Brazil. A graduate in journalism, she is regional coordinator of university students in southwest Bahia. She loves her sister, Thâmisa, and the coast. **May 22**

Edith Fitch, a retired teacher living in Lacombe, Alberta, Canada, volunteers in the archives at Canadian University College. She enjoys life and thanks God for every new day. **May 26**

Janice Fleming-Williams, a certified family life educator, has been teaching for over 35 years. She lives with husband, Gordon, on St. Thomas (U.S. Virgin Islands) and has two sons. **Oct. 16**

Lana Fletcher and her husband live in Washington but spend winters in California with the family of their eldest daughter, who teaches at the Loma Linda School of Dentistry. **Mar. 6**

Patricia Buxton Flores lives in Trenton, New Jersey, and attends the Morrisville Presbyterian Church. This mother and grandmother keeps busy presenting workshops on storytelling. **Oct. 5**

Sherilyn R. Flowers, born in Belize, now calls Los Angeles home. She has authored *Personal Omens Expressing My Soul (P.O.E.M.S.),* published by Outskirts Press. She loves God. **Jan. 18**

Elizeth de Carvalho Fonseca, a retired teacher, lives with her husband in Brazil. They have three children and one grandson. She enjoys Bible studies and praying with others. **May 1**

Marea I. Ford and husband, Lee, live in Tennessee. She survived colon cancer and enjoys her five grandchildren and their families. Her hobbies include crocheting and new recipes. **June 13**

Gail Frampton, a freelance artist, lives in Ontario, Canada. She enjoys time with God in the great outdoors, working with young people, and encouraging them along God's path. **July 27**

Andrea Francis teaches high school in Providenciales, Turks and Caicos. She is actively involved in church life, and in children's and young adult ministries. Her passion is to nurture. **Feb. 16**

Antoinette Franke, in her 60s, writes from Stafford, Virginia. She and her husband have two grown children. About 45 years ago God touched her with His saving grace. Praise God! **Nov. 7**

Forsythia Catane Galgao served as a missionary in Africa (Ethiopia and Madagascar) for 25 years. She coordinates the ESL program at Pacific International University in Thailand. **Jan. 16**

Edna Maye Gallington has published her first book, *Watching From the Shadows*. A member of Toastmasters International, she speaks often. Visit her blogs at www.ednagallington.com. **Feb. 1**

Claudette Garbutt-Harding, originally from Belize, lives in Orlando, Florida. She has been a kindergarten through college educator for over 40 years and is married to Keith. **July 10**

Georgina George, from Dominica in the Caribbean, completed an education program at Canadian University in Lacombe, Alberta, where she lives with her daughters. She coordinates church music programs. **June 8**

Nancy A. Gerard works in fund-raising/alumni relations at Georgia-Cumberland Academy. She and her husband, Greg, have two adult children. She is active in church and community. **Sept. 22**

Yan Siew Ghiang attends Balestier Seventh-day Adventist Church in Singapore. She had completed her Pathfinder Leadership Award Course. **Jan. 9, Mar. 23**

Evelyn Glass and husband, Darrell, live in Minnesota on the farm where Darrell was born. She has three grown children and two grandchildren, and wrote *Women in the Bible and Me*. **Aug. 9**

Sandra Golding is a business consultant in the United Kingdom. Active in women's ministries, her passions are writing, event management, and international development work. **Oct. 7**

Hannelore Gomez, from Panama, currently teaches Spanish in a Virginia high school. Her hobbies are reading and traveling. Knowing the gospel has been her greatest blessing. **June 18**

Alexis A. Goring, a freelance writer/photographer who has interviewed well-known people, joins her grandmother (Annie B. Best) and mother (Cynthia Best-Goring) in this book. **May 9**

Mayla Magaieski Graepp, a scholarship recipient, studies in Brazil and works at the White Center as a research assistant. She likes to run and to publish Christ-centered articles. **June 27**

Cecelia Grant is a Seventh-day Adventist medical doctor, retired from government service. She lives in Kingston, Jamaica, where she enjoys gardening and counseling young people. **Oct. 24**

Jasmine E. Grant, a retired social worker in Jamaica, New York, was a senior counselor for 18 years working with pregnant addicts. She is involved with several church ministries. **July 19**

Mary Jane Graves lost her husband to cancer in 2009 after 58 years of a happy marriage. She is looking forward to the day when they can be together again. She lives in North Carolina. **July 2**

Marjorie Gray-Johnson resides in Port Saint Lucie, Florida. She has three adult children, six grandchildren, and an 85-year-old mother. A nurse, she is pursuing graduate degrees. **Aug. 31**

Ellie Postlewait Green, a retired nurse, has coauthored books and written articles. She has presented evangelistic series and has a husband, two children, and three grandchildren. **Dec. 22**

Carol J. Greene, a grandmother of four and the great-grandmother of one, writes from Palm Bay, Florida. Her daily telephone ministry is one of her greatest delights. **Nov. 20**

Glenda-mae Greene writes from her wheelchair in Florida. She is a retired university educator. Crafting devotionals, a way of drawing closer to God, is one of her greatest passions. **Nov. 19**

Gloria Gregory is dean of the College of Education and Leadership at Northern Caribbean University in Jamaica. She and husband, Milton, are involved in team ministry. **Apr. 26**

Meibel Mello Guedes, a retired pastor's wife, was one of Brazil's women's ministries pioneers. She writes books and articles, lectures widely, and lives in Curitiba, Paraná, Brazil. **June 23**

Maria Bellesi Guilhem, retired from church work, enjoys time with her pastor husband, three children, and four grandchildren. She lives in São Carlos, SP, and visits the elderly. **Mar. 28**

Kera Gwebu, born in Zimbabwe, now lives in Elizabeth City, North Carolina. Married with two adult children, she was a nursing professor at Oakwood University for many years. **Oct. 17**

Diantha Hall-Smith, a daughter of God, writes from California where resides with her husband serving in the U.S. Air Force. A mother of two, she enjoys writing and traveling. **Aug. 12**

Juli Hamilton writes from Calhoun, Georgia, and lives with the love of her life. They have five children and two grandchildren, and she teaches 18 more at Coble Elementary School. **Oct. 23**

Peggy Curtice Harris, is board chair of W.A.S.H. (www.w-a-s-h.org). You can find two of her books at www.adventsource.org and five others she has authored at www.authorhouse.com. **Dec. 11**

Marian M. Hart-Gay, a retired elementary teacher and nursing home administrator, lives in Avon Park, Florida, with her new husband. They enjoy mission trips and their 17 grandchildren. **Jan. 6**

Helen Heavirland writes from Oregon. Her book *Zion: Champion for God* tells of a Christian woman's unlikely ministry. Heavirland enjoys local and foreign mission work. **Feb. 22**

Muriel Heppel, a retired teacher, lives in British Columbia. After her husband's death in 2009, she relocated to McBride where she had taught over 50 years earlier. She loves birding. **Nov. 21**

Denise Dick Herr teaches English at Canadian University College in Alberta, Canada. She enjoys reading, traveling, and the potential that each day brings. **Apr. 28, July 18, Nov. 17**

Andrea D. Hicks is founder of FOCUS (Fellowship of Christians Unique and Single) Ministries, is a motivational speaker, and works for a dental radiography company in New York. **Oct. 13**

Vashti Hinds-Vanier, born in Guyana, South America, recently celebrated her 50th anniversary of becoming a nurse. She lives in New York, travels widely, and enjoys her grandson, Jaden. **Oct. 12**

Denise Hochstrasser is married and has three adult daughters and three grandchildren. She travels widely as Women's Ministries director at the Inter-European Division in Bern. **July 3**

Roxy Hoehn writes from Topeka, Kansas. A minister's daughter and a minister's wife, Roxy has moved often. The move she really anticipates is the move up to heaven. **Apr. 20, June 4, Nov. 24**

Karen Holford, a freelance writer, family therapist, mother, and grandmother, lives in Scotland. She loves collecting vintage linens and wandering the Scottish hills with her husband. **Dec. 21**

Tamyra Horst, a wife, mom, and sought-after speaker, serves as Communication director and Women's Ministries director for the Pennsylvania Conference. **Mar. 3, May 13, Dec. 4**

Jacqueline Hope HoShing-Clarke, PhD, an educator at North Caribbean University (Jamaica), is married and has two adult children and a grandson, Demetrio Josiah. **Apr. 8**

Gloria P. Hutchinson is a retired nurse who resides in Palm Bay, Florida, where she attends church. She conducts Bible study classes for the children, helping them to know Jesus. **Nov. 13**

Cecilia Moreno de Iglesias, director for Women's Ministries in the Inter-American Division, is Ecuadorian by birth and Colombian by adoption. She is a wife and mother. **Sept. 17**

Shirley C. Iheanacho, a retiree, mother, and grandmother, writes from Huntsville, Alabama. She and Morris have been married more than 45 years and have daughters and grandsons. **Feb. 28**

Consuelo Roda Jackson, of Tappannock, Virginia, volunteers at an academy library and is grateful both for the library experience and BS degree she earned from Union College. **Oct. 14**

Joan D. L. Jaensch and husband, Murray, live in South Australia. They have two married sons, two granddaughters, two grandsons, one great-grandson, and one great-granddaughter. **Mar. 12**

Tammy Jamieson, with her husband, Jason, raises three boys in Brooks, Alberta, Canada. Along with being a full-time mother, she teaches college business and computer courses. **June 20**

Greta Michelle Joachim-Fox-Dyett, living in Trinidad and Tobago, is a wife, mother, artist, potter, writer, and teacher. She is currently reading for her second degree in fine arts. **Mar. 10**

Corleen Johnson, married to Paul, lives in Oregon. For 14 years she was Oregon Conference Women's Ministries director. She volunteers as prayer coordinator for the North Pacific Union Conference. **Apr. 4**

Elaine J. Johnson lives in Alabama and is active in her small country church. She has 4 children, 12 grandchildren, and 3 great-grandchildren. She enjoys "computering." **Jan. 29**

Erna Johnson, the director for Women's Ministries in the South Pacific Division, is married to Eddy, a pastor. She is trilingual and loves her children, her grandchildren, and ministry. **Jan. 22**

Jeannette Busby Johnson lives in Maryland, which has many of the same letters as "Montana" (where she grew up) but none of the mountains. She has three children, six grandchildren, and a dignified coon hound, Ludwig. **Feb. 4, June 1, Dec. 23**

Kathy Jo Duterrow Jones, born in Seattle, has served God throughout Alaska; Michigan; Maryland; Alberta, Canada; and Idaho. She loves ministering to the needs of others. **Mar. 2**

Angie Joseph is a pastor's wife, codirector of Lay Evangelism in the Iowa-Missouri Conference, a speaker at women's retreats, and Bible instructor. **Feb. 26**

Gerene I. Joseph, wife of Sylvester, is mother of two teens. Formerly Women's and Children's Ministries director (North Caribbean Conference), she is now director of Education. **July 21**

Nadine A. Joseph is working on PhD degree at Adventist International Institute of Advanced Studies in the Philippines. You can visit her Web site at www.nadinejoseph.com. **Sept. 24**

Carolyn K. Karlstrom, a Bible worker, gives Bible studies, teaches, and preaches. She is married to Rick, has a sweet cat named Minuet, and is a published freelance writer. **Apr. 11**

Jean Kelly lives with her retired pastor husband in Huntsville, Alabama. She has two adult children, three adult grandchildren, and two great-grandchildren. She loves to entertain Sabbath dinner guests. **Aug. 6**

Sonia Kennedy-Brown lives in Ontario, Canada, and is a retired nurse and teacher. She is presently working on her biography. She likes to read and dabble in writing poetry. **Nov. 2**

Iris L. Kitching enjoys creative endeavors, spoken word poetry performances, and writing. She works in presidential section at the General Conference of Seventh-day Adventists and is married to Will. **Apr. 6, Oct. 18**

Bogadi Koosaletse writes from Botswana, Africa. She is a retired principal education officer, a head elder, and a published author (Associated Printers), who loves witnessing for God. **Jan. 30**

Betty Kossick, a longtime newspaper/magazine journalist, lives with husband, Johnny, in Apopka, Florida. For more information on her books, e-mail her at bkwrites4u@hotmail.com. **June 10**

Patricia Mulraney Kovalski lives in Chattanooga, Tennessee, but quite a bit of the time, is in Michigan, visiting children, grandchildren, and two great-grandsons. She enjoys crafts. **July 23**

Mabel Kwei, a retired university and college lecturer, did missionary work in Africa for many years with her pastor husband and their three children. She now lives in New Jersey. **Oct. 25**

Sally Lam-Phoon, the Children's, Family, and Women's Ministries director for the Northern Asia-Pacific Division of Seventh-day Adventists, is married to Pastor Chek-Yat and has two married daughters and two grandchildren. **Apr. 14, Nov. 3**

Barbara Lankford is a child of God, a daughter, a wife, a mother, and a grandmother. She and her husband, Jerry, live in Burley, Idaho, and have been married for over 46 years. **Aug. 25**

Janet Lankheet, a mother of four and former news reporter, is married to Roger. She pursued religious education and entered editorial work for her church, traveling worldwide as a credentialed minister and local elder. **Sept. 19**

Iani Dias Lauer-Leite lives in Bahia, Brazil. She is a college professor. At church she likes to help in music and prayer ministries. **Jan. 13**

Desireé Lee is an inspirational speaker, author, and convicted felon. From Snellville, Georgia, she now works to provide at-risk youth and teens with tools for a better future. **May 30**

Wilma Kirk Lee, MSW, LCSW, founded the Houston Healthy Marriage Coalition (Houston, Texas) and is married to pastor husband, W. S. Lee. She is a mother and grandmother. **Sept. 8**

Loida Gulaja Lehmann, originally from the Philippines, got married in Germany. She and her husband are members in the International Church in Darmstadt and support lay ministry. **Aug. 11**

Naomi Naylor Lokko is a neonatal intensive care unit nurse in Ardmore, Alabama, where she and her husband, Charles, raised their five children. She enjoys studying the Word of God. **Nov. 10**

Sharon Long (Brown), originally from Trinidad, makes her home in Alberta, Canada. A longtime child welfare social worker, she is married to Miguel Brown and has four adult children and two adult granddaughters. **Feb. 25**

Rhodi Alers de López, an author and singer, writes from Massachusetts. Her ministry, ExpreSsion Publishing Ministries, aims to inspire others to a closer relationship with Jesus. **Nov. 12**

Mary Louis is a retired social worker living in Sonora, California, where she attends St. Patrick's

Church. She is active in visitation of the sick and homebound and likes to write. **July 20**

Lynn Mfuru Lukwaro was born and raised in Tanzania. She and her husband, Gureni, live in Sharjah, United Arab Emirates, with their two beautiful daughters. **May 27**

Rhona Grace Magpayo enjoys early retirement. A former optician, she has a passion for helping people see better. She is married to Celestino, a retired U.S. Navy master chief. **May 20**

Debbie Maloba is the Women's and Children's Ministries director for the East-Central Africa Division of Seventh-day Adventists. She and husband, Jim, have five children. They are based in Nairobi, Kenya, where she loves to train women in leadership. **June 29**

Eunice Michiles Malty is married and lives in Brasilia, Midwestern Brazilian Region. She was a parliamentarian for 16 years. She enjoys travel, church activities, and floral design. **Sept. 20**

Nokuthula Maphosa-Mutumhe, the oldest of seven children, had a difficult childhood. Yet it served to bring her to God early in life. Now married, she has two children. **July 8**

Rojean Vasquez Marcia lives in Thailand, where she teaches and attends the Asia-Pacific International University (AIU) Church. She also ministers at an AIDS hospice. **Jan. 27**

Carolyn Venice Marcus resides in North Carolina. She is married with two adult children. A retired health care professional, she enjoys walking, traveling, and choral music. **Oct. 27**

Carol Jean Marino, a "Jackie of all trades," has, among other things, taught ESL in South Korea. A volunteer at her local library, she attends church in Palisade, Colorado. **Aug. 2**

Lillian Marquez de Smith writes from Ocala, Florida, and has studied in the A.I.C.E. program through Cambridge University in England. She loves to experiment in the kitchen. **June 6**

Tamara Marquez de Smith writes from Florida, where she lives with her husband and two daughters, Lillian and Cassandra. A native New Yorker, she uses her gifts for God. **Nov. 18**

Clarissa J. Marshall is a part-time caregiver and copy editor for the *Journal of Health & Healing* and W.D. Frazee Sermons. She hopes to encourage others through writing. **June 28**

Marilyn Thompson Marshall, a mother and grandmother from Trinidad, is pursuing an education degree from University of New Brunswick. She is a women's ministries leader. **Mar. 9**

Marion V. Clarke Martin is a retired physician who writes from Panama. She stays busy helping a son with health issues and her granddaughter. She is active in her church. **June 21**

Orpha Gumbo Maseko was born in Tsholotsho, Zimbabwe, and holds an MSA in pastoral care and is a PhD candidate in education leadership. She currently lives in Indiana. **Feb. 12**

Premila Masih serves the Southern Asia Division as Women's Ministries director. She is married to Pastor Hidayat Masih, SS/PM director. They have two adult children. **Feb. 3**

Gail Masondo is a wife, mother, women's/children's advocate, chaplain, songwriter, Life in Recovery coach, author, and international speaker. She resides in Johannesburg, South Africa. **Oct. 20**

Rose G. S. Matos is married and has two beautiful daughters. She likes to read and write. She lives in Sumaré-São Paulo, Brazil. **Feb. 10**

Ruth Mbabazi, a mother of three, is a student at Mbarara University in western Uganda. She formerly worked as a clinician in an HIV/AIDS clinic. She likes gospel music. **Dec. 20**

Laurie McClanahan writes from Flatrock, North Carolina, where old age and retirement have taken over after years of selling books and serving as chaplain and Bible instructor. **Aug. 18**

Vidella McClellan is retired in beautiful British Columbia, Canada. She is a wife, mother, and grandmother, and has one grandchild and two great-grandchildren. She loves gardening. **Dec. 5**

Kristin McGuire lives in Maine, where she enjoys being a wife and mother. She is a teachers' assistant and cook at her children's school and also gives Bible studies and writes. **Dec. 6**

Mary McIntosh, PhD, is a writer, freelance editor, and teacher from Washougal, Washington. A published author, she has been women's ministries leader at her church for eight years. **Aug. 24**

Judelia Medard-Santiesteban is an English teacher from the island of St. Lucia. She is pursuing studies in guidance and counseling, which she plans to use in ministry. **Feb. 13**

Vicki Mellish is an occupational therapist living in Ontario, Canada. She is looking forward to introducing her nieces and nephews to Aunt Florence in the earth made new. **Jan. 11**

Annette Walwyn Michael, a mother of three, grandmother of seven, is married to her retired pastor-husband, Reginald, and writes from St. Croix in the Virgin Islands. **Jan. 12**

Quilvie G. Mills is a retired community professor. She and her husband attend the Port St. Lucie Church in Florida, where she serves as a musician and Bible class teacher. **Nov. 6**

Marcia Mollenkopf, a retired teacher, lives in Klamath Falls, Oregon. She enjoys church involvement and has served in both adult and children's divisions. **July 9, Aug. 23**

Esperanza Aquino Mopera, RN, founder of Polillo Life Enhancement Program and president of Polillo Life Enhancement Organization Inc., helps families utilize local resources. **Apr. 16**

Lourdes Morales-Gudmundsson is a professor of Spanish Language and Literature at La Sierra University. A published author, ordained elder, and women's ministries director, she is currently president of the Association of Adventist Women. **Mar. 30, Mar. 31, Nov. 22, Nov. 23**

Valerie Hamel Morikone, along with being a pastor's wife, is Women's Ministries director for the Mountain View Conference in West Virginia, where she also works full time. **May 4**

Nilva de F. Oliveira da Boa Morte lives in the state of Mato Grosso, Brazil, with her husband, Jucinei Claudio C. da Boa Morte. She teaches art and works in the state health department. **June 25**

Bonnie Moyers lives with her husband and two cats in Staunton, Virginia. This freelance writer is a mother of two, a grandmother of three, and a musician for several area churches. **Jan. 4**

Joelcira F. Müller-Cavedon, a mother, has remarried and divides herself between Germany and Brazil. She is helping to form an international church in the Stuttgart region. **Jan. 21**

Tanya Muganda works as an administrative assistant in the Children's Ministries Department at the Seventh-day Adventist Church World headquarters in Silver Spring, Maryland. **Aug. 27**

Judith M. Mwansa, originally from Zambia, currently lives in Maryland. She and her husband, Pardon, serve at the General Conference of Seventh-day Adventists and have great adult children. She enjoys traveling. **Apr. 1**

Caroline Naumann is married and has two children. She has studied at Seminar Schloss Bogenhofen and the University of Innsbruck. She works with children at a crisis center. **Jan. 26**

Regina Ncube was born in Zimbabwe but is now settled in the United Kingdom. This mother of two young adults is a primary school teacher, who has also worked with health, social care, and with young women. **Feb. 23**

Bienvisa Ladion Nebres, from the Philippines, teaches in Thailand. She enjoys recalling the experiences she had working with her husband in Africa and composing poetry. **Jan. 25**

Anne Elaine Nelson, a retired teacher, corrects testing for schools. She has 4 children, 14 grandchildren, and 5 great-grandchildren. She is active in her Michigan church. **Sept. 29**

Samantha Nelson, married to a pastor, Steve, is vice president/CEO of the Hope of Survivors, a nonprofit assisting victims of clergy sexual abuse (http://thehopeofsurvivors.com). **Oct. 22**

Judith P. Nembhard both taught and served in administration at the high school and university levels. She writes, has published a work of Christian fiction, and lives in Chattanooga. **Apr. 25**

Linda Nottingham, semiretired, teaches a church Bible study class, serves as a mentor to businesswomen, and was a 2012 Honoree of the Florida Commission on the Status of Women. **Feb. 11**

Sarah Nyende was Women's Ministries director for the Uganda Union and Central Uganda Conference. Mother of four, she is a teacher, counselor, and human resource manager. **Mar. 4**

Beth Versteegh Odiyar of Kelowna, British Columbia, has managed the family chimney sweep business since 1985. She has twin sons, a daughter, and delightful grandchildren. **Mar. 20**

Joyce O'Garro, a 79-year-old retired laboratory technician, has also taught from kindergarten to college and still teaches piano. She has adult children and three grandchildren. **July 15**

Daniela Santos de Oliveira, born in Sao Paulo, Brazil, is married; teaches music; and likes singing, cooking, and going to the beach. She loves animals and being with family and friends. **Nov. 26**

Lourdes S. de Oliveira, a mother of three and grandmother of one, has been married for 37 years.

She is a retired civil servant and lives in Hortolândia and Serra Negra, São Paulo. **Sept. 26**

Jemima Dollosa Orillosa lives in Maryland with her husband, Danny. Jemima is a proud grandmother of a baby girl, Aryia Carrin. Jemima's passion is organizing mission trips. **Jan. 31**

Sharon Oster is a retired teacher assistant living in Evans, Colorado, with her retired pastor husband. She enjoys car trips to the Rocky Mountains and is a mother and grandmother. **Aug. 13**

Raisa Ostrovskaya writes from Russia where she serves as the Women's Ministries director for Euro-Asia Division. Her husband is a pastor. They have four sons. She likes poetry, cooking, and reading. **Feb. 27**

Hannele Ottschofski lives in southern Germany. She has four daughters and five grandchildren. A speaker for the Hope Channel, she organizes women's events and has compiled four women's devotionals. **Feb. 7**

Sharon Michael Palmer, MD, is married to Army Specialist Matthew Palmer. They reside in Fort Benning, Georgia. Sharon is a practicing family physician. **Jan. 24**

Ofelia A. Pangan is a retired ESL teacher living in Clovis, California, with her pastor husband, Abel. They have had ministry adventures in Laos, Thailand (21 years), and Canada. **Oct. 21**

Revel Papaioannou enjoys helping her 83-year-old pastor husband with a variety of church work in Berea, Greece. She volunteers part time in the local library. **June 30**

Bonnie R. Parker resides in Yucaipa, California, with husband, Richard. She is a homemaker, former teacher, office manager in her husband's dental office, mother, and grandmother. **July 17**

Barbara Parkins lives in New South Wales, Australia, when she is not in Kenya with the Maasai and running her school, rescue center, and women's community center. **Feb. 20**

Eliane Ester Stegmiller Paroschi, a pastor's wife and mother of two daughters, has taught at the Adventist college in Engenheiro Coelho, Sao Paulo, Brazil, where she lives. **Apr. 22**

Carmen Virgínia dos Santos Paulo is a specialist in linguistics and teaching and a health and socio-educational agent. She likes to read, sing, and speak of God's love to others. **Jan. 23**

Evelyn G. Pelayo works with her husband at Adventist University Zurcher in Madagascar. A graduate of Mountain View College (Philippines), she is a mother and grandmother. **May 10**

Sueli da Silva Pereira is a business manager who works in city hall. She serves her church by working with the youth, teens, and Pathfinders. She is married and has three children. **Sept. 11**

Céleste Perrino-Walker is a much-published author, editor, and textile artist. She is married with kids. To learn more, follow her blog at reindeerstationfarm.blogspot.com. **May 24, Aug. 19**

Betty Glover Perry is a retired anesthetist who writes from North Carolina, where she lives with her husband, a retired pastor. They are great-grandparents. She loves music. **Feb. 19, Sept. 21**

Diane Pestes, an international speaker and servant of God, is known for her commitment to Christ and ability to memorize Scripture. Diane resides in Oregon (www.dianepestes.com). **June 26**

Cheri Peters, an author (*Miracle From the Streets*) and host of popular TV program *Celebrating Life in Recovery* (on 3ABN), founded True Step Ministries, which helps people break free of damage from the past. **Feb. 8, May 12**

Marilyn Petersen is a retired elementary teacher and church organist. She loves animals and enjoys reading and writing. She has a daughter and two granddaughters. **Apr. 17**

Angèle Peterson lives in Ohio and enjoys finding spiritual lessons in everyday life. She currently serves as church treasurer/clerk and usher and anticipates Christ's soon return. **Dec. 3**

Kathy Peterson and husband, Dallas, live in Greeley, Colorado, enjoying retirement. A former high school special education assistant, she enjoys her grandkids and great-grandkids. **Dec. 13**

Karen Phillips lives in Omaha, Nebraska. A single mother of four, she works as a human resource/safety manager and actively leads a weekly women's Bible study. **Sept. 9**

Maureen Thomas Pierre lives in Meridianville, Alabama. She is a teacher who enjoys gardening, decorating, writing poetry, and reading the Bible for special nuggets. **Sept. 27**

Birdie Poddar is a retiree who originally comes from Northeast India but settled in South India. She has two adult children and five grandchildren. She has a handcrafted card ministry. **June 3**

Prudence LaBeach Pollard is author of *Raise a Leader, God's Way,* which is available from adventistbookcenter.com or as an e-book from amazon.com. **Dec. 27, Dec. 28, Dec. 29**

Cynthia J. Prime, an author and inspirational speaker, lives with husband, Phillip, in Indianapolis, Indiana. She is CEO and cofounder of Saving Orphans through Healthcare and Outreach (SOHO). **Apr. 23, Apr. 24**

Janine Schwanz Ramos is an educator in Vitória, ES, Brazil. She attends the Church of Jardim Camburi, where she has taught in the children's Sabbath School department for 24 years. **July 24**

Sharmila Rasanayagam-Osuri lives in Kensington, Maryland, with her husband, Vaynu Osuri; her son, Rahul; and daughter, Riya. Originally from Sri Lanka, she enjoys reading and music. **July 14**

Donna Reese, a retired speech and language pathologist, is a wife, grandmother, and private pilot. She enjoys an active lifestyle in the California foothills and is a published writer. **Aug. 4**

Katia Garcia Reinert, an advanced practice nurse originally from Brazil, lives in Maryland and serves as the Health Ministries director for the Seventh-day Adventist Church in North America. **Sept. 1, Dec. 14**

Darlenejoan McKibbin Rhine, born in Nebraska, raised in California, and educated in Tennessee, has now retired from the *Los Angeles Times.* Widowed, she has one son. **Jan. 7**

Jill Rhynard is retired in Vernon, British Columbia, Canada. Due to a disability, life has some challenges, but she enjoys traveling and has two married sons who live in the States. **July 13**

Karen Richards writes from England, where she is a teacher of a reception class working with children aged 4 and 5. She has been married for 27 years and has two grown daughters. **May 11**

Marli Ritter-Hein was born in Sao Paulo, Brazil, to a German father and an Italian mother. She married Nestor Esteban, an Argentinian doctor, with whom she went to Nepal as a missionary with their two small boys. They are now missionaries in Asuncion, Paraguay. **Sept. 3**

Jenny Rivera, a registered nurse, writes from Brisbane, Australia, where she is an active, musical member of the South Brisbane church. She is proud of her nieces and nephews. **Feb. 29**

Taniesha Robertson-Brown is a teacher living in the Turks and Caicos Islands and married to her husband, Courtney. She is grateful that he supports her ministry and writing endeavors. **Nov. 28**

Terry Wilson Robinson lives in Hendersonville, North Carolina, with her husband, Harry. She teaches disabilities awareness in schools, in churches, and for other organizations. **Nov. 1**

Dixil L. Rodriguez is a university professor and volunteer chaplain, who lives in Argyle, Texas. **May 5, Oct. 8**

Sayuri Ruiz Rodriguez is a daughter of the King of kings and has the best earthly parents ever! She is a pastor's wife (the most amazing heavenly adventure!) in Grants Pass, Oregon. **Aug. 3**

Kirsten Anderson Roggenkamp is a mother, grandmother, and teacher. Retired from Monterey Bay Academy, she lives in Loma Linda with her new husband, Clyde Roggenkamp. **May 28**

Melodie Roschman studies journalism and English literature at Andrews University. She wants to emulate C. S. Lewis, her spiritual mentor, by becoming both a professor and a writer. **Apr. 10**

Mahuya Roy has served as the Shepherdess, Women's Ministries, and Health Ministries director of Bangladesh Adventist Union Mission since 2011. She lives in the capital city of Dhaka. **Oct. 28**

Kollis Salmon-Fairweather, originally from Jamaica, West Indies, now lives in Florida with her husband. A retired nurse, she coordinates a Bible class and has held many church offices. **Feb. 5**

Clair Sanches-Schutte, a mother of two sons, is married to John, a pastor and psychologist. She is the director of Women's, Children's, and Family Ministries for the Trans-European Division in England. **Aug. 14**

Deborah Sanders lives in Alberta, Canada, with her husband, Ron, and son, Sonny. She hopes to publish her book of sacred memories, entitled *Saints-in-Training.* **Feb. 18**

Jennifer Jill Schwirzer, a speaker, writer, and musician, resides with husband, Michael, in Philadelphia, where she is in private counseling practice. They have two daughters, Alison and Kimberly. Her latest book is *13 Weeks to Peace* (Pacific Press®). **Apr. 27, Dec. 2**

Shirley P. Scott, a retiree from Oakwood University, serves as Women's Ministries director for the South Central Conference of Seventh-day Adventists and resides with her husband, Lionel, in Huntsville, Alabama. She has three adult children and two granddaughters. **June 15**

Omobonike Sessou is the director of Women's/Children's Ministries of the West-Central Africa Division, in Abidjan, Ivory Coast. Mother of three, she is married to Pastor Sessou. **Dec. 7**

Laurice Shafer lives in Washington State with her husband, John, and 91-year-old mother. Her book *Living Loved* is available as a free download at http://livingloved.com. **Apr. 13**

Cathy Shannon is a wife, mother, and academy art and home economics teacher. Born in the Midwest, Cathy lives in the South (Tennessee) but looks forward to her heavenly home. **Feb. 14**

Donna Lee Sharp writes from Yuba City, California, though her family is scattered across North America. She enjoys playing the piano and organ as ministry and bird watching. **Jan. 20**

Cheryl Jane Shelton lives in Georgia and teaches nutrition classes. Her vegan cookbook received an award from the National Women's Press. She has a son and grandson. **Apr. 18**

Rose Neff Sikora, retired after 45 years of nursing, lives with her husband, Norman, in North Carolina. Her adult daughter, Julie, has three lovely children: Tyler, Olivia, and Grant. **July 4**

Luciana Barbosa Freitas da Silva is secretary of the Department of Personal Ministries of the Pernambuco Conference. She is wife of Elias, mother of Bianca, and attends the church at Beira Mar, Recife, PE, Brazil. **Aug. 26**

Tamara Lemes Marins Silva is a married nurse who likes to use social media to share about Jesus. In church she teaches a children's class. She lives in Minas Gerais, Brazil. **Oct. 19**

Ella Louise Smith Simmons, a vice president at the General Conference of Seventh-day Adventist in Silver Spring, Maryland, is the first female to hold this position. A former university educator, provost, academic vice president, and professor, she is married to Nord. They have two children, three grandchildren, and one great-grandson. **Jan. 19, Aug. 1, Sept. 5**

Pauline Sinclair, originally from Jamaica, writes from Antigua, where she and her husband enjoy their two daughters. She is passionate about soul winning and likes to sing. **Nov. 11**

Heather-Dawn Small is the director for Women's Ministries at the General Conference of Seventh-day Adventists. She is married to Pastor Joseph Small and is the mother of Dalonne and Jerard. She loves air travel, reading, and scrapbooking. **Jan. 2, Apr. 5, July 16, Oct. 4**

Yvonne Curry Smallwood, a published writer, resides in Maryland and enjoys crocheting, journaling, writing, reading, and spending time with her granddaughter, Jordan. **Apr. 21**

Thamer Cassandra Smikle lives in Spanish Town, St. Catherine, Jamaica, with her husband, Wayne, and four beautiful children. She works as auditor at Jamaica Customs Agency. **Sept. 12**

Eileen Snell, a retired nurse, lives in Arizona, though she grew up in Kenya. Her interests include traveling, spending time with family and friends, and singing solos or in choirs. **Aug. 20**

Neide de Sá Soares, living in Brazil, is an educator, Sabbath School director, and church secretary. She cultivates friendships in family and society. She likes helping people. **Oct. 10**

Edna Ferreira de Souza loves raising her three children. She works as a real estate advisor. She is working as a regional director of Adventist Youth. She loves to cook for friends. **July 7**

Sylvia Stark, an artist, musician, and published writer, lives in Tennessee. Her artwork is displayed in the States and in South America. She enjoys backpacking, camping, and yard work. **May 16**

Leonardine Steinfelt, born in Washington, has lived and worked in three foreign countries. She likes to visit her three daughters, her grandchildren, and a bunch of great-grandchildren. **June 12**

Ardis Dick Stenbakken, the recent editor for these devotional books, is hoping to find time to pursue some hobbies since her retirement as director of Women's Ministries at the General Conference of Seventh-day Adventists. She and her husband, Dick, love spending time with their family. **Feb. 21, Mar. 27, Nov. 29**

Keisha D. Sterling works as a registered pharmacist and entrepreneur. Through God's grace, she serves women and supports youth, church building, health, and leadership ministries. **Sept. 23**

Carol Stickle writes from Kelowna, British Columbia, Canada. She has pursued several different careers. She loves visiting her adult grandchildren and preteen granddaughter. **Oct. 3**

Charity Stone is from Washington State and has served as a Bible worker in Philadelphia. She plans to attend the seminary at Andrews University in preparation for God's call on her life. **Aug. 21**

Naomi Striemer lives in Tennessee with her husband, Jordan, and dog, Bella. This author, Christian singer/songwriter, and speaker tours globally ministering to many. **Jan. 28, May 17**

Carolyn Rathbun Sutton, Jim's wife, enjoys editing these devotional books, the proceeds of which all go to scholarships for collegiate-age women in developing countries. **Mar. 7, Sept. 14, Nov. 4**

Loraine F. Sweetland, a retired widow in Tennessee, lives with her 14-year-old dog, Sugar. Loraine hopes to others who struggle with chronic kidney disease, as she does. **Mar. 14**

Aleksandra Tanurdzic, born in Bosnia, met her future husband at Belgrade Theological Seminary in Serbia. Now a chaplain in the Chicago area, she enjoys her beautiful daughter. **Dec. 1**

Arlene R. Taylor, an internationally known author, speaker, and brain function specialist, works with three hospitals in California. She also engages in research through her nonprofit corporation, Realizations Inc. Her electronic Brain Bulletin is free of charge at www.arlenetaylor.org **Jan. 5, June 24, Sept. 25**

Rose Joseph Thomas, an educator, lives in Altamonte Springs, Florida, with her husband, Walden, and daughter, Crystal Rose. Her son, Samuel Joseph, studies at Southern Adventist University. **Nov. 14**

Bula Rose Haughton Thompson, the first of fraternal twins, writes from Mandeville, Jamaica. A dental assistant, she enjoys pre-retirement and is married to a wonderful man, Norman. **Nov. 9**

Ethlyn Thompson, recently retired, started the first and largest vegetarian restaurant in Jamaica. Married with four children and four grandchildren, she serves, worships, and gardens in Kingston. **May 19**

Rebecca Timon, the administrative assistant to Heather-Dawn Small, director of the General Conference Women's Ministries, has one married son and loves Bible study. **Mar. 24, Mar. 25**

Joey Norwood Tolbert works at the Samaritan Center in Ooltewah, Tennessee; teaches humanities; and sings with Message of Mercy. She is married to Matthew and has two children. **Aug. 15**

Adel Arrabito Torres, a nurse, lives with her two boys and husband in Michigan, where he is attending seminary. She loves missions and is writing a book about her parents. **Feb. 17**

Nancy Ann (Neuharth) Troyer is married to Chaplain Don Troyer, a U.S. Army lieutenant colonel. They have one daughter, Steph, and live in Banning, California, where she enjoys singing, photography, and writing. **Sept. 30**

Haleigh Van Allen has three siblings and spent two years in Honduras as a missionary. She lives in Virginia, where she is studying elementary education. She wants to work for the Lord. **Oct. 9**

Marge Vande Hei is the mother of three and a grandmother of two. She has always lived in Green Bay, Wisconsin, and has been married for over 34 years to her high school sweetheart. **Apr. 29**

Angelina Vandiver is the proud mother of her daughter, Tori. She works in health care IT as a financial analyst. She enjoys being creative and loves a good challenge. **Dec. 26**

Monica Vesey, the daughter of missionaries, lives Berkshire, England, with her husband and daughter. She has taught for years and helped countless children overcome dyslexia. **Mar. 15**

Lidia Graepp Voos lives in Brazil with her pastor husband and coordinates her district's women's ministries. A mother of two, she enjoys people, ministry, sewing, and music. **July 26**

Luann Wainwright-Dill, a married musician and education officer for the Bermuda Public School System, directs Proclaim It! and also produces Bermuda's premiere show choir program. **Nov. 5**

Barbara J. Walker, of Jackson, Mississippi, serves as clerk and elder in her church and as the South Central Conference Women's Ministries director for Mississippi. She coordinates Morning Manna, a prayer ministry. **Aug. 17**

Cora A. Walker is a retired nurse, editor, and freelance writer who lives in McDonough, Georgia. She is mother of Andre V. Walker and enjoys swimming and classical music. **Feb. 6**

Anna May Radke Waters, a retired administrative secretary, puts eight grandchildren and her husband at the top of her list of hobbies. She answers prayer requests for Bibleinfo.com. **Jan. 17**

Elizabeth Darby Watson, an associate professor of social work, writes, speaks, and loves children's ministry. Dr. Watson's professionalism and assertiveness contributed to her success as a single parent of three children. She has five wonderful grandchildren. **Dec. 12**

Daniela Weichhold, originally from Germany, works as an administrative assistant at the EU headquarters in Brussels, Belgium. During leaves of absence, she has received medical missionary training. She enjoys the outdoors, singing, and playing the piano. **June 22**

Lyn Welk-Sandy lives in Australia, where she works as a grief counselor. She enjoys making music and caravanning around Outback Australia with her husband, Keith. **Mar. 29, Oct. 2**

Eunice E. West-Haynes, born in the West Indies, traveled to England, becoming a nurse and midwife, then practicing there and in the States for many years. She retired to Miami, Florida. **May 3**

Penny Estes Wheeler, retired, feels blessed that she had a career doing what she loved most—editing and writing. She and her husband, Gerald, enjoy traveling to visit grandchildren. **Nov. 16**

Sandra Widulle is married with two children. She loves to write and is engaged in children's ministry and in the creative decoration of the church that she attends in Germany. **Apr. 30**

Hyveth Williams is a minister of the gospel, whose ministry crosses racial and religious boundaries. Author of four books, she is a professor and director of the Homiletics program at the Adventist theological seminary at Andrews University. **July 29, July 30, July 31**

Kimasha Pauline Williams, a recent graduate of the University of the Southern Caribbean, lives in St. Maarten and is the communications officer at the St. Maarten Medical Center. **Mar. 17**

Wendy Williams lives in Ohio. Her favorite pastimes are writing, photography, traveling, hiking with her husband, and eating the world's supply of chocolate. **Sept. 2**

Rhoda Wills, a 32-year classroom veteran, says students gave her a profound understanding of the word *retirement.* She enjoys abandoning retirement projects for quick, delicious naps. **Apr. 7**

Violet Crockwell Wilson, a member of the Oakwood University Church in Huntsville, Alabama, has four children, nine grandchildren, and eight great-grandchildren. **Nov. 25**

Dalores Broome Winget is a retired 30-year elementary teacher living in Warwick, Pennsylvania, with husband, Richard. This much-published writer has two children and two granddaughters. **July 22**

Linda-Luiselle B. Yapi took developmental studies at Valley View University in Ghana. A presenter of French programming for Adventist World Radio, she really enjoys ministry. **Nov. 15**

Maxine Young is a writer from New York City. She is currently creating the e-book version of her booklet about God's promises to sufferers of chronic illness. **May 31**

Shelly-Ann Patricia Zabala serves in Women's and Children's Ministries in the New York Conference of Seventh-day Adventists. She and her pastor husband, Florencio, have two energetic boys and minister in the Syracuse, New York area. **May 18**

Candace Zook is the director of Inter-Faith Circle of Women and does marketing for several nonprofit organizations. This Indiana-based speaker and writer has seven grandchildren. **Jan. 10, July 5**